WHO WAS WHEN?

WHO WAS WHEN?
A DICTIONARY OF CONTEMPORARIES

MIRIAM ALLEN DE FORD
and JOAN S. JACKSON

THIRD EDITION

THE H.W. WILSON COMPANY • NEW YORK • 1976

TO THE MEMORY OF MAYNARD SHIPLEY

WHO HAD THE FIRST IDEA OF THIS BOOK

Library of Congress Cataloging in Publication Data

De Ford, Miriam Allen
  Who was when?

  Includes index.
  SUMMARY: Lists 10,000 celebrated individuals from
500 B.C. to the present both by date and by field of
activity. An alphabetical listing follows.
  1. Biography. 2. Chronology, Historical—Tables.
[1. Biography. 2. Chronology, Historical—Tables]
I. Jackson, Joan S., joint author. II. Title.
CT103.D4 1976   902'.02   76-2404
ISBN 0-8242-0532-4

PREFACE

This third edition of WHO WAS WHEN carries the original concept of the late Miriam Allen de Ford through the year 1974. (The first edition brought the work through 1938, the second through 1949.)

WHO WAS WHEN is a quick reference guide to 10,000 celebrated individuals from 500 B.C. to the present. Contemporaries are aligned in two dimensions: by date (whether of birth or death) and by broad field of activity. Between the birth and death dates of any individual there can be found the names and dates of those in the same or any other field. All the names charted in the main text can be found in a single alphabetical index at the end; birth and death dates are noted to facilitate location of names in the text.

As a reference tool, the book will answer such questions as the following: Who was writing music or painting pictures when Shakespeare was alive? Could Newton have influenced Descartes? Who was the king of England when Columbus discovered America? Could the Brontë sisters have visited Jane Austen? Which crowned heads of Europe might have attended a summit meeting in 1776? Were other notable political leaders born in the same year as Franklin D. Roosevelt? Artists? Actors? Writers?

Readers can also use the book to gain a general picture of the cultural, political, or religious life of any given era, from a year to a century or more. In this connection, it is instructive to observe how interests change from period to period. Look at the nineteenth century, when scientists and authors flourish; or the sixteenth, where the crowded sections are those devoted to painters; or the thirteenth, when theologians hold sway. Economists and inventors are few until the eighteenth century; times of widespread and in-

cessant warfare provide a plethora of military leaders. One might almost write a history of the world from a study of this skeleton of its story through almost 2,500 years.

No attempt has been made to give the names of all the rulers of every European country, or of all the popes; only those best known are included. Coverage of deceased English and American chiefs of state is broader: all kings and reigning queens of England and all presidents of the United States are listed. With a few exceptions, Roman emperors are listed as rulers of Rome to 330 A.D., of the East or West to 962, and of the Holy Roman Empire after that date. At what precise point monarchs ceased to reign over (for example) the Franks and became rulers of France has been determined flexibly. In the case of British monarchs, before William the Conqueror only Alfred the Great is listed as a king of England.

Most of the categories are self-explanatory. A few, however, may need amplification. Included under Government and Law are leaders who actually (for a time at least) governed. Unsuccessful revolutionists are grouped with economists, political theorists, inventors, and men of finance and business in the column headed Industry, Commerce, Economics, Finance, Invention, Labor. The category Philosophy and Religion includes not only philosophers, saints, popes, and preachers, but also antireligionists and rationalists. Under Miscellaneous are grouped all those who did not fit in anywhere else. Here are actors, most engineers, philanthropists; but also kings' mistresses, impostors, charlatans, and criminals, as well as other unclassifiable persons whose names nevertheless belong in any biographical tabulation.

After 1850, those coming under the former head of

Travel and Exploration are included under Miscellaneous so that Literature, the longest list, can be printed in double-column form. Changes in other headings — Military, Naval, and Aviation Affairs; Science, Technology, and Medicine; Literature and Journalism; Visual Arts — mirror the growing complexity and shifting emphases of the modern era.

Each individual is listed under a single category. Those who achieved fame in more than one field will be found in the column reflecting their major endeavor. Thus, readers seeking a name in one column may occasionally find that it is in another.

Names may be abbreviated in the text, but they are given in the index in full, as commonly used. Two individuals with identical names are differentiated by description. Alternative forms, nicknames, pseudonyms, and the given and family names of nobles are in parentheses. Pseudonyms are enclosed in quotation marks unless actually used as real names. French, German, and Italian titles of nobility are in the vernacular; others are noted in English equivalents.

Names with particles — de, von, etc. — are indexed under the surnames, rather than the particles, except for persons (mostly American or British) who spelled the particles with capitals and integrated them with surnames.

Because of limitations of space, names were limited to those most likely to be of permanent interest. Standard authorities were used to establish questionable dates and to resolve problems of spelling and transliteration. In the preparation of this edition Miriam Allen de Ford collaborated with Joan S. Jackson.

INSTRUCTIONS FOR USE

WHO WAS WHEN consists of two sections: a main section of chronological charts covering the years from 500 B.C. to 1974 A.D. and an index section containing the names of all individuals in the charts and giving their birth and death dates. On every page of the charts, the years for which information is given are printed in boldface, in proper chronological order, down the lefthand column. The guide dates appearing in heavy type at the upper outer corner of every page indicate the years covered on the page and the one facing it.

To learn the contemporaries of any individual, first find his or her birth and death dates by looking in the index. Then turn to the two pages in the chart section on which these dates fall. Examine these pages *and all the pages in between*. On them you will find the names of the individual's contemporaries grouped in columns according to activity or profession. A name followed by "b." signifies a birth date; a name printed in italics and followed by "d." signifies a death date. Other abbreviations used in the charts are fl., flourished; a., acceded; abd., abdicated; dep., deposed. Note that in the case of monarchs and popes, date of accession is used instead of birth date; if they abdicated or were deposed that date is used instead of date of death. The abbreviation H.R.E. refers to the Holy Roman Empire.

It is possible that a contemporary could have been born before and died after the individual you are interested in. Therefore, in order to obtain the widest range of contemporaries, consult the pages that precede the individual's year of birth and follow the date of death.

ABBREVIATIONS MOST FREQUENTLY USED

abd. abdicated	dep. deposed	H.R.E. Holy
a. acceded	d. died	Roman Empire
b. born	fl. flourished	

WHO WAS WHEN?

Year B.C.	Government and Law	Military and Naval Affairs	Industry Commerce Economics Finance Invention Labor	Travel and Exploration	Philosophy and Religion	Science and Medicine	Education Scholarship History	Literature	Painting and Sculpture	Music	Miscellaneous
500				Hanno fl.	Archelaus of Miletus fl. Habakkuk fl. Malachi fl. Obadiah fl. *Pythagoras d.* Xenophanes fl.	Anaxagoras b. Atreya fl. Empedocles b. Hippo fl. Nabu-rimanni fl.	Hecataeus of Miletus fl. Scylax of Coryanda fl.		Phidias b.		
495								Sophocles b.			
490	Pericles b.										
488	*Cleomenes I (Sparta) d.* Leonidas (Sparta) a.	Miltiades d.						*Anacreon d.*			
486	*Darius the Great (Persia) d.* Xerxes (Persia) a.										
485	Gelon (Syracuse) a.	M. Furius Camillus b.									
484							Herodotus b.				
483					*Buddha d.*		Gorgias b.				
481					Protagoras b.						
480	*Leonidas (Sparta) d.*				Diagoras fl.			Euripides b.			
478	*Gelon (Syracuse) d.*				*Confucius d.*						
477		*Pausanias d.*									
475					*Heraclitus d.*						
471							Thucydides b.				
470					*Parmenides d?*				Polygnotus b.		Aspasia b.
469					Socrates b.						
468	*Aristides d.*							*Simonides of Ceos d.*			
465	Artaxerxes I (Persia) a. *Xerxes (Persia) d.*				Crates fl.						
460					Democritus b. Philolaus fl.	Hippocrates b.		*Bacchylides d.?*			
459											Lysias b.
456								*Aeschylus d.*			

Year B.C.	Government and Law	Military and Naval Affairs	Industry Commerce Economics Finance Invention Labor	Travel and Exploration	Philosophy and Religion	Science and Medicine	Education Scholarship History	Literature	Painting and Sculpture	Music	Miscellaneous
450	Appius Claudius Crassus fl. Critias b.	Alcibiades b.			Euclid b.	Hippocrates of Chios fl.		*Epicharmus d.*	Polyclitus fl.		
449	*Themistocles d.*	*Cimon d.*									
448								Aristophanes b.			
444					Antisthenes b.						
443								*Pindar d.*			
440								Pherecrates fl.	*Polygnotus d.*		
439		*L.Q. Cincinnatus d.*									
436											Isocrates b.
435								Philoxenus b.			
434						Xenophon b.					
432									*Phidias d.*		
431		Thrasybulus b.									
430						*Empedocles d.*					
429	*Pericles d.*										
428						*Anaxagoras d.*					
427					Plato b.						
425	*Artaxerxes I (Persia) d.*						*Herodotus d.*				
424	Darius II (Persia) a.										
423		Cyrus the Younger b.						*Cratinus d.*			
422	*Cleon d.*										
420									Zeuxis		Isaeus b.
418	Epaminondas b.										
412					Diogenes b.						
411		Timoleon b.			*Protagoras d.*						
410											*Aspasia d.*
409						Eudoxus b.					

Year B.C.	Government and Law	Military and Naval Affairs	Industry Commerce Economics Finance Invention Labor	Travel and Exploration	Philosophy and Religion	Science and Medicine	Education Scholarship History	Literature	Painting and Sculpture	Music	Miscellaneous
408	Dion (Syracuse) b.								Apollodorus fl.		
407					Speusippus b.						
406								Euripides d. Sophocles a.			
405	Dionysius (Syracuse) a.				Zeno of Elea fl.						
404	Artaxerxes II (Persia) a. Darius II (Persia) d.	Alcibiades d.			Nehemiah b.						
402	Critias d. Phocion b.										
401	Agesilaus II (Sparta) a.	Clearchus d. Cyrus the Younger d.			Ezra fl.		Ctesias fl.		Protogenes fl.		
400		Parmenio b.			Diodorus Cronus fl. Xenophanes d.	Archytas b.	Thucydides d.		Apelles fl. Parrhasius fl.		
399	Archelaus (Macedonia) d.				Socrates d.						
398		Antipater b.									
396					Xenocrates b.						
395		Lysander d. Tissaphernes d.									
389	Aeschines b.	Thrasybulus d.									
385											
384					Aristotle b.						Demosthenes b.
380								Aristophanes d. Philoxenus d.			Lysias d.
377						Hippocrates d.					
375							Gorgias d.				
374					Euclid d.						
372					Mencius b. Theophrastus b.						
367	Dionysius (Syracuse) d.					Kidinnu fl.					
365		M. Furius Camillus d.			Antisthenes d.	Archytas d.			Praxiteles fl.		
364		Pelopidas d.									

362–272 B.C.

Year B.C.	Government and Law	Military and Naval Affairs	Industry Commerce Economics Finance Invention Labor	Travel and Exploration	Philosophy and Religion	Science and Medicine	Education Scholarship History	Literature	Painting and Sculpture	Music	Miscellaneous
362	Epaminondas d.				Democritus d.						
361	Agesilaus II (Sparta) d. Lysimachus (Thrace) b.							Philemon b.			
360		Eumenes b.			Pyrrho of Elis b.						
359	Artaxerxes II (Persia) d. Philip II (Macedonia) a.				Nehemiah d.						
355	Demochares b.	Timotheus d.					Theopompus fl. Xenophon d.				
353	Dion (Syracuse) d.					Eudoxus d.					
350					Theodorus of Cyrene fl.				Lysippus fl.		Isaeus d.
348		Iphicrates d.									
347					Plato d.						
345							Timaeus b.				
343								Menander b.			
342					Epicurus b.						
339					Speusippus d.						
338	Agis III (Sparta) fl.										Isocrates d.
337		Timoleon d.									
336	Philip II (Macedonia) d.				Zeno b.						
335	Alexander the Great (Macedonia) a.										
330		Parmenio d.									
323	Alexander the Great (Macedonia) d. Ptolemy I (Egypt) a.				Diogenes d.						
322					Aristotle d.						Demosthenes d.
321	Chandragupta (India) a.										
320						Pytheas fl.		Callimachus b.			
319		Antipater d.									

Year B.C.	Government and Law	Military and Naval Affairs	Industry Commerce Economics Finance Invention Labor	Travel and Exploration	Philosophy and Religion	Science and Medicine	Education Scholarship History	Literature	Painting and Sculpture	Music	Miscellaneous
317	Agathocles (Syracuse) a. Phocion d.										
316		Eumenes d.									
314	Aeschines d.				Xenocrates d.						
312	Appius Claudius Caecus fl.										
307	Seleucus I (Syria) a.										
306	Antigonus Cyclops (Macedonia) a.										
301	Antigonus Cyclops (Macedonia) d.										
300	Pyrrhus (Epirus) a.				Cleanthes b. Euhemerus fl. Hegesias óf Magnesia fl.	Erasistratus fl. Euclid fl. Herophilus fl.					
296	Chandragupta (India) d.										
294	Demetrius (Macedonia) a.										
290		Fabius Maximus d.						Menander d.			
289	Agathocles (Syracuse) d.				Mencius d.						
287					Theophrastus d.	Archimedes b.					
284								Livius Andronicus b.			
283	Demetrius (Macedonia) d. Ptolemy I (Egypt) d. Ptolemy II (Egypt) a.										
281	Lysimachus (Thrace) d.										
280					Chrysippus b. Timon of Phlius fl. Zenodotus fl.		Manetho fl.	Sositheus fl.			
276						Eratosthenes b.					
275	Demochares d.										
272	Asoka b.										

Year B.C.	Government and Law	Military and Naval Affairs	Industry Commerce Economics Finance Invention Labor	Travel and Exploration	Philosophy and Religion	Science and Medicine	Education Scholarship History	Literature	Painting and Sculpture	Music	Miscellaneous
270	Hiero II (Syracuse) a.	Hamilcar Barca b.			Epicurus d. Pyrrho of Elis d.	Aristarchus of Samos fl.					
268		M. Claudius Marcellus b.									
264					Zeno d.			Naevius b.			
263								Philemon d.			
262						Apollonius of Perga b.					
254							Fabius Pictor b.	Plautus b.			
253		Philopoemen b.									
250		M. Atilius Regulus d.			Strato fl.		Berossus fl. Timaeus d.	Theocritus fl.			
247	Ptolemy II (Egypt) d.	Hannibal b.									
241	Attalus I (Pergamum) a.										
240		Hanno the Great fl.						Callimachus d.			
239								Ennius b.			
237		Scipio Major b.									
235	Cleomenes III (Sparta) a.										
234	Cato the Elder b.										
232	Asoka d.										
229		Hamilcar Barca d. L. Emilianus Paulus b.									
228		T. Quinctius Flaminius b.									
223	Antiochus the Great (Syria) a.										
220					Cleanthes d.			M. Pacuvius b.			
219	Cleomenes III (Sparta) d.										
217	C. Flaminius d.										
216	Hiero II (Syracuse) d.										
212						Archimedes d.					

Year B.C.	Government and Law	Military and Naval Affairs	Industry Commerce Economics Finance Invention Labor	Travel and Exploration	Philosophy and Religion	Science and Medicine	Education Scholarship History	Literature	Painting and Sculpture	Music	Miscellaneous
208		M. Claudius Marcellus d.									
207	Nabis (Sparta) a.	Hasdrubal d.									
206					Chrysippus d.						
204	Massinissa (Numidia) a.							Livius Andronicus d.			
203											
201							Fabius Pictor d.? Polybius b.	Herodas fl.			
200						Apollonius of Perga d.					
197	Attalus I (Pergamum) d. Eumenes II (Pergamum) a.										
195						Eratosthenes d.					
194	Nabis (Sparta) d.?							Naevius d.			
192					Critolaus b.						
190								Terence b.			
187	Antiochus the Great (Syria) d.										
185	Scipio Minor b.										
184		Philopoemen d.						Plautus d.			
183		Hannibal d. Scipio Major d.									
180						Hipparchus b.					
178											
176	Antiochus Epiphanes (Syria) a.										
174		T. Quinctius Flaminius d.									
170		Mattathias fl.									
169								Ennius d.			
167	Persius (Macedonia) d.										
166								Statius Caecilius d.			

Year B.C.	Government and Law	Military and Naval Affairs	Industry Commerce Economics Finance Invention Labor	Travel and Exploration	Philosophy and Religion	Science and Medicine	Education Scholarship History	Literature	Painting and Sculpture	Music	Miscellaneous
164	Antiochus Epiphanes (Syria) d.										
163	T. Sempronius Gracchus b.										
160		L. Emilianus Paulus d.			Aristobulus of Paneas fl.						
159	Eumenes II (Pergamum) d.							Terence d.			
158							Aristarchus of Samothrace b.				
155		C. Marius b.									
154							Stilo Praeconinus b.				
153	C. Sempronius Gracchus b.										
152		Q. Lutatius Catulus b.									
150						Heron of Alexandria b.?		Aristides of Miletus b. Moschus fl.			
149	Cato the Elder d. Massinissa (Numidia) d.										
143	M. Antonius (Elder) b. Ptolemy VII (Egypt) a.										
140	M. Licinius Crassus (Elder) b.										
138		L. Cornelius Sulla b.									
135		Judas Maccabaeus d.									
133	T. Sempronius Gracchus d.										
130					Poseidonius b.			Nicander fl. M. Pacuvius d.			
129	Scipio Minor d.										
126											Q. Roscius b.
125						Hipparchus d.					
124	C. Aurelius Cotta b.										

Year B.C.	Government and Law	Military and Naval Affairs	Industry Commerce Economics Finance Invention Labor	Travel and Exploration	Philosophy and Religion	Science and Medicine	Education Scholarship History	Literature	Painting and Sculpture	Music	Miscellaneous
121	C. Sempronius Gracchus d. Mithradates the Great (Pontus) a. P. Sulpicius Rufus b.										
120							Polybius d.				
116	Ptolemy VII (Egypt) d.							M. Terentius Varro b.			
115	M. Licinius Crassus (Younger) b.										
112	Jugurtha (Numidia) a.										
110					Critolaus d.						Lucullus b.
109	M. Livius Drusus d.						T. Pomponius Atticus b.				
108											Catiline b.
106	Jugurtha (Numidia) dep. Pompey b.							Cicero b.			
105	John Hyrcanus I d.							D. Laberius b.			
104	Aristobulus I (Jews) a.										
102	Aristobulus I (Jews) d.										
100	Julius Caesar b. L. Appuleius Saturninus d.				Aenesidemus fl.	Heron of Alexandria d.?	Dionysius Thrax fl.	Aristides of Miletus d. Bion fl. Publilius Syrus fl.			
99							Cornelius Nepos b.				
98							P. Nigidius Figulus b.	Lucretius b.			
95					Cato the Younger b.			Lucius Afranius fl.			
93	Publius Clodius b.										
91	M. Licinius Crassus (Elder) d.										
88	P. Sulpicius Rufus d.						Aristarchus of Samothrace d.				
87	M. Antonius (Elder) d.	Q. Lutatius Catulus d.									

Year B.C.	Government and Law	Military and Naval Affairs	Industry Commerce Economics Finance Invention Labor	Travel and Exploration	Philosophy and Religion	Science and Medicine	Education Scholarship History	Literature	Painting and Sculpture	Music	Miscellaneous
86		C. Marius d.					Sallust b.				
85	M. Junius Brutus b.										
84		L. Cornelius Cinna d.						Caius Catullus b.			
83	Mark Antony b.										
82	M. Rufus Caelius b. Q. Mucius Scaevola d.							Licinius Macer Calvus b.			
78		L. Cornelius Sulla d.									
77	Antigonus (Jews) d.										
76								C. Asinius Pollio b.			
74							Stilo Praeconinus d.				
73	C. Aurelius Cotta d.										
72		Q. Sertorius d.									
71			Spartacus d.								
70					Hillel b.			Cornelius Gallus b. Virgil b.			Maecenas b.
69	Cleopatra b.										
65								Horace b.			
63	M. V. Agrippa b. Mithradates the Great (Pontus) d.					Strabo b.	Didymus b.				
62											Catiline d. Q. Roscius d.
59							Livy b.				
56											Lucullus d.
55								Lucretius d.			
54	Seneca the Elder b.						Dionysius of Halicarnassus b.	Caius Catullus d. Tibullus b.			
53	M. Licinius Crassus (Younger) d.										
52	Publius Clodius d.										
50		Lucius Afranius fl.			Poseidonius d.			Propertius b.			

Year B.C.	Government and Law	Military and Naval Affairs	Industry Commerce Economics Finance Invention Labor	Travel and Exploration	Philosophy and Religion	Science and Medicine	Education Scholarship History	Literature	Painting and Sculpture	Music	Miscellaneous
48	M. Rufus Caelius d. Pompey d.						P. Nigidius Figulus d.				
47		Aulus Gabinius d.						Licinius Macer Calvus d.			
46	Juba (Numidia) d.				Cato the Younger d.						
44	Julius Caesar d.										
43								Cicero d. D. Laberius d. Ovid b.			
42	M. Junius Brutus d. C. Cassius Longinus d.							C. Helvius Cinna d.			
40	Herod the Great (Jews) a.										
38		N. C. Drusus b.									
37	Orodes (Parthia) d.										
34	Aristobulus III (Jews) d.						Sallust d.				
32							T. Pomponius Atticus d.				
30	Mark Antony d. Cleopatra d. John Hyrcanus II d.				Hillel b.		Diodorus Siculus fl.		Agesander fl.		
29	Augustus (Rome) a.										
27								M. Terentius Varro d.			
26								Cornelius Gallus d.			
24							Cornelius Nepos d.				
20					Philo Judaeus b.						
19							M. Velleius Paterculus b.	Virgil d.			
17		Arminius b.						Tibullus d.			
15		Germanicus Caesar b.						Propertius d.			Vitruvius fl.
12	M. V. Agrippa d.										
9		N. C. Drusus d.									
8								Horace d.			Maecenas d.
7					Jesus Christ b.?		Dionysius of Halicarnassus d.				
4	Herod the Great (Jews) d. Herod Antipas (Jews) a.				Seneca the Younger b.						
1					Apollonius of Tyana fl.			Meleager fl.			

1–101 A.D.

Year A.D.	Government and Law	Military and Naval Affairs	Industry Commerce Economics Finance Invention Labor	Travel and Exploration	Philosophy and Religion	Science and Medicine	Education Scholarship History	Literature	Painting and Sculpture	Music	Miscellaneous
1					St. James fl. St. John fl. St. John the Baptist fl. St. Mark fl. St. Matthew fl. St. Peter fl. St. Thomas fl.	Celsus fl. Theodosius fl.		Valerius Maximus fl.			
5								*C. Asinius Pollio d.*			
10					*Hillel d.*		*Didymus d.*				
14	*Augustus (Rome) d.* Tiberius (Rome) a.										
15		L. Virginius Rufus b.									
16											Agrippina II b.
17							*Livy d.*	*Ovid d.*			
19		*Germanicus Caesar d.*									
21		*Arminius d.*									
22						*Strabo d.*					Messalina b.
23							Pliny the Elder b.				
25								Silius Italicus b.			
30					St. Clement b. *Jesus Christ d.?*						
31							*Velleius Paterculus d.*				
34								Persius b.			
35								Quintilian b.			
37	Caligula (Rome) a. *Tiberius (Rome) d.*	Agricola b.						Josephus b.			
39	*Herod Antipas (Jews) d.* *Seneca (Elder) d.*							Lucan b.			
40		Frontinus b.			Dio Chrysostom b. St. Luke fl.	Columella fl.		Martial b. Phaedrus fl.			
41	*Caligula (Rome) d.* Claudius (Rome) a. Herod Agrippa a.										
44	*Herod Agrippa d.*										

Year A.D.	Government and Law	Military and Naval Affairs	Industry Commerce Economics Finance Invention Labor	Travel and Exploration	Philosophy and Religion	Science and Medicine	Education Scholarship History	Literature	Painting and Sculpture	Music	Miscellaneous
45								Statius b.			
46								Plutarch b.			
48											*Messalina d.*
54	*Claudius (Rome) d.* Nero (Rome) a.				*Philo Judaeus d.*		Curtius Rufus fl.				
55						Dioscorides fl.	Tacitus b.				
59											*Agrippina II d.*
60		Caractacus fl.			Epictetus b.			Juvenal b.			
62	*Boadicea d.*				*St. Paul d.*			*Persius d.* Pliny the Younger b.			
65					*Seneca (Younger) d.*			*Lucan d.*			
66					*Thrasea d.*			*Petronius d.*			
67		*Corbulo d.*									
68	Galba (Rome) a. *Nero (Rome) d.*										
69	*Galba (Rome) d.* Otho (Rome) a. and d. Vespasian (Rome) a. *Vitellius (Rome) a. and d.*				St. Ploycarp b.						
79	Titus (Rome) a. *Vespasian (Rome) d.*						*Pliny the Elder d.*				
81	Domitian (Rome) a. *Titus (Rome) d.*										
86	Antoninus Pius (Rome) a.										
93		*Agricola d.*									
95					*St. Dionysius the Areopagite d.*		*Josephus d.*				
96	*Domitian (Rome) d.* Nerva (Rome) a.				Arrian b.			*Statius d.*			
97		*L. Virginius Rufus d.*									
98	*Nerva (Rome) d.* Trajan (Rome) a.										
100					*St. Clement d.* Justin Martyr b.		Fronto b.	*Quintilian d.*			
101					Athenagoras fl. Peregrinus Proteus fl.	Pausanias fl.	Appian fl. Phlegon fl. Suetonius fl.	Iamblichus fl *Silius Italicus d.*			

Year A.D.	Government and Law	Military and Naval Affairs	Industry Commerce Economics Finance Invention Labor	Travel and Exploration	Philosophy and Religion	Science and Medicine	Education Scholarship History	Literature	Painting and Sculpture	Music	Miscellaneous
102								Martial d.			
103		Frontinus d.									
107					St. Ignatius of Antioch d.						
110	Gaius b.										
114								Pliny the Younger d.			
115					Dio Chrysostom d.						
117	Hadrian (Rome) a. Trajan (Rome) d.										
120					Epictetus d.	Soranus fl.	Tacitus d.	Plutarch d.			
125								Apuleius b. Lucian b.			
130					St. Irenaeus b.	Galen b.		Aulus Gellius b.			
138	Hadrian (Rome) d.										
140								Juvenal d.			
142	Papinianus b.										
150					Aquila fl. Clement of Alexandria b. Marcion fl. Valentinus fl.	Aretaeus of Cappadocia fl. Caraca of Cashmir fl.	Dio Cassius b.				
155					St. Polycarp d.						
160					Tertullian b.						
161	Antoninus Pius (Rome) d. Marcus Aurelius (Rome) a.										
165					Justin Martyr d.						
170	Ulpian b.				Celsus fl.		Fronto d.	Philostratus b.			
176					St. Cecilia d.						
180	Marcus Aurelius (Rome) d. Commodus (Rome) a. Gaius d.				Arrian d. Hegesippus fl.	Ptolemy fl.		Aulus Gellius d.			
185					Origen b.						

Year A.D.	Government and Law	Military and Naval Affairs	Industry Commerce Economics Finance Invention Labor	Travel and Exploration	Philosophy and Religion	Science and Medicine	Education Scholarship History	Literature	Painting and Sculpture	Music	Miscellaneous
192	Commodus (Rome) d.										
193	Pertinax (Rome) a. and d. Severus (Rome) a.										
200					St. Cyprian b.	Galen d.		Apuleius d.? Longus fl. Lucian d.			
202					St. Cosmas fl. St. Irenaeus d. Plotinus b.						
210					Gregory Thaumaturgus b.						
211	Caracalla (Rome) a. Geta (Rome) a. Severus (Rome) d.										
212	Geta (Rome) d. Papinianus d.						Serenus Sammonicus d.				
213					Longinus b.						
216					Mani b.						
217	Caracalla (Rome) d.										
218	Heliogabalus (Rome) a.										
220					Clement of Alexandria d.		Herodianus fl.				
222	Alexander Severus (Rome) a. Heliogabalus (Rome) d.										
228	Ulpian d.										
230					St. Hippolytus d. Sabellius fl. Tertullian d.		Diogenes Laërtius fl.				
233							Porphyry b.				
235	Alexander Severus (Rome) d. Maximinus I (Rome) a.						Dio Cassius d.				
238	Gordianus (Rome) a. and d. Maximinus I (Rome) d.										
245								Philostratus d.			

Year A.D.	Government and Law	Military and Naval Affairs	Industry Commerce Economics Finance Invention Labor	Travel and Exploration	Philosophy and Religion	Science and Medicine	Education Scholarship History	Literature	Painting and Sculpture	Music	Miscellaneous
249	Decius (Rome) a.										
250					*St. Christopher d.*	Diophantus fl.		Commodianus fl.			
251	*Decius (Rome) d.* Gallus (Rome) a.				St. Anthony b.						
253	Gallienus (Rome) a. *Gallus (Rome) d.* Valerianus (Rome) a.										
254					*Origen d.*						
257					Gregory the Illuminator b.						
258					*St. Cyprian d.* *St. Lawrence d.*						
260	*Valerianus (Rome) d.*				Eusebius of Caesarea b. Lactantius b. Paulo of Samosata fl.						
264					*Dionysius of Alexandria d.*						
266	*Odaenathus (Palmyra) d.*										
267	Zenobia (Palmyra) a.										
268	Claudius Gothicus (Rome) a. *Gallienus (Rome) d.*										
270	Aurelian (Rome) a. *Claudius Gothicus (Rome) d.*				*Gregory Thaumaturgus d.* *Plotinus d.* *St. Valentine d.*						
272	Zenobia (Palmyra) dep.				St. Januarius b.						
273					*Longinus d.*						
275	*Aurelian (Rome) d.* Tacitus (Rome) a.										
276	Probus (Rome) a. *Tacitus (Rome) d.*				*Mani d.*						
282	*Probus (Rome) d.*										
283	Carinus (Rome) a.										
284	*Carinus (Rome) d.* Diocletian (Rome) a.										

Year A.D.	Government and Law	Military and Naval Affairs	Industry Commerce Economics Finance Invention Labor	Travel and Exploration	Philosophy and Religion	Science and Medicine	Education Scholarship History	Literature	Painting and Sculpture	Music	Miscellaneous
286	Maximian (Rome) a.				St. Maurice d.						
288					St. Sebastian d.						
291					St. Agnes b. St. Hilarion b.	Pappus of Alexandria fl.					
292					St. Pachomius b.						
293	Carausius d.										
296					St. Athanasius b.						
301						Serenus of Antissa fl.		Heliodorus of Tricca fl.			
303					St. George d.						
304					St. Agnes d.		Porphyry d.				
305	Diocletian (Rome) abd. Galerius (Rome) a. Maximian (Rome) d.				St. Januarius d.						
306	Constantine I (The Great—Rome) a. Maxentius (Rome) a.										
307	Licinius (Rome) a.				St. Catherine of Alexandria d.						
308	Maximinus II (Rome) a.										
309					St. Pamphilius d.						
310								Ausonius b.			
311	Galerius (Rome) d.				Ulfilas b.						
312	Maxentius (Rome) d.				Lucian d.						
314	Maximinus II (Rome) d.						Libanius b.				
315					St. Cyril of Jerusalem b. St. Epiphanius b. St. Hilary of Poitiers b. St. Martin of Tours b.		Himerius b.				
320					Ephraem Syrus b.						
323											
324	Licinius (Rome) d.										

Year A.D.	Government and Law	Military and Naval Affairs	Industry Commerce Economics Finance Invention Labor	Travel and Exploration	Philosophy and Religion	Science and Medicine	Education Scholarship History	Literature	Painting and Sculpture	Music	Miscellaneous
325							Marcellinus Ammianus b.				
328					St. Gregory of Nazianzus b.						
329					St. Basil b.						
331					St. Gregory of Nyssa b.						
337	Constans I (Emp. West) a. *Constantine the Great (Rome) d.* Constantius (Emp. East) a.				*Gregory the Illuminator d.*						
340					St. Ambrose b. *Eusebius of Caesarea d.* Iamblichus fl. St. Jerome b. *Lactantius d.* Tyrannius Rufinus b.		Victorinus fl.				
345					*St. Nicholas d.* Symmachus b.						
346					*St. Pachomius d.*						
347					St. John Chrysostom b.						
348							Prudentius b.				
350	*Constans I (Emp. West) d.*				Theodore of Mopsuestia b.		Donatus fl.				
352					Pope (St.) Liberius a.						
353					St. Paulinus b.						
354					St. Augustine b.						
356					*St. Anthony d.?*						
360					Joannes Cassianus b. Pelagius b.						
361	*Constantius (Emp. East) d.* Julian the Apostate (Emp. East) a.										
363	Jovian (Emp. West) a. *Julian the Apostate (Emp. East) d.*				Severus Sulpicius b.						

Year A.D.	Government and Law	Military and Naval Affairs	Industry Commerce Economics Finance Invention Labor	Travel and Exploration	Philosophy and Religion	Science and Medicine	Education Scholarship History	Literature	Painting and Sculpture	Music	Miscellaneous
364	Jovian (Emp. West) d. Flavius Valens (Emp. East) a. Valentinian I (Emp. West) a.										
365								Claudian b.			
366					Pope (St.) Damascus a. Pope (St.) Liberius d.						
367					St. Hilary of Poitiers d.						
370	Alaric (Visigoths) b.				Ephraem Syrus d.	Hypatia b.					
372					St. Hilarion d.						
373					St. Athanasius d. Synesius b.						
375	Gratian (Rome) a. Valentinian I (Emp. West) d.										
376					St. Cyril of Alexandria b.						
378	Flavius Valens (Emp. East) d.										
379	Theodosius I (Emp. East) a.				St. Basil d.						
380					Eutyches b.						
381					St. Meletius of Antioch d.						
383	Gratian (Rome) d.				Ulfilas d.						
384					Pope (St.) Damascus d.						
385					Priscillian d.						
386					St. Cyril of Jerusalem d. Theodoret b.		Himerius d.				
389					St. Gregory of Nazianzus d. St. Patrick b.						
390					Prosper of Aquitaine b. St. Simeon Stylites b.		Servius Honoratus fl.				

93029

Year A.D.	Government and Law	Military and Naval Affairs	Industry Commerce Economics Finance Invention Labor	Travel and Exploration	Philosophy and Religion	Science and Medicine	Education Scholarship History	Literature	Painting and Sculpture	Music	Miscellaneous
392							Marcellinus Ammianus d.				
393					Eunomius d.		Libanius d.				
394								Ausonius d.			
395	Honorius (Emp. West) a. Theodosius I (Emp. East) d.										
396					St. Gregory of Nyssa d.						
397					St. Ambrose b. St. Martin of Tours d.						
400					Hermias Sozomen b.						
401					Macrobius fl. Syrianus fl.			Rutilius fl.			
402					St. Epiphanius d. Pope Innocent I a.						
403					St. Hilary of Arles b.						
405					Salvian b.						
406	Attila (Huns) b.										
407					St. John Chrysostom d.						
408		Flavius Stilicho d.					Zosimus b.	Claudian d.			
410	Alaric (Visigoths) d.				Proclus b. Tyrannius Rufinus d. Symmachus d.			Prudentius d.			
414					Synesius d.						
415					Orosius fl.	Hypatia d.					
417					Pope Innocent I d.						
418					Pope Boniface I a.						
420					St. Jerome d. Pelagius d.						
422					Pope Boniface I d. St. Genevieve b.						
423	Honorius (Emp. West) d.				Pope Celestine I a.						

Year A.D.	Government and Law	Military and Naval Affairs	Industry Commerce Economics Finance Invention Labor	Travel and Exploration	Philosophy and Religion	Science and Medicine	Education Scholarship History	Literature	Painting and Sculpture	Music	Miscellaneous
425	Valentinian III (Emp. West) a.				Severus Sulpicius d.						
428					Theodore of Mopsuestia d.						
429	Genseric (Vandals) a.										
430					Apollinaris Sidonius b.						
431					St. Augustine d. St. Paulinus d.						
432					Pope Celestine I d.						
435					Joannes Cassianus d.						
437					St. Remigius b.						
440					Pope (St.) Leo I a.						
443					Hermias Sozomen d.						
444					St. Cyril of Alexandria d.						
449					St. Hilary of Arles d.						
450	Vortigern (Britons) fl.				St. Vincent of Lerins d.		Zosimus d.				
451					Nestorius d.						
453	Attila (Huns) d.				St. Bridget b.						
455	Valentinian III (Emp. West) d.	Horsa d.									
456					Eutyches d.						
457	Leo I (Emp. East) a. Majorian (Emp. West) a.				Theodoret d.						
458	Childeric I (Franks) a.										
459					St. Simeon Stylites d.						
461	Majorian (Emp. West) d.				Pope (St.) Leo I d.						
463					St. Patrick d.						
465					Prosper of Aquitaine d.						

Year A.D.	Government and Law	Military and Naval Affairs	Industry Commerce Economics Finance Invention Labor	Travel and Exploration	Philosophy and Religion	Science and Medicine	Education Scholarship History	Literature	Painting and Sculpture	Music	Miscellaneous
474	Zeno (Emp. East) a.							Ennodius b.			
475	Basilicus (Emp. East) a. Leo I (Emp. East) d. Romulus Augustulus (Emp. West) a.				Boëthius b. St. Clotilda b.		Joannes Stobaeus fl.	Dracontius fl.			
476	Odoacer (Italy) a. Romulus Augustulus (Emp. West) dep.										
477	Basilicus (Emp. East) d. Genseric (Vandals) d.										
480					St. Benedict of Nursia b. Damascius b.						
481	Childeric I (Franks) d. Clovis (Franks) a.										
485					Proclus d.						
488		Hengest d.			Apollinaris Sidonius d.						
490	Cassiodorus b.						Procopius b.				
491	Anastasius I (Emp. East) a. Zeno (Emp. East) d.										
492					Salvian d.						
493	Odoacer (Italy) d. Theodoric (Ostrogoths) a.										
501				Cosmas of Alexandria fl.				Corippus fl.			
505		Belisarius b.									
508	Theodora b.										
511	Childebert I (Franks) a. Clovis (Franks) d.										
512					St. Geneviève d.						
516								Gildas b.			
518	Anastasius I (Emp. East) d.										

Year A.D.	Government and Law	Military and Naval Affairs	Industry Commerce Economics Finance Invention Labor	Travel and Exploration	Philosophy and Religion	Science and Medicine	Education Scholarship History	Literature	Painting and Sculpture	Music	Miscellaneous
520					St. Cloud b.						
521					St. Columba b.			Ennodius d.			
523					St. Bridget d.						
525					Boëthius d.						
526	Theodoric (Ostrogoths) d.										
527	Justinian (Emp. East) a.										
530								Fortunatus b.			
531	Khosru I (Persia) a.										
533					St. Remigius d.						
535					Damascius d.?						
538					St. Gregory of Tours b.						
541	Totila (Ostrogoths) a.										
543					St. Benedict of Nursia d. St. Columban b.						
544					St. Clotilda d.						
545	Tribonian d.										
548	Theodora d.										
552	Totila (Ostrogoths) d.										
555					Pope Pelagius I a.						
558	Childebert I (Franks) d. Clotaire I (Franks) a.										
560	Ethelbert (Kent) a.				St. Cloud d.		Isidore of Seville b.				
561	Alboin (Lombards) a. Chilperic I (Franks) a. Clotaire I (Franks) d. Sigebert (Franks) a.				Pope Pelagius I d.						

Year A.D.	Government and Law	Military and Naval Affairs	Industry Commerce Economics Finance Invention Labor	Travel and Exploration	Philosophy and Religion	Science and Medicine	Education Scholarship History	Literature	Painting and Sculpture	Music	Miscellaneous
562							Procopius d.				
565	Justinian (Emp. East) d.	Belisarius d.									
568				Zemarchus fl.							
570					Mohammed b.		Gildas d.				
573	Alboin (Lombards) d.										
575	Childebert II (Franks) a. Sigebert (Franks) d.										
579	Khosru I (Persia) d.										
580					St. Maximus b.						
582	Mauricius (Emp. East) a.										
584	Chilperic I (Franks) d. Clotaire II (Franks) a.										
585	Cassiodorus d.										
590					Pope (St.) Gregory I a.						
591	Khosru II (Persia) a.										
592											
594					St. Gregory of Tours d.						
595	Childebert II (Franks) d.										
597					St. Columba d.						
601						Paulus of Aegina fl.					
602	Mauricius (Emp. East) d. Phocas (Emp. East) a.				Theodore of Canterbury b.						
604					Pope (St.) Gregory I d.						
605					St. Oswald b.		Hsüan Tsang b.				
606					Fatima b.						
609								Fortunatus d.			

Year A.D.	Government and Law	Military and Naval Affairs	Industry Commerce Economics Finance Invention Labor	Travel and Exploration	Philosophy and Religion	Science and Medicine	Education Scholarship History	Literature	Painting and Sculpture	Music	Miscellaneous
610	Heraclius (Emp. East) a. Phocas (Emp. East) d.										
615					St. Columban d.						
616	Ethelbert (Kent) d.										
617	Edwin (Northumbria) a.										
625					St. Adamnan b. Pope Honorius I a.						
626											
628	Khosru II (Persia) d.										
629	Clotaire II (Franks) d. Dagobert I (Franks) a.										
632					Fatima d. · Mohammed d.						
633	Edwin (Northumbria) d. Penda (Mercia) a.										
635					St. Wilfrid b.						
636							Isidore of Seville d.				
638					Pope Honorius I d.						
639	Dagobert I (Franks) d.										
641	Constans II (Emp. East) a.										
642	Heraclius (Emp. East) d.				St. Oswald d.						
646					St. Gall d.						
650					St. Winifred d.						
651					Aidan d.						
656					St. Hubert b.						
657					St. Willibrord b.						
662					St. Maximus d.						
664							Hsüan Tsang d.				

665-839 A.D.

Year A.D.	Government and Law	Military and Naval Affairs	Industry Commerce Economics Finance Invention Labor	Travel and Exploration	Philosophy and Religion	Science and Medicine	Education Scholarship History	Literature	Painting and Sculpture	Music	Miscellaneous
665	Penda (Mercia) d.										
668	Constans II (Emp. East) d.										
673							Bede b.				
680					St. Boniface b.			Caedmon d.			
682					St. Agathon d.						
587					St. Cuthbert d.						
690					St. Aimé d. John of Damascus b. Theodore of Canterbury d.						
701								Li Po b.			
704					St. Adamnan d.						
709					St. Wilfrid d.						
711	Roderic (Visigoths) d.										
717	Charles Martel (Franks) a. Leo III (Emp. East) a.										
720							Paulus Diaconus b.				
721						Geber b.					
727					St. Hubert d.						
735							Alcuin b. Bede d.				
738					St. Willibrord d.						
740	Constantine V (Emp. West) a.										
741	Charles Martel (Franks) d. Leo III (Emp. East) d.				Pope Zacharias a.						
742	Charlemagne b.										
745	Constantine V (Emp. West) d.						Waquidi b.				
752	Pepin le Bref (Franks) a.				Pope Zacharias d.						

Year A.D.	Government and Law	Military and Naval Affairs	Industry Commerce Economics Finance Invention Labor	Travel and Exploration	Philosophy and Religion	Science and Medicine	Education Scholarship History	Literature	Painting and Sculpture	Music	Miscellaneous
754					John of Damascus d.						
755					St. Boniface d.						
762								Li Po d.			
768	Pepin le Bref (Franks) d.										
770							Eginhard b.				
775	Abu Ja'far Almansur										
776						Geber d.					
780	Irene (Empress of East) a.				Al-Mokanna d. St. Walpurgis d.						
786	Hārūn-al-Rashid a.										
795					Pope (St.) Leo III a.						
796	Offa (Mercia) d.										
798					St. Ignatius of Constantinople b.						
800					Turpin d.		Paulus Diaconus d.	Cynewulf fl.			
802	Egbert (English) a. Irene (Empress of East) dep.										
804							Alcuin d.				
809	Hārūn-al-Rashid d.										
813	Leo V (Emp. East) a.										
814	Charlemagne d. Louis I (France) a.										
815					Scotus Erigena b.						
816					Pope (St.) Leo III d.						
820	Leo V (Emp. East) d.				Photius b.						
823							Waqidi d.				
827											
829	Theophilus (Emp. East) a.										
839	Egbert (English) d. Ethelwulf (W. Saxons) a.										

840–928 A.D.

Year A.D.	Government and Law	Military and Naval Affairs	Industry Commerce Economics Finance Invention Labor	Travel and Exploration	Philosophy and Religion	Science and Medicine	Education Scholarship History	Literature	Painting and Sculpture	Music	Miscellaneous
840	Louis I (France) d.						Eginhard d.				
842	Theophilus (Emp. East) d.										
843	Lothair I (Emp. West) a.										
847					Pope Leo IV a.						
848					Dionysius of Tel-Mahrē d.						
849					Walafrid Strabo d.						
850	Hatto b.					Mohammed al-Batani fl.					
853	Boris I (Bulgaria) a.										
855	Edmund (East Anglia) a. Lothair I (Emp. West) d.				Pope Leo IV d.						
858	Ethelbald (W. Saxons) a. Ethelwulf (W. Saxons) d.				Pope Nicholas I a.						
860	Ethelbald (W. Saxons) d. Ethelbert (W. Saxons) a.										
862					St. Swithin d.						
866	Basil I (Emp. East) a. Ethelbert (W. Saxons) d. Ethelred I (W. Saxons) a.										
867					Pope Nicholas I d.						
870	Edmund (East Anglia) d.									Al Farabi b.	
871	Alfred the Great (England) a. Ethelred I (W. Saxons) d.										
872	Harald I (Norway) a.				Pope John VIII a.						
875	Charles II (Emp. West) a.										
876	Carloman (Bavaria and Italy) a.										

Year A.D.	Government and Law	Military and Naval Affairs	Industry Commerce Economics Finance Invention Labor	Travel and Exploration	Philosophy and Religion	Science and Medicine	Education Scholarship History	Literature	Painting and Sculpture	Music	Miscellaneous
877	Charles II (Emp. West) d.				Scotus Erigena d.						
878					St. Ignatius of Constantinople d.						
880	Carloman (Bavaria and Italy) d.										
881	Charles III (Emp. West) a.										
882					Pope John VIII d.						
886	Basil I (Emp. East) d. Leo VI (Emp. East) a.										
888	Arnulf (Emp. West) a. Charles III (Emp. West) d.										
889	Boris I (Bulgaria) d.										
891					Photius d.		Ya'qūbi d.				
892					Seadiah ben Joseph b.						
899	Arnulf (Emp. West) d. Edward the Elder (English) a.										
900	Alfred the Great (England) d.					Bubacher fl.					
909					St. Dunstan b.						
911	Leo VI (Emp. East) d.										
912	Constantine VII (Emp. East) a.										
913	Hatto d.										
914					Pope John X a.						
919	Heinrich I (Germany) a.										
922	Robert I (Franks) a.										
923	Robert I (Franks) d.				St. Bernard de Menthon b.						
924	Edward the Elder (English) d. Ethelstan (Saxons) a.				Berengarius d.						
928					Pope John X d.						

933–1018 A.D.

Year A.D.	Government and Law	Military and Naval Affairs	Industry Commerce Economics Finance Invention Labor	Travel and Exploration	Philosophy and Religion	Science and Medicine	Education Scholarship History	Literature	Painting and Sculpture	Music	Miscellaneous
933	Harald I (Norway) d.										
935	Haakon I (Norway) a.						Hrotsvitha b.				
936	Heinrich I (Germany) d.										
940	Ethelstan (English) d.							Firdousi b.			
942					Seadiah ben Joseph d.						
943	Howel Dda (Wales) a.										
946	Edred (English) a.										
950	Howel Dda (Wales) d.									Al Farabi d.	
955	Edred (English) d.				Pope John XII a.			Aelfric b.			
956					St. Vladimir b.						
959	Constantine VII (Emp. East) d. Edgar (English) a.										
960	Basil II (Emp. East) a.										
961	Haakon I (Norway) d.										
962	Otto I (H.R.E.) a.										
964					Pope John XII d.						
965						Ibn-al-Haitham b.					
967	Otto II (H.R.E.) a.										
971		Mahmud of Ghazni b.									
973	Otto I (H.R.E.) d.					Al-Biruni b.					
975	Edgar (English) d. Edward the Martyr (English) a.										
978	Edward the Martyr (English) d. Ethelred II (English) a.										
980						Avicenna b.					
981	Olaf the Red (Northumbria) d.										

Year A.D.	Government and Law	Military and Naval Affairs	Industry Commerce Economics Finance Invention Labor	Travel and Exploration	Philosophy and Religion	Science and Medicine	Education Scholarship History	Literature	Painting and Sculpture	Music	Miscellaneous
983	*Otto II (H.R.E.) d.* Otto III (H.R.E.) a.										
985	Sweyn (Denmark) a.										
987	Hugh Capet (Franks) a.										
988					*St. Dunstan d.*						
990							Rabbi Jonah b.			Guido of Arezzo fl.	
992	Boleslav I (Poland) a.										
995	Olaf I (Norway) a.										
996	*Hugh Capet (Franks) d.* Robert II (Franks) a.										
997	Stephen I (Hungary) a.										
999					Pope Silvester II a.						
1000	*Olaf I (Norway) d.*			Leif Ericsson fl.	Adalbert b.						
1002	Brian Boru (Ireland) a. Henry II (H.R.E.) a. *Otto III (H.R.E.) d.*			Thorfinn Karlsefni fl.			*Hrotsvitha d.*				
1003					*Pope Silvester II d.*						
1005					Lanfranc b.						
1007					St. Pietro Damiani b.						
1008					*St. Bernard de Menthon d.*						
1012					St. Wulfstan b.						
1014	*Brian Boru (Ireland) d.* *Sweyn (Denmark) d.*										
1015		Robt. Guiscard b.			*St. Vladimir d.*						
1016	*Edmund II (English) a. and d.* *Ethelred II (English) d.* Olaf II (Norway) a.										
1017	Canute (English and Danes) a.										
1018								Michael Psellus b.			

1020–1072 A.D.

Year A.D.	Government and Law	Military and Naval Affairs	Industry Commerce Economics Finance Invention Labor	Travel and Exploration	Philosophy and Religion	Science and Medicine	Education Scholarship History	Literature	Painting and Sculpture	Music	Miscellaneous
1020						Constantine the African b. *Ibn-al-Haitham d.*		*Aelfric d.* *Firdousi d.*			
1023								*Wulfstan d.*			
1024	*Henry II (H.R.E.) d.*				Avicebrón b.						
1025	*Basil II (Emp. East) d.* *Boleslav I (Poland) d.*										
1027	Conrad II (H.R.E.) a.										
1030	*Olaf II (Norway) d.*	*Mahmud of Ghazni d.*			Saint Bruno b.						
1031	Henri I (France) a. *Robert II (Franks) d.*										
1033					St. Anselm b.						
1034	Duncan I (Scotland) a.										
1035	*Canute (English and Danes) d.* Hardicanute (English and Danes) a. Harold I (English) a. *Robert the Devil d.*										
1036					Odo of Bayeux b.						
1037						*Avicenna d.*					
1038	*Stephen I (Hungary) d.*										
1039	*Conrad II (H.R.E.) d.* Henry III (H.R.E.) a.										
1040	*Duncan I (Scotland) d.* Harold I (English) d. Macbeth (Scotland) a.	The Cid b.					Rashi b.				Lady Godiva b.
1042	Edward the Confessor (English) a. *Hardicanute (English and Danes) d.*										
1045	Raymund of Toulouse b.				St. Margaret b.						
1046	Matilda of Tuscany b.										

Year A.D.	Government and Law	Military and Naval Affairs	Industry Commerce Economics Finance Invention Labor	Travel and Exploration	Philosophy and Religion	Science and Medicine	Education Scholarship History	Literature	Painting and Sculpture	Music	Miscellaneous
1047	Harald III (Norway) a.										
1048						Al-Biruni d.					
1049					Pope (St.) Leo IX a.						
1050					Roscellinus b.		Rabbi Jonah d.				
1053	Godwine d.										
1054					Pope (St.) Leo IX d.						
1055					Pope Victor II a.						
1056	Ferdinand I (Castile and Leon) a. Henry III (H.R.E.) d. Henry IV (H.R.E.) a.										
1057	Isaac I (Emp. East) a.				Pope Victor II d.		Joannes Xiphilinus fl.				
1058	Boleslav II (Poland) a. Macbeth (Scotland) d.				Avicebron d. Ghazali b. Pope Nicholas II a.						
1059	Isaac I (Emp. East) d. Malcolm III (Scotland) a.										
1060	Henri I (France) d. Philippe I (France) a.						Eadmer b.				
1061		Godefroy de Bouillon b.			Pope Nicholas II d.						
1065	Ferdinand I (Castile and Leon) d.										
1066	Edward the Confessor (English) d. Harald III (Norway) d. Harold II (English) a. and d. Tostig (Northumberland) d. William the Conqueror (England) a.										
1071											
1072	Alfonso I (Castile) a. Roger I (Sicily) a.	Hereward the Wake fl.			Adalbert d. St. Pietro Damiani d.						

Year A.D.	Government and Law	Military and Naval Affairs	Industry Commerce Economics Finance Invention Labor	Travel and Exploration	Philosophy and Religion	Science and Medicine	Education Scholarship History	Literature	Painting and Sculpture	Music	Miscellaneous
1073					Pope (St.) Gregory VII a.						
1075							Orderic Vitali b.				
1077	Ladislaus I (Hungary) a.										
1078		Tancred b.									
1079					Abelard b.			Michael Psellus d.			Héloïse b.
1080							William of Malmesbury b.				Lady Godiva d.
1081	Alexius I (Emperor of East) b. Boleslav II (Poland) d. Suger b.										
1084					St. Charles of Flanders b.						
1085		Robt. Guiscard d.			Pope (St.) Gregory VII d.	Judah ben Samuel Halevi b.					
1086					Pope Victor III a.						
1087	William the Conqueror (England) d. William II (England) a.				Pope Victor III d.	Constantine the African d.					
1088					Pope Urban II a.						
1089					Lanfranc d.						
1090					St. Bernard de Clairvaux b.						
1091					Avenzoar b.						
1092								Abenezra b.			
1093	Malcolm III (Scotland) d.				St. Margaret d.						
1094					St. Malachy b.						
1095	Kolomon (Hungary) a. Ladislaus I (Hungary) d.				St. Wulfstan d.						
1096					Hugh of St. Victor b.						
1097					Odo of Bayeux d.						
1098					St. Hildegarde b.						

Year A.D.	Government and Law	Military and Naval Affairs	Industry Commerce Economics Finance Invention Labor	Travel and Exploration	Philosophy and Religion	Science and Medicine	Education Scholarship History	Literature	Painting and Sculpture	Music	Miscellaneous
1099	Raymund of Antioch b.	*The Cid d.*			Pope Paschal II a. *Pope Urban II d.*	Edrisi b.					
1100	Albrecht I (Brandenburg) b. Baldwin I (Jerusalem) a. Henry I (England) a. *Philippe I (France) d. William II (England) d.*	*Godefroy de Bouillon d.*			Arnold of Brescia b. St. Gilbert of Sempringham b. Peter Lombard b.		Wace b.	Geoffrey of Monmouth b.			
1101	*Roger I (Sicily) d.*			Daniel of Kiev fl.	*St. Bruno d.*			*Bertrand de Born fl.* Blondel fl. John Tzetzes fl.			Héloïse b.
1102	Boleslav III (Poland) a. Matilda (England) b.										
1105	*Raymund of Toulouse d.*						*Rashi d.*				
1106	*Henry IV (H.R.E.) d. Henry V (H.R.E.) a.*										
1108	Enrico Dandolo b. Louis VI (France) a.										
1109	*Alfonso I (Castile) d.*				*St. Anselm d.*						
1111					*Ghazali d.*						
1112		*Tancred d.*									
1115	*Matilda of Tuscany d.*				*Peter the Hermit d.*			John of Salisbury b.			
1116	*Kolomon (Hungary) d.*										
1117	Mohammed Nureddin b.										
1118	*Alexius I (Emp. East) d. Baldwin I (Jerusalem) d.* Baldwin II (Jerusalem) a.				Thos. à. Becket b. *Pope Paschal II d.*						
1119								Fārid Ud-Dīn Attār b.			
1120	Vacarius b.										
1121					*William of Champeaux d.*						
1122					*Roscellinus d.*						
1123								*Omar Khayyām d.*			

1124–1178 A.D.

Year A.D.	Government and Law	Military and Naval Affairs	Industry Commerce Economics Finance Invention Labor	Travel and Exploration	Philosophy and Religion	Science and Medicine	Education Scholarship History	Literature	Painting and Sculpture	Music	Miscellaneous
1124	David I (Scotland) a.						Eadmer d.				
1125	Henry V (H.R.E.) d.										
1126					Averroes b.						
1127					St. Charles of Flanders d. St. Felix b.						
1128	Absalon b. Ranulf Flambard d.										
1129							Alured of Beverley d.				
1130	Roger II (Sicily) a.				Pope Innocent II a.						
1131	Baldwin II (Jerusalem) d.										
1133	Lothair II (H.R.E.) a.										
1135	Henry I (England) d. Stephen (England) a.				St. Hugh of Lincoln b. Moses Maimonides b.						
1137	Lothair II (H.R.E.) d. Louis VI (France) d. Louis VII (France) a.										
1138	Conrad III (Germany) a. Saladin b.				Avempace fl.						
1139	Boleslav III (Poland) d.				Roger of Salisbury d.						
1140	Alfonso I (Portugal) a.				Thurstan d.	Judah ben Samuel Halevi d.		Chrétien de Troyes b. Walter Mape b. Nizāmī b.			
1141					Hugh of St. Victor d.						
1142					Abelard d.		Orderic Vitali d.				Héloïse d.
1143	Baldwin III (Jerusalem) a. Manuel I (Emp. East) a.				Pope Innocent II d.		William of Malmesbury d.				
1145					Pope Eugenius III a. Joachim of Floris b.						
1146							Giraldus Cambrensis b.				
1147											
1148				Kiu Chang-Chun b.	St. Malachy d.						

Year A.D.	Government and Law	Military and Naval Affairs	Industry Commerce Economics Finance Invention Labor	Travel and Exploration	Philosophy and Religion	Science and Medicine	Education Scholarship History	Literature	Painting and Sculpture	Music	Miscellaneous
1149	Raymund of Antioch d.										
1150					Bernard Sylvestris fl.		Saxo Grammaticus b.				
1151	Suger d.										
1152	Conrad III (Germany) d.										
1153	David I (Scotland) d.				St. Bernard de Clairvaux d. Pope Eugenius III d.						
1154	Henry II (England) a. Roger II (Sicily) d. Stephen (England) d. William I (Sicily) a.				Pope Adrian IV a. Robt. Pulleyn d.			Geoffrey of Monmouth d.			
1155	Frederick I (H.R.E.) a.				Arnold of Brescia d.						
1157	Valdemar I (Denmark) a.					Alexander Neckam b.					
1159					Pope Adrian IV d.						
1160							Geoffroy de Villehardouin b.				
1161					Theobald d.						
1162	Baldwin III (Jerusalem) d. Genghis Khan b.			Abdallatif b.	Avenzoar d.						
1164					Peter Lombard d.						
1165	William (Scotland) a.							Wolfram von Eschenbach b.			
1166	William I (Sicily) d. William II (Sicily) a.										
1167	Matilda (England) d.							Abenezra d.			
1170	Albrecht I (Brandenburg) d. Canute II (Denmark) a.				Thos. à Becket d. St. Domenic de Guzman b.			Hartmann von Aue b.			
1175					St. Edmund Rich b. Robt. Grosseteste b.		Michael Scot b. Wace d.	Marie de France fl.			
1176		Earl Richard of Pembroke d.									
1178	Mohammed Nureddin d.										

1179–1223 A.D.

Year A.D.	Government and Law	Military and Naval Affairs	Industry Commerce Economics Finance Invention Labor	Travel and Exploration	Philosophy and Religion	Science and Medicine	Education Scholarship History	Literature	Painting and Sculpture	Music	Miscellaneous
1179					*St. Hildegarde d.*	*Yāqūt b.*	*Snorri Sturlason b.*				
1180	*Louis VII (France) d.* *Manuel I (Emp. East) d.* Philippe II (France) a.				*Walter of St. Victor d.*	*Edrisi d.*		*John of Salisbury d.*			
1182	*Valdemar I (Denmark) d.*			G. de Piano Carpini b.	St. Francis of Assisi b.						
1184								*Sa'dī b.*			
1185	*Alfonso I (Portugal) d.* Isaac II (Emp. East) a.				Pope Urban III a.						
1187	*Raymund of Tripoli d.* Saladin a.				*Pope Urban III d.*						
1189	*Henry II (England) d.* Richard I (England) a. *William II (Sicily) d.*				St. Gilbert of Sempringham d.						
1190	*Frederick I (H.R.E.) d.* *Ranulf de Glanvill d.*										
1191	Henry VI (H.R.E.) a.							*Chrétien de Troyes d.*			
1193	Saladin d.				Albertus Magnus b. St. Clare b.		*Eustathius d.*				
1195					St. Anthony of Padua b.			John Garland b.			
1197	*Henry VI (H.R.E.) d.* *Wm. de Longchamp d.*				St. Richard b.						
1198	Philipp (Germany) a. *Roderick (Ireland) d.*				*Averroes d.* Pope Innocent III a.			Walther von der Vogelweide b.			
1199	John (England) a. *Richard I (England) d.*										
1200	*Vacarius d.*				St. Hugh of Lincoln d.		Matthew of Paris b.				
1201	*Absalon d.*					Sakarja ben Mohammed fl.		Layamon fl. Thibaut IV (Navarre) b.			
1202	*Canute II (Denmark) d.* Valdemar II (Denmark) a.				Joachim of Floris d.			*Nizāmī d.*			

Year A.D.	Government and Law	Military and Naval Affairs	Industry Commerce Economics Finance Invention Labor	Travel and Exploration	Philosophy and Religion	Science and Medicine	Education Scholarship History	Literature	Painting and Sculpture	Music	Miscellaneous
1204	Isaac II (Emp. East) d.				Moses Maimonides d.						
1205	Enrico Dandolo d. Hubert Walter d.										
1206							Saxo Grammaticus d.				
1207					St. Elizabeth b.			Rumi b.			
1208	Simon de Montfort b. Philipp (Germany) d.										
1209	Otto IV (H.R.E.) a.							Walter Mape d.			
1210								Jean Bodel d. Gottfried von Strassburg fl. Hartmann von Aue d.			
1211							Jocelin de Brakelond d.				
1212					St. Felix d.						
1213							Geoffroy de Villehardouin d.				
1214	William (Scotland) d.					Roger Bacon b.					
1215	Otto IV (H.R.E.) d.			William of Rubruquis b.							
1216	Henry III (England) a. John (England) d. Kublai Khan b.				Pope Innocent III d.						
1217	Haakon IV (Norway) a.					Alexander Neckam d.					
1218					St. Thomas de Cantilupe b.						
1219	Earl William of Pembroke d.										
1220	Frederick II (H.R.E.) a. Heinrich VII (Germany) a.						Giraldus Cambrensis d.	Thomas of Erceldoune b. Wolfram von Eschenbach d.			
1221					St. Bonaventura b. St. Domenic de Guzman d.						
1223	Philippe II (France) d.										

1224–1273 A.D.

Year A.D.	Government and Law	Military and Naval Affairs	Industry Commerce Economics Finance Invention Labor	Travel and Exploration	Philosophy and Religion	Science and Medicine	Education Scholarship History	Literature	Painting and Sculpture	Music	Miscellaneous
1224								Sire de Joinville b.			
1225					Amalric d. St. Thomas Aquinas b.						
1226	Louis IX (France) a.				St. Francis of Assisi d.		Abul Faraj b.				
1227	Genghis Khan d.			Kiu Chang Chun d.	Pope Gregory IX a.						
1228					Stephen Langton d.			Walther von der Vogelweide d.			
1229						Yāqūt d.		Farīd Ud-Dīn Attār d.			
1231				Abdallatif d.	St. Anthony of Padua d. St. Elizabeth d.						
1232							Michael Scot d.				
1235	Béla IV (Hungary) a.				Raymond Lully b. Siger de Brabant b.	Arnaud de Villeneuve b.	Gervase of Tilbury d.				
1236					Roger of Wendover d.						
1237											
1239											
1240	David II (Wales) a.				St. Edmund Rich d.			Jean de Meung b.	Giovanni Cimabue b.		
1241	Valdemar II (Denmark) d.				Pope Gregory IX d.		Snorri Sturlason d.				
1242	Heinrich VII (Germany) d.										
1243	Hubert de Burgh d.				Pope Innocent IV a. Jacques de Molay b.						
1245					Alexander of Hales d.			Rutebeuf b.	Giovanni Pisano b.		
1246	David II (Wales) d.										
1247				Giovanni di Montecorvino b.							
1249					William of Auvergne d.						
1250	Conrad IV (Germany) a. Frederick II (H.R.E.) d.				Pietro d'Abano b.		Wm. Rishanger b.	Sordello fl.			
1252	Alfonso X (Leon and Castile) a.			G. de Piano Carpini d.							

Year A.D.	Government and Law	Military and Naval Affairs	Industry Commerce Economics Finance Invention Labor	Travel and Exploration	Philosophy and Religion	Science and Medicine	Education Scholarship History	Literature	Painting and Sculpture	Music	Miscellaneous
1253	Ottakar II (Bohemia) a.				St. Clare d. Robert Grosseteste d. St. Richard d. St. Yves of Britanny b.			Thibaut IV (Navarre) d.			
1254	Conrad IV (Germany) d.			Marco Polo b.	Pope Innocent IV d.						
1257								Cecco d'Ascoli b.			
1258	Manfred (Sicily) a.										
1259	Osman I (Turkey) b.						Matthew of Paris d.				
1260	Michael VIII (Emp. East) a.				Johannes Eckhart b.		Robert of Gloucester b.		Gaddo Gaddi b.		
1262	Hugh le Despenser b.										
1263	Haakon IV (Norway) d.										
1264					Vincent of Beauvais d.						
1265	Simon de Montfort d.				Pope Clement IV a. Duns Scotus b.			Dante b.			
1266	Charles I (Naples and Sicily) a. Conradin (Jerusalem) a. Manfred (Sicily) d.										Beatrice b.
1268	Henry de Bracton d. Conradin (Jerusalem) d.				Pope Clement IV d.						
1269							Sir John de Baliol d.				
1270	Béla IV (Hungary) d. Louis IX (France) d. Philippe III (France) a. Stephen II (Hungary) a.				Nicolaus of Lyra b.				Andrea Pisano b.		
1272	Edward I (England) a. Henry III (England) d. Ladislaus IV (Hungary) a. Stephen II (Hungary) d.	Sir Wm. Wallace b.						John Garland d.			
1273	Rudolf I (Germany) a.						Abulfeda b.	Rumi d.			

1274–1321 A.D.

Year A.D.	Government and Law	Military and Naval Affairs	Industry Commerce Economics Finance Invention Labor	Travel and Exploration	Philosophy and Religion	Science and Medicine	Education Scholarship History	Literature	Painting and Sculpture	Music	Miscellaneous
1274					St. Thomas Aquinas d. St. Bonaventura d.						
1275							Giovanni Villani b.				
1276									Giotto b.		
1277	Earl Thomas of Lancaster b.										
1278	Marino Falieri b. Ottakar II (Bohemia) d.										
1280		Roger di Flor b.			Albertus Magnus d.				Pietro Lorenzetti b.		
1282	David III (Wales) a. Don Juan Manuel b. Michael VIII (Emp. East) d.				St. Thomas de Cantilupe b.		Richard of Bury b.				
1283	David III (Wales) d.							Juan Ruiz b.			
1284	Alfonso X (Leon and Castile) d.				Siger de Brabant d.				Simone Martini b. Niccola Pisano d.		
1285	Charles I (Naples and Sicily) d. Philippe III (France) d. Philippe IV (France) a.							Rutebeuf d.			
1286		Sir James Douglas b.		Odoric b.			Abul Faraj d.				
1288					Gersonides b.			Robert Mannyng b.			
1290	Jacob van Artevelde b. Ladislaus IV (Hungary) d.				Richard Rolle de Hampole b.		Marsilius of Padua b. Walter of Coventry fl.				Beatrice d.
1291	Rudolf I (Germany) d.							Sa'di d.			
1292	John de Baliol (Scotland) a.										
1293				William of Rubruquis d.	Jan van Ruysbroek b.						
1294	Kublai Khan d.				Pope Boniface VIII a. Pope Celestine V a. and abd.	Roger Bacon d.					
1296	Frederick III (Sicily) a.										

Year A.D.	Government and Law	Military and Naval Affairs	Industry Commerce Economics Finance Invention Labor	Travel and Exploration	Philosophy and Religion	Science and Medicine	Education Scholarship History	Literature	Painting and Sculpture	Music	Miscellaneous
1297								Thomas of Erceldoune d.			
1299							Ranulf Higdon b.				
1300				Sir John Mandeville b. Ugolino Vivaldo fl.	William of Occam b. Heinrich Suso b. Johann Tauler b.		Robert of Gloucester d.	Hafiz b. Guillaume de Machaut b.	Taddeo Gaddi b. Ambrogio Lorenzetti b.		
1302					St. Bridget of Sweden b.				Giovanni Cimabue d.		
1303					Pope Boniface VIII d. St. Yves of Britanny d.						
1304				Ibn Batuta b.				Petrarch b.			
1305		Sir Wm. Wallace d.			Pope Clement V a.			Jean de Meung d.			
1306	Robert Bruce (Scotland) a.	Roger di Flor d.									
1307	Edward I (England) d. Edward II (England) a.										
1308	Henry VII (H.R.E.) a.				Duns Scotus d.				Orcagna b.		
1311	John (Bohemia) a.										
1312							William Rishanger d.				
1313	Henry VII (H.R.E.) d. Cola di Rienzi b.					Arnaud de Villeneuve d.		Giovanni Boccaccio b.			
1314	Louis IV (H.R.E.) a. Philippe IV (France) d.				Pope Clement V d. Jacques de Molay d. Bernard Saisset d.				Giovanni Pisano d.		
1315	John de Baliol (Scotland) d.				Raymond Lully d.						
1316					Pietro d'Abano d. Pope John XXII a.				John Barbour b.		
1317	Philippe V (France) a.							Sire de Joinville d.			
1320	Ladislaus I (Poland) a.	Bertrand DuGuesclin b.			John Wycliffe b.						
1321								Dante d.			

Year A.D.	Government and Law	Military and Naval Affairs	Industry Commerce Economics Finance Invention Labor	Travel and Exploration	Philosophy and Religion	Science and Medicine	Education Scholarship History	Literature	Painting and Sculpture	Music	Miscellaneous
1322	Charles IV (France) a. Earl Thomas of Lancaster d. Philippe V (France) d.										
1323				Marco Polo d.			William of Wykeham b.				
1325			Francesco Pegolotti fl.					John Gower b.			
1326	Hugh le Despenser d. Osman I (Turkey) d.										
1327	Edward II (England) d. Edward III (England) a.				Johannes Eckhart d. St. Roch d.			Cecco d'Ascoli d. Philippe de Mézières b.			
1328	Charles IV (France) d. Philippe VI (France) a.										
1329	Robert Bruce (Scotland) d. David II (Scotland) a.										
1330		Sir James Douglas d. Edward the Black Prince b.						Ulrich Bonner fl	Aretino Spinello b.		
1331		Gaston de Foix b.		Odoric d.			Abulfeda d.				
1332							Ibn Khaldūn b. P. López de Ayala b.	Wm. Langland b.	Gaddo Gaddi d.		
1333	Casimir III (Poland) a. Ladislaus I (Poland) d. Tamerlane b.										
1334					Pope John XXII d.						
1337	Frederick III (Sicily) d.							Jean Froissart b.	Giotto d.		
1338								Robert Mannyng d.			
1340	Philip van Artevelde b. Earl John of Lancaster b. Valdemar IV (Denmark) a.			Giovanni de' Marignolli fl.	Gerhard Groot b. Nicolaus of Lyra d.			Geoffrey Chaucer b. Eustache Deschamps b.			
1341	Duke Edmund of York b.										

Year A.D.	Government and Law	Military and Naval Affairs	Industry Commerce Economics Finance Invention Labor	Travel and Exploration	Philosophy and Religion	Science and Medicine	Education Scholarship History	Literature	Painting and Sculpture	Music	Miscellaneous
1342	Philip the Bold (Burgundy) b. Louis I (Hungary) a.						Marsilius of Padua d.				
1343	Joanna I (Naples) a.										
1344					Gersonides d.	al-Damiri b.			Simone Martini d.		
1345	Jacob van Artevelde d.						Richard of Bury d.				
1346	John (Bohemia) d.										
1347	Charles IV (H.R.E.) a. John VI (Emp. East) a. Louis IV (H.R.E.) d.				St. Catherine of Siena b.						
1348				Giovanni di Montecorvino d.	John de Stratford d.		Giovanni Villani d.		Ambrogio Lorenzetti d. Pietro Lorenzetti d. Andrea Pisano d.		
1349	Don Juan Manuel d.				Richard Rolle de Hampole d. William of Occam d.						
1350	Sir Wm. Gascoigne b. Philippe VI (France) d. Witold b.				Pierre d'Ailly b.		Andrew of Wyntoun b.	Laurence Minot fl. Juan Ruiz d.			
1352					Pope Innocent VI a.						
1353											
1354	John VI (Emp. East) dep. Cola di Rienzi d.										
1355	Marino Falieri d. Duke Thomas of Gloucester b.						Manuel Chrysoloras b.				Iñez de Castro d.
1359	Murad I (Turkey) a. Owen Glendower b.										
1360	Jean II (France) a.	Jan Žižka b.									
1361					Johann Tauler d.						
1362					Pope Innocent VI d. Pope Urban V a.						
1363					Jean de Gerson b.		Ranulf Higdon d.				

1364–1399 A.D.

Year A.D.	Government and Law	Military and Naval Affairs	Industry Commerce Economics Finance Invention Labor	Travel and Exploration	Philosophy and Religion	Science and Medicine	Education Scholarship History	Literature	Painting and Sculpture	Music	Miscellaneous
1364	Charles V (France) a. Jean II (France) d.	Sir Henry Percy b.					Henry Chicheley b. Ahmed el-Makrîzî b.	Christine de Pisan b.			
1365	Robert Le Maçon b.				Jerome of Prague b.						
1366	1st Duke of Norfolk b.				Heinrich Suso d.				Hubert van Eyck b. Taddeo Gaddi d.		
1368									Orcagna d.		
1369					John Huss b.						
1370	Casimir III (Poland) d.	Sir John Chandos d.	Coster b.		Pope Urban V d.			John Lydgate b. Thos. Occleve b.	Jan van Eyck b.		
1371	David II (Scotland) d. Robert II (Scotland) a.										
1372	Francesco Foscari b.			Sir John Mandeville d.							
1373	Duke Edward of York b.				St. Bridget of Sweden d.						
1374								Petrarch d.			
1375	Valdemar IV (Denmark) d.							Giovanni Boccaccio d.	Robt. Campin b.		
1376		Edward the Black Prince d.									
1377	Edward III (England) d. Olgierd d. Richard II (England) a.				Henry Beaufort b. Sir John Oldcastle b. ?			Guillaume de Machaut d.	Filippo Brunelleschi b.		
1378	Charles IV (H.R.E.) d. Wenceslaus (H.R.E.) a.	Sir John Fastolf b.		Ibn Batuta d.	Pope Urban VI a.		John Hardyng b.		Jacopo Della Quercia b. Lorenzo Ghiberti b.		
1379											
1380	Charles V (France) d. Charles VI (France) a.	Bertrand DuGuesclin d.		Anselme D'Isalguier b.	Thomas à Kempis b. St. Bernardine b. St. Catherine of Siena d. Peter Payne b.			Fernão Lopes b. Poggio b.			
1381	Thomas Arundel b. Margaret (Norway, etc.) a.		John Ball d. Wat Tyler d.	Hans Schiltberger b.	Jan van Ruysbroek d.						

Year A.D.	Government and Law	Military and Naval Affairs	Industry Commerce Economics Finance Invention Labor	Travel and Exploration	Philosophy and Religion	Science and Medicine	Education Scholarship History	Literature	Painting and Sculpture	Music	Miscellaneous
1382	*Philip van Artevelde d.* *Joanna I (Naples) d.* *Louis I (Hungary) d.* 13th Earl of Warwick b.										
1384					*Gerhard Groot d.* *John Wycliffe d.*		*John of Fordun d.*				
1385	João I (Portugal) a.										
1386	Ladislaus II (Poland) a.								Donatello b.		
1387		Hunyadi János b.							Fra Angelico b.		
1388		Earl Thomas of Salisbury b.						Juliana Berners fl. *Hafiz d.* Antoine de LaSale b.			
1389	Bayazid I (Turkey) a. Duke of Bedford b. *Murad I (Turkey) d.*				Pope Boniface IX a. *Pope Urban VI d.*						
1390	*Robert II (Scotland) d.*							*Sir Thomas Clanvowe d.*			
1391	Duke Humphrey of Gloucester b. Manuel II (Emp. East) a.	*Gaston de Foix III d.*						Duc Charles d'Orleans b.			
1392								Alain Chartier b.			
1394	Ulugh-Beg b.	*Sir John Hawkwood d.*		Henry the Navigator b.							
1395			Jacques Coeur b.		John Bessarion b.		William Waynflete b.	*John Barbour d.* Reginald Pecock b.			
1396	Philip the Good (Burgundy) b. Duke Wm. of Suffolk b.										
1397	*Duke Thomas of Gloucester d.*								Vittore Pisano b. Paolo Uccello b.		
1398			Johann Gutenberg b.				Francesco Filelfo b.				
1399	Henry IV (England) a. *Earl John of Lancaster d.* *1st Duke of Norfolk d.* *Richard II (England) dep.*		Wm. Canynge b.								

1400–1431 A.D.

Year A.D.	Government and Law	Military and Naval Affairs	Industry Commerce Economics Finance Invention Labor	Travel and Exploration	Philosophy and Religion	Science and Medicine	Education Scholarship History	Literature	Painting and Sculpture	Music	Miscellaneous
1400	Wenceslaus (H.R.E.) dep.						Nicolaus Cusanus b. Theodorus Gaza b.	Geoffrey Chaucer d. Wm. Langland d.	Jacopo Bellini b. Luca Della Robbia b. Stephan Lochner b. Rogier van der Weyden b.		Johann Fust b.
1401		Francesco Sforza b.					Georgius Pletho fl.		Masaccio b.		
1402	Gian Galeazzo Visconti d. Duke Edmund of York d.										
1403	Bayazid I (Turkey) d. Skanderbeg b.	Jean Dunois b. Sir Henry Percy d.									
1404	Philip the Bold (Burgundy) d. Duke Edmund of Somerset b.				Pope Boniface IX d.		William of Wykeham d.				Gilles de Rais b.
1405	Tamerlane d.					al-Damiri d.		Philippe de Mézières d.			
1406	James I (Scotland) a.				Pope Gregory XII a.		Ibn Khaldûn d. Laurentius Valla b.		Filippo Lippi b. Claus Sluter d.		
1407	Sir Thomas de Littleton b.						P. López de Ayala d.	Eustache Deschamps d.			
1408								John Gower d.			
1409	René I (Anjou) b.										Agnes Sorel b.
1410	Sigismund (H.R.E.) a.				Pope John XXIII (anti-Pope) a.			Jean Froissart d.	Dierik Bouts b. Aretino Spinello d.		
1411	Duke Richard of York b.	Antoine Chabannes b.									
1412	Margaret (Norway, etc.) d.	Joan of Arc b.									
1413	Henry IV (England) d. Henry V (England) a.										
1414	Albrecht III (Brandenburg) b. Thos. Arundel d. Joanna II (Naples) a.										

Year A.D.	Government and Law	Military and Naval Affairs	Industry Commerce Economics Finance Invention Labor	Travel and Exploration	Philosophy and Religion	Science and Medicine	Education Scholarship History	Literature	Painting and Sculpture	Music	Miscellaneous
1415	Duke Edward of York d.				Pope Gregory XII d. John Huss d. Pope John XXIII (anti-Pope) dep.		Manuel Chrysoloras d. Wm. Worcester b.		Antonio Vivarini b.		
1416	Owen Glendower d.				St. Francis of Paola b. Jerome of Prague d.				Jean Fouquet b.		
1417	Jacoba (Holland) a.				Pope Martin V a. Sir John Oldcastle d.						
1419	Sir Wm. Gascoigne d.			Nicolo de Conti b.							
1420	John Morton b.			Anselme D'Isalguier d.	Pierre d'Ailly d. Tomás Torquemada b. Johann Wessel b.		Andrew of Wyntoun d.		Petrus Christus b. Piero Della Francesca b. Benozzo Gozzoli b.		
1422	Charles VI (France) d. Charles VII (France) a. Henry V (England) d. Henry VI (England) a.								Il Pesellino b.		Wm. Caxton b.
1423											Dick Whittington d.
1424		Jan Žizka d.									
1425	Manuel II (Emp. East) d.								Claus de Werve fl.		
1426									Hubert van Eyck d. Maso Finiguerra b.		
1427									Alessio Baldovinetti b.		
1428	Earl of Warwick ("Kingmaker") b.	Earl Thomas of Salisbury d.							Jacopo Della Quercia d. Masaccio d.		
1429					Jean de Gerson d.				Gentile Bellini b. Antonio Pollaiuolo b.		
1430	Margaret of Anjou b. Witold d.								Antonello b. Giovanni Bellini b. Carlo Crivelli b. Justus of Ghent b. Andrea Mantegna b. Hans Memling b. Cosimo Tura b.		
1431		Joan of Arc d.			Pope Eugenius IV a. Pope Martin V d.		Wm. Elphinstone b.	Christine de Pisan d. François Villon b.	Mino di Giovanni b.		

1432–1460 A.D.

Year A.D.	Government and Law	Military and Naval Affairs	Industry Commerce Economics Finance Invention Labor	Travel and Exploration	Philosophy and Religion	Science and Medicine	Education Scholarship History	Literature	Painting and Sculpture	Music	Miscellaneous
1432	Jacoba (Holland) dep.							Luigi Pulci b.	Bartolommeo Vivarini b.		
1433	Charles the Bold (Burgundy) b. João I (Portugal) d.				Marsilio Ficino b.			Alain Chartier d.			
1434	Ladislaus II (Poland) d. Ladislaus III (Poland) a.							Matteo Boiardo b.	Michael Wohlgemuth b.		
1435	Duke of Bedford d. Joanna II (Naples) d.								Andrea del Verrocchio b.		
1436	F. Jiménez de Cisneros b.					Regiomontanus b.					
1437	James I (Scotland) d. James II (Scotland) a. Sigismund (H.R.E.) d.				Isaac Abrabanel b.				Andrea Della Robbia b.		
1438									Francesco del Cossa b. Velt Stoss b. Jacopo Della Quercia d.		
1439	13th Earl of Warwick d.										
1440			Coster d.	Hans Schiltberger d.					Jan van Eyck d. Hugo van der Goes b.		Gilles de Rais d.
1442						Rudolph Agricola b. Ahmed el-Makrîzî d.	Earl Rivers b.		Luca Signorelli b.		
1443		Robt. Le Maçon d.			Pierre Cauchon d.		Henry Chicheley d.				
1444	Ladislaus III (Poland) d.			Nicolo de Conti d.	St. Bernardine d.				Sandro Botticelli b. Bramante b. Robt. Campin d.		
1445									Antonio Liberale b. Martin Schongauer b.		
1446							William Grocyn b.?		Filippo Brunelleschi d. Perugino b. Alvise Vivarini b.		
1447	Casimir IV (Poland) a. Duke Humphrey of Gloucester d.				Henry Beaufort d. Pope Eugenius IV d. Pope Nicholas V a.		Philippe de Comines b.				

Year A.D.	Government and Law	Military and Naval Affairs	Industry Commerce Economics Finance Invention Labor	Travel and Exploration	Philosophy and Religion	Science and Medicine	Education Scholarship History	Literature	Painting and Sculpture	Music	Miscellaneous
1448	Richard Fox b.										
1449	Duke of Clarence b. Archibald Douglas b. Lorenzo de ' Medici b. *Ulugh-Beg d.*								Domenico Ghirlandajo b.		
1450	Christian I (Denmark) a. Sir John Fortescue (lawyer) fl. *Duke Wm. of Suffolk d.*	*Jack Cade d.*		Affonso d'Albuquerque b. John Cabot b. Pedro da Covilhâo b. B. Diaz de Novaes b. João Fernandes fl.	Jacobus Faber b. Wm. Warham b.	Basil Valentine fl.		Henry Bradshaw b. *Thos. Occleve d.*	Jerom Bosch b. Giambono fl. Bartolomeo Montagna b.	Joaquin Des Prés b. Heinrich Isaac b.	Aldus Manutius b. *Agnes Sorel d.*
1451	Mohammed II (Turkey) a.			Christopher Columbus b. Amerigo Vespucci b.				*John Lydgate d.*	Stephan Lochner d.		
1452	Frederick III (H.R.E.) a.				Girolamo Savonarola b.				Leonardo da Vinci b.		
1453	Caterina Sforza b.	Gonzalo de Cordoba b. *Earl of Shrewsbury d.*		Alfonso d'Albuquerque b.							
1454								Politian b.	Pinturicchio b.		
1455	Duke Edmund of Somerset d.				*Pope Nicholas V d.* *Peter Payne d.*		Johann Reuchlin b.		*Fra Angelico d.* *Lorenzo Ghiberti d.* *Vittore Pisano d.* Peter Vischer (Elder) b.		
1456		*Hunyadi Janos d.*	*Jacques Coeur d.*								
1457	Francesco Foscari d.						Peter Martyr b. *Laurentius Valla d.*	Sebastian Brant b.	Filippino Lippi b. *Il Pesellino d.*		
1458	George of Poděbrad (Bohemia) a. Matthias I (Hungary) a.				Pope Pius II a.			Jacopo Sannazaro b.			
1459		*Sir John Fastolf d.*			John Fisher b.		*Poggio d.*		Lorenzo di Credi b.		
1460	*James II (Scotland) d.* James III (Scotland) a. *Duke Richard of York d.*			Pedro Cabral b. Sebastián del Cano b. Vasco da Gama b. *Henry the Navigator d.* Juan Ponce de León b.			*Fernão Lopes d.*	Wm. Dunbar b. *Reginald Pécock d.* John Skelton b.	Adam Krafft b. Andrea Sansovino b. Andrea Da Solario b.		Johannes Frobenius b.

1461–1484 A.D.

Year A.D.	Government and Law	Military and Naval Affairs	Industry Commerce Economics Finance Invention Labor	Travel and Exploration	Philosophy and Religion	Science and Medicine	Education Scholarship History	Literature	Painting and Sculpture	Music	Miscellaneous
1461	Charles VII (France) d. Edward IV (England) a. Henry VI (England) dep. Louis XI (France) a.								V. Domenico d.		
1462	Ivan III (Muscovy) a.				Pietro Pomponazzi b.			Antoine de LaSale d.	Piero di Cosimo b.		
1463							Conde di Pico della Mirandola b.				
1464					Pope Paul II a. Pope Pius II d.		Nicolaus Cusanus d.		Maso Finiguerra d. Rogier van der Weyden d.		
1465					Johann Tetzel b.		John Hardyng d.	Duc d'Orléans d. Francois Villon d.?	Vittorio Carpaccio b. Geertgen van Haarlem b. Hans Holbein (Elder) b. ?		
1466		Francesco Sforza d.			Desiderius Erasmus b.				Donatello d. Quentin Matsys b.		Johann Fust d.
1467	Philip the Good (Burgundy) d.				John Colet b.				Giovanni Boltraffio b.		Luigi Cornaro b.
1468	Skanderbeg d.	Andrea Doria b. Jean Dunois d.	Johann Gutenberg d.				Wm. Lilye b.				
1469			Jakob Fugger d.					Lord Berners b. Niccolo Machiavelli b.	Giovanni Della Robbia b. Filippo Lippi d.		
1470							Pietro Bembo b. Virgil·Polydore b.	Robt. Henryson fl. Gil Vicente b.	Jacopo Bellini d. Vincenzo Catena b.		
1471	George of Poděbrad (Bohemia) d. Earl of Warwick ("Kingmaker") d.			Francisco Pizarro b.	Thos. à. Kempis d. Pope Paul II d. Pope Sixtus IV a.			Sir Thos. Malory d.	Albrecht Dürer b.		
1472					John Bessarion d.				Lucas Cranach b. Jan Mabuse b. Pietro Torrigiano b.		
1473		Chevalier Bayard b. 3rd Duke of Norfolk b.				Nicolaus Copernicus b.			Petrus Christus d.		
1474	Ferdinand I (Spain) a. Isabella I (Spain) a. Cuthbert Tunstall b.		Wm. Canynge d.		Lorenzo Campeggio b.		Bartolome de Las Casas b.	Lodovico Ariosto b. Gavin Douglas b.			Perkin Warbeck b.

Year A.D.	Government and Law	Military and Naval Affairs	Industry Commerce Economics Finance Invention Labor	Travel and Exploration	Philosophy and Religion	Science and Medicine	Education Scholarship History	Literature	Painting and Sculpture	Music	Miscellaneous
1475	Thos. Wolsey b.			V. Nuñez de Balboa b.				Pierre Gringoire b.? John Rastell b.	Fra Bartolommeo b. *Dierik Bouts d.*, Barnardino Luini b. Michelangelo b. Joachim de Patinir b. *Paolo Uccello d.*		
1476		Cesare Borgia b.		Sebastian Cabot b.		*Regiomontanus d.*		Alexander Barclay b.			*Jean Gobelin d.*
1477	*Charles the Bold (Burgundy) d.*				Hieronymus Emser b.		Aventinus b.		Girolamo de Pacchia b. Il Sodoma b. Titian b.		Lambert Simnel b.
1478	*Duke of Clarence d.* Sir Thos. More b.				Johann Faber b.		*Theodorus Gaza d.* G. de Oviedo y Valdéz b. Jacob Sylvius b.	Baldassare Castiglione b.	Giorgione b.		
1479							Jean Grolier b.		*Antonello d.* G. Dosso Dossi b.		
1480	*René I (Anjou) d.*	Goetz von Berlichingen b.		Fernando Magellan b.	Lars Anderson b. Johann Faust b.		Marco Vida b.	Matteo Bandello b. Harry the Minstrel fl. Christiern Pedersen b. Wm. Stewart b.	Veneto Bartolommeo b. Giovanni Caroto b. Joos van Cleve b. *Francesco del Cossa d.* *Jean Fouquet d.* *Justus of Ghent d.* Lorenzo Lotto b. Marcantonio b. Jacopo Palma b.		Lucrezia Borgia b.
1481	Bayazid II (Turkey) a. *Christian I (Denmark) d.* *Sir Thos. de Littleton d.* *Mohammed II (Turkey) d.*	Franz von Sickingen b.					*Francesco Filelfo d.*		Benvenuto Tisi b.		Baldassare Peruzzi b.
1482	Boabdil (Moors) a. *Margaret of Anjou d.* Geo. Martinuzzi b.				John Oecolampadius b.	*Wm. Worcester d.*		Bernardim Ribeiro b.	*Luca Della Robbia d.* *Hugo van der Goes d.*		
1483	*Edward IV (England) d.* *Edward V (England) a. and d.* *Louis XI (France) d.* Richard III (England) a.				Martin Luther b.	Girolamo Fracastoro b.	Francesco Guicciardini b.	*Earl Rivers d.*	Ridolfo Ghirlandajo b. Il Pordenone b. Raphael b.		Old Parr b.
1484	Duke Chas. of Suffolk b.				*Pope Sixtus IV d.* Georg Spalatin b. Ulrich Zwingli b.			*Luigi Pulci d.* F. de Sá de Mirandola b. J. C. Scaliger b.	*Mino di Giovanni d.* Gaudenzio Ferrari b. *Antonio Vivarini d.*		

1485-1508 A.D.

Year A.D.	Government and Law	Military and Naval Affairs	Industry Commerce Economics Finance Invention Labor	Travel and Exploration	Philosophy and Religion	Science and Medicine	Education Scholarship History	Literature	Painting and Sculpture	Music	Miscellaneous
1485	Catherine of Aragon b. Thos. Cromwell b. Henry VII (England) a. Antonio de Mendoza b. *Richard III (England) d.*	Hernando Cortez b.		G. Ramusio b.	Hugh Latimer b.		*Rudolph Agricola d.* Beatus Rhenanus b.		Michael Pacher fl. Sebastiani del Piombo b.		
1486	*Albrecht III (Brandenburg) d.*				Johann Eck b. Franz Lambert b.	C. Agrippa von Nettesheim b.	*Wm. Waynflete d.*		Andrea del Sarto b. Jacopo Sansovino b.		Mother Shipton b.
1487					Jos. Caro b. Bernardino Ochino b.				Peter Vischer (Younger) b.		
1488	*James III (Scotland) d.* James IV (Scotland) a.	*Antoine Chabannes d.*			Miles Coverdale b.	Otto Brunfels b.			*Andrea del Verrocchio d.*		
1489					Thos. Cranmer b. Guillaume Farel b. Ulrich von Hutten b. Thos. Münzer b. Johann Wessel b.		Sebastian Münster b.				
1490	Albrecht (Prussia) b. *Matthias I (Hungary) d.*	Duc de Bourbon b.		A. Nuñez Cabeza de Vaca b.	Bernt Knipperdollinck b. Karl von Schwenkfeld b.		Sir Thos. Elyot b. Olaus Magnus b. Juan Sepulveda b.	Vittoria Colonna b. Sir David Lyndsay b. François Rabelais b.		Robt. Wilkinson fl.	
1491	Guillaume Du Bellay b.			Jacques Cartier b.	Martin Bucer b. St. Ignatius de Loyola b.				*Friedrich Herlin d. Martin Schongauer d.*		*Wm. Caxton d.*
1492	Boabdil (Moors) dep. *Casimir IV (Poland) d. Lorenzo de' Medici d.*				Johann Agricola b. Pope Alexander VI a. Menno Simons b. Wm. Tyndale b.	Edward Wotton b.	B. Díaz del Castillo b. Juan Luis Vives b.	Pietro Aretino b. Margaret of Navarre b.	*Piero Della Francesca d.* Bernert van Orley b. Giulio Romano b.		
1493	*Frederick III (H.R.E.) d.* Stephen Gardiner b. Maximilian I (H.R.E.) a.	Duc de Montmorency b.		*Martin Pinzon d.*		Paracelsus b.		Agnolo Firenzuola b.	*Carlo Crivelli d. Geertgen van Haarlem d.*		
1494		Jean de la Valette b.		Johannes Leo b.	Juan de Ávila b. David Beaton b.		*Conde di Pico della Mirandola d.*	*Matteo Boiardo d. Politian d.* Hans Sachs b.	Correggio b. *Domenico Ghirlandajo d.* Lucas van Leyden b. Jacopo da Pontormo b.		
1495	Baber (India) a. Emanuel I (Portugal) a. Huáscar b.			Pedro de Alvarado b.	Thos. Bilney b.			Luigi Alamanni b. John Bale b. Clément Marot b.	*Hans Memling d. Cosimo Tura d.*	John Traverner	

Year A.D.	Government and Law	Military and Naval Affairs	Industry Commerce Economics Finance Invention Labor	Travel and Exploration	Philosophy and Religion	Science and Medicine	Education Scholarship History	Literature	Painting and Sculpture	Music	Miscellaneous
1496	Sir Anthony St. Leger b.						João de Barros b.	Sir Richard Maitland b.			François Bonivard b.
1497					Philipp Melanchthon b.			John Heywood b.	Benozzo Gozzoli d. Hans Holbein (Younger) b.		
1498				John Cabot d.	Andreas Osiander b. Girolamo Savonarola d. Tomás Torquemada d.				Il Moretto b. Antonio Pollaiuolo d.		
1499				Hernando De Soto b.	Marsilio Ficino d. Sebastian Franck b. Johannes Lasco b. Laurentius Petri b.		Edward Halle b.		Alessio Baldovinetti d. Bartolommeo Vivarini d.		Perkin Warbeck d.
1500	Atahualpa (Inca) b. John Morton d.	Peder Skram b.		Francisco de Orellana b. B. Diaz de Novaes d.	Alesius b. Richard Cox b. John Hooper b.? Peter Martyr b. Reginald Pole b. Nicholas Ridley b. John Rogers b. Thos. Sternhold b. Juan de Valdes b.		Aonio Paleario b.	Bonaventure Des Periers b.	Benvenuto Cellini b. Perino del Vaga b.		
1501		G. Jiménez de Quesada b.				Jerome Cardan b. Leonhard Fuchs b.					
1502	Duke of Northumberland b.	Vitellozzo Vitelli d.									
1503	Wilhelm von Grumbach b. Montezuma II (Mexico) a.				Pope Alexander VI d. Pope Julius II a.			Garcilaso de la Vega b. Sir Thos. Wyat b.	Alvise Vivarini d.		Nostradamus b.
1504	Isabella I (Spain) d. Margaret (Scotland) a.				Patrick Hamilton b. Matthew Parker b.		Florentius Volusenus b.		Filippino Lippi d. Parmigiano b.		
1505	Ivan III (Muscovy) d.	Sorley Boy Macdonnell b.			John Knox b.		Giles Tschudi b.	Nicholas Udall b.	Léonard Limousin b.		
1506	Sigismund I (Poland) a. Duke Edward of Somerset b.			Christopher Columbus d.	Elizabeth Barton b. St. Francis Xavier b.	Niccolo Tartaglia b.	Geo. Buchanan b. John Leland b. Johannes Sleidanus b.		Andrea Mantegna d.		
1507	Anne Boleyn b. Michel de l'Hopital b. Sir Ralph Sadler b. Viglius b.	Cesare Borgia d.			St. Francis of Paola d.	Guillaume Rondelet b.			Gentile Bellini d.		
1508		Duke of Alva b. Lord Seymour of Sudeley b.			Isaac Abrabanel d. Bernardino Telesio b.			Jean Daurat b.			

1509–1531 A.D.

Year A.D.	Government and Law	Military and Naval Affairs	Industry Commerce Economics Finance Invention Labor	Travel and Exploration	Philosophy and Religion	Science and Medicine	Education Scholarship History	Literature	Painting and Sculpture	Music	Miscellaneous
1509	Henry VII (England) d. Henry VIII (England) a. Philip of Hesse a. Caterina Sforza d.				John Calvin b. Étienne Dolet b. John Erskine b. John of Leiden b.		Philippe de Comines d.		Adam Krafft d. Luis de Morales b. Daniele Volterra b.		
1510	Francisco de Almeida d. Francesco Borgia b. Alessandro de' Medici b.			F. Vásquez de Coronado b. Mendéz Pinto b. Ludovico di Varthema fl.	John Story b.	Robt Recorde b. ?		John Caius b. Lord Vaux of Harrowden b.	Jacopo Bassano b. Sandro Botticelli d.	Andrea Gabrieli b.	Bernard Palissy b.
1511					Michael Servetus b.				Bartolomeo Ammanati b. Giorgione d. Giorgio Vasari b.		
1512	Bayazid II (Turkey) d. Selim I (Turkey) a.			Gerardus Mercator b. Amerigo Vespucci d.							
1513	Christian II (Denmark) a. James IV (Scotland) d. James V (Scotland) a.				Pope Julius II d. Pope Leo X a. Geo. Wishart b.		Robt. Fabyan d.	Jacques Amyot b. Henry Bradshaw d.	Pinturicchio d.		Richard Grafton b.
1514	Archibald Douglas d. Sir Francis Knollys b.						Sir John Cheke b. Wm. Elphinstone d.		Bramante d.		
1515	François I (France) a. Mary of Lorraine b. Sir Nicholas Throckmorton b.	Gonzalo de Cordoba d. Sir Andrew Wood d.		Affonso d'Albuquerque d.	St. Philip Neri b. St. Theresa b.	Cordus Valerius b. Andreas Vesalius b.	Roger Ascham b. Pierre Ramus b.		Tilman Riemenschneider fl.	Thos. Tallis b.	Aldus Manutius d. Christophe Plantin b.
1516	Ferdinand I (Spain) d.				John Foxe b.	Konrad von Gesner b. Johann Wier b.			Giovanni Bellini d. Giovanni Boltraffio d. Jerom Bosch d.		
1517	F. Jiménez de Cisneros d.			V. Nuñez de Balboa d.	Bernard Gilpin b.	Ambroise Paré b.		Earl of Surrey b.	Fra Bartolommeo d.	Gioseffo Zarlino b.	
1518	Hubert Languet b.				Robt. Crowley b. Ninian Winzet b.	Pierre Belon b.			Tintoretto b.		Andrea Palladio b.
1519	Charles V (H.R.E.) a. Duc de Guise b. Maximilian I (H.R.E.) d. Catherine de' Medici b.	Gaspard de Coligny b.	Sir Thos. Gresham b.	A. P. Menéndez b.	Theodore Beza b. John Colet d. Edmund Grindal b. Johann Tetzel d.	Andrea Cesalpino b.	P. de Cieza de León b. Wm. Grocyn d.	Nicholas Grimald b.	Leonardo da Vinci d. Michael Wohlgemuth d.		Lucrezia Borgia d.
1520	Montezuma II (Mexico) d.			Jean Ribaut b.				Thos. Churchyard b. Wm. Dunbar d. Jorge Montemayor b.	Pieter Breughel b. Jean Goujon b. Raphael d. Andrea da Solario d.		

Year A.D.	Government and Law	Military and Naval Affairs	Industry Commerce Economics Finance Invention Labor	Travel and Exploration	Philosophy and Religion	Science and Medicine	Education Scholarship History	Literature	Painting and Sculpture	Music	Miscellaneous
1521	Lord Burleigh b. *Emanuel I (Portugal) d.* *Selim I (Turkey) d.* *Soliman I (Turkey) a.*	*Juan López de Padilla d.*		*Fernando Magellan d.* *Juan Ponce de León d.*	Petrus Canisius b. *Pope Leo X d.*			*Sebastian Brant d.* Pontus de Tyard b.	*Piero di Cosimo d.*	*Joaquin Des Prês d.* *Heinrich Isaac d.?*	Sir Thos. Wyat (Younger) b.
1522	Comte de Egmont b.				Pope Adrian VI a. John Jewel b.	Ulisse Aldrovandi b.	*Wm. Lilye d.* *Johann Reuchlin d.*	*Gavin Douglas d.* Joachim DuBellay b.	*Vittorio Carpaccio d.* Jean Cousin b. *Pietro Torrigiano d.*		
1523	Christian II (Denmark) dep. Gustavus Vasa (Sweden) a. Thos. Randolph b.	*Franz von Sickingen d.*			*Pope Adrian VI d.* *Pope Clement VII a.* *Ulrich von Hutten d.*	Gabriello Fallopio b.			*Gerard David d.* *Bartolomeo Montagna d.* *Luca Signorelli d.*		
1524		*Chevalier Bayard d.*		*Vasco da Gama d.*	Thos. Erastus b.		*Sir Richard Sutton d.*	Luis de Camoëns b. Geo. Gascoigne b. Pierre de Ronsard b. Thos. Tusser b.	Paolo Farinato b. Giambologna b. *Hans Holbein (Elder) d.* *Joachim de Patinir d.* *Perugino d.*		
1525	Wm. Maitland b. Earl of Morton b. Earl of Sussex b.				*Thos. Münzer d.* *Pietro Pomponazzi d.* Lelio Socinus b.		*Peter Martyr d.* John Stow b.				*Richard de la Pole d.*
1526	John (Hungary) a.	Marquis de Santa Cruz b.		*Pedro Cabral d.* *Sebastian del Cano d.*			John Lesley b.	Louise Labé b.	*Antonio Liberale d.* Jean Navarette b.	Giovanni da Palestrina b.	
1527	Sir John Perrot b.	*Duc de Bourbon d.*		Abraham Ortelius b.	*Hieronymus Emser d.*			*Niccolo Machiavelli d.* Luis Ponce de León b.	Luca Cambiasi b.	Francisco Guerrero b.	John Dee b. *Johannes Frobenius d.*
1528	Emmanuel Philibert b. *Richard Fox d.*				*Patrick Hamilton d.*		Henri Estienne b.	Antônio Ferreira b.	*Andrea Della Robbia d.* *Albrecht Dürer d.* *Jacopo Palma d.* Veronese b. *Peter Vischer (Younger) d.*		
1529	Sir Henry Sidney b.					Francesco Patrizzi b.		*Baldassare Castiglione d.* Étienne Pasquier b. *John Skelton d.*	*Giovanni Della Robbia d.* *Andrea Sansovino d.* *Peter Vischer (Elder) d.* Taddeo Zuccaro b.		
1530	*Baber (India) d.* Sir Francis Walsingham b. *Thos. Wolsey d.*	Prince de Condé I b.	Jean Bodin b.		*Franz Lambert d.* John Whitgift b.		Sir Thos. Hoby b. Jean Nicot b. Nicholas Sanders b.	*Jacopo Sannazaro d.*	*Marcantonio d.* *Quentin Matsys d.*		
1531	Sir John Fortescue (statesman) b. Earl of Murray b.	François de La Noue b.			*Thos. Bilney d.* *John Oecolampadius d.* *Ulrich Zwingli d.*				*Andrea del Sarto d.* *Vincenzo Catena d.*		

1532–1553 A.D.

Year A.D.	Government and Law	Military and Naval Affairs	Industry Commerce Economics Finance Invention Labor	Travel and Exploration	Philosophy and Religion	Science and Medicine	Education Scholarship History	Literature	Painting and Sculpture	Music	Miscellaneous
1532	Earl of Leicester b. *Huáscar (Peru) d.*	Sir John Hawkins b.		*Vicente Pinzon d.?*	*Wm. Warham d.*			Jean de Baïf b. Etienne Jodelle b.	*Bernardino Luini d.*	Orlando di Lasso b.	Sir Thos. Lucy b. Amy Robsart b.
1533	*Atahualpa (Inca) d.* Marguerite de Valois b. William I (Orange) b.					*Girolamo Fracastoro d.*		*Lodovico Ariosto d. Lord Berners d.* A. d'Ercilla y Zuñiga b. Michel de Montaigne b.	*Lucas van Leyden d. Veit Stoss d.*		David Rizzio b.
1534					Elizabeth Barton d. Pope Clement VII d. Isaac Luria b. Pope Paul III a.	Otto Brunfels d.	Aventinus d. Wm. Harrison b.	Robert Garnier b. Fernando de Herrera b.	*Correggio d. Jan Mabuse d.*		Wynken de Worde d.
1535	*Sir Thos. More d.*			Sir Martin Frobisher b.	*John Fisher d.*	C. Agrippa von Nettesheim d.	Pierre Brantôme b.	Sir Thos. North b.			*Lambert Simnel d.?*
1536	Anne Boleyn d. Earl of Bothwell b. *Catherine of Aragon d.* 4th Duke of Norfolk b.	Earl of Nottingham b.		Juan Fernández b.	*Desiderius Erasmus d. John of Leiden d. Bernt Knipper- dollinck d. Wm. Tyndale d.*			*John Rastell d.* Jean Vauquelin de la Fresnaye b. Thomas Sackville b. *Gil Vicente d.*			*Baldassare Peruzzi d.*
1537	Lady Jane Grey b. *Alessandro de' Medici d.* Cosimo I de'Medici a.				*Jacobus Faber d.*	Giralomo Fabrizio b.			*Lorenzo di Credi d.* Nicholas Hilliard b.		
1538					Caesar Baronius b. St. Carlo Borromeo b.			*Pierre Gringoire d.* Giovanni Batista Guarini b. Reginald Scot b.			
1539				Sir Humphrey Gilbert b.	Lorenzo Campeggio d. Fausto Socinus b.		Garcilaso de la Vega b.		*Il Pordenone d.*		
1540	*Thos. Cromwell d.* Baron Ellesmere b. Christopher Hatton b. *John (Hungary) d.* Antonio Perez b.	Sir Francis Drake b. Hugh O'Neill b.			Edmund Campion b. *Johann Faust d.*	William Gilbert b. Franciscus Vieta b.	*Francesco Guicciardini d.* J. J. Scaliger b. *Juan Luis Vives d.*	Pierre de Chastelard b. Barnabe Googe b. Pierre Larivey b. Wm. Painter b. Barnabe Rich b. Geo. Turberville b.	Denis Calvaert b. *Joos van Cleve d. Girolamo del Pacchia d. Parmigiano d.*	William Byrd b. Tomasso Victoria b.	Louis Elzevir b.
1541	Wm. Davison b. Earl Walter of Essex b. *Margaret (Scotland) d.* Maurice (Saxony) a. Jan Zamojski b.	Louis de Crillon b.		*Pedro de Alvarado d. Francisco Pizarro d.*	Pierre Charron b. *Johann Faber d. Juan de Valdés d.*	Paracelsus d.					
1542	*Catherine Howard d. James V (Scotland) d.* Mary (Scotland) b. and a.			*Hernando De Soto d.*	Roberto Bellarmino b. St. Juan de la Cruz b.			*Sir Thos. Wyat d.*	*G. Dosso Dossi d.* Il Greco b. *Bernert van Orley d.*		
1543	Guillaume Du Bellay d.				*Johann Eck d. Sebastian Franck d.*	*Nicolaus Copernicus d.* Costanzo Varoli b.		John Still b.	*Hans Holbein (Younger) d.* Federigo Zuccaro b.		

Year A.D.	Government and Law	Military and Naval Affairs	Industry Commerce Economics Finance Invention Labor	Travel and Exploration	Philosophy and Religion	Science and Medicine	Education Scholarship History	Literature	Painting and Sculpture	Music	Miscellaneous
1544						Cordus Valerius d.		Bonaventure Des Periers d. Guillaume Du Bartas b. Clément Marot d. Torquato Tasso b. Geo. Whetstone b.	Gillis van Coninxloo b.		
1545	Lord Darnley b. Duke Chas. of Suffolk d.	Principe de Farnese b.		Pedro da Covilhâo d. d.	Georg Spalatin d.		Sir Thos. Bodley b. Andrew Melville b.	Nicholas Breton b. Agnolo Firenzuola d. Johann Fischart b. Gabriel Harvey b.	Jean Clouet d.	John Taverner d.	
1546					David Beaton d. Étienne Dolet d. Martin Luther d. Robt. Parsons b. Geo. Wishart d.	Tycho Brahe b.	Sir Thos. Elyot d.	Philippe Des Portes b.	Gaudenzio Ferrari d. Giulio Romano d.		
1547	Edward VI (England) a. François I (France) d. Henri II (France) a. Henry VIII (England) d. Ivan IV (Muscovy) a. J. van Oldenbarne-veldt b.	Hernando Cortez d. Don John of Austria b.					Beatus Rhenanus d. Pietro Bembo d. Edward Halle d. Justus Lipsius b. Florentius Volusenus d.	Miguel de Cervantes b. Vittoria Colonna d. Earl of Surrey d.	Perino del Vaga d. Sebastiani del Piombo d.		
1548	Sigismund I (Poland) d. Sigismund II (Poland) a.				Giordano Bruno b. Francisco Suarez b.	Simon Stevinus b.					
1549		Lord Seymour of Sudeley d.		Francisco de Orellana d.	Philippe de Mornay b. Pope Paul III d. Thos. Sternhold d.		Antonio Herrera b. Sir Henry Savile b.	Giles Fletcher Sr. b. Margaret of Navarre d.	Il Sodoma d.		
1550	Powhatan b.			John Davis b. Sebastián Vizcaino b.	Robt. Browne b. Tomás Sanchez b.	John Napier b.	Jacob Sylvius d.?	Juan de la Cueva b. Alexander Montgomerie b. Alexander Scott fl. Wm. Stewart d.	Hendrik van Steenwyk b.		
1551	Geo. Martinuzzi d.				Martin Bucer d.		Wm. Camden b.				
1552	Sir Edward Coke b. Alberico Gentili b. Antonio de Mendoza d. Duke Edward of Somerset d.			Johannes Leo d. Sir Walter Raleigh b.	Lars Anderson d. Andreas Osiander d. Matteo Ricci b. St. Francis Xavier d.	Paolo Sarpi b.	Théodore D'Aubigné b. John Leland d. Sebastian Münster d. John Speed b.	Alexander Barclay d. Gabriello Chiabrera b. Bernardim Ribeiro d. Edmund Spenser b.			
1553	Edward VI (England) d. Mary I (England) a. Maurice (Saxony) d. Duke of Northumberland d.			Richard Hakluyt b.	Philaret b. Michael Servetus d.		J.-A. de Thou b.	John Florio b. François Rabelais d.	Lucas Cranach d.		

1554–1573 A.D.

Year A.D.	Government and Law	Military and Naval Affairs	Industry Commerce Economics Finance Invention Labor	Travel and Exploration	Philosophy and Religion	Science and Medicine	Education Scholarship History	Literature	Painting and Sculpture	Music	Miscellaneous
1554	Lady Jane Grey d.	Duc de Mayenne b. 3rd Duke of Norfolk d.		F. Vasquez de Coronado d. Sir Hugh Willoughby d.	Richard Hooker b.			Lord Brooke b. Stephen Gosson b. John Lyly b. Christiern Pedersen d. Sir Philip Sidney b.	Il Moretto d.		Francis Throckmorton b. Sir Thos. Wyat (Younger) d.
1555	Stephen Gardiner d. Earl of Totnes b.			Thos. Cavendish b.	Lancelot Andrews b. Henry Garnett b. John Hooper d. Hugh Latimer d. Pope Paul IV a. Nicholas Ridley d. John Rogers d.	Edward Wotton d.	Virgil Polydore d.	Richard Carew b. Sir David Lyndsay d. François de Malherbe b.	Veneto Bartolommeo d. Giovanni Caroto d. Lodovico Carracci b.		
1556	J. Akbar (India) b. Charles V (H.R.E.) abd. Ferdinand I (H.R.E.) a. Philip II (Spain) a.	Gaspard Bauhin b.			Thos. Cranmer d. St. Ignatius de Loyola d.	Henry Briggs b. Guillaume Rondelet d.	Johannes Sleidanus d.	Luigi Alamanni d. Nicholas Udall d. Lord Vaux of Harrowden d.	Lorenzo Lotto d. Jacopo da Pontormo d.		
1557	Sebastião (Portugal) a.			Sebastian Cabot d. Jacques Cartier d. A. Nuñez Cabeza da Vaca d. G. Ramusio d.		Niccolo Tartaglia d.	Sir John Cheke d. G. de Oviedo y Valdéz d.	Pietro Aretino d. Alexander Hume b. Thos. Watson b.	Agostino Carracci b.	Thos. Morley b.	
1558	Elizabeth (England) a. Mary I (England) d.				Reginald Pole d.	Robt. Recorde d.	Olaus Magnus d.	Abraham Fraunce b. Robt. Greene b. Thos. Kyd b. Thos. Lodge b. Geo. Peele b. F. de Sá de Mirandola d. J. C. Scaliger d.			
1559	Frederick II (Denmark) a. Henri II (France) d. Sir Anthony St. Leger d. Cuthbert Tunstall d.	Graf von Tilly b.			Menno Simons d. Pope Paul IV d. John Penry b. Pope Pius IV a.	Realdo Columbus d.		Isaac Casaubon b. Geo. Chapman b.	Benvenuto Tisi d.		
1560	Eric XIV (Sweden) a. Charles IX (France) a. Gustavus Vasa (Sweden) d. Mary of Lorraine d. Duc de Sully b.	Andrea Doria d.			Jacobus Arminius b. Johannes Lasco d. Philipp Melanchthon d.		P. de Cieza de León d. "Admirable" Crichton b.	Joachim Du Bellay d. Wm. Fowler b. John Rolland fl.	Annibale Carracci b.		Amy Robsart d.
1561					Francis Bacon b. Karl von Schwenkfeld d.	Sanctorius b.		L. Gongora y Argote b. Sir John Harington b. Jorge Montemayor d. Robt. Southwell b.	Ridolfo Ghirlandajo d.	Jacopo Peri b.	Mother Shipton d.
1562		Goetz von Berlichingen d.			Geo. Abbot b. Peter Martyr d. Lelio Socinus d.	Gabriello Fallopio d. Christian Longomontanus b.		Matteo Bandello d. Henry Constable b. Saml. Daniel b. Nicholas Grimald d. Lope de Vega Carpio b.		John Bull b.	
1563	Duc de Guise d. Sir Ralph Winwood b.				Alesius d.			John Bale d. Pierre de Chastelard d. Michael Drayton b. Joshua Sylvester b.			George Heriot b.

Year A.D.	Government and Law	Military and Naval Affairs	Industry Commerce Economics Finance Invention Labor	Travel and Exploration	Philosophy and Religion	Science and Medicine	Education Scholarship History	Literature	Painting and Sculpture	Music	Miscellaneous
1564	Ferdinand I (H.R.E.) d. Maximilian II (H.R.E.) a. Manus O'Donnell d.				John Calvin d. Bernardino Ochino d.	Pierre Belon d. G. Galileo b. Andreas Vesalius d.		Christopher Marlowe b. Wm. Shakespeare b.	Michelangelo d. Francisco Pacheco b.		
1565	Earl Robert of Salisbury b.	Jean de la Valette d.		Jean Ribaut d. Sir Anthony Shirley b.	Guillaume Farel d. Pope Pius IV d. John Spottiswoode b.	Konrad von Gesner d.	Jean Grolier d.		M. da Caravaggio b.		
1566	Wm. Brewster b. Earl Robt. of Essex b. Selim II (Turkey) a. Soliman I (Turkey) d.			Sir Ferdinando Gorges b.	Johann Agricola d. Pope Pius V a.	M. A. de Dominis b. Leonhard Fuchs d.	Sir. Thos. Hoby d. Bartolome de Las Casas d. Marco Vida d.	Louise Labé d.	Jean Goujon d. Daniele Volterra d. Taddeo Zuccaro d.		Edward Alleyn b. Luigi Cornaro d. Nostradamus d. David Rizzio d.
1567	Lord Darnley d. Wilhelm von Grumbach d. Philip of Hesse d. Earl of Stirling b.	Duc de Montmorency d.		Saml. de Champlain b.	St. Francis de Sales b.			Thos. Nashe b.	Michiel van Mierevelt b.	Thos. Campion b. Claudio Monteverdi b.	Richard Burbage b.
1568	Albrecht (Prussia) d. Comte de Egmont d. Eric XIV (Sweden) d.				Tomaso Campanella b. Miles Coverdale d.		Roger Ascham d.	Honoré d'Urfé b. Sir Henry Wotton b.	Guiseppe Cesari b.		
1569	Jahangir b.	Prince de Condé I d. Marquis de Spinola b.			Juan de Ávila d.			Sir John Davies b. Antônio Ferreira d. Alexander Hardy b.	Pieter Breughel d.		
1570	Earl of Murray d.				John Welsh b.		João de Barros d. Aonio Paleario d.	Thos. Middleton b.	Jacopo Sansovino d.		François Bonivard d. Guy Fawkes b.
1571	Sir Nicholas Throckmorton d.				John Jewel d. John Story d.	Johann Kepler b.	Sir Robt. Cotton b. Wolfgang Ratich b.	Sir Robt. Ayton b. "Tirso de Molina" b.	Benvenuto Cellini d.		
1572	Francesco Borgia d. 4th Duke of Norfolk d. Hugh Roe O'Donnell b. Sigismund II (Poland) d.	Gaspard de Coligny d.			Pope Gregory XIII a. John Knox d. Cyril Lucaris b. Isaac Luria d. Pope Pius V d.		Pierre Ramus d. Giles Tschudi d.	Thos. Dekker b.	François Clouet d.		Richard Grafton d.
1573	Michel de l'Hôpital d. Wm. Maitland d. Maximilian the Great (Bavaria) b. Marie de' Medici b.				Wm. Laud b. Laurentius Petri d.			John Caius d. John Donne b. Étienne Jodelle d. Ben Jonson b. Mathurin Régnier b.			Robt. Catesby b. Inigo Jones b.

1574–1589 A.D.

Year A.D.	Government and Law	Military and Naval Affairs	Industry Commerce Economics Finance Invention Labor	Travel and Exploration	Philosophy and Religion	Science and Medicine	Education Scholarship History	Literature	Painting and Sculpture	Music	Miscellaneous
1574	Charles IX (France) d. Henri III (France) a. Cosimo I de' Medici d. Murad III (Turkey) a. Selim II (Turkey) d.			Sir Robert Dudley b. A. P. Menéndez d.	Robert Fludd b.	Bartolommeo Eustachio d.	Juan Sepulveda d.	John Day b. Jos. Hall b. Thomas Heywood b. ?	Giorgio Vasari d.	John Wilbye b.	
1575	Stephen Báthori (Poland) a. Arabella Stuart b.	Duc d'Angoulême b.		Saml. Purchas b.	Jakob Boehme b. Jos. Caro d. Matthew Parker d.	Costanzo Varoli d.	Michael O'Clery b.	John Marston b. Wm. Stevenson d. Cyril Tourneur b. Henry Willobie b.	Guido Reni b.	Thos. Weelkes b. ?	
1576	Thos. Dudley b. Earl Walter of Essex d. Maximilian II (H.R.E.) d. Rudolf II (H.R.E.) a.				Giovanni Diodati b. St. Vincent de Paul b.	Jerome Cardan d.	Enrico Davila b.	Henry Peacham b. Hans Sachs d.	Francisco Herrera b. Titian d.		
1577	Lord Delaware b. Earl of Gowrie b. Viglius d.				Gerhard Vossius b.	J. B. van Helmont b.		Robt. Burton b. Jacob Cats b. Thos. Coryat b. Geo. Gascoigne d. Wm. Vaughan b.	Léonard Limousin d. Peter Paul Rubens b.		Beatrice Cenci b.
1578	Earl of Bothwell d. Sebastião (Portugal) d.	Don John of Austria d.				Wm. Harvey b.		Geo. Sandys b.			François Ravaillac b.
1579		F. de Bassompierre b. G. Jiménez de Quesada d.	Sir Thos. Gresham d.		John Cameron b. Francis Rous b.	M. A. Severino b.		Luis de Camoëns d. John Fletcher b.	Jean Navarette d. Frans Snyders b.		
1580	Lord Baltimore b. Gábor Bethlen b. Earl of Bristol b. Emmanuel Philibert d. Massassoit b. Peter Minuit b.	Earl of Leven b.		John Smith b.			Danl. Heinsius b. Raphael Holinshed d. Nicholas de Peiresc b.	J. d'Alarćon y Mendoza b. Edward Fairfax b. John Heywood d. F. Quevedo y Villegas b. John Taylor b. Thos. Tusser d. John Webster b.			Andrea Palladio d.
1581	Hubert Languet d. Earl of Morton d. Sir Thos. Roe b.	Peder Skram d.			Edmund Campion d. Richard Cox d. Jas. Ussher b.	Gasparo Aselli d. Edmund Gunter b.	B. Díaz del Castillo d. Nicholas Sanders d.	P. C. Hooft b. Sir Thos. Overbury b.	Z. Domenichino b. Frans Hals b.		
1582		Duke of Alva d.			Wm. Juxon b. St. Theresa d. John Williams b.		Geo. Buchanan d. "Admirable" Crichton d.	Phineas Fletcher b.	David Teniers (Elder) b.		

Year A.D.	Government and Law	Military and Naval Affairs	Industry Commerce Economics Finance Invention Labor	Travel and Exploration	Philosophy and Religion	Science and Medicine	Education Scholarship History	Literature	Painting and Sculpture	Music	Miscellaneous
1583	*Earl of Desmond d.* Hugo Grotius b. Count Oxenstjerna b. *Earl of Sussex d.*	Albrecht von Wallenstein b.		*Sir Humphrey Gilbert d.* *Mendéz Pinto d.*	Simon Episcopius b. *Thos. Erastus d.* *Bernard Gilpin d.* *Edmund Grindal d.* Alexander Henderson b. Lord Herbert of Cherbury b.			Sir John Beaumont b. Philip Massinger b.		Orlando Gibbons b.	Bonaventure Elzevir b.
1584	Feodor I (Russia) a. *Ivan IV (Muscovy) d.* John Pym b. John Selden b. *William I (Orange) d.*	Miles Standish b.		Wm. Baffin b.	*St. Carlo Borromeo d.* John Cotton b.		André Duchesne b. Thos. Erpenius b. John Hales b.	Francis Beaumont b.	Caspar de Crayer b.		*Francis Throckmorton d.*
1585	Cardinal de Richelieu b.				*Pope Gregory XIII d.* Cornelius Jansen b. Pope Sixtus V a. Lucilio Vanini b.			William Drummond b. *Pierre de Ronsard d.* Wm. Rowley b.	*Luca Cambiasi d.* Cornelis de Vos b.	*Thos. Tallis d.*	
1586	Abbas I (Persia) a. Mohammed Kuprili b. John Mason b. *Sir Henry Sidney d.* *Stephen Báthori (Poland) d.*			Pietro Della Valle b.	Georg Calixtus b. Thos. Hooker b.			John Ford b. *Sir Richard Maitland d.* *Sir Philip Sidney d.*	Geo. Jameson b. *Luis de Morales d.*	*Andrea Gabrielli d.*	Théophraste Renaudot b.
1587	*Mary (Scotland) d.* *Sir Ralph Sadler d.* Sigismund III (Poland) a. Earl Robert of Warwick b.				*John Foxe d.*			Joost van den Vondel b. *Geo. Whetstone d.*			
1588	Christian IV (Denmark) a. *Frederick II (Denmark) d.* *Earl of Leicester d.* Pierre Séguier b. John Winthrop (Elder) b.	*Marquis de Santa Cruz d.*			*Robt. Crowley d.* Thos. Hobbes b. *Bernardino Telesio d.*	*Johann Wier d.*	Claudius Salmasius b.	Jean Daurat d. Giles Fletcher, Jr. b. Ivan Gundulić b. F. de La Mothe le Vayer b. Geo. Wither b.	José Ribera b. *Veronese d.*		Marquise de Rambouillet b.
1589	John Endicott b. *Henri III (France) d.* Henri IV (France) a. *Catherine de'Medici d.* Sir Henry Vane (Elder) b.	Duc de Soubise b.						*Jean de Baif d.*			*Bernard Palissy d.* *Christophe Plantin d.*

1590–1607 A.D.

Year A.D.	Government and Law	Military and Naval Affairs	Industry Commerce Economics Finance Invention Labor	Travel and Exploration	Philosophy and Religion	Science and Medicine	Education Scholarship History	Literature	Painting and Sculpture	Music	Miscellaneous
1590	Wm. Bradford b. Earl of Holland b. *Thos. Randolph d.* Earl of Somerset b. *Sir Francis Walsingham d.*	*Sorley Boy Macdonnell d.* Owen Roe O'Neill b.			Anne Hutchinson b. *Pope Sixtus V d.*	*Ambroise Paré d.*		*Guillaume Du Bartas d.* M. de Faria y Sousa b. *Johann Fischart d. Robert Garnier d.*	*Jean Cousin d.* Simon Vouet b.	Ludovico Zacconi fl. *Gioseffo Zarlino d.*	Thos. Morton b.
1591	*Christopher Hatton d.* Wm. Lenthall b.	*Francois de La Noue d.*			Uriel Acosta b. *St. Aloysius d.* Pope Clement VIII a. *St. Juan de la Cruz d. John Erskine d.* J. Schall von Bell b.	Willebrord Snell b.		Wm. Browne b. Robt. Herrick b. *Luis Ponce de Leon d.* Théophile b.			
1592	1st Duke of Buckingham b. Sir John Eliot b. *Sir John Perrot d.* Peter Stuyvesant b.	*Principe di Farnese d.*		Thos. Cavendish d.	John Comenius b. Nicholas Ferrar b. *Ninian Winzet d.*	Pierre Gassendi b.	Chas. Chauncy b.	*Robt. Greene d. Michel de Montaigne d.* Francis Quarles b. *Thos. Watson d.*	*Bartolomeo Ammanati d. Jacopo Bassano d.* Jacques Callot b.		Abraham Elzevir b.
1593	Earl of Strafford b. Antony Van Diemen b.				*John Penry d.*		*Wm. Harrison d.*	*Jacques Amyot d.* Geo. Herbert b. *Christopher Marlowe d.* Izaak Walton b.	Jacob Jordaens b. Louis Le Nain b.		
1594	John Hampden b.	Graf von Pappenheim b.		*Sir Martin Frobisher d. Gerardus Mercator d.*				*Barnabe Googe d. Thos. Kyd d. Wm. Painter d.* Sieur de Saint-Amant b.	Nicolas Poussin b. *Tintoretto d.*	*Orlando di Lasso d. Giovanni da Palestrina d.*	Stephen Daye b.
1595	*Murad III (Turkey) d.* Edward Winslow b.	*Sir John Hawkins d.*			*St. Philip Neri d.* Thos. Weld b.			Thos. Carew b. Jean Chapelain b. Thos. May b. *Robt. Southwell d. Torquato Tasso d.*		John Wilson b.	Pocahontas b.
1596	Praise God Barebones b. Geo. Jenatsch b. *Sir Francis Knollys d.*	*Sir Francis Drake d.*	Jean Bodin d.		René Descartes b. Richard Mather b.		*John Lesley d.*	*A. d'Ercilla y Zuñiga d.* Sir Constantijn Huygens b. Jas. Shirley b. *Henry Willobie d.*	Pietro da Cortona b. Jan van Goyen b.	Henry Lawes b.	
1597		Martin van Tromp b.			*Petrus Canisius d.*	Francis Glisson b. *Francesco Patrizzi d.*		*Fernando de Herrera d.* Martin von Opitz b. *Geo. Peele d.*			
1598	Duke of Argyll b. Boris Godunov (Russia) a. *Lord Burleigh d.* Duc César de Choiseul b. *Feodor I (Russia) d. Philip II (Spain) d.* Oliver St. John b. Wm. Strode b.			*Abraham Ortelius d.*			*Henri Estienne d.*	Georg Stjernhjelm b. Vincent Voiture b.	Giovanni Bernini b. Francisco de Zurbaran b.		François Mansart b.

Year A.D.	Government and Law	Military and Naval Affairs	Industry Commerce Economics Finance Invention Labor	Travel and Exploration	Philosophy and Religion	Science and Medicine	Education Scholarship History	Literature	Painting and Sculpture	Music	Miscellaneous
1599	Oliver Cromwell b. Lord Holles b.	Robt. Blake b. Principe di Piccolomini b.						Reginald Scot d. Edmund Spenser d.	Sir Anthony Van Dyck b. Diego Velásquez b.	Francisco Guerrero d.	Beatrice Cenci d.
1600	Earl of Gowrie d. Wm. Prynne b. Hannibal Sehested b.	Sir Richard Grenville b.			Giordano Bruno d. Richard Hooker d. Saml. Rutherford b.	Jean Nicot d.		P. Calderón b. Richard Flecknoe b. John Ogilby b.	Jacques Blanchard b. Claude Lorrain b. Andrea Sacchi b.		Sir Thos. Lucy d.
1601	Anne of Austria b. Earl Robert of Essex d.	Lord Newark b.	Marquess of Worcester b.			Tycho Brahe d.		John Earle b. Thos. Nashe d. Sir Thos. North d. Georges de Scudéry b.	Alonzo Cano b.		
1602	J. Akbar (India) d. Henry Marten b. Jules Mazarin b. Hugh Roe O'Donnell d.			Juan Fernández d.	William Chillingworth b. John Lightfoot b.	Otto von Guencke b. Gilles de Roberval b.			Agostino Carracci d. Philippe de Champaigne b.	Francesco Cavalli b.	Wm. Lilly b.
1603	Ahmed I (Turkey) a. Elizabeth (England) d. James I (Scotland) a.			Abel J. Tasman b.	Pierre Charron d.	Andrea Cesalpino d. Sir Kenelm Digby b. Wm. Gilbert d. Franciscus Vieta d.			Aernout van der Neer b. Hendrik van Steenwyk d.	Thos. Morley d.	
1604	Charles IX (Sweden) a. Marquess of Clanricarde b.	Maurice of Nassau b.			John Eliot b. Menasseh ben Israel b. Fausto Socinus d. John Whitgift d. Roger Williams b.	Johann Glauber b.	Edward Pococke b.	Thos. Churchyard d.		Giacomo Carissimi b.	
1605	Boris Godunov (Russia) d. Bulstrode Whitelocke b. Jan Zamojski d.		Jean Tavernier b.	John Davis d.	Theodore Beza d. Pope Clement VIII d. Nikon b. Pope Paul V a.		John Stow d.	Sir Thos. Browne b. Simon Dach b. John Gauden b. Wm. Habington b. Pontus de Tyard d. Thos. Randolph b.			Robt. Catesby d.
1606	Leonard Calvert b. Duke of Hamilton b. Thos. Harrison b. Hans Svane b. John Winthrop (Younger) b.				Henry Garnett d.		Justus Lipsius d.	Pierre Corneille b. Sir Wm. Davenant b. Philippe Des Portes d. John Lyly d. Edmund Waller b.	Adriaen Brouwer b. Paolo Farinato d. Jan van Heem b. Rembrandt b.		Guy Fawkes d.
1607	Sir John Fortescue (statesman) d.	Michel deRuyter b.			Caesar Baronius d.	Ulisse Aldrovandi d.	John Harvard b. John Rushworth b.	Madeleine de Scudéry b. John Still d.	Gillis van Coninxloo d. Wenzel Hollar b.		

1608–1624 A.D.

Year A.D.	Government and Law	Military and Naval Affairs	Industry Commerce Economics Finance Invention Labor	Travel and Exploration	Philosophy and Religion	Science and Medicine	Education Scholarship History	Literature	Painting and Sculpture	Music	Miscellaneous
1608	Sir Wm. Berkeley b. *Wm. Davison d.* *Alberico Gentili d.*	Geo. Monk b.			Thos. Fuller b. Antonio Vieira b.	Giovanni Borelli b. Evangelista Torricelli b.		Sir Richard Fanshawe b. F. Manuel de Mello b. John Milton b. *Thos. Sackville d.* *Jean Vauquelin de la Fresnaye d.*	*Giambologna d.*		*John Dee d.*
1609	Earl Edward of Clarendon b. Sir Matthew Hale b. Henrietta Maria b.				*Jacobus Arminius d.* Lodowick Muggleton b. Benj. Whichcote b.		*J. J. Scaliger d.*	Paul Fleming b. *Alexander Hume d.* Jean de Rotrou b. Sir John Suckling b.	*M. da Caravaggio d.* *Annibale Carracci d.* Saml. Cooper b. *Federigo Zuccaro d.*		
1610	Sir Geo. Carteret b. Viscount Falkland b. *Henri IV (France) d.* Louis XIII (France) a. Duke of Ormonde b.	Marquis de Duquesne b. Sieur de Saint-Évremond b.			Jean Labadie b. *Robt. Parsons d.* *Matteo Ricci d.* *Tomás Sanchez d.*	John Pell b.		*Juan de la Cueva d.* Sieur DuCange b. *Alexander Montgomerie d.* Paul Scarron b. *Geo. Turberville d.*	Wm. Dobson b. Pierre Mignard b. Adriaen van Ostade b. David Teniers (Younger) b. Willem Vandevelde (Elder) b.		*François Ravaillac d.*
1611	*Charles IX (Sweden) d.* Gustavus Adolphus (Sweden) a. Jas. Harrington b. *Antonio Perez d.* Lord Warriston b.	Henry Ireton b. *Duc de Mayenne d.* Viscomte de Turenne b.		Ralph Fitch d. Henry Hudson d.	Robt. Leighton b.		Johann Gronovius b. Sir Thos. Urquhart b.	*Giles Fletcher, Sr. d.* J. F. Sarasin b.	B. Franceschini b. Jan Fyt b.	*Tomasso Victoria d.*	
1612	Matthias (H.R.E.) a. *Rudolf II (H.R.E.) d.* *Earl Robert of Salisbury d.*	Lord Fairfax of Camerón b. Marquess of Montrose b.			Antoine Arnauld b. John Pearson b.			Anne Bradstreet b. Saml. Butler b. *Giovanni Batista Guarini d.* *Sir John Harington d.* Thos. Killigrew b. *Pierre Larivey d.*			
1613	Mikhail (Russia) a. Sir Henry Vane (Younger) b.	Karl von Wrangel b.			Jeremy Taylor b.		*Sir Thos. Bodley d.*	John Cleveland b. *Henry Constable d.* Richard Crashaw b. Duc de la Rochefoucauld b. *Sir Thos. Overbury d.* *Mathurin Regnier d.*	Gerard Douw b. B. van der Helst b. André LeNôtre b. Claude Perrault b.		
1614	Jean de Retz b. Viscount Stafford b.		John Lilburne b.			Thos. Wharton b. John Wilkins b.	*Pierre Brantôme d.*	*Isaac Casaubon d.* *Wm. Fowler d.*	*Il Greco d.*		
1615	*Marguerite de Valois d.* *Arabella Stuart d.*	*Louis de Crillon d.* Duc de Schomberg b.		*Sebastián Vizcaino d.*	Richard Baxter b. John Biddle b.			*Étienne Pasquier d.*	Govert Flinck b. Salvator Rosa b.		

Year A.D.	Government and Law	Military and Naval Affairs	Industry Commerce Economics Finance Invention Labor	Travel and Exploration	Philosophy and Religion	Science and Medicine	Education Scholarship History	Literature	Painting and Sculpture	Music	Miscellaneous
1616	Duke of Lauderdale b. Sir Roger L'Estrange b. John Thurloe b.	*Hugh O'Neill d.*		*Richard Hakluyt d.*	John Owen b.	Thos. Bartholin b. John Wallis b.	*Garcilaso de la Vega d.*	Francis Beaumont d. Miguel de Cervantes d. Sir John Denham b. Andreas Gryphius b. *Wm. Shakespeare d.* Jacob Steendam b.	Sebastien Bourdon b. Giovanni Castiglione b. Carlo Dolci b. William Faithorne b. Eustache LeSueur b.		*Philip Henslowe d.*
1617	*Ahmed I (Turkey) d. Baron Ellesmere d. Sir Ralph Winwood d.*	Edmund Ludlow b.			Ralph Cudworth b. *Francisco Suarez d.*	Jeremiah Horrocks b. *John Napier d.*	*J.-A. de Thou d.*	Thos. Coryat d. *Barnabe Rich d.*	Bartolomé Murillo b. Gerard Ter Borch b.		*Louis Elzevir d. Pocahontas d.*
1618	Earl of Arlington b. *Lord Delaware d. Powhatan d.*	Geo. Walker b.		*Sir Walter Raleigh d.*	Jas. Nayler b. Jas. Sharp b.			Abraham Cowley b. Richard Lovelace b. Ferrante Pallavicino b. *Joshua Sylvester d.*	Sir Peter Lely b.		
1619	J. B. Colbert b. Ferdinand II (H.R.E.) a. *Matthias (H.R.E.) d. J. van Olden-barneveldt d.* Viscount Stair b.	John Lambert b. Prince Rupert b.			Jean Claude b. *Lucilio Vanini d.*	*Giralomo Fabrizio d.*		Cyrano de Bergerac b. *Saml. Daniel d.* Antoine Furetière b. G. Tallemant des Réaux b.	*Denis Calvaert d. Lodovico Carracci d. Nicholas Hilliard d.* Chas. Le Brun b. Philip Wouwerman b.		*Richard Burbage d.*
1620	Comte de Frontenac b.				Jean Picard b. *Simon Stevinus d.*			John Evelyn b.	Albert Cuyp b.	*Thos. Campion d.* Pierre Perrin b.	Marquis de Cinq-Mars b. Ninon de Lenclos b.
1621	Comte de Gramont b. Philip IV (Spain) a. 1st Earl of Shaftesbury b.	Prince Louis de Condé II b. Sir Wm. Penn b.			*Roberto Bellarmino d. Pope Paul V d.*	Thos. Willis b.		Jean de La Fontaine b. Andrew Marvell b. Earl Roger of Orrery b.	Jacques Courtois b. G. van den Eckhout b. Isack van Ostade b. J. B. Weenix b.		
1622	Count De la Gardie b. Algernon Sidney b.	Masaniello b.		*Wm. Baffin d.* Bernhardus Varenius b.	Johann Clauberg b. *St. Francis de Sales d.* Thos. Vaughan b.	Jean Pecquet b.	*Andrew Melville d. Sir Henry Savile d.*	Molière b. Henry Vaughan b.	Pierre Puget b.		
1623	Cornelis DeWitt b. Murad IV (Turkey) a. Sir Wm. Scroggs b.		Sir Wm. Petty b.		*Philippe de Mornay d.* Blaise Pascal b. Pope Urban VIII a.	*Paolo Sarpi d.*	*Wm. Camden d.*	*Giles Fletcher, Jr. d.*		*Wm. Byrd d. Thos. Weelkes d.*	
1624	Sir Geo. Downing b. Richard Nicolls b.	*Gaspard Bauhin d. Earl of Nottingham d.*			*Jakob Boehme d.* Geo. Fox b. François de LaChaise b. Matthew Poole b.	*M. A. de Dominis d.* Thos. Sydenham b.	*Thos. Erpenius d.*	*Stephen Gosson d.* Paul Pellisson b.			*Geo. Heriot d.*

Year A.D.	Government and Law	Military and Naval Affairs	Industry Commerce Economics Finance Invention Labor	Travel and Exploration	Philosophy and Religion	Science and Medicine	Education Scholarship History	Literature	Painting and Sculpture	Music	Miscellaneous
1625	Charles I (England) a. Jan De Witt b. *James I (England) d.*	Earl of Sandwich b.			John Cameron d. John Fell b. Pierre Nicole b. *John Welsh d.*	Jean Cassini b.	*Antonio Herrera d.*	Thomas Corneille b. *John Fletcher d. John Florio d. Thos. Lodge d.* Thos. Stanley b. *Honoré d'Urfé d. John Webster d.*	Robert Nanteuil b. Paul Potter b.	*Orlando Gibbons d.*	
1626	Richard Cromwell b. William II (Orange) b.			*Saml. Purchas d.*	*Lancelot Andrewes d. Francis Bacon d.* Sabbatai Zevi b.	*Gasparo Aselli d. Edmund Gunter d.* Francesco Redi b. *Willebrord Snell d.*	John Aubrey b.	*Nicholas Breton d. Sir John Davies d.* Sir Robt. Howard b. Mme. de Sévigné b. *Théophile d. Cyril Tourneur d.*	Jan Steen b.		*Edward Alleyn d.*
1627	*Jahangir (Delhi) d.* Shah Jahan (Delhi) a.				Jacques Bossuet b. John Rogers b.	Robt. Boyle b.		*Sir John Beaumont d. L. Gongora y Argote d. Thos. Middleton d.* Duchesse de Montpensier b.	Jan Siberechts b.		
1628	*Abbas I (Persia) d. 1st Duke of Buckingham d.* 2nd Duke of Buckingham b. Sir Wm. Coventry b. Sir Wm. Temple b.	Duc de Luxembourg b.				Marcello Malpighi b. John Ray b.		Lord Brooke d. John Bunyan b. *François de Malherbe d.* Chas. Perrault b.	Carlo Cignani b. François Girardon b. Jacob van Ruysdael b.	*John Bull d.*	
1629	*Gábor Bethlen d. Earl of Totnes d.*	Niels Juel b. Cornelis van Tromp b.				Christiaan Huygens b.	*John Speed d.*	*Richard Carew d.*			
1630		*Marquis de Spinola d.* Earl of Tyrconnel b.			John Howe b. John Tillotson b.	Isaac Barrow b. *Henry Briggs d. Johann Kepler d.* J. Kunkel von Löwenstjern b. Olaf Rudbeck b.	*Theodore D'Aubigné d.* Pierre Huet b.	Chas. Cotton b. *Gabriel Harvey d.* Edward Phillips b.			Marquise de Brinvilliers b.
1631	Duke of Leeds b.			*John Smith d.*	Richard Cumberland b. John Locke b. Michael Wigglesworth b.		*Sir Robt. Cotton d. Enrico Davila d.*	J. G. Cotta b. *John Donne d. Michael Drayton d.* John Dryden b. *Alexander Hardy d.* Katherine Philips b.	Ludolph Backhuysen b.		
1632	*Lord Baltimore d.* Christina of Sweden a. *Sir John Eliot d. Gustavus Adolphus (Sweden) d.* Ladislaus IV (Poland) a. Duc de Lauzun b. Samuel von Pufendorf b. *Sigismund III (Poland) d.*	*Graf von Pappenheim d. Graf von Tilly d.*			Louis Bourdaloue b. Benedict Spinoza b.	Anton van Leeuwenhoek b.	Jean Mabillon b. Anthony à Wood b.	Marquis de Coulanges b. Countess of Wharton b.	Luca Giordano b. Nicolas Maes b. Adam van der Meulen b. Jan Vermeer b.		Sir Christopher Wren b.

Year A.D.	Government and Law	Military and Naval Affairs	Industry Commerce Economics Finance Invention Labor	Travel and Exploration	Philosophy and Religion	Science and Medicine	Education Scholarship History	Literature	Painting and Sculpture	Music	Miscellaneous
1633	Marquess of Halifax b.	Sébastien de Vauban b.			George Abbot d. Robt. Browne d. J. H. Heidegger b. Philaret d. Robt. South b.			Abraham Fraunce d. Geo. Herbert d. Saml. Pepys b.	Willem Vandevelde (Younger) b.	Jacopo Peri d.	
1634	Sir Edward Coke d.	Albrecht von Wallenstein d.			Pasquier Quesnel b.			Geo. Chapman d. Comtesse de LaFayette b. John Marston d. Thos. Randolph d.	Eglon van der Neer b.		
1635	Count Griffenfeld b. John Mason d.			Saml. de Champlain d. Sir Anthony Shirley d.	Philipp Spener b. Edward Stillingfleet b.	Johann Becher b. Robt. Hooke b. Francis Willughby b.	Wolfgang Ratich d.	Sir George Etherege b. Edward Fairfax d. Lope de Vega Carpio d. Philippe Quinault b.	Jacques Callot d. Franz van Mieris b. J. B. Tubi b.		Thos. Betterton b. Mme. de Maintenon b. Sir Henry Morgan b. Old Parr d.
1636	Sir Geo. Mackenzie b.				Jos. Glanvill b. Hermann Witsius b.	Sanctorius d.		Nicolas Boileau b.	Adriaan Vandevelde b.		
1637	Ferdinand II (H.R.E.) d. Ferdinand III (H.R.E.) a.	Nicholas de Catinat b. Marquis de Chauteau—Renauit b.		Jacques Marquette b.	Nicholas Ferrar d. Robt. Fludd d. Thos. Ken b. Cyril Lucaris d.	Jan Swammerdam b.	Nicholas de Peiresc d. Sébastien de Tillemont b.	Gabriello Chiabrera d. Ben Jonson d. Thos. Traherne b.	Jan van der Heyden b.		John Kyrle b.
1638	Earl Henry of Clarendon b. Peter Minuit d.			Cornelius Jansen d. Nicolas de Malebranche b. Richard Simon b. Danl. Whitby b.		Jas. Gregory, (Earlier) b. Frederic Ruysch b. Nicolaus Steno b.	John Harvard d.	Sir Robt. Ayton d. Ivan Gundulić d.	Jacques Blanchard d. Adriaen Brouwer d. Meyndert Hobbema b.	Francis Pilkington d. John Wilbye d.	
1639	Geo. Jenatsch d. King Philip b. Lord Russell b.				Tomaso Campanella d. Increase Mather b. John Spottiswoode d.			J. d'Alarcón y Mendoza d. John Ford d. Martin von Opitz d. Jean Racine b.	Antonio Verrio b.	J. B. Lully b.	
1640	1st Duke of Devonshire b. Friedrich Wilhelm (Brandenburg) a. Murad IV (Turkey) d. Earl of Stirling d. Earl Robt. of Sunderland b.	Mazeppa b.		Louis Hennepin b.	Claude Fleury b. Miguel de Molinos b.		André Duchesne d.	Aphra Behn b. Robt. Burton d. John Day d. Paul Fleming d. Philip Massinger d. Sir Henry Wotton d. Wm. Wycherley b.	Giuseppe Cesari d. Antoine Coysevox b. Peter Paul Rubens d.		
1641	Marquis de Louvois b. Earl of Rochester b. Earl Lawrence of Romney b. Earl of Strafford d. Duc de Sully d.	Baron van Coehoorn b.	Sir Dudley North		Henri Arnaud b.	Reinier DeGraaf b. Nehemiah Grew b. Jeremiah Horrocks d. Sir Robt. Sibbald b. Raymond Vieussens b.	Abraham Pierson b. Thos. Rymer b.	Thos. Dekker d. Thos. Heywood d. Wm. Vaughan d.	Z.Domeninchino d. Jean Drouilly b. Michiel van Mierevelt d. Sir Anthony Van Dyck d.		Mme. de Montespan b.

1642–1658 A.D.

Year A.D.	Government and Law	Military and Naval Affairs	Industry Commerce Economics Finance Invention Labor	Travel and Exploration	Philosophy and Religion	Science and Medicine	Education Scholarship History	Literature	Painting and Sculpture	Music	Miscellaneous
1642	*Marie de' Medici d.* *Cardinal de Richelieu d.*	*Duc de Soubise d.* Comte de Tourville b.				*G. Galileo d.* Sir Isaac Newton b.		*Wm. Rowley d.* Thos. Shadwell b. *Sir John Suckling d.*	*Guido Reni d.*		Chas. Buhl b. *Marquis de Cinq-Mars d.*
1643	*Viscount Falkand d.* *John Hampden d.* *Louis XIII (France) d.* Louis XIV (France) a. *John Pym d.*			Sieur de La Salle b.	*Simon Episcopius d.* *Anne Hutchinson d.*	John Mayow b.	Gilbert Burnet b. *Michael O'Clery d.* John Strype b.	*Wm. Browne d.* *Henry Peacham d.*		*Claudio Monteverdi d.*	Claude Duval b.
1644	*Wm. Brewster d.* Lord Jeffreys b. Wm. Penn b. *Sir Thos. Roe d.*	Duc de Villeroi b.			*William Chillingworth d.* *Pope Urban VIII d.*	*J. B. van Helmont d.* Ole Roemer b.		François de Choisy b. *Ferrante Pallavicino d.* *Francis Quarles d.* *Geo. Sandys d.*	*Geo. Jameson d.*	Antonio Stradivari b.	Duchesse de La Vallière b. John Partridge b.
1645	Alexis (Russia) a. Earl of Godolphin b. *Hugo Grotius d.* *Mikhail (Russia) d.* Earl of Portland b. *Earl of Somerset d.* *Wm. Strode d.* *Antony Van Diemen d.*			Louis Joliet b.	*Wm. Laud d.*			*Thos. Carew d.* Jean de La Bruyère b. *F. Quevedo y Villegas d.*		Alessandro Stradella b.	Thos. Guy b. Capt. Kidd b.
1646		*François de Bassompierre d.*	Sieur de Boisguillebert b.		*Alexander Henderson d.*	John Flamsteed b. G. W. Leibnitz b.	Jean Hardouin b.		*Wm. Dobson d.* Sir Godfrey Kneller b.		J. H. Mansard b. *Thos. Morton d.*
1647	Nathaniel Bacon b. *Leonard Calvert d.* Earl Chas. of Sunderland b.	*Masaniello d.* Earl of Torrington b.		*Sir Ferdinando Gorges d.*	*Uriel Acosta d.* Marie Alacocque b. Pierre Bayle b. *Thos. Hooker d.*	*Christian Longomontanus d.* Denis Papin b. *Evangelista Torricelli d.*		*P. C. Hooft d.*			
1648	*Christian IV (Denmark) d.* Nicolas Desmarets b. Frederick III (Denmark) a. *Ladislaus IV (Poland) d.*	Marquis de Ruvigny b.			Jeanne Guyon b. *Lord Herbert of Cherbury d.* Humphrey Prideaux b.		Elihu Yale b.	Earl John of Rochester b. Elkanah Settle b. *"Tirso de Molina" d.* *Vincent Voiture d.* Marquess of Wharton b.	M. A. Franceschini b. *Louis Le Nain d.*	John Blow b.	
1649	*Charles I (England) d.* *Duke of Hamilton d.* *Earl of Holland d.* *John Winthrop (Elder) d.*	John Graham of Claverhouse b. Duke of Monmouth b. *Owen Roe O'Neill d.*		*Sir Robt. Dudley d.*	William Carstairs b. *Giovanni Diodati d.* *Gerhard Vossius d.*			*Richard Crashaw d.* *Wm. Drummond d.* *M. de Faria y Sousa d.*	*Isaack van Ostade d.* *David Teniers (Elder) d.* *Simon Vouet d.*		Titus Oates b.

Year A.D.	Government and Law	Military and Naval Affairs	Industry Commerce Economics Finance Invention Labor	Travel and Exploration	Philosophy and Religion	Science and Medicine	Education Scholarship History	Literature	Painting and Sculpture	Music	Miscellaneous
1650	William II (Orange) d.	Duc d'Angoulême d. Duke of Marlborough b. Marquess of Montrose d. Sir Geo. Rooke b. Sir Cloudesley Shovell b.		Bernhardus Varenius d.	Jeremy Collier b. René Descartes d. Sir Jonathan Trelawny b. John Williams d.	John Radcliffe b.		Phineas Fletcher d. Thos. May d. Jean de Rotrou d.			Nell Gwyn b.
1651	Maximilian the Great (Bavaria) d. Sir Wm. Phips b.	Jean Barth b. Henry Ireton d.		Engelbrecht Kaempfer b.	St. Jean Baptiste de la Salle b.	Abraham Sharp b.	André Dacier b.	F. de la M. Fénelon b.	Cornelis de Vos d.		
1652	Saml. Sewall b.			Wm. Dampier b. Pietro Della Valle d.	John Cotton d.	Archibald Pitcairne b. Augustus Rivinus b.		Richard Brome d. Thos. Otway b. Nahum Tate b.	José Ribera d.		Abraham Elzevir d. Bonaventure Elzevir d. Inigo Jones d.
1653	Earl of Bristol d. Thos. Dudley d. André de Fleury b.	John Benbow b. Martin van Tromp d. Claude de Villars b.					Claudius Salmasius d.	Tom D'Urfey b. John Oldham b. John Taylor d.	J. B. Poultier b.	Arcangelo Corelli b. Agostino Steffani b.	Théophraste Renaudot d.
1654	Charles X (Sweden) a. Christina (Sweden) abd. Count Oxenstjerna d. John Selden d. Sir Henry Vane (Elder) d.	Duc de Vendôme b.				Jacques Bernoulli b.		Wm. Habington d. J. F. Sarasin d.	Francisco Pacheco d. Paul Potter d.		
1655	Christian Thomasius b. Edward Winslow d.					Pierre Gassendi d.	Jas. Blair b. Danl. Heinsius d. Bernard de Montfaucon b.	Cyrano de Bergerac d. Andrew Fletcher b.	Eustache Le Sueur d.		
1656	Guillaume Dubois b.	François Lefort b. Principe di Piccolomini d. Miles Standish d.			Georg Calixtus d. Matthew Tindal b. Jas. Ussher d.	Edmund Halley b. M. A. Severino d. J. P. de Tournefort b.	John Hales d.	Jos. Hall d. J. F. Regnard b.	Jan van Goyen d. Francisco Herrera d. Nicolas Largilliere b.		
1657	Wm. Bradford d. Marquess of Clanricarde d. Ferdinand III (H.R.E.) d. Sophia (Russia) b.	Robt. Blake d.	John Lilburne d.	A. de la M. Cadillac b.	Jean Le Clerc b. Menasseh ben Israel d. John Norris b.	Wm. Harvey d.		John Dennis b. Bernard de Fontenelle b.	Ogata Korin b. Frans. Snyders d.		
1658	Aurungzebe b. Oliver Cromwell d. Leopold I (H.R.E.) a. Mary of Modena b. Earl of Warwick (Robt. Rich) d.	Sir Richard Grenville d. Earl of Peterborough b. Thos. Pride d.	Wm. Paterson b.					John Cleveland d. Richard Lovelace d.	Nicolas Coustou b.	Henry Purcell b.	

1659–1675 A.D.

Year A.D.	Government and Law	Military and Naval Affairs	Industry Commerce Economics Finance Invention Labor	Travel and Exploration	Philosophy and Religion	Science and Medicine	Education Scholarship History	Literature	Painting and Sculpture	Music	Miscellaneous
1659				Abel J. Tasman d.	Francis Rous d.		Thos. Creech b.	Simon Dach d. Daniel Defoe b.		Alessandro Scarlatti b.	
1660	Charles II (England) a. Charles X (Sweden) d. Lord Colepeper d. Thos. Harrison d. Duke of Shrewsbury b.	Philip Skippon d.			Danl. Jablonski b. Jas. Nayler d. St. Vincent de Paul d. Thos. Weld d.	Friedrich Hoffmann b. Sir Hans Sloane b. Georg Stahl b.	Sir Thos. Urquhart d.	Jacob Cats d. Paul Scarron d. Thos. Southerne b.	Govert Flinck d. Diego Velasquez d. J. B. Weenix d.		
1661	Duke of Argyll d. Earl of Halifax b. Robt. Harley b. Mohammed Kuprili d. Massassoit d. Jules Mazarin d.	Earl of Leven d.		Sieur de Iberville b.	Thos. Fuller d. Saml. Rutherford d.	David Gregory b. François Poupart b.	Chas. Rollin b.	Sieur de Saint-Amant d.	Jan Fyt d. Andrea Sacchi d.		
1662	Francis Atterbury b. Wm. Lenthall d. Sir Henry Vane (Younger) d.				John Biddle d. Blaise Pascal d. James Renwick b.		Richard Bentley b. Thos. Innes b.	Adam Billaut d. John Gauden d.		Henry Lawes d.	Count Königsmark b.
1663	Lord Warriston d.	Eugène of Savoy b.	Thos. Newcomen b.		August Francke b. Wm. Juxon d. Jean Massillon b. Cotton Mather b.			Pierre Motteux b.			Anne Bracegirdle b. Wm. Bradford b.
1664								Andreas Gryphius d. Katherine Philips d. Matthew Prior b. Sir John Vanbrugh b.			
1665	Carlos II (Spain) a. Earl of Cowper b. John Endicott d. Philip IV (Spain) d.				Johann Clauberg d. John Rogers d.	Rudolf Camerarius b. Sir Kenelm Digby d.		John Earle d.	Giuseppe Crespi b. Nicolas Poussin d.		Marquise de Rambouillet d.
1666	Anne of Austria d. Henrietta Maria d. Hannibal Sehested d. Shah Jahan (Delhi) d.				J. Schall von Bell d. Thos. Vaughan d.	Wm. Cowper b.		Sir Richard Fanshawe d. F. Manuel de Mello d. Jas. Shirley d. Countess of Winchilsea b.	Frans Hals d.		François Mansart d.
1667		Lord Lovat b.	Marquess of Worcester d.		Jeremy Taylor d.	Giorgio Baglivi b. Jean Bernoulli b. Abraham Demoivre b. Wm. Whiston b.		John Arbuthnot b. Abraham Cowley d. Georges de Scudéry d. Jonathan Swift b. Geo. Wither d.	Alonzo Cano d.		Susannah Centlivre b. Thos. Coram b.

Year A.D.	Government and Law	Military and Naval Affairs	Industry Commerce Economics Finance Invention Labor	Travel and Exploration	Philosophy and Religion	Science and Medicine	Education Scholarship History	Literature	Painting and Sculpture	Music	Miscellaneous
1668	Georg von Görtz b. Hans Svane d. John Thurloe d.				G. B. Vico b.	Hermann Boerhaave b. Johann Glauber d.	Johann Fabricius b.	Mary Astell b. Sir Wm. Davenant d. Alain René Lesage b.	Philip Wouwerman d.	François Couperin b.	Stephen Daye d.
1669	Wm. Prynne d.	Geo. Monk d.			Richard Mather d. John Toland b. Thos. Woolston b.	Jacob Winslöw b.		Sir John Denham d.	Pietro da Cortona d. Caspar de Crayer d. Rembrandt d. Francisco de Zurbaran d.		
1670	Frederick III (Denmark) d.	Duke of Berwick b. Sir Wm. Penn d.			John Comenius d.	Olaf Celsius b.		Wm. Congreve b. Bernard de Mandeville b. J. B. Rousseau b.	Giovanni Castiglione d. B. van der Helst d.		Claude Duval d.
1671	3rd Earl of Shaftesbury b.	Lord Fairfax of Cameron d. Stenka Razin d.	John Law b.				Johann Gronovius d.	Colley Cibber b.	Sébastien Bourdon d.		Rob Roy b.
1672	Cornelis De Witt d. Jan De Witt d. Prince Menshikov b. Richard Nicolls d. Peter the Great (Russia) a. Peter Stuyvesant d.	Earl of Sandwich d. Pierre Seguier d.				E. F. Geoffroy b. John Wilkins d. Francis Willughby d.	Chas. Chauncy d. Ludovico Muratori b.	Jos. Addison b. Anne Bradstreet d. F. de La Mothe le Vayer d. Antoine de Lamotte b. Sir Richard Steele b. Jacob Steendam d. Georg Stjernhjelm d. G. Tallemante de Reaux d.	Saml. Cooper d. Adriaan Vandevelde d.		Edmund Hoyle b.
1673	Oliver St. John d.	Geo. Wade b.				Johann Dippel b. Thomas Wharton d.	John Oldmixon b.	Molière d.	Salvator Rosa d.		
1674	Earl Edward of Clarendon d. John III (Poland) a. Duc Philippe II d'Orléans b. 2nd Viscount Townshend b.	Prince Gallitzin b.			Jean Labadie d. Henry Sacheverell b. Isaac Watts b.	Eustachio Manfredi b. Jean Pecquet d.	Wm. Byrd b. Thos. Ruddiman b.	Jean Chapelain d. Prosper de Crébillon b. Robt. Herrick d. John Milton d. Nicholas Rowe b. Thos. Traherne d.	Philippe de Champaigne d. G. van den Eeckhout d.	Giacomo Carissimi d. John Wilson d.	Beau Nash b.
1675	Duc César de Choiseul d. Bulstrode Whitelocke d.	Earl of Cadogan b. Viscomte de Turenne d.		Jacques Marquette d.	Saml. Clarke b. John Lightfoot d.	Reinier DeGraaf d. James Gregory, (Earlier) d. Giles de Roberval d. Thos. Willis d.		Ambrose Philips b. Duc de Saint-Simon d. Wm. Somerville b.	Gerard Douw d. Jan Vermeer d.	Pierre Perrin d.	Lord Mohun b.

1676–1693 A.D.

Year A.D.	Government and Law	Military and Naval Affairs	Industry Commerce Economics Finance Invention Labor	Travel and Exploration	Philosophy and Religion	Science and Medicine	Education Scholarship History	Literature	Painting and Sculpture	Music	Miscellaneous
1676	Alexis (Russia) d. Nathaniel Bacon d. Feodor III (Russia) a. Sir Matthew Hale d. King Philip d. Alexander Spotswood b. Sir Robt. Walpole b. John Winthrop (Younger) d.	Prinz von Anhalt-Dessau b. Prince Rákóczy b. Michel de Ruyter d. Karl von Wrangel d.			Anthony Collins b. Benj. Hoadly b. Pope Innocent XI a. Sabbatai Zevi d.		Pietro Giannone b. Earl Chas. of Orrery b.	John Ogilby d. John Philips b.	Jacques Courtois d. Sir Jas. Thornhill b.	Francesco Cavalli d.	Marquise de Brinvilliers d. Alexander Selkirk b.
1677	Sir Wm. Berkeley d. Jas. Harrington d.	Otto Traun b.			Benedict Spinoza d.	Isaac Barrow d. Francis Glisson d. Stephen Hales b.			Guillaume Coustou b. Wenzel Hollar d. Aernout van der Neer d.		
1678	Viscount Bolingbroke b.						Thos. Hearne b. Simon Ockley b.	Geo. Farquhar b. Richard Flecknoe d. Andrew Marvell d. Thomas Stanley d.	Jacques Caffieri b. Jacob Jordaens d. Robt. Nanteuil d.		
1679	Jean de Retz d. Roger Wolcott b.	Maurice of Nassau d.			Thos. Chubb b. Thos. Hobbes d. Matthew Poole d. Jas. Sharp d. Christian von Wolff b.	Giovanni Borelli d. John Mayow d.	Robert Wodrow b.	Earl Roger of Orrey d. Thos. Parnell b. Joost van den Vondel d.	Jan Steen d.		Geo. Psalmanazar b.
1680	Praise God Barebones d. Sir Geo. Carteret d. Lord Holles d. Henry Marten d. Viscount Stafford d.			Vitus Behring b.	Arthur Collier b. Joseph Glanvill d.	Thos. Bartholin d. Jan Swammerdam d.	Ephraim Chambers b.	Saml. Butler d. "Philippe Destouches" b. Duc de La Rochefoucauld d. Earl John of Rochester d.	Giovanni Bernini d. Sir Peter Lely d. Philip Van Dyck b.	Antonio Vivaldi b.	
1681		Jean Cavalier b.			Nikon d.			P. Calderón d.	Franz van Mieris d. Gerard Ter Borch d.	Alessandro Stradella d.	Wm. Lilly d.
1682	Feodor III (Russia) d. Duke of Lauderdale d.	Lord Newark d. Prince Rupert d.			Pierre de Charlevoix b.	Johann Becher d. John Hadley b. Giovanni Morgagni b. Jean Picard d.	Jacopo Facciolati b.	Sir Thos. Browne d.	Claude Lorrain d. Bartolomé Murillo d. Jacob van Ruysdael d.		Jonathan Wild b.
1683	J. B. Colbert d. Lord Russell d. Sir Wm. Scroggs d. 1st Earl of Shaftesbury d. Algernon Sidney d. Uncas d.	John Lambert d.			Conyers Middleton b. John Owen d. Benj. Whichcote d. Roger Williams d.	René de Réaumur b.		Thos. Killigrew d. John Oldham d. Izaak Walton d. Edward Young b.	Antoine Pesne b.	Giuseppe Guarnieri b. Jean Rameau b.	Anne Oldfield b.
1684	Sir Geo. Downing d.				Jean Astruc b. Nathaniel Lardner b. Robt. Leighton d.			Pierre Corneille d. Marguerite de Launay b. Baron von Holberg b.	Jan van Heem d. J. B. Vanloo b. Antoine Watteau b.		Joe Miller b.

Year A.D.	Government and Law	Military and Naval Affairs	Industry Commerce Economics Finance Invention Labor	Travel and Exploration	Philosophy and Religion	Science and Medicine	Education Scholarship History	Literature	Painting and Sculpture	Music	Miscellaneous
1685	Earl of Arlington d. Charles II (England) d. James II (England) a.	Duke of Monmouth d.			Bishop Berkeley b.	John Pell d. Brook Taylor b.		John Gay b. Thos. Otway d. Countess of Wharton d.	J. M. Nattier b. Adriaen van Ostade d.	J. S. Bach b. G. F. Händel b.	Wm. Kent b.
1686	Sir Wm. Coventry d. Count De la Gardie d. Count Osterman b.	Prince Louis de Condé II d.			Hans Egede b. John Fell d. Wm. Law b. John Pearson d.	Gabriel Fahrenheit b. Otto von Guencke d. Nicolaus Steno d.		Allan Ramsay b. Thos. Tickell b.	Carlo Dolci d.	Nicola Porpora b.	
1687	2nd Duke of Buckingham d. Sir Wm. Wyndham b.		Sir Wm. Petty d.	Sieur de La Salle d.	Jean Claude d.	Robert Simson b.	Wm. Stukeley b.	Chas. Cotton d. Sir Constantijn Huygens d. Edmund Waller d.		J. B. Lully d.	Nell Gwyn d.
1688	Friedrich Wilhelm (Brandenburg) d. James II (England) dep. Nadir Shah b. Duke of Ormonde d.	Marquis de Duquesne d.		Sieur de Vincennes b.	Ralph Cudworth d. James Renwick d. Emanuel Swedenborg b.	Cadwalader Colden b.	Sieur Du Cange d. Lewis Theobald b.	John Bunyan d. Antoine Furetière d. Pierre de Marivaux b. Alexander Pope b. Philippe Quinault d.	Claude Perrault d. John Smybert b.		Jas. Edw. (Old Pretender) b. Sir Henry Morgan d.
1689	Lord Jeffreys d. Mary II (England) a. William III (England) a.	John Graham of Claverhouse d.	Jean Tavernier d.		Pope Innocent XI d. Baron de Montesquieu b.	Thos. Sydenham d.		Aphra Behn d. Lady M. W. Montagu b. Alexis Piron b. Saml. Richardson b.	B. Franceschini d.		
1690	Earl John of Granville b.	Duc de Schomberg d. Geo. Walker d.	Wm. Ged b.		Marie Alacocque d. John Eliot d.		John Rushworth d.		Chas. Le Brun d. Adam van der Meulen d. David Teniers (Younger) d.		
1691	Marquis de Louvois d. Sir Geo. Mackenzie d.	Peder Tordenskjöld b. Cornelis van Tromp d. Earl of Tyrconnel d.	Sir Dudley North d.		Richard Baxter d. Geo. Fox d.	Robt. Boyle d.	Edward Pococke d.	Thos. Amory b. Sir George Etherege d.	Albert Cuyp d. Wm. Faithorne d.		Edward Cave b.
1692					Joseph Butler b.			J. G. Cotta d. Comtesse de LaFayette d. Thos. Shadwell d.	G. B. Tiepolo b.	Giuseppe Tartini b.	Wm. Caslon b. Adrienne Lecouvreur b. John Rich b.
1693	Count Bestuzhev b. Robt. Dinwiddie b.	Edmund Ludlow d. Patrick Sarsfield d.			Georg Bilfinger b.	Jas. Bradley b.		Eliza Haywood b. Geo. Lillo b. Duchesse de Montpensier d. Paul Pellisson d.	Nicolas Maes d. Willem Vandevelde (Elder) d.		Jas. Quin b. Christopher Sower b.

1694–1712 A.D.

Year A.D.	Government and Law	Military and Naval Affairs	Industry Commerce Economics Finance Invention Labor	Travel and Exploration	Philosophy and Religion	Science and Medicine	Education Scholarship History	Literature	Painting and Sculpture	Music	Miscellaneous
1694	Mary II (England) d. Samuel von Pufendorf d. Wm. Shirley b.	Lord Murray b.	François Quesay b.		Antoine Arnauld d. Francis Hutcheson b. St. Paul of the Cross b. Hermann Reimarus b. John Tillotson d.	Marcello Malpighi d.		Lord Chesterfield b. François de Voltaire b.	Pierre Puget d. Michael Rysbrach b.	Leonardo Leo b.	Peter Collinson b. Count Königsmark d.
1695	Marquess of Halifax d. Sir Wm. Phips d. Viscount Stair d.	Edward Braddock b. Duc de Luxembourg d.			Pierre Nicole d.	Christiaan Huygens d.	Anthony á Wood d.	J. C. Günther b. Jean de La Fontaine d. Henry Vaughan d.	Pierre Mignard d. Louis Roubillac b.	Henry Purcell d.	
1696	John III (Poland) d.	Jas. Keith b. Jas. Oglethorpe b. Sir Wm. Pepperell b. Maurice de Saxe b.			Lord Kames b. St. Alfonso de Liguori b.		Wm. Oldys b.	Lord Hervey of Ickworth b. Jean de La Bruyère d. Edward Phillips d. Mme. de Sévigné d.			
1697	Augustus II (Poland) a. Charles XII (Sweden) a.	Lord Anson b. Niels Juel d.			Miguel de Molinos d. Antônio Vieira d.	Bernhard Albinus b. Jean de Anville b. Alexander Monro b. Francesco Redi d.	John Aubrey d. Geo. Sale b.	Robt. Patlock b. Abbé Prévost b. Richard Savage b.	Antonio Canaletto b. Wm. Hogarth b.		Marquise du Deffand b. J. P. Zenger b.
1698	Comte de Frontenac d.				Jean Calas b. J. H. Heidegger d. Lodowick Muggleton d.	Colin Maclaurin b. Pierre Maupertuis b.	Sébastien de Tillemont d. Wm. Warburton b.	Sir Robt. Howard d. "Metastasio" b. Erik Pontopiddan b.	Jean Drouilly d.		
1699	Count Griffenfeld d. Marquis dá Pombal b. Sir Wm. Temple d.	François Lefort d. Johann von Ziethen b.			Edward Stillingfleet d.	John Bartram b.		Robt. Blair b. Thomas Longman b. Jean Racine d. Joseph Spence b.	Jean Chardin b. Pierre Subleyras b.	Johann Hasse b.	Mme. de Geoffrin b.
1700	Graf von Brühl b. Carlos II (Spain) d. Philip V (Spain) a.		Peter Fanuel b.	Louis Hennepin d.? Louis Joliet d.	Pope Clement XI a. Graf von Zinzendorf b.	Daniel Bernoulli b. Saml. Klingenstierna b. Abraham Trembley b. Paul Werlhof b.	Thos. Creech d.	John Dryden d. John Dyer b. Johann Gottsched b. Jas. Thomson b.	Lambert Adam b. André LeNôtre d. J. B. Tubi d.		
1701	Friedrich I (Prussia) a.	Comte de Tourville d.			Alexander Cruden b.	Ruggiero Boscovich b. Anders Celsius b.		Madeleine de Scudéry d.		K. H. Graun b.	Capt. Kidd d.
1702	Anne (England) a. Marqués de la Ensenada b. Earl Robt. of Sunderland d. William III (England) d.	Jean Barth d. John Benbow d.				Olaf Rudbeck d.		David Mallet b.	Jean Liotard b. Pietro Longhi b.		Jack Sheppard b.
1703	Ahmed III (Turkey) a.	Sieur de Saint-Évremond d.			Jonathan Edwards b. John Wesley b.	Robt. Hooke d. J. Kunkel von Löwenstjern d. John Wallis d.		Henry Brooke b. Robt. Dodsley b. José d'Isla b. Saml. Pepys d. Chas. Perrault d.	François Boucher b. Eglon van der Neer d. Jan Siberechts d.		

Year A.D.	Government and Law	Military and Naval Affairs	Industry Commerce Economics Finance Invention Labor	Travel and Exploration	Philosophy and Religion	Science and Medicine	Education Scholarship History	Literature	Painting and Sculpture	Music	Miscellaneous
1704	*Sir Roger L'Estrange d. Earl of Romney d. Sophia (Russia) d.* Stanislaus I (Poland) a.	John Byng b. *Baron van Coehoorn d.*			*Jacques Bossuet d. Louis Bourdaloue d. John Locke d.* August Spangenberg b.			Chas. Duclos b. Wm. Hamilton b.			Eugene Aram b.
1705	Lord Holland b. *Leopold I (H.R.E.) d.* Earl Mansfield (Wm. Murray) b.	Lord Hawke b.			David Hartley b. *Philipp Spener d.* Abraham Tucker b. *Michael Wigglesworth d.*	Peter Artedi b. *Jacques Bernoulli d. John Ray d.*		Antonio da Silva b.	*Luca Giordano d.* August von Rosenhof b. Chas. Vanloo b.	Farinelli b.	*Ninon de Lenclos d. Titus Oates d.* John Wood b.
1706	Benj. Franklin b.			*Sieur de Iberville d.*	*Pierre Bayle d. John Howe d.*	*Giorgio Baglivi d.* John Dollond b.		*John Evelyn d.*		B. Galuppi b.	John Baskerville b. Dick Turpin b.
1707	*Aurungzebe d. 1st Duke of Devonshire d. Comte de Gramont d.* Stephen Hopkins b.	Benj. Robins b. *Sir Cloudesley Shovell d. Sébastien de Vauban d.*			Countess of Huntingdon b. Chas. Wesley b.	Comte de Buffon b. Leonhard Euler b. Linnaeus b. Pierre Lyonet b. Sir John Pringle b.	Johann Ernesti b. Johann Ihre b. *Jean Mabillon d. Abraham Pierson d.*	*Geo. Farquhar d.* Henry Fielding b. Robt. Foulis b. Carlo Goldoni b.	*Willem Vandevelde (Younger) d. Antonio Verrio d.*		*Mme. de Montespan d.*
1708	Wm. Pitt (Lord Chatham) b.				*Hermann Witsius d.*	*David Gregory d.* Albrecht von Haller b. *J. P. de Tournefort d.*		Olof von Dalin b. Friedrich von Hagedorn b.	*Ludolph Backhuysen d.*	*John Blow d.*	*J.-H. Mansard d.*
1709	*Earl Henry of Clarendon d. Earl of Portland d.* Stanislaus I (Poland) abd.	*Mazeppa d. Sir Geo. Rooke d.*	Étienne de Silhouette b.		*François de La Chaise d.* Julien de La Mettrie b.	*Wm. Cowper d. François Poupart d.*	Charles de Brosses b.	*Thomas Corneille d.* Saml. Johnson b. *John Philips d.*	*Meyndert Hobbema d.*		
1710				Jonathan Carver b.	Thos. Reid b.	Jas. Ferguson b. *Ole Roemer d.*	Floyer Sydenham b.	Chas. Favart b. *J. F. Regnard d.*		Thos. A. Arne b. Wm. Boyce b. Giovanni Pergolesi b.	*Thos. Betterton d. Duchesse de La Vallière d.* Comte de Saint-Germain b.
1711	Charles VI (H.R.E.) a. Thos. Hutchinson b. Prinz von Kaunitz–Rietberg b. *Earl Lawrence of Rochester d.* Earl of Temple b.	Edward Boscawen b. Richard Gridley b. Freiherr von der Trenck b.			David Hume b. *Thos. Ken d.* H. M. Muhlenberg b. *John Norris d.*	Johann Lieberkühn b.	Eleazer Wheelock b.	*Nicolas Boileau d.* Mikhail Lomonósov b.			Kitty Clive b.
1712	Graf Johann von Bernstorff b. *Richard Cromwell d. Earl of Godolphin d.* Geo. Grenville b. *Duke of Leeds d.*	*Nicholas de Catinat d.* Marquis de Montcalm b. *Duc de Vendôme d.*			Antonio Genovesi b. *Richard Simon d.*	*Jean Cassini d.* Nehemiah Grew a. *Denis Papin d. Sir Robt. Sibbald d.*	C. M. de l'Epée b.	Francesco Algarotti b. Andrew Foulis b. J. J. Rousseau b.	*Jan van der Heyden d.*		*Lord Mohun d.*

1713–1726 A.D.

Year A.D.	Government and Law	Military and Naval Affairs	Industry Commerce Economics Finance Invention Labor	Travel and Exploration	Philosophy and Religion	Science and Medicine	Education Scholarship History	Literature	Painting and Sculpture	Music	Miscellaneous
1713	Earl of Bute b. *Friedrich I (Prussia) d.* Friedrich Wilhelm I (Prussia) a. *3rd Earl of Shaftesbury d.*				Denis Diderot b. Junípero Serra b.	Alexis Clairault b. Giovanni Della Torre b. Nicolas de Lacaille b. *Archibald Pitcairne d.*	Edward Capell b. *Thos. Rymer d.*	Alison Cockburn b. Guillaume Raynal b. Laurence Sterne b.	Allan Ramsay b.	*Arcangelo Corelli d.*	
1714	*Anne (England) d.* Earl of Camden b. George I (England) a. René Maupeou b.		*Sieur de Boisguillebert d.*		Alexander Baumgarten b. Geo. Whitefield b.	Percival Pott b. *John Radcliffe d.*		Jas. Hervey b. Lord Monboddo b. Wm. Shenstone b.	J. B. Pigalle b. Joseph Vernet b. Richard Wilson b.	K. P. E. Bach b. Christoph Gluck b.	Peg Woffington b.
1715	*Earl of Halifax d.* *Louis XIV (France) d.* Louis XV (France) a.	Sir Wm. Johnson b.		*Wm. Dampier d.*	Étienne de Condillac b. Claude Helvétius b. *Nicolas de Malebranche d.*	Peter Kalm b. Pierre Le Monnier b.	*Gilbert Burnet d.* Giacobbo Pereire b. Ephraim Williams b.	*F. de la M. Fénelon d.* Christian Gellert b. John Hawkesworth b. *Nahum Tate d.* Marquis de Vauvenargues b. *Marquess of Wharton d.* Wm. Whitehead b.	*François Girardon d.*		Robt. Damiens b. *John Partridge d.*
1716	Viscount Sackville b.	*Marquis de Château-Renault d.* *Earl of Torrington d.*		*Engelbrecht Kaempfer d.*	*Wm. Carstairs d.* *Robt. South d.*	L. J. Daubenton b. *G. W. Leibnitz d.* Jas. Lind b. *Raymond Vieussens d.*	Johann Reiske b.	*Marquis de Coulanges d.* *Andrew Fletcher d.* Thos. Gray b. John Hill b. Jean de Saint-Lambert b. *Wm. Wycherley d.*	Étienne Falconet b. *Ogata Kōrin d.*		
1717	Maria Theresa b. Comte de Vergennes b.	Lord Amherst b. Baron Heathfield b.	Joseph Foullon b.		*Jeanne Guyon d.* Johann Michaelis b.	J. le R. d'Alembert b. Matthew Stewart b.		Elizabeth Carter b. Horace Walpole b.	Johann Winckelmann b.	Johann Stamitz b.	David Garrick b.
1718	*Charles XII (Sweden) d.* *Mary of Modena d.* Count Panin b. *Wm. Penn d.* Lord Rodney b. *Duke of Shrewsbury d.*	Esek Hopkins b. Israel Putnam b.			*Richard Cumberland d.* Paul Rabaut b.	Maria Agnesi b. John Canton b. Wm. Hunter b.		*Pierre Motteux d.* *Thos. Parnell d.* *Nicholas Rowe d.*			Thos. Chippendale b.
1719	Duc Étienne de Choiseul b. *Georg von Görtz d.*		*Wm. Paterson d.*	*Sieur de Vincennes d.*	*St. Jean Baptiste de la Salle d.* *Pasquier Quesnel d.*	*John Flamsteed d.*	Sir Thos. Newdigate b.	*Joseph Addison d.* Jacques Cazotte b. Michel Sedaine b.	*Carlo Cignani d.* *J. B. Poultier d.*		*Mme. de Maintenon d.* Thos. Sheridan b.

Year A.D.	Government and Law	Military and Naval Affairs	Industry Commerce Economics Finance Invention Labor	Travel and Exploration	Philosophy and Religion	Science and Medicine	Education Scholarship History	Literature	Painting and Sculpture	Music	Miscellaneous
1720	Pontiac b. Victor Amadeus I (Sardinia) a.	*Marquis de Ruvigny d. Peder Tordenskjold d.*			John Woolman b.	Charles de Bonnet b. Baron Karl de Geer b. Gilbert White b.	*Simon Ockley d.*	Saml. Foote b. Jupiter Hammon b. Charlotte Lennox b. *Countess of Winchilsea d.*	Bernardo Canaletto b. *Antoine Coysevox d.* Giambattista Piranesi b.		Charles Edward (Young Pretender) b. Baron von Münchhausen b.
1721	*Nicolas Desmarets d.* Chrétien de Malesherbes b. Edmund Pendleton b. Roger Sherman b.	Thos. Gage b. Johann Kalb b. Freiherr von Seydlitz b.			*Henri Arnaud d. Pope Clement XI d.* Saml. Hopkins b. *Sir Jonathan Trelawny d.*	*Rudolf Camerarius d.*	Jos. de Guignes b. *Pierre Huet d.* Wm. Robertson b. *Elihu Yale d.*	Mark Akenside b. Wm. Collins b. *Matthew Prior d.* Tobias Smollett b.	*Antoine Watteau d.*		Mme. de Pompadour b. *Alexander Selkirk d.*
1722	Saml. Adams b. Hyder Ali b. *Earl Chas. of Sunderland d.* Chas. Yorke b.	John Burgoyne b. *Duke of Marlborough d.*			*John Toland d.*	Leopold Auenbrugger b. Théophile de Bordeu b. Pieter Camper b.	*André Dacier d.* David Ruhnken b.	Conde di Gozzi b. Christopher Smart b.			Flora Macdonald b.
1723	Sir Wm. Blackstone b. *Earl of Cowper d. Guillaume Dubois d. Duc de Lauzun d.* Wm. Livingston b. *Duc Philippe II d'Orléans d.* Peyton Randolph b. John Witherspoon b.		Adam Smith b.		Johann Basedow b. Adam Ferguson b. *Claude Fleury d.* Baron d'Holbach b. *Increase Mather d.* Richard Price b.	Markus Bloch b. *Anton van Leeuwenhoek d.* Johann Mayer b. *Augustus Rivinus d.*		*Tom D'Urfey d.* Baron von Grimm b. *J. C. Günther d.* Jean Marmontel b.	*Sir Godfrey Kneller d.* Sir Joshua Reynolds b.		*Susannah Centlivre d. Sir Christopher Wren d.*
1724	Ahmed Shah b. *Robt. Harley d.* Henry Laurens b.	Viscount Hood b. Marquis de Ségur b.			Immanuel Kant b. *Humphrey Prideaux d. Henry Sacheverell d.*	Anton Büsching b. John Michell b. John Smeaton b.	John Ash b.	*François de Choisy d.* Wm. Gilpin b. G. F. Klopstock b. *Elkanah Settle d.* Frances Sheridan b.			*Thos. Guy d. John Kyrle d. Jack Sheppard d.* Richard Tattersall b.
1725	Catherine I (Russia) a. Lord Clive b. Graf von Hertzberg b. John Logan b. Geo. Mason b. Jas. Otis b. *Peter the Great (Russia) d.* 3rd Viscount Townshend b.	Pasquale Paoli b. Comte de Rochambeau b. John Thomas b.		Geo. Glas b.	John Newton b. Johann Semler b.			Wm. Mason b.	J. B. Greuze b.	*Alesandro Scarlatti d.*	Giovanni Casanova b. *Henry Stuart d. Jonathan Wild d.*
1726	Lord Hailes b. Oliver Wolcott b. Geo. Wythe b.	*Earl of Cadogan d.* Earl Howe b.			*Jeremy Collier d.* Philip Otterbein b. *Danl. Whitby d.*	Jas. Hutton b. Thos. Pennant b.		Louise d'Epinay b. *Sir John Vanbrugh d.*	Danl. Chodowiecki b.	Chas. Burney b.	Sir Wm. Chambers b. John Howard b.

1727–1739 A.D.

Year A.D.	Government and Law	Military and Naval Affairs	Industry Commerce Economics Finance Invention Labor	Travel and Exploration	Philosophy and Religion	Science and Medicine	Education Scholarship History	Literature	Painting and Sculpture	Music	Miscellaneous
1727	Jas. Bowdoin b. *Catherine I (Russia) d.* *George I (England) d.* George II (England) a. John Wilkes b.	Jas. Wolfe b.	Robert Turgot b.		*August Francke d.* Johann Gassner b.	Jean Deluc b. *Sir Isaac Newton d.*	Ezra Stiles b.	Hester Chapone b.	G. B. Cipriani b. Thomas Gains—borough b.	Neil Gow b.	
1728	Ceasar Rodney b. *Christian Thomasius d.*	Horatio Gates b. John Stark b.	Ferdinando Galiani b. John Wilkinson b.	Jas. Cook b.	*Cotton Mather d.* Johann von Zimmermann b.	Antoine Baume b. Joseph Black b. John Hunter b.		Oliver Goldsmith b. Mercy Warren b. Thos. Warton b.	Raphael Mengs b.	Nicola Piccinni b. *Agostino Steffani d.*	Robt. Adam b. Chevalier d'Eon b.
1729	Edmund Burke b. *Prince Menshikov d.* Suraj-ud-Dowlah (Bengal) b. Wm. Tryon b.	Viscount Howe b. P. de Suffren Saint-Tropez b. Count Savorov b.	*John Law d.* *Thos. Newcomen d.*	L. A. de Bougain-ville b.	*Saml. Clarke d.* *Anthony Collins d.* Moses Mendels-sohn b. Saml. Seabury b.	Lazaro Spallanzani b.	*Jean Hardouin d.* Christian Heyne b.	Gotthold Lessing b. Giuseppe Parini b. Thos. Percy b. Clara Reeve b. *Sir Richard Steele d.*	*M. A. Franceschini d.*		
1730	*Ahmed III (Turkey) d.* *Saml. Sewall d.* Victor Amadeus I (Sardinia) abd.	*Prince Gallitzin d.* Baron von Steuben b. *Duc de Villeroi d.*	Josiah Wedgwood b.	A. de la M. Cadillac d.	Johann Hamann b.	Johann Hedwig b. Jan Ingenhousz b. Charles Mason b. Charles Messier b. Otto Müller b. Benj. West b.	Thos. Tyrwhitt b.	*Wm. Congreve d.*			*Adrienne Lecouvreur d.* *Anne Oldfield d.*
1731	William Franklin b. Lord Thurlow b.	Wm. Moultrie b. Robert Rogers b.				Wm. Aiton b. Henry Cavendish b. Erasmus Darwin b. *E. F. Geoffroy d.* *Frederic Ruysch d.* *Brook Taylor d.*	*Earl Chas. of Orrery d.* Francis Grose b. ?	*Mary Astell d.* Wm. Cowper b. *Danl. Defoe d.* *Antoine de Lamotte d.*	Pierre Julien b.		
1732	*Francis Atterbury d.* John Dickinson b. Henry Flood b. Warren Hastings b. Sir Elijah Impey b. Lord Kenyon b. Richard Henry Lee b. Jacques Necker b. Lord North b. Geo. Washington b.	Francis Marion b.	Sir Richard Arkwright b.		*Arthur Collier d.*	Peter Forskål b. Joseph de Lalande b. Nevil Maskeleyne b. José Mutis b. David Rittenhouse b.	Angelo Fabroni b.	Pierre de Beaumarchais b. *Richard Cumberland d.* Wm. Falconer b. *John Gay d.*	J.H. Fragonard b.	Josef Haydn b.	*Chas. Buhl d.* Geo. Colman (Elder) b. Julie de Lespinasse b.
1733	*Augustus II (Poland) d.* Earl of Rosslyn b.	Philip Schuyler b.		Karsten Niebuhr b.	*Matthew Tindal d.* *Thomas Woolston d.*	Richard Kirwan b. Josef Koelreuter b. Franz Mesmer b. Joseph Priestley b. Caspar Wolff b.		*Bernard de Mandeville d.* C. M. Wieland b.	*Nicolas Coustou d.*	*François Couperin d.*	

Year A.D.	Government and Law	Military and Naval Affairs	Industry Commerce Economics Finance Invention Labor	Travel and Exploration	Philosophy and Religion	Science and Medicine	Education Scholarship History	Literature	Painting and Sculpture	Music	Miscellaneous
1734	Chas. de Calonne b. Francis Lightfoot Lee b. Count Orlov b. Cardinal de Rohan b. J. Roland de la Platière b.	Sir Ralph Abercromby b. *Duke of Berwick d.* Sir John Jervis b. Prince Repnin b. Thos. Sumter b. *Claude de Villars d.*	Robt. Morris b.			Paul Barthez b. *Johann Dippel d. Eustachio Manfredi d. Georg Stahl d.*	*Robert Wodrow d.*	John Dennis d. Francisco de Nascimento b.	Geo. Romney b. *Sir Jas. Thornhill d.* Joseph Wright b.		Jean Riesener b. *Rob Roy d.*
1735	John Adams b. Graf Andreas von Bernstorff b.'	Prince de Ligne b. *Earl of Peterborough d. Prince Rákóczy d.* Paul Revere b. Earl of St. Vincent b.	Thos. Coutts b.	Danl. Boone b. Tobias Furneaux b.	Robt. Raikes b.	*Peter Artedi d.* Torbern Bergman b.	*Thos. Hearne d.*	John Arbuthnot d. Jas. Beattie b. St. J. de Crèvecœur b., John Langhorne b. J. A. Musäus b.	Thos. Banks b.		Granville Sharp b.
1736	Patrick Henry b. Baron von Thugut b.	*Eugène of Savoy d.* Richard Montgomery b.	Jas. Watt b.		*Jean Le Clerc d.* Ann Lee b.	Jean Bailly b. Chas. de Coulomb b. *Gabriel Fahrenheit d.* Thos. Fowler b. Comte de Lagrange b. Danl. Solander b.	*Johann Fabricius d. Geo. Sale d.* Geo. Steevens b. J. Horne Tooke b.	Jas. Macpherson b. G. Senac de Mailhan b.		*Giovanni Pergolesi d.*	
1737	Chas. Carroll b. Silas Deane b. John Hancock b. Marquess (Wm.) Lansdowne b. Thos. Paine b. Earl of Shelburne b.		Johan Struensee b.		Alexander Geddes b.	Luigi Galvani b.	Edward Gibbon b. *John Strype d.*	Heinrich von Gerstenberg b. Francis Hopkinson b. Bernardin de Saint-Pierre b.	John S. Copley b. Joseph Nollekens b.	*Antonio Stradivari d.*	Frances Abington b.
1738	John Beresford b. Chevalier de Boufflers b. *2nd Viscount Townshend d.*	Sir Henry Clinton b. Marquess of Cornwallis b.	Marchese di Beccaria b.			*Hermann Boerhaave d.* Sir Wm. Herschel b.		"Peter Pindar" b.	Benj. West b.		Joseph Guillotin b. *Joe Miller d.*
1739	Alexander McGillivray b. Prince Potemkin b. John Rutledge b.	Ethan Allen b. Chas. Dumouriez b. Andrew Pickens b.	P. S. Du Pont deNemours b.			Wm. Bartram b.		Hugh Kelly b. J. F. de Laharpe b. *Geo. Lillo d. Antonio da Silva d.* John Walter b.		Benj. Cooke b. K. Ditters von Dittersdorf b.	*Dick Turpin d.*

1740–1751 A.D.

Year A.D.	Government and Law	Military and Naval Affairs	Industry Commerce Economics Finance Invention Labor	Travel and Exploration	Philosophy and Religion	Science and Medicine	Education Scholarship History	Literature	Painting and Sculpture	Music	Miscellaneous
1740	Armand Camus b. *Charles VI (H.R.E.) d.* Frederick the Great (Prussia) a. *Frederick Wilhelm I (Prussia) d.* Ivan VI (Russia) a. Arthur Lee b. *Alexander Spotswood d.* Jas. N. Tandy b. Jonathan Trumbull b. *Sir Wm. Wyndham d.*	*Jean Cavalier d.* John Sullivan b.	Sir Francis Baring b. Joseph Montgolfier b.		Pope Benedict XIV a. J. F. Oberlin b. Augustus Toplady b.	Horace de Saussure b.	*Ephraim Chambers d.*	Karl Bellmann b. Jas. Boswell b. Sir Philip Francis b. Jung-Stilling b. Isabel Pagan b. Marquis de Sade b. *Thos. Tickell d.*	John Smart b.		Giambattista Bodoni b.
1741	Samuel Chase b. Elizabeth (Russia) a.	Benedict Arnold b. Joseph Warren b.	Arthur Young b.	*Vitus Behring d.* J. F. La Pérouse b.	*Danl. Jablonski d.*	J. K. Lavater b. Peter Pallas b.	Edmund Malone b. *Bernard de Montfaucon d.* *Chas. Rollin d.*	Sébastien Chamfort b. Wm. Combe b. Johann Merck b. Hester Thrale Piozzi b. *J. B. Rousseau d.*	Jas. Barry b. Henry Fuseli b. J. A. Houdon b. Angelica Kauffmann b. Chas. W. Peale b.	André Grétry b. Giovanni Paisello b.	Elisha Perkins b. Emel'yan Pugachev b.
1742	Joseph Brant b. Charles VII (H.R.E.) a. Jas. Wilson b.	Gerhard von Blücher b. Nathanael Greene b.			Chas. Dupuis b. *Jean Massillon d.*	*Edmund Halley d.* *Friedrich Hoffmann d.* Nicolas Le Blanc b. Georg Lichtenberg b. K. W. Scheele b. *Abraham Sharp d.*	*Nathan Bailey d.* *Richard Bentley d.* *John Oldmixon d.* Roch Sicard b.	*Wm. Somerville d.*	John Kay b.		Philip Astley b.
1743	Francis Dana b. *André de Fleury d.* Thos. Jefferson b. John Lowell b. P.–D. Toussaint l'Ouverture b. Graf von Toll b.	C. de Latour d'Auvergne b. Seth Warner b.	Edmund Cartwright b. *Peter Fanuel d.* John Fitch b. Mayer Anselm Rothschild b.		Marquis de Condorcet b. Friedrich Jacobi b. Wm. Paley b. Marquis de Saint-Martin b.	René Haüy b. Martin Klaproth b. Antoine Lavoisier b. K. P. Thunberg b.	*Jas. Blair d.*	A. L. Barbauld b. *Henry Carey d.* Hannah Cowley b. Princess Dashkova b. Gavrila Derzhavin b. Johannes Ewald b. *Lord Hervey of Ickworth d.* *Richard Savage d.*		Luigi Boccherini b. *Antonio Vivaldi d.*	Alessandro di Cagliostro b. David Röntgen b.
1744	Lord Wm. Auckland b. Elbridge Gerry b. Jean Paul Marat b. Josiah Quincy b.	Sir Wm. Cornwallis b. Thos. Mifflin b.			J. G. von Herder b. Rowland Hill b. *G. B. Vico d.*	Sir Joseph Banks b. *Anders Celsius d.* Pierre Desault b. *John Hadley d.* Jean de Lamarck b.	*Wm. Byrd d.* *Thos. Innes d.* *Lewis Theobald d.*	Richard L. Edgeworth b. Thomaz Gonzaga b. *Alexander Pope d.*	David Allan b.	*Leonardo Leo d.*	Abigail Adams b.
1745	*Charles VII (H.R.E.) d.* John Jay b. Timothy Pickering b. John Sevier b. Lord Stowell b. *Sir Robt. Walpole d.*	John Barry b. Sir Robt. Calder b. Anthony Wayne b.	Comte de Roederer b.		Francis Asbury b. Henry Edgeworth b. Johann Griesbach b.	Geo. Attwood b. Philippe Pinel b. Benj. Rush b. Ale Alessandro Volta b.	Lindley Murray b. Henry Rutgers b.	Wm. Hayley b. Thos. Holcraft b. Henry Mackenzie b. Hannah More b. John Nichols b. Henry Pye b. *Jonathan Swift d.*	*J. B. Vanloo d.*	Charles Dibdin b. *Giuseppe Guarnieri d.* Johann Salomon b.	

Year A.D.	Government and Law	Military and Naval Affairs	Industry Commerce Economics Finance Invention Labor	Travel and Exploration	Philosophy and Religion	Science and Medicine	Education Scholarship History	Literature	Painting and Sculpture	Music	Miscellaneous
1746	Henry Grattan b. Sir Wm. Jones b. Robt. Livingston b. Jean Pache b. *Philip V (Spain) d.* Chas. C. Pinckney b. Jean Portalis b.	Viscount Keith b. Thaddeus Kosciusko b. J. P. G. Muhlenberg b.			*Thos. Chubb d. Francis Hutcheson d.* Jean Maury b.	*Colin Maclaurin d.* Gaspard Monge b. Giuseppe Piazzi b.	Johann Pestalozzi b. Danl. A. Wyttenbach b.	*Robt. Blair d.* Michael Bruce b. Comtesse de Genlis b. *Thos. Southerne d.*	*Guillaume Coustou d.* Francisco Goya b. *Nicolas Largilliere d.*		Mme. DuBarry b. *J. P. Zenger d.*
1747	E. Dubois-Crancé b. A. Fouquier-Tinville b. *Nadir Shah d.* Duc d'Orléans ("Philippe Égalité") b. *Count Osterman d.* Theodore Sedgwick b.	*Prinz von Anhalt-Dessau d.* Armand de Biron b. John Paul Jones b. *Lord Lovat d.* Danl. Shays b.	*Duc de La Rochefoucauld-Liancourt d.*		*Thos. Coke d.*	Johann Bode b. Antonio Scarpa b.	Saml. Parr b.	John Aikin b. Gottfried Bürger b. *Alain René Lesage d.* John O'Keeffe b. Anna Seward b. *Marquis de Vauvenargues d.*	*Giuseppe Crespi d.*		"Lord" Timothy Dexter b.
1748	Count Reventlow b. Comte de Sieyès b.	Baron Lynedoch b. Count Pulaski b. *Otto Traun d.* *Geo. Wade d.*	Jeremy Bentham b.		Elias Hicks b. Dietrich Tiedemann b. *Isaac Watts d.* Adam Weishaupt b.	*Jean Bernoulli d.* Claude de Berthollet b. A. L. de Jussieu b. John Playfair b. F. Vicq d'Azyr b.	*Pietro Giannone d.*	Thos. Day b. John Logan b. Graf Christian zu Stolberg b. *Jas. Thomson d.*	Jacques David b.		*Anne Bracegirdle d. Wm. Kent d.*
1749	Domenico Azuni b. Earl of Clare b. Chas. James Fox b. Comte de Mirabeau b. Tippoo Sahib (Mysore) b.	Peter Gansevoort b. *Freiherr von der Trenck d.*	*Wm. Ged d.* John Stevens b.	Auguste Chouteau b.		Jean Delambre b. Edward Jenner b. Danl. Rutherford b.	David Ramsay b. Joseph Strutt b.	Vittorio Alfieri b. Dominique Garat b. J. W. von Goethe b. *Ambrose Philips d.* Charlotte Smith b. Isaiah Thomas b.	*Pierre Subleyras d.* Abt Vogler b.	Domenico Cimarosa b.	Princesse de Lamballe b.
1750	*Viscount Bolingbroke d.* J. Collot d'Herbois b. John P. Curran b. Lord Erskine b. Henri Grégoire b. Prinz von Hardenberg b. William Windham b.	Jan De Winter b. Francisco Miranda b. Henry Knox b. *Maurice de Saxe d.*	Thos. Spence b.		*Georg Bilfinger d.* Johann Jahn b. *Conyers Middleton d.* Joanna Southcott b.	Déodat de Dolomieu b. Caroline Herschel b. Marquis de LaPlace b. C. C. Sprengel b. Abraham Werner b.	*Ludovico Muratori d.*	Lady Anne Barnard b. *Marguerite De Launay d.* P. Fabre d'Eglantine b. Robt. Fergusson b. Graf Friedrich zu Stolberg b. John Trumbull b. Tomás de Yriarte b.		*J. S. Bach d.* Antonio Salieri b.	Stephen Girard b.
1751	Earl of Eldon b. Frederick Adolphus (Sweden) a. Jas. Madison b.	John André b. Count Platov b. *Benj. Robins d.*	Pierre Bertin b. Marquis de Jouffroy d'Abbans b.	John Ledyard b.	*Julien de La Mettrie d.*		Sir Nathaniel Wraxall b.	R. B. Sheridan b. Johann Voss b.	*John Smybert d.*		*Thos. Coram d.* Lord Geo. Gordon b. Thos. Sheraton b.

1752–1762 A.D.

Year A.D.	Government and Law	Military and Naval Affairs	Industry Commerce Economics Finance Invention Labor	Travel and Exploration	Philosophy and Religion	Science and Medicine	Education Scholarship History	Literature	Painting and Sculpture	Music	Miscellaneous
1752	Luke Hansard b. Graf von Haugwitz b. Gouverneur Morris b. Count Potockí b. Antoine Santerre b.		Joseph Jacquard b.	Geo. Rogers Clark b.	*Joseph Butler d.* Timothy Dwight b. Johann Eichhorn b.	Johann Blumenbach b. Adrien Legendre b. *Wm. Whiston d.*	Johannes von Müller b.	Fanny Burney b. Thos. Chatterton b. Philip Freneau b. Friedrich von Klinger b. St. George Tucker b.	John Raphael Smith b.	Muzio Clementi b. Niccolo Zingarelli b.	*Wm. Bradford d.* Betsy Ross b.
1753	Jean de Cambacérès b. Edmund Randolph b. Pierre Vergniaud b.	Louis F. Berthier b. Wm. Bligh b. L. N. M. Carnot b.	François Blanchard b.		*Bishop Berkeley d.* Dugald Steward b.	Franz Achard b. Jas. Gregory (Later) b. Count Rumford b. *Sir Hans Sloane d.* Earl of Stanhope b.	Andrew Bell b. Josef Dobrovsky b.	Rhijnvis Feith b. Elizabeth Inchbald b. Wm. Roscoe b. Phillis Wheatley b.	Sir Wm. Beechey b. *Phillip Van Dyck d.*		
1754	C. de Talleyrand-Périgord b.	Marquess of Hastings b. Sir Banistre Tarleton b.	Comte de Maistre b. Wm. Murdock b. Sir John Sinclair b.	Georg Forster b.	Andrew Fuller b. *Christian von Wolff d.*	*Abraham Demoivre d.* J. L. Proust b.		Joel Barlow b. Geo. Crabbe b. *"Philippe Destouches" d.* Wm. Drennan b. *Henry Fielding d. Friedrich von Hagedorn d. Wm. Hamilton d. Baron von Holberg d.* Joseph Joubert b.	Asmus Carstens b. Utamaro b.		Zaro Agha b.? Thos. Bowdler b. *Edward Cave d.* Moses Cleaveland b. Pierre L'Enfant b. *Mme. Roland b. John Wood d.*
1755	B. Barère de Vieuzac b. Comte de Barras b. Baron de Cloots b. Alexander Hamilton b. Jacques Hebert b. Rufus King b. Marie Antoinette b. John Marshall b. Olaf Wallqvist b.	*Edward Braddock d.* Louis de Casabianca b. Count von Fersen b. Nathan Hale b. Aloys von Reding b. Johann von Scharnhorst b. Thos. Truxtun b.		Sir Alexander Mackenzie b.	*Baron de Montesquieu d.*	Nicolas Conte b. Antoine de Fourcroy b. Saml. C. F. Hahnemann b. Jas. Parkinson b. Saml. Sömmering b.	*Ephraim Williams d.*	Jean Florian b. Anne Grant b. *Thomas Longman d. Duc deSaint-Simon d.*	*Jacques Caffieri d.* John Flaxman b. Thos. Stothard b. Gilbert Stuart b. Mme. Vigée-Lebrun b.		A. Brillat-Savarin b. Sarah Siddons b.
1756	J. Billaud Varenne b. F. Boissy d'Anglas b. Aaron Burr b. J. B. Carrier b. Duc de Champagny b. Georges Couthon b. J. Pétion de Villeneuve b.	Lord Gambier b. Vicomte de Noailles b.	John L. McAdam b.			*Olaf Celsius d.* Jean Chaptal b. Friedrich Chladni b. Comte de Lacépède b. *Johann Lieberkuhn d.*		Willem Bilderdijk b. Jas. Currie b. Wm. Gifford b. Wm. Godwin b. *Eliza Haywood d.*	Sir Henry Raeburn b. Thos. Rowlandson b. John Trumbull b.	Wolfgang Amadeus Mozart b.	Maria Fitzherbert b. Edmund Lodge b.

Year A.D.	Government and Law	Military and Naval Affairs	Industry Commerce Economics Finance Invention Labor	Travel and Exploration	Philosophy and Religion	Science and Medicine	Education Scholarship History	Literature	Painting and Sculpture	Music	Miscellaneous
1757	Ercole Consalvi b. Marquis de Lafayette b. Nathaniel Macon b. Sir Saml. Romilly b. Viscount Sidmouth b. Robt. Smith b. Baron vom und zu Stein b. *Suraj-ud-Dowlah (Bengal) d.*	*John Byng d.* Viscount Exmouth b. Lord de Saumarez b. Jas. Wilkinson b.			Richard Brothers b. Pierre Cabanis b. *David Hartley d.* Georg Rapp b. Comte de Volney b.	Erik Acharius b. *René de Réaumur d.*	*Thos. Ruddiman d.*	Wm. Blake b. *Colley Cibber d.* Marquis de Fontanes b. *Bernard de Fontenelle d.*	Antonio Canova b. Jas. Gillray b. *Antoine Pesne d.* Jas. Sowerby b.	Ignatz Pleyel b. *Johann Stamitz d.*	*Robt. Damiens d.* John Philip Kemble b.
1758	Fisher Ames b. Jas. Monroe b. Chas. Pinckney b. Red Jacket b. ? Maximilien de Robespierre b.	John Armstrong b. *Jas. Keith d.* André Masséna b. Christian von Massenbach b. Horatio Nelson b. Sir Thos. Picton b.		Geo. Vancouver b.	*Pope Benedict XIV d.* *Jonathan Edwards d.* *Hans Egede d.*	F. J. Gall b. Heinrich Olbers b.	Baron de Sacy b. Thos. Taylor b. Noah Webster b.	*John Dyer d.* Elizabeth Hamilton b. *Jas. Hervey d.* *Allan Ramsay d.*	Johann von Dannecker b. Raphael Morghen b. Alexander Nasmyth b. Pierre Prud'hon b. Carle Vernet b.		*Christopher Sower d.*
1759	Carlos III (Spain) a. Alexander J. Dallas b. Georges Danton b. Ferdinand IV (Naples) a. Lord Grenville b. Wm. Pitt (Younger) b. Juan de Rozas b.	*Marquis de Montcalm d.* *Sir Wm. Pepperell d.* *Jas. Wolfe d.* Graf von Yorck von Wartenburg b.	Thos. Cooper b.			*Pierre Maupertuis d.* Johann Reil b.	Richard Porson b. F. A. Wolf b.	Wm. Beckford b. Robt. Burns b. Alexander Chalmers b. *Wm. Collins d.* Johann von Schiller b. Mary Wollstonecraft b.	*Lambert Adam d.* Jean Audebert b. *August von Rosenhof d.*	*K. H. Graun d.* *G. F. Händel d.* Geo. Thomson b.	Wm. Wilberforce b.
1760	François Babeuf b. Camille Desmoulins b. *George II (England) d.* George III (England) a. Marquis of Wellesley b.	Graf von Gneisenau b. *Lord Murray d.*	Comte de Saint-Simon b.		*Graf von Zinzendorf d.*	*Jacob Winslöw d.*	Karl Böttiger b.	Mathew Carey b. Ivan Dmitriev b. Constantine Rhigas b. Claude Rouget de Lisle b. M. L. Weems b.	K. Hokusai b.	Luigi Cherubini b. Jan Dussek b. Jean LeSueur b.	*Eugene Aram d.* Thos. Clarkson b. Marie Tussaud b. *Peg Woffington d.*
1761	Antoine Barnave b. Pierre Daunou b. Albert Gallatin b.	*Edward Boscawen d.* Archduke Karl Ludwig b. Sir John Moore b.			*Pierre de Charlevoix d.* *Benj. Hoadly d.* *Wm. Law d.* Heinrich Paulus b.	Matthew Baillie b. *John Dollond d.* *Stephen Hales d.* Jedidiah Morse b. Jean Louis Pons b. Caspar Wistar b.	*Wm. Oldys d.* François Raynouard b.	Richard Alsop b. August von Kotzebue b. José Macedo b. *Saml. Richardson d.* Marquise de Souza-Botelho b. Karl Tauchnitz b.	John Opie b.	Henri Berton b.	Lady Emma Hamilton b. *Beau Nash d.* *John Rich d.*
1762	Catherine the Great (Russia) a. *Elizabeth (Russia) d.* Spencer Perceval b. *Peter III (Russia) a. and d.*	*Lord Anson d.* Sir Saml. Hood b. J. B. Jourdan b. Chas. Pichegru b.			*Alexander Baumgarten d.* *Jean Calas d.* J. G. Fichte b. Edmund Rice b.	*Jas. Bradley d.* *Nicolas de Lacaille d.* Pierre Latreille b. *Johann Mayer d.*	Malcolm Laing b.	Joanna Baillie b. Wm. L. Bowles b. André de Chénier b. *Prosper de Crébillon d.* *Lady M. W. Montagu d.* Christian Vulpius b.	*Louis Roubillac d.*		Marchese di Cagnola b. Geo. Colman (Younger) b. Dorothea Jordan b.

1763–1772 A.D.

Year A.D.	Government and Law	Military and Naval Affairs	Industry Commerce Economics Finance Invention Labor	Travel and Exploration	Philosophy and Religion	Science and Medicine	Education Scholarship History	Literature	Painting and Sculpture	Music	Miscellaneous
1763	Graf von Brühl d. / Pierre Chaumette b. / Jean Drouet b. / Lord Fitzgerald b. / Joseph Fouché b. / Edmond Genêt b. / Earl John of Granville d. / Empress Josephine b. / Jas. Kent b. / T. Wolfe Tone b. / Duke Frederick Augustus of York b.	Jean Moreau b. / Joseph Poniatowski b. / Silvestre Villeneuve b.	John Jacob Astor b. / William Cobbett b.		Joseph Fesch b. / Pierre Royer-Collard b.	Peter Forskål d. / Louis Vauquelin b.		Janos Bacsányi b. / Mary Berry b. / Jean Bouilly b. / Olof von Dalin d. / Pierre de Marivaux d. / Abbé Prévost d. / Jean Paul Richter b. / Saml. Rogers b. / Wm. Shenstone d.	Geo. Morland b.	E.-N. Méhul b. / Stephen Storace b.	Chas. Bulfinch b. / Geo. Psalmanazar d. / François Talma b.
1764	Friedrich von Gentz b. / Earl Charles Grey b. / Ivan VI (Russia) d. / Edward Livingston b. / Wm. Pinkney b. / Lord Plunket b. / Conde di Pozzo di Borgo b. / Nikolai de Rezánov b. / Stanislaus II (Poland) a.	Comte de Dessaix b. / Wm. Eaton b. / Marquis de Saint-Cyr b. / Sir Wm. Sidney Smith b.	Rudolf Ackermann b.		Baronesse von Krüdener b.	John Abernethy b.		Francesco Algarotti d. / Jens Baggesen b. / Blaise de Chénier b. / N. de Cienfuegos b. / Robt. Dodsley d. / Mary Lamb d. / Erik Pontopiddan d. / Ann Radcliffe b. / Regina M. Roche b.	Wm. Hogarth d. / Johann Schadow b.	Jean Rameau d.	Mme. de Pompadour d.
1765	Joseph II (H.R.E.) a. / Sir Jas. Mackintosh b. / Stephen Van Rensselaer b.	Comte d'Erlon b. / Alexandre Macdonald b.	Robt. Fulton b. / Eli Whitney b.	Geo. Glas d.	Franz Baader b.	Alexis Clairault d. / Karl Kielmeyer b. / Saml. Klingenstierna d. / Johann Pfaff b. / Jas. Smithson b.	Henry T. Colebrooke b. / John Lempriere b. / Wm. Stukeley d. / Wm. Taylor b.	Manuel Bocage b. / Mikhail Lomonosov d. / David Mallet d. / Edward Young d.	Chas. Vanloo d.		Herman Blennerhasset b.
1766	Christian VII (Denmark) a. / José Francia b. / Comte de Las Cases b. / Duc de Richelieu b.	J. B. Bessières b. / Marquis de Grouchy b. / Count Radetzky b. / C. Victor-Perrin b.			Jean Astruc d. / F. Maine de Biran b.	John Dalton b. / Christian Ideler b. / Baron de Larrey b. / Sir John Leslie b. / Thos. Malthus b. / Alexander Wilson b. / W. H. Wollaston b.	John Adolphus b. / Carlo Botta b. / Jean Lacretelle b.	A.-V. Arnault b. / Robt. Bloomfield b. / Isaac D'Israeli b. / Johann Gottsched d. / Nikolai Karamzin b. / Lady Caroline Nairne b. / Frances Sheridan d. / Mme. de Staël b.	J. M. Nattier d.	John W. Callcott b. / Saml. Wesley b.	Wm. Caslon d. / James Edward (Old Pretender) d. / Jas. Ouin d.
1767	John Quincy Adams b. / Chas. Barbaroux b. / Black Hawk b. / H. B. Constant de Rebecque b. / Manuel de Godoy b. / Andrew Jackson b. / Louis de Saint-Just b. / Jean Tallien b. / 3rd Viscount Townshend d. / Roger Wolcott d.	Andreas Hofer b.	Jacques Laffitte b. / J. B. Say b. / Étienne de Silhouette d.			Alexander Monro d. / John Pond b. / Nicolas de Saussure b. / Paul Werlhof d.	Wilhelm von Humboldt b.	Michael Bruce d. / Maria Edgeworth b. / Wm. Patlock d. / A. W. von Schlegel b.	Conde di Cicognara b. / J. B. Isabey b.	Nicola Porpora d.	

Year A.D.	Government and Law	Military and Naval Affairs	Industry Commerce Economics Finance Invention Labor	Travel and Exploration	Philosophy and Religion	Science and Medicine	Education Scholarship History	Literature	Painting and Sculpture	Music	Miscellaneous
1768	*Count Bestuzhev d.* Joseph Bonaparte b. *Caroline of Brunswick d.* Tecumseh b.	Viscount Beresford b. L. Desaix de Veygoux b. Lazare Hoche b.			Adam Eschenmayer b. *Nathaniel Lardner d.* *Hermann Reimarus d.* Friedrich Schleiermacher b.	Sir Astley Cooper b. *Robert Simson d.*	Thos. Creevy b. Sharon Turner b.	F. R. de Chateaubriand b. Ivan Krylov b. *Joseph Spence d.* *Laurence Sterne d.* Friedrich Werner b.	José Alvarez b. *Antonio Canaletto d.* John Crome b. *Johann Winckelmann d.*		*Peter Collinson d.* Charlotte Corday b.
1769	Graf Christian von Bernstorff b. Louis de Bourrienne b. Viscount Castlereagh b. DeWitt Clinton b. Napoleon I (Bonaparte) b. *Pontiac d.* K. Zacharias von Lingenthal b.	Sir Thos. M. Hardy b. Barthélemi Joubert b. Michel Ney b. Nicolas Soult b. Duke of Wellington b.			Pope Clement XIV a. *Antonio Genovesi d.*	Baron de Cuvier b. Alexander von Humboldt b. Wm. Smith b.	*Jacopo Facciolati d.*	Ernest Arndt b. *Wm. Falconer d.* John H. Frere b. *Christian Gellert d.* Jane Marcet b. Amelia Opie b. Anne Royall b.	Sir Thos. Lawrence b. *G. B. Tiepolo d.*		*Edmund Hoyle d.*
1770	Sir Francis Burdett b. Geo. Canning b. Prince Czartoryski b. *Robt. Dinwiddie d.* *Geo. Grenville d.* Wm. Huskisson b. Basil Montagu b. Alexandre Pétion b. Sequoya b. *Chas. Yorke d.*	Sir Hudson Lowe b.		Wm. Clark b. Wm. Moorcraft b.	*Alexander Cruden d.* Demetrius Gallitzin b. Pasquale Galluppi b. G. W. F. Hegel b. *Geo. Whitefield d.*	*Bernhard Albinus d.* Alexandre Brongniart b. Ignaz Döllinger b.	J. J. Jacotot b.	*Mark Akenside d.* *Thos. Chatterton d.* John Foster b. Jas. Hogg b. Friedrich Holderlin b. Joseph Hopkinson b. Francis Scott Key b. Étienne de Sénancour b. Wm. Wordsworth b.	*François Boucher d.* Baron de Gérard b. Thos. Hope b. *Michael Rysbrach d.* Bertel Thorwaldsen b.	Ludwig van Beethoven b. *Giuseppe Tartini d.*	Arthur Thistelwood b.
1771	*Frederick Adolphus (Sweden) d.* Gustavus III (Sweden) a. *Wm. Shirley d.*	Joseph Chlopicki b. Prinz K. zu Schwarzenberg b.	Robert Owen b. Francis Place b. Alois Senfelder b. Richard Trevithick b.	Mungo Park b.	*Claude Helvétius d.*	François Bichât b. Ephraim McDowell b. *Giovanni Morgagni d.* Karl Rudolphi b.	Friedrich Creuzer b. John Lingard b.	Chas. Brockden Brown b. Thos. J. Dibdin b. Thos. G. Fessenden b. *Thos. Gray d.* N. Lemercier b. Jas. Montgomery b. Sir Walter Scott b. *Christopher Smart d.* Sydney Smith b. *Tobias Smollett d.* R. Varnhagen von Ense b. Dorothy Wordsworth b.	Baron de Gros b.	Johann Cramer b.	Fra Diavolo b.
1772	*Graf Johann von Bernstorff d.* Wm. H. Crawford b. Duc d'Enghien b. Lord Lyndhurst b. Count Speransky b. Anton Thibaut b. Wm. Wirt b.	Comte de Clausel b. Viscount Hill b. Comte de La Rochejacquelin b. Louis Suchet b.	François Fourier b. David Ricardo b. *Johan Struensee d.*		Friedrich von Schlegel b. *Emanuel Swedenborg d.* *John Woolman d.*	*John Canton d.* Jean Esquirol b. Karl Gartner b. E. Geoffroy Saint-Hilaire b.	Josiah Quincy b.	Friedrich Brockhaus b. Henry F. Cary b. S. T. Coleridge b. *Chas. Duclos d.* Sándor Kisfaludy b. "Novalis" b. Manuel Quintana b. Mary Tighe b.			Pierce Egan b.

1773–1784 A.D.

Year A.D.	Government and Law	Military and Naval Affairs	Industry Commerce Economics Finance Invention Labor	Travel and Exploration	Philosophy and Religion	Science and Medicine	Education Scholarship History	Literature	Painting and Sculpture	Music	Miscellaneous
1773	Ahmed Shah d. Wm. Henry Harrison b. Prinz von Metternich b. John Randolph b. Comte de Villele b. Hugh L. White b.	Comte de Bourmont b. Comte de Gérard b. John Rodgers b. *Freiherr von Seydlitz d.*	F.-X. Droz b.		Jacob Fries b. Henrik Steffens b.	Aimé Bonpland b. Nathaniel Bowditch b. Sir Thos. Brisbane b. Robt. Brown b. Thos. Young b.	Jas. Mill b. Jean de Sismondi b.	*Lord Chesterfield d.* Sophie Cottin b. Paul Courier b. *John Hawkesworth d.* Lord Jeffrey b. Robt. Treat Paine b. *Alexis Piron d.* Ludwig Tieck b.			Henry Hunt b.
1774	Lord Ashburton b. *Lord Clive d.* *Lord Holland d.* *Louis XV (France) d.* Louis XVI (France) a. Danl. D. Tompkins b.	Wm. Bainbridge b. *Sir Wm. Johnson d.* Jean Savary b.	Friedrich König b. *François Quesnay d.* Thos. Tooke b.	Matthew Flinders b. Meriwether Lewis b.	*Pope Clement XIV d.* Ram Mohan Roy b. *Abraham Tucker d.*	Francis Baily b. Sir Chas. Bell b. Jean Biot b. Leopold von Buch b.	Giuseppi Mezzofanti b. *Johann Reiske d.*	Archibald Constable b. *Robt. Fergusson d.* *Oliver Goldsmith d.* Robt. Southey b. Robt. Tannahill b. Christopher Wordsworth (Elder) b.		John Braham b. Gasparo Spontini b.	
1775	Lucien Bonaparte b. Paul von Feuerbach b. Danl. O'Connell b. *Josiah Quincy d.* *Peyton Randolph d.*	Earl of Dundonald b. *Richard Montgomery d.* J. de Palafox y Melzi b. *Joseph Warren d.*			Lyman Beecher b. *St. Paul of the Cross d.* Pope Pius VI a. *Lorenzo Ricci d.* Friedrich von Schelling b.	André Ampère b.	Georg Grotefend b. John Leyden b. Chas. Richardson b.	Jane Austen b. Sir Alexander Boswell b. *Andrew Foulis d.* *John Hill d.* Chas. Lamb b. Walter Savage Landor b. Matthew G. Lewis b. Chas. Lloyd b. Henry Crabb Robinson b. Mary M. Sherwood b. Jas. Smith b. Joseph Blanco White b.	François Granet b. J. M. W. Turner b. Sir Richard Westmacott b.	François Boieldieu b. Wm. Crotch b. Manuel García b.	*John Baskerville d.* Chas. Kemble b. *Emel'yan Pugachev d.* François Vidocq b.
1776	Jean Pierre Boyer b. Conde di Capo d'Istria b. Lord Moncrieff b.	*Nathan Hale d.* *John Thomas d.*		Lady Hester Stanhope b.	J. F. Herbart b. *David Hume d.*	Amerigo Avogadro b. *Théophile de Bardeu d.* *Cadwalader Colden d.* *Jas. Ferguson d.* Chas. Mirbel b. C. Nees von Esenbeck b. Gerard Troost b.	Thos. F. Dibdin b. Barthold Niebuhr b.	Pierre Ballanche b. Wm. Blackwood b. *Robt. Foulis d.* Josef von Gorres b. E. T. W. Hoffman b. Jane Porter b.	John Constable b. John Vanderlyn b.		George Birkbeck b. *Julie de Lespinasse d.* Chas. Mathews b. Johann Spurzheim b.
1777	Henry Clay b. Casimir Perier b. Roger Taney b.	Sir Benj. D'Urban b.		Sir John Ross b.		*John Bartram d.* Henri Blainville b. Karl F. Gauss b. *Albrecht von Haller d.* C. C. deLatour b. H. C. Oersted b. Louis Thénard b.	*Charles deBrosses d.* Henry Hallam b. John Pickering b.	Thos. Campbell b. *Saml. Foote d.* Baron de la Motte Fouqué b. *Hugh Kelly d.* Heinrich von Kleist b.	Christian Rauch b.		*Mme. deGeoffrin d.* Wm. Henry Ireland b. Jeanne Récamier b. Chas. Mayne Young b.
1778	Louis Bonaparte b. Lord Brougham b. Robt. Emmet b. Saml. Hoar b. Bernardo O'Higgins b. *Wm. Pitt (Lord Chatham) d.* Jose de San Martin b.		*Jas. Hargreaves d.*	Giovanni Belzoni b.	*Augustus Toplady d.*	Thos. Brown b. Augustin de Candolle b. Sir Humphry Davy b. J. L. Gay-Lussac b. *Baron Karl deGeer d.* *Linnaeus d.* John C. Warren b.	George Crabb b. Friedrich Jahn b. Joseph Lancaster b.	Clemens Brentano b. Ugo Foscolo b. Wm. Hazlitt b. John Murray b. Jas. Kirke Paulding b. *J. J. Rousseau d.* *François de Voltaire d.*	Rembrandt Peale b. *Giambattista Piranesi d.* John Thomson b.	*Thos. A. Arne d.* Johann Hummel b.	Beau Brummell b.

Year A.D.	Government and Law	Military and Naval Affairs	Industry Commerce Economics Finance Invention Labor	Travel and Exploration	Philosophy and Religion	Science and Medicine	Education Scholarship History	Literature	Painting and Sculpture	Music	Miscellaneous
1779	Lord Cockburn b. *Lord Elphinstone d.* Viscount Melbourne b. Karl von Savigny b. Joseph Story b. *Earl of Temple d.*	Stephen Decatur b. Viscount Gough b. *Count Pulaski d.*	Simon Bernard b.	*Jas. Cook d.* Zebulon M. Pike b.	*Johann Gassner d.* Ludolph Treviranus b.	*John Ash d.* *J. J. Berzelius b.* *Peter Kalm d.* Lorenz Oken b. Karl Ritter b. Benj. Silliman b.	Peter M. Roget b. *Wm. Warburton d.* *Eleazer Wheelock d.*	John Galt b. *John Langhorne d.* Clement C. Moore b. Thos. Moore b. Adam Oehlenschläger b. Horace Smith b.	Washington Allston b. *Jean Chardin d.* *Raphael Mengs d.*	*Wm. Boyce d.*	Chas. J. Apperley b. *Thos. Chippendale d.* *David Garrick d.* Joseph Grimaldi b.
1780	*Sir Wm. Blackstone d.* Élie Decazes b. *Thos. Hutchinson d.* *John Logan d.* *Maria Theresa d.* Prince de Polignac b. Ranjit Singh b. Richard Rush b.	*John André d.* Karl von Clausewitz b. *Johann Kalb d.* David Porter b.	Robt. Torrens b.	*Jonathan Carver d.*	John Abercrombie b. Thos. Chalmers b. Wm. Ellery Channing (Elder) b. *Étienne de Condillac d.* Wilhelm DeWette b.	J. J. Audubon b. Chas. Badham b. Johann Döbereiner b. Mary Somerville b.	*Johann Ihre d.* *Giacobbo Pereire d.*	Pierre de Béranger b. John W. Croker b. Geo. Croly b. Wm. Hone b. Chas. Nodier b. Frances Trollope b.	*Bernardo Canaletto d.* J. A. Ingres b.	Angelica Catalani b.	*Marquise du Deffand d.* Elizabeth Fry b. Jean Laffite b. *Comte de Saint-Germain d.*
1781	*Marqués de la Ensenada d.* Sir Thos. Raffles b.	Eugene de Beauharnais b. *Lord Hawke d.* Jas. Lawrence b.	Geo. Stephenson b. *Robert Turgot d.*	*Tobias Furneaux d.*	Bernhard Bolzano b. Ismail Hadji Maulvi-Mohammed b. Karl Krause b.	*Daniel Bernoulli d.* Sir David Brewster b. René Laënnec b. S.-D. Poisson b. David Young b.	*Edward Capell d.* *Johann Ernesti d.* Friedrich Raumer b.	Lucy Aikin b. Adelbert von Chamisso b. Ebenezer Elliott b. *Johannes Ewald d.* *Jose d'Isla d.* *Gotthold Lessing d.* Johann Wyss b.	Sir Francis Chantrey b.	Anthony P. Heinrich b. Vincent Novello b.	
1782	Thos. H. Benton b. John C. Calhoun b. Lewis Cass b. *Hyder Ali d.* *Marquis da Pombal d.* Martin Van Buren b. Danl. Webster b.	Sir Chas. Napier b. Ivan Paskevich b. Sir Robt. Sale b.			*Lord Kames d.* Wm. Miller b. Robt. Morrison b.	*Jean de Anville d.* *Giovanni Della Torre d.* *Sir John Pringle d.* *Danl. Solander d.*	Friedrich Froebel b.	Susan E. Ferrier b. Robert de Lamennais b. Chas. R. Maturin b. *"Mestasio" d.* José de Olmedo b. Ann Taylor b. Esaias Tegner b.	Sir Wm. Allan b. John S. Cotman b. John Pye b. *Richard Wilson d.*	Daniel Auber b. *Farinelli d.* John Field b. Nicolo Paganini b.	
1783	Simón Bolívar b. Augustin de Iturbide b. *Count Orlov d.* *Jas. Otis d.* *Count Panin d.* Sir Jonathan Pollock b.	Thos. Macdonough b. Guglielmo Pepe b. Sir Fredk. Ponsonby b. Saml. C. Reid b. Conde di Santarosa b.			Reginald Heber b.	*Jean d'Alembert d.* *Leonhard Euler d.* *Wm. Hunter d.* François Magendie b. Constantine Rafinesque b.	Erik Geijer b.	*Henry Brooke d.* *Louise d'Epinay d.* Nikolai Grundtvig b. Washington Irving b. Lady Sydney Morgan b. "Stendhal" b. Jane Taylor b. Vasili Zhukovsky b.	Peter von Cornelius b. David Cox b. Saml. Prout b. Thos. Sully b.	*Johann Hasse d.*	
1784	Earl of Aberdeen b. Lord Geo. Auckland b. Jerôme Bonaparte b. Ernst I (Saxe-Coburg-Gotha) b. Viscount Palmerston b. *Caesar Rodney d.* Zachary Taylor b.	Sir Richard Church b. *Seth Warner d.* Graf von Wrangel b.		Johann Burckhardt b.	*Denis Diderot d.* *Ann Lee d.* *Junípero Sperra d.* Robt. Taylor b.	*Torbern Bergman d.* Friedrich Bessel b. Christopher Hansteen b. *Otto Müller d.* *Abraham Trembley d.* Wm. Yarrell b.	Wm. Allen b. Joseph E. Worcester b.	Bernard Barton b. Adam Black b. Allan Cunningham b. Leigh Hunt b. *Saml. Johnson d.* J. S. Knowles b. Wm. Tennant b. *Phillis Wheatley d.*	*Allan Ramsay d.* François Rude b. Peter de Wint b.	Louis Spohr b.	*Princess Liewen b.* Sir Moses Montefiore b.

1785–1792 A.D.

Year A.D.	Government and Law	Military and Naval Affairs	Industry Commerce Economics Finance Invention Labor	Travel and Exploration	Philosophy and Religion	Science and Medicine	Education Scholarship History	Literature	Painting and Sculpture	Music	Miscellaneous
1785	Duc Achille de Broglie b. José Carrera b. *Duc Étienne de Choiseul d.* *Stephen Hopkins d.* *Viscount Sackville d.* Henry Wheaton b.	Viscount Hardinge b. Sir Wm. Napier b. *Jas. Oglethorpe d.* Oliver H. Perry b.			Peter Cartwright b.	Carl Agardh b. J. J. Audubon b. Pierre Dulong b. Wm. Prout b. Adam Sedgwick b. *Matthew Stewart d.*	Friedrich Dahlmann b. Jakob Grimm b.	Daniel Appleton b. Bettina von Arnim b. Thos. De Quincey b. Alessandro Manzoni b. M. M. Noah b. Thos. Love Peacock b. John Pierpont b. Karl Varnhagen von Ense b. Henry Kirke White b. *Wm. Whitehead d.* John Wilson b. Saml. Woodworth b. John Younger b.	*Giovanni Cipriani d.* *Pietro Longhi d.* *J. B. Pigalle d.* Sir David Wilkie b.	*Baldassare Galuppi d.*	*Kitty Clive d.* Lady Caroline Lamb b.
1786	*Frederick the Great (Prussia) d.* Friedrich Wilhelm II (Prussia) a. Louis J. Papineau b. Viscount Stratford de Redcliffe b.	*Nathanael Greene d.* Baron von Haynau b. Winfield Scott b. *Johann von Ziethen d.*		David Crockett b. Sir John Franklin b.	*Moses Mendelssohn d.*	François Arago b. Sir Wm. Hooker b. Thos. Nuttall b. Jas. C. Prichard b. Jas. Rush b. *Karl Wilhelm Scheele d.*	Gabor Döbrentei b. Wilhelm Grimm b. *Thos. Tyrwhitt d.* Johannes Voigt b.	Thos. Barnes b. Lady Callcott b. Andras Fáy b. John Cam Hobbhouse b. Justinus Kerner b. Iancu Vacarescu b. G. C. Verplanck b.	Benj. R. Haydon b. Wm. Mulready b.	Sir Henry Bishop b. Carl Maria von Weber b.	*Geo. Hepplewhite d.*
1787	John J. Crittenden b. Baron von Stockmar b. *Comte de Vergennes d.*	*Thos. Gage d.* Sir Harry G. W. Smith b.	Ludwig Börne b. Sir Saml. Cunard b. Louis Daguerre b. *Ferdinando Galiani d.* Conde di Rossi b. Robt. L. Stevens b.	Otto von Kotzebue b. Sir John Richardson b.	Edward Cardwell b. *St. Alfonso de Liguori d.* *Henry M. Muhlenberg d.* Richard Whately b.	*Ruggiero Boscovich d.* Wm. D. Conybeare b. Sir John Forbes b. Josef von Fraunhofer b. *Chas. Mason d.* Georg Ohm b. Johannes Purkinje b. Thos. Say b.	Thos. H. Gallaudet b. François Guizot b. Rasmus Rask b. *Floyer Sydenham d.* Emma Willard b.	Saml. Bailey b. Chas. Cowden Clarke b. R. H. Dana, Sr., b. V. S. Karajich b. Mary R. Mitford b. *J. A. Musäus d.* Bryan Waller Procter b. Isaac Taylor b. Johann Uhland b.	Wm. Etty b.	*Christoph Gluck d.*	Edmund Kean b.
1788	Marco Bozzaris b. *Carlos III (Spain) d.* Carlos IV (Spain) a. Jas. Gadsden b. Geo. McDuffie b. Sir Robt. Peel b. *Wm. Tryon d.*	Lord Raglan b. *P. deSuffren Saint-Tropez d.*	Étienne Cabet b.	Basil Hall b. *Jean-François LaPérouse d.* *John Ledyard d.*	Alexander Campbell b. *Johann Hamann d.* Sir Wm. Hamilton b. Adoniram Judson b. Arthur Schopenhauer b. *Chas. Wesley d.*	Antoine C. Becquerel b. *Comte de Buffon d.* Augustin Fresnel b. Pierre Pelletier b. *Percivall Pott d.* Baron von Reichenbach b. Sir Edward Sabine b.	Jacques Boucher de Crèvecoeur b. Jean P. Remusat b.	Richard Barham b. Lord Byron b. Sarah J. Hale b. Theodore Hook b. Karoly Kisfaludy b. *John Logan d.* Sir Francis Palgrave b. Silvio Pellico b. Friedrich Ruckert b.	Wm. Collins b. David d'Angers b. *Thomas Gainsborough d.* Sir John W. Gordon b. Karl W. von Heidegger b.	*Karl P. E. Bach d.*	Geo. Combe b. *Charles Edward (Young Pretender) d.* Joseph Gurney b. *Thos. Sheridan d.*
1789	*Silas Deane d.* Selim III (Turkey) a.	*Ethan Allen d.* Ibrahim Pasha b.	*Joseph Foullon d.* Friedrich List b. Richard Oastler b.	Francis R. Chesney b. Wm. Scoresby b.	Hiram Bingham, Sr., b. *Baron d'Holbach d.* Johann Neander b.	Wm. Bond b. Richard Bright b. *Pieter Camper d.* Karl Carus b. Baron de Cauchy b. *Pierre Lyonet d.* Antoine Serres b.	Cesare Balbo b. *C. M. de l'Epée d.* Jared Sparks b.	*Thos. Amory d.* Countess of Blessington b. Jas. Fenimore Cooper b. *Thos. Day d.* Chas. W. Dilke b. Thos. Pringle b. Catharine Sedgwick b. Sir Jas. Stephen b. Richard Henry Wilde b.	Jean Charles Langlois b. *Jean Liotard d.* John Martin b. Friedrich Overbeck b. Friedrich Schadow b. *Joseph Vernet d.* Horace Vernet b.		Eleazar Williams b.

Year A.D.	Government and Law	Military and Naval Affairs	Industry Commerce Economics Finance Invention Labor	Travel and Exploration	Philosophy and Religion	Science and Medicine	Education Scholarship History	Literature	Painting and Sculpture	Music	Miscellaneous
1790	John Austin b. *Jas. Bowdoin d.* Earl of Ellenborough b. *Benj. Franklin d.* *Joseph II (H.R.E.) d.* Keokuk b. Leopold II (H.R.E.) a. *Wm. Livingston d.* John Ross b. John Tyler b.	Manuel Enceladus b. *Adam Smith d.* *Baron Heathfield d.* *Israel Putnam d.*	Nassau Senior b.	Jacques Arago b. Jules Dumont D'Urville b. Sir Wm. Parry b.	*Johann Basedow d.* Richard Carlile b. Israel Hwasser b. Father Mathew b.	Jean Champollion b. John F. Daniell b. Marshall Hall b. August Möbius b.		Alexander H. Everett b. Fitz–Greene Halleck b. Johannes C. Hauch b. Alphonse de Lamartine b. José Rivera b. ? *Thos. Warton d.* *Tomás de Yriarte d.* Josef von Zedlitz b.	John Gibson b.		*John Howard d.* *Flora Macdonald d.*
1791	Jas. Buchanan b. Baron von Bunsen b. *Henry Flood d.* Duff Green b. Empress Marie Louise b. Prince Mavrokordatos b. *Comte de Mirabeau d.* *Prince Potemkin d.* Richard L. Sheil b. Count Szecheny b.		Peter Cooper b. Saml. F. B. Morse b.		*Countess of Huntingdon d.* *Johann Michaelis d.* *Richard Price d.* *Johann Semler d.* *John Wesley d.*	Jean Cruveilhier b. Johann Encke b. Michael Faraday b.	Franz Bopp b. John Elliotson b. *Francis Grose d.* Henry H. Milman b. Patrick F. Tytler b.	Sergei Aksakov b. Karl F. Dahlgren b. Emile Deschamps b. Friedrich Forster b. Franz Grillparzer b. Johann L. Heiberg b. *Francis Hopkinson d.* Chas. Knight b. Karl T. Körner b. *Johann Merck d.* John Howard Payne b. Edward Quillinan b. Duque de Rivas b. Augustin Scribe b. Lydia H. Sigourney b. Geo. Ticknor b. Chas. Wolfe b.	*Étienne Falconet d.* Théodore Géricault b.	Karl Czerny b. Giacomo Meyerbeer b. *Wolfgang Amadeus Mozart d.*	Henry Betty b.
1792	Jas. G. Birney b. *Earl of Bute d.* Lord Campbell b. Earl of Durham b. Baldomero Espartero b. Sir Jas. Graham b. *Gustavus III (Sweden) d.* Gustavus IV (Sweden) a. *Lord Hailes d.* *Henry Laurens d.* *Arthur Lee d.* *Leopold II (H.R.E.) d.* *Geo. Mason d.* *René Maupeou d.* *Lord North d.* Earl Russell b. Thaddeus Stevens b.	*John Burgoyne d.* Lord Clyde b. *John Paul Jones d.* *Lord Rodney d.* Prince Ypsilanti b.	*Sir Richard Arkwright d.* Abbott Lawrence b. *John Smeaton d.*	Stephen Austin b.	Ferdinand Baur b. Victor Cousin b. Chas. G. Finney b. Johann Gieseler b. Edward Irving b. John Keble b. *August Spangenberg d.*	Chas. Babbage b. Karl von Baer b. Thos. Bell b. Sir John Herschel b. Isaac Lea b. Sir Roderick Murchison b.	Sir Archibald Alison b. François Isambert b. Matthew Vassar b. Karl Zumpt b.	Sir John Bowring b. *Jacques Cazotte d.* Johann Eckermann b. *Chas. Favart d.* T.J. Hogg b. Wm. Howitt b. Fredk. Marryat b. P.B. Shelley b. Seba Smith b. E.J. Trelawny b.	Geo. Cruikshank b. John Linnell b. *Sir Joshua Reynolds d.*	Lowell Mason b. Gioachino Rossini b.	*Robert Adam d.* William Burke b. *Princesse de Lamballe d.*

1793–1798 A.D.

Year A.D.	Government and Law	Military and Naval Affairs	Industry Commerce Economics Finance Invention Labor	Travel and Exploration	Philosophy and Religion	Science and Medicine	Education Scholarship History	Literature	Painting and Sculpture	Music	Miscellaneous
1793	Antoine Barnave d. Khan Dost Mohammed b. John Hancock d Louis XVI (France) d. Louis XVII (France) a. Earl Mansfield (Wm. Murray) d. Jean Paul Marat d. Marie Antoinette d. Alexander McGillivray d. Duc d'Orléans ("Philippe Égalité") d. Jean Roland de la Platière d. Juan de Rosas b. Roger Sherman d. John Slidell b. Pierre Vergniaud d. Wm. C. Wentworth b.	Armand de Biron d.	Henry C. Carey b.	Sam Houston b. Alexander G. Laing b.		Thomas Addison b. Wm. Aiton d. Jean Bailly d. Charles de Bonnet d. Anton Büsching d. Michel Chasles b. Geo. Green b. Edward Hitchcock b. John Hunter d. Dionysius Lardner b. Nikolai Lobachevsky b. John Michell d. Martin Rathke b. Friedrich von Struve b. Gilbert White d.	Karl Lachmann b. David Laing b. Wm. Robertson d. Henry R. Schoolcraft b.	Karl Almqvist b. John Clare b. Jean Delavigne b. Carlo Goldoni d. S.G. Goodrich b. Felicia D. Hemans b. Wm. Maginn b. Jan Frans Willems b.	Sir Chas. L. Eastlake b. Clarkson Stanfield b.	Benj. Cooke d.	Charlotte Corday d. Mme. DuBarry d. Lord Geo. Gordon d. Wm. Chas. Macready b. Lucretia Mott b. Mme. Roland d.
1794	Charles Barbaroux d. Earl of Camden d. J. B. Carrier d. Pierre Chaumette d. Lord Chelmsford b. Baron de Cloots d. Georges Couthon d. Georges Danton d. Camille Desmoulins d. Edward Everett b. Hans Hassenpflug b. Jacques Hébert d. Sir Wm. Jones d. Prinz von Kaunitz-Rietberg d. Richard Henry Lee d. Chrétien de Malesherbes d. J. Pétion de Villeneuve d. Maximilien de Robespierre d. Louis de Saint-Just d. Baron von Steuben d. John Witherspoon d.	Comte de La Rochejacquelin d. Matthew Perry b.	Cesare Beccaria d. Feargus O'Connor b. Cornelius Vanderbilt b.	Georg Forster d. Baron von Wrangel b.	Jean d'Aubigné b. Marquis de Condorcet d. Paul Rabaut d.	Jean Flourens b. Elias Fries b. Antoine Lavoisier d. Jas. Lind d. Wm. Lonsdale b. Eilhardt Mitscherlich b. Heinrich Pander b. François Raspail b. Félix Vicq d'Azyr d. Wm. Whewell b. Caspar Wolff d.	Friedrich Diez b. Edward Gibbon d. Geo. Grote b.	Maria G. Brooke b. Wm. Cullen Bryant b. Gottfried Bürger d. Wm. Carleton b. Sébastien Chamfort d. André de Chénier d. Alison Cockburn d. Philippe Fabre d'Églantine d. Jean Florian d. Fulke Greville b. Anna B. Jameson b. Paul de Kock b. J. G. Lockhart b.	J. Schnorr von Karolsfeld b.		Geo. Colman (Elder) d. Thos. G. Wainewright b.

Year A.D.	Government and Law	Military and Naval Affairs	Industry Commerce Economics Finance Invention Labor	Travel and Exploration	Philosophy and Religion	Science and Medicine	Education Scholarship History	Literature	Painting and Sculpture	Music	Miscellaneous
1795	*Antoine Fouquier–Tinville d.* Joshua R. Giddings b. *Graf von Hertzberg d.* Kamehameha I (Hawaii) a. *Louis XVII (France) d. ?* Wm. L. Mackenzie b. Jas. K. Polk b. Stanislas II (Poland) abd.	*Sir Henry Clinton d.* Sir Henry Havelock b. *Francis Marion d.* *Robt. Rogers d.* A.L. de Santa Anna b. Robt. F. Stockton b. Antonio de Sucre b. *John Sullivan d.*	Sir Rowland Hill b. *Josiah Wedgwood d.* Francis Wright b.	Chas. Sturt b.	*Johann von Zimmerman d.*	*Pierre Desault d.* Gérard Deshayes b. Christian Ehrenberg b. Peter A. Hansen b. Jas. G. Percival b. Moritz Romberg b. Ernst H. Weber b.	Thos. Arnold b. Leopold von Ranke b. *Ezra Stiles d.* Jacques Thierry b.	*Karl Bellmann d.* James Gordon Bennett b. *Jas. Boswell d.* Thos. Carlyle b. Geo. Darley b. Jos. Rodman Drake b. Karl Follen b. Alexander Griboyedov b. Jas. Harper b. John Keats b. John P. Kennedy b. Sir Thos. Talfourd b.	Antoine Barye b. Ary Scheffer b.		*Alessandro di Cagliostro d.* Geo. Peabody b. *Richard Tattersall d.*
1796	*Catherine the Great (Russia) d.* *Jean d'Herbois Collot d.* Adolphe Cremieux b. Reverdy Johnson b. Paul I (Russia) a. Edward G. Wakefield b.	*Richard Gridley d.* Jacques de Saint-Arnaud b. Karl von Steinmetz b. *Anthony Wayne d.*	Barthelemy Enfantin b.	Sir Geo. Back b.	Théodore Jouffroy b. Johann Möhler b. Wm. A. Muhlenberg b. *Thos. Reid d.* *Saml. Seabury d.* John Williams b.	Nicolas Carnot b. Geo. Catlin b. Sir Henry De la Beche b. J.F.W. Johnston b. Johann Poggendorf b. Adolphe Quetelet b. Anders Retzius b. *David Rittenhouse d.* John Torrey b.	Horace Mann b. François Mignet b. Wm. H. Prescott b. Karl Christian Rafn b. Agnes Strickland b.	Michael Banim b. Henry G. Bohn b. *Robt. Burns d.* Hartley Coleridge b. Thos. C. Haliburton b. Karl Immermann b. *Jas. Macpherson d.* J.G. Palfrey b. Graf von Platen b. *Guillaume Raynal d.*	*David Allan d.* Jean Corot b.	Gottfried Loewe b. *Stephen Storace d.*	Junius Brutus Booth b. *Sir Wm. Chambers d.* Jas. Lick b. Jas. R. Planche b.
1797	*François Babeuf d.* *Graf Andreas von Bernstorff d.* *Edmund Burke d.* *Friedrich Wilhelm II (Prussia) d.* Friedrich Wilhelm III (Prussia) a. *Lazare Hoche d.* Hugh S. Legaré b. *Francis Lightfoot Lee d.* Josef von Radowitz b. Louis Thiers b. *John Wilkes d.* *Oliver Wolcott d.*	*Lord Amherst d.* Edwin V. Sumner b.	Pierre Leroux b.	Ida Pfeiffer b.	Christoffer Boström b. Chas. Hodge b. Immanuel Ilmoni b. A. Rosmini-Serbati b. Alexandre Vinet b.	Jean Audouin b. Andrew Combe b. Joseph Henry b. *Jas. Hutton d.* Sir Chas. Lyell b.	Chas. Anthon b. Mary Lyon b. Sir Anthony Panizzi b. Connop Thirlwall b. Sir John Wilkinson b.	Thos. H. Bayly b. Annette von Droste-Hülshoff b. Wilhelm Häring b. Heinrich Heine b. Saml. Lover b. *Wm. Mason d.* Wm. Motherwell b. *Michel Sedaine d.* Mary W. Shelley b. Alfred de Vigny b. *Horace Walpole d.* A.A. Watts b. Thurlow Weed b. *Mary Wollstonecraft d.*	Paul Delaroche b. *Joseph Wright d.*	Gaetano Donizetti b. Franz Peter Schubert b.	*Baron von Münchhausen d.* Gerrit Smith b. Lucia Vestris b.
1798	Jules Dufaure b. *Lord Fitzgerald d.* Jas. M. Mason b. *Theobald Wolfe Tone d.* *Jas. Wilson d.*	*Louis de Casabianca d.* John A. Dix b. Chas. Wilkes b.	*John Fitch d.*	*Geo. Vancouver d.*	Friedrich Beneke b. Auguste Comte b.	Jean de Beaumont b. *Luigi Galvani d.* Macedonio Melloni b. David Moir b. Franz Neumann b. *Thos. Pennant d.* Lord Wrottesley b.	Alexander Csoma de Körös b. Alexander Dyce b. Jules Michelet b. Frantisek Palacký b. *David Ruhnken d.*	John Banim b. Isaac DaCosta b. Henrik Hertz b. August Hoffmann b. Jacques Jasmin b. Giacomo Leopardi b. Adam Mickiewicz b. Robt. Pollok b. *Constantine Rhigas d.*	*Asmus Carstens d.* Eugène Delacroix b. Eugène Verboeckhoven b.		*Giovanni Casanova d.* John St. John Long b.

1799–1805 A.D.

Year A.D.	Government and Law	Military and Naval Affairs	Industry Commerce Economics Finance Invention Labor	Travel and Exploration	Philosophy and Religion	Science and Medicine	Education Scholarship History	Literature	Painting and Sculpture	Music	Miscellaneous
1799	Rufus Choate b. Earl of Derby b. *Patrick Henry d.* *Tippoo Sahib d.* *George Washington d.*	*Earl Howe d.* *Barthélemi Joubert d.* Andres Pretorius b.	Amasa Walker b.	James Bowie b. René Caillé b.	Bronson Alcott b. Johann von Döllinger b. *Pope Pius VI d.* Richard Rothe b. Friedrich Tholuck b.	*Maria Agnesi d.* Friedrich Argelander b. *Joseph Black d.* *Markus Bloch d.* Sir Chas. Fellows b. *Johann Hedwig d.* *Jan Ingenhousz d.* Wm. Lassell b. *Pierre Lemonnier d.* Georg Lichtenberg d. John Lindley b. F. Poey y Aloy b. *Horace de Saussure d.* *Lazaro Spallanzani d.* Jas. Syme b.	Geo. Finlay b. Stanislas Julien b. Heinrich Leo b.	Honoré de Balzac b. *Pierre de Beaumarchais d.* João d'Almeida Garrett b. Thomas Hood b. Mary Howitt b. G.P.R. James b. *Jean Marmontel d.* *Lord Monboddo d.* Karl A. Nicander b. *Giuseppe Parini d.* Alexander Pushkin b. Marie Roch Reybaud b. Wm. Thom b. Rodolphe Töpffer b. Chas. J. Wells b.		*Karl von Dittersdorf d.* Jacques F. Halévy b.	*Elisha Perkins d.*
1800	Aga Khan I (Bombay) b. Caleb Cushing b. Millard Fillmore b. Chas. Rogier b. *John Rutledge d.* Prinz F. zu Schwarzenberg b. Benj. F. Wade b. *Olaf Wallqvist d.* Lord Westbury b.	*Louis Desaix de Veygout d.* *C. de Latour d'Auvergne d.* *Thos. Mifflin d.* Graf von Moltke b. *Count Suvorov d.*	Chas. Goodyear b. Platt R. Spencer b. Wm. H.F. Talbot b.		Theodor Fliedner b. Pope Pius VII a. Alonzo Potter b. Edward B. Pusey b.	*L. J. Daubenton d.* Jean Dumas b. Ebenezer Emmons b. John E. Gray b. Francis Lieber b. Henri Milne-Edwards b. Félix Pouchet b. Earl of Rosse b. Franz Unger b. Friedrich Wöhler b.	Geo. Bancroft b. Catherine Beecher b. *Joseph de Guignes d.* Christian Lassen b. Geo. Long b. Wm. H. McGuffey b. *Geo. Steevens d.*	Wm. Barnes b. Robt. Bell b. Antonio Castilho b. *Wm. Cowper d.* Catherine S. Crowe b. Gergely Czuczor b. Louis Hachette b. *Jupiter Hammon d.* Thos. B. Macaulay b. Jacques Migne b. Sir Henry Taylor b. Mihaly Vörösmarty b.	Jean Audebert d. Wm. Simson b.	Ludwig von Köchel b. *Nicola Piccinni d.*	John Brown b. Nat Turner b.
1801	Alexander I (Russia) a. L.H. Carnot b. *Paul I (Russia) d.* Wm. H. Seward b. Robt. J. Walker b.	*Sir Ralph Abercromby d.* *Benedict Arnold d.* David G. Farragut b. *Prince Repnin d.* *Marquis de Ségur d.* Lord Strathnairn b.	Frédéric Bastiat b. Robt. Dale Owen b.	Karl Baedeker b.	Vincenzo Gioberti b. Maximilien Littré b. Julius Müller b. Cardinal Newman b. Brigham Young b.	Sir Geo. Airy b. Adolphe Brongniart b. Thos. Clark b. Antoine Cournot b. Auguste De la Rive b. *Déodat de Dolomieu d.* Félix Dujardin b. Gustav Fechner b. *Tnos. Fowler d.* *J. K. Lavater d.* Johannes P. Müller b. Jos. Plateau b. Julius Plücker b. Alfred Volkmann b.	Saml. Gridley Howe b. Edward W. Lane b. Theodore Dwight Woolsey b.	Fredrika Bremer b. *Hester Chapone d.* Karl Ebert b. Abraham Hayward b. *"Novalis" d.*	Richard Bonnington b. *Danl. Chodowiecki d.* Harry Inman b.	Vincenzo Bellini b. *Domenico Cimarosa d.*	Count D'Orsay b. Sir Joseph Paxton b.
1802	Lord Bentinck b. *Charles de Calonne d.* *Earl of Clare d.* Sir Alexander Cockburn b. Franz Karl (Austria) b. Earl Henry Grey b. *Lord Kenyon d.* Louis Kossuth b. *John Lowell d.* Don Miguel b. Friedrich Stahl b. Chas. P. Villiers b.	Louis Cavaignac b. *Esek Hopkins d.* Adolphe Niel b.			Horace Bushnell b. *Alexander Geddes d.* J. B. Lacordaire b. Phineas Quimby b. Arnold Ruge b. Friedrich Trendelenburg b. Isaac Williams b. Cardinal Wiseman b.	Niels Henrik Abel b. *François Bichât d.* *Erasmus Darwin d.* Heinrich Magnus b. Hugh Miller b. Sir Chas. Wheatstone b.	Paul Botta b. Ernst Ettmüller b. Mark Hopkins b. Karl Lehrs b. Elias Lönnrot b. August Pott b. Karl Simrock b. *Joseph Strutt d.*	Thos. Aird b. Leonard Bacon b. Robt. Chambers b. Lydia M. Child b. Sara Coleridge b. Alexandre Dumas, Père, b. Wilhelm Hauff b. Victor Hugo b. Letitia E. Landon b. Jacob van Lennep b. Harriet Martineau b. Alessandro Poerio b. W. M. Praed b. Geo. Ripley b.	Sir Edwin Landseer b. *George Romney d.* Ludwig Schwanthaler b.		Dorothea Dix b. Elijah Lovejoy b.

Year A.D.	Government and Law	Military and Naval Affairs	Industry Commerce Economics Finance Invention Labor	Travel and Exploration	Philosophy and Religion	Science and Medicine	Education Scholarship History	Literature	Painting and Sculpture	Music	Miscellaneous
1803	Samuel Adams d. Sir Jas. Brooke b. Ferencs Deák b. Robt. Emmet d. Wm. Smith O'Brien b. Edmund Pendleton d. Cardinal de Rohan d. Jas. N. Tandy d. P.-D. Toussaint l'Ouverture d.	John Barry d. Albert Sidney Johnston b. Graf von Roon b.	John Ericsson b. Robt. Stephenson b. A. T. Stewart b.	John A. Sutter b.	Orestes A. Brownson b. Georg Ewald b. J. G. von Herder d. Saml. Hopkins d. Marquis de Saint-Martin d. Dietrich Tiedemann d.	Jas. Challis b. Christian Doppler b. Heinrich Dove b. Baron von Liebig b. Jacques Sturm b. Wm. S. Sullivant b.	Rawdon Brown b. Angelo Fabroni d. August Gfrörer b. Henri Ollendorff b. Wm. J. Thoms b.	Jacob Abbott b. Vittorio Alfieri d. Jas. Beattie d. Thos. L. Beddoes b. Geo. Borrow b. E. G. Bulwer-Lytton b. R. W. Emerson b. Margerie Fleming b. Gerald Griffin b. Robt. S. Hawker b. Richard Hengist Horne b. Douglas Jerrold b. G. F. Klopstock d. J. F. de Laharpe d. Jas. C. Mangan b. Chas. Jas. Mathews b. Prosper Mérimée b. Edgar Quinet b. Jean de Saint-Lambert d. G. Senac de Meilhan d. Robt. Surtees b. Fyodor Tyutchev b.	Alexandre Decamps b. Robt. Weir b.	Hector Berlioz b. Mikhail Glinka b.	
1804	Armand Camus d. Dessalines (Haiti) a. Benj. Disraeli b. Duc d'Enghien d. Alexander Hamilton d. Jos. Howe b. Daniele Manin b. Jacques Necker d. Osceola b. Franklin Pierce b.	Vicomte de Noailles d. Chas. Pichegru d. Philip Schuyler d.	Richard Cobden b.	Richard Lander b.	Ludwig Feuerbach b. Immanuel Kant d.	Antoine Baumé d. Stephan Endlicher b. Otto Erdmann b. Karl Jacobi b. Alexander K. Johnson b. Sir Richard Owen b. Joseph Priestley d. Carl Rokitansky b. Matthias Schleiden b. Karl von Siebold b. Wilhelm Weber b.	Johan Madvig b. Elizabeth Peabody b.	Cesare Cantù b. Wm. Gilpin d. Delphine de Girardin b. L. A. Godey b. Francesco Guerrazzi b. Nathaniel Hawthorne b. Charlotte Lennox d. Francis S. Mahony b. J.L. Runeberg b. C. A. Sainte-Beuve b. "George Sand" b. Eugène Sue b. Chas. Whitehead b.	"Paul Gavarni" b. Pierre Julien d. Geo. Morland d. Richard Redgrave b. Moritz von Schwind b. Sir John Steel b.	Johann Strauss (Elder) b. C. Traviès de Villers b.	Zerah Colburn b. Neal Dow b. Framjee Patel b. Maria Taglioni b.
1805	John Beresford d. Wm. G. Brownlow b. David Dudley Field b. Wm. Lloyd Garrison b. Marquess (Wm.) Lansdowne d. Ferdinand de Lesseps b. Giuseppe Mazzini b. Count Potocki d. Earl of Rosslyn d. Earl of Shelburne d. David Urquhart b.	Lord Cornwallis d. Wm. Moultrie d. Horatio Nelson d.	Louis Blanqui b. Johann K. Rodbertus b.		Jas. Martineau b. F.D. Maurice b. Wm. Paley d. Karl Rosenkranz b. Joseph Smith b. Saml. Wiberforce b.	Alexander Braun b. Nicolas Conte d. Robt. Fitzroy b. Thos. Graham b. Sir Wm. Rowan Hamilton b. Johann von Lamont b. Hugo von Mohl b. Alexander von Nordmann b. Michael Sars b. Rudolf Wagner b.	Julius Fürst b. C. E. A. Gayarré b. Francis Newman b. Earl of Stanhope b.	John C.S. Abbott b. Comtesse d'Agoult b. Wm. H. Ainsworth b. Hans Christian Andersen b. Manuel Bocage d. Thos. Cooper b. Jas. Currie d. Eugénie de Guérin b. Johann von Schiller d. Alexis de Tocqueville b. Thos. Wade b.	Thos. Banks d. Horatio Greenough b. J. B. Greuze d. Wm. von Kaulbach b. Hiram Powers b.	Luigi Boccherini d.	J.E.R. Houdin b.

1806–1810 A.D.

Year A.D.	Government and Law	Military and Naval Affairs	Industry Commerce Economics Finance Invention Labor	Travel and Exploration	Philosophy and Religion	Science and Medicine	Education Scholarship History	Literature	Painting and Sculpture	Music	Miscellaneous
1806	*Dessalines (Haiti) d.* Wm. Pitt Fessenden b. *Charles James Fox d.* Friedrich Augustus I (Saxony) a. Benito Juárez b. Sir Geo. Cornewall Lewis b. Maximilian I (Bavaria) a. *Wm. Pitt (Younger) d.* Graf von Réchberg–Rothenlowen b. *Lord Thurlow d.* *Geo. Wythe d.*	Count Batthyányi b. *Horatio Gates d.* *Henry Knox d.* Sir Henry M. Lawrence b. Leonidas Polk b. *Silvestre Villeneuve d.* Henry A. Wise b.	Pierre LePlay b. *Robert Morris d.* John A. Roebling b. Max Stirner b.	*Mungo Park d.*	Alexander Duff b. John Stuart Mill b. Hermann Ulrici b.	Alexander D. Bache b. *Paul Barthez d.* *Charles de Coulomb d.* Augustus DeMorgan b. Guillaume Duchenne b. *Josef Koelreuter d.* *Nicolas Leblanc d.* Matthew F. Maury b.	Lorenz Diefenbach b. Wilhelm Freund b. Herman Merivale b. *Sir Roger Newdigate d.* Friedrich Ritschl b. Johann Zeuss b.	Robt. M. Bird b. Elizabeth Barrett Browning b. *Elizabeth Carter d.* Ernst von Feuchtersleben b. *Émile de Girardin b.* *Conde di Gozzi d.* Chas. F. Hoffman b. Heinrich Laube b. Chas. Jas. Lever b. Wm. Gilmore Simms b. *Charlotte Smith d.* Emile Souvestre b. John Sterling b. *Henry Kirke White d.* N. P. Willis b.	*Jas. Barry d.* Wm. Dyce b. *Jean Honoré Fragonard d.* Solomon Hart b. Sir Geo. Harvey b. Danl. Maclise b. Horatio McCulloch b. David Scott b. *Utamaro d.* Antoine Wiertz b.	Sir Julius Benedict b.	*Moses Cleaveland d.* *Timothy Dexter d.* *Fra Diavolo d.* Edwin Forrest b. *Jean Riesener d.* *Thos. Sheraton d.*
1807	Chas. F. Adams b. *Joseph Brant d.* Giuseppe Garibaldi b. Jules Grévy b. A. Ledru–Rollin b. *Jean Portahs d.* *Nikolai de Rezanov d.*	Joseph E. Johnston b. Robert E. Lee b. *J.P.G. Muhlenberg d.* *Pasquale Paoli d.* *Comte de Rochambeau d.*		Sir Robt. McClure b.	Henry Edgeworth d. *John Newton d.*	Louis Agassiz b. *Geo. Attwood d.* Theodor Bischoff b. Arnold Guyot b. *Joseph de Lalande d.* Auguste Laurent b.	Ezra Cornell b. Hans von der Gabelentz b. Richard Hildreth b. John M. Kemble b.	Jacques Bertrand b. *Sophie Cottin d.* Lady Dufferin b. Tomaz Gonzaga b. *Baron von Grimm d.* Jónas Hallgrimsson b. H.W. Longfellow b. Robt. Montgomery b. *Clara Reeve d.* Fredk. Tennyson b. Richard Chenevix Trench b. Saml. Warren b. J. G. Whittier b. Christopher Wordsworth (Younger) b.	Narcisse de la Peña Díaz b. *Angelica Kauffmann d.* *John Opie d.* Friedrich Vischer b.	*Neil Gow d.*	*David Röntgen d.* *Henry Stuart d.*
1808	*Fisher Ames d.* Johann Bluntschli b. Carlos IV (Spain) abd. Salmon P. Chase b. *Christian VII (Denmark) d.* Jefferson Davis b. *John Dickinson d.* Ferdinand VII (Spain) a. Hamilton Fish b. Andrew Johnson b. Mahmud II (Turkey) a. Joachim Murat (Naples) a. *Selim III (Turkey) d.*	Comte de Mac–Mahon b.	Victor Considerant b. MacGregor Laird b. Jas. Nasmyth b. F. Schulze-Delitzsch b. *John Wilkinson d.*	Thos. Cook b.	*Pierre Cabanis d.* Jas. F. Ferrier b. Cardinal Manning b. Hans Martensen b. David Strauss b.	Henry I. Bowditch b. Bernhard von Cotta b. Hugh Falconer b. *José Mutis d.* Chas. Pritchard b. Friedrich Stannius b.	Wm. Cureton b. Johann Droysen b. Chas. Merivale b. *Richard Porson d.* Jas. Spedding b.	Jules Barbey d'Aurevilly b. Willis Gaylord Clark b. José de Espronceda b. Jean Karr b. "Gérard de Nerval" b. Caroline Norton b. Saml. F. Smith b. Chas. Tennysi Chas. Tennyson Turner b.	Honoré Daumier b. John Sartain b.	Michael W. Balfe b. Maria Malibran b. Franz Schubert (Later) b.	Enoch Pratt b.

Year A.D.	Government and Law	Military and Naval Affairs	Industry Commerce Economics Finance Invention Labor	Travel and Exploration	Philosophy and Religion	Science and Medicine	Education Scholarship History	Literature	Painting and Sculpture	Music	Miscellaneous
1809	Armand Barbès b. Charles XIII (Sweden) a. Jules Favre b. Wm. E. Gladstone b. Gustavus IV (Sweden) abd. Hannibal Hamlin b. *Sir Elijah Impey d.* Abraham Lincoln b. *Thos. Paine d.* *Antoine Santerre d.* *Jonathan Trumbull d.* Robert Winthrop b.	Philip St. G. Cooke b. John A. Dahlgren b. *Sir John Moore d.* Raphael Semmes b.	*François Blanchard d.* Louis Delescluze b. Baron de Haussmann b. Cyrus H. McCormick b. P. J. Proudhon b. Sir Travers Twiss b.	Kit Carson b. *Meriwether Lewis d.*	Bruno Bauer b. Saml. A. Crowther b. *Charles Dupuis d.* Alessandro Gavazzi b.	*Leopold Auenbrugger d.* Charles Darwin b. Jas. D. Forbes b. *Antoine de Fourcroy d.* Jas. Glaisher b. Oswald Heer b. Jakob Henle b. S. L. Lovén b. Benj. Peirce b. Chas. G. W. St. John b. Sir Erasmus Wilson b.	Frederick A. P. Barnard b. Theodor Benfey b. John Hill Burton b. *Johannes von Müller d.* Wm. F. Skene b.	T. S. Arthur b. Park Benjamin b. John S. Blackie b. Thos. H. Chivers b. *Nicasio de Cienfuegos d.* *Hannah Cowley d.* Edward Fitzgerald b. Giuseppe Giusti b. Nikolai Gogol b. Thos. G. Hake b. *Thos. Holcraft d.* O. W. Holmes (Sr.) b. Lord Houghton b. A. W. Kinglake b. Mariano de Larra b. Mark Lemon b. Frederik Paludan-Müller b. Albert Pike b. Edgar Allan Poe b. *Anna Seward d.* Lord Tennyson b.		*Josef Haydn d.* Felix Mendelssohn-Bartholdy b.	John W. Griffiths b. Fanny Kemble b. Geo. Selwyn b. Alexis Soyer b.
1810	Camillo di Cavour b. Cassius M. Clay b. Horatio Seymour b. Comte de Walewski b. *Wm. Windham d.*	*Count von Fersen d.* *Andreas Hofer d.* John B. Magruder b. Lord Napier of Magdala b. Francisco Serrano b. Robt. Toombs b.	*Sir Francis Baring d.* *Joseph Montgolfier d.* Edward V. Neale b. Félix Pyat b. Ernestine Rose b. Louis Wolowski b.	Antoine Abbadie b.	Henry Alford b. Theodore Parker b.	*Henry Cavendish d.* Henry Christy b. Asa Gray b. J. Quatrefages deBréau b. H. V. Regnault b. Theodor Schwann b. Geo. Waterhouse b.	John S. Brewer b. Elihu Burritt b. Andrew Findlater b. A. Herculano de Carvalho b. Karl Lepsius b. Henri Martin b. Comte de Montalembert b. Sir Henry C. Rawlinson b. Thos. Wright b.	Nicolaus Becker b. *Chas. Brockden Brown d.* John Brown b. Lewis Gaylord Clark b. Jas. Freeman Clarke b. *Princess Dashkova d.* Sir Francis H. Doyle b. Sir Saml. Ferguson b. Ferdinand Freiligrath b. Margaret Fuller b. Elizabeth C. Gaskell b. Maurice de Guerin b. Alfred de Musset b. A. R. Rangabé b. Fritz Reuter b. *Robt. Tannahill d.* *Mary Tighe d.* Thos. Adolphus Trollope b. Martin Farquhar Tupper b.		Ole Bull b. Frédéric Chopin b. Félicien David b. Giuseppe Mario b. Karl Otto Nicolaï b. Robert Schumann b. Saml. Sebastian Wesley b.	P. T. Barnum b. Fanny Eissler b. *Chevalier d'Éon d.*

1811–1816 A.D.

Year A.D.	Government and Law	Military and Naval Affairs	Industry Commerce Economics Finance Invention Labor	Travel and Exploration	Philosophy and Religion	Science and Medicine	Education Scholarship History	Literature	Painting and Sculpture	Music	Miscellaneous
1811	Judah P. Benjamin b. John Bright b. *Samuel Chase d.* Henri Christophe (Haiti) a. *Francis Dana d.* Edouard Laboulaye b. Lord Lawrence b. Duc de Morny b. Duc de Reichstadt b. Domingo Sarmiento b. Viscount Sherbrook b. Jón Sigurdsson b. Chas. Sumner b.	Achille Bazaine b. *Wm. Eaton d.* Friedrich Hecker b. Tsêng Kuo-Fan b.	Louis Blanc b. John H. Noyes b. Jas. Young b.	*Louis de Bougainville d.*	Henry James, Sr. b. Jas. McCosh b. Wendell Phillips b. *Robt. Raikes d.* Archibald C. Tait b.	Robt. von Bunsen b. John W. Draper b. Johann Dzierzon b. Sir Wm. Grove b. Jas. Hall b. Jos. B. Jukes b. Urbain Leverrier b. *Nevil Maskeleyne d.* *Peter Pallas d.* Karl Reichert b. Sir Jas. Y. Simpson b. Hugh E. Strickland b.	Henry Barnard b. Jean Duruy b. Vicomte de Falloux b. *John Leyden d.* H. G. Liddell b.	Gilbert à Beckett b. *Blaise de Chénier d.* *Richard Cumberland d.* Alfred Domett b. *Majorie Fleming d.* Théophile Gautier b. Horace Greeley b. Karl F. Gutzkow b. Arthur H. Hallam b. H. P. Holst b. *Heinrich von Kleist d.* Fanny Lewald b. *Robt. Treat Paine d.* Sara Parton b. *Thos. Percy d.* Jules Sandeau b. Wm. Bell Scott b. Harriet Beecher Stowe b. W. M. Thackeray b.	Chas. W. Cope b. Jules Dupré b. Jean Flandrin b. *John Smart d.*	Giulia Grisi b. Franz Liszt b. Ambroise Thomas b.	Delia Bacon b. Henry Bergh b. Chas. John Kean b. Sir Geo. Gilbert Scott b.
1812	Earl of Canning b. Geo. T. Curtis b. Luigi Farini b. Ilya Garashanin b. Sir Geo. Grey b. Carl C. Hall b. *Spencer Perceval d.* Earl of Selborne b. Alexander H. Stephens b.	*Jan De Winter d.* *Peter Gansevoort d.*	Stephen Pearl Andrews b. Alexander Herzen b. Richard M. Hoe b. Alfred Krupp b. *Mayer Anselm Rothschild d.* Chas. Tiffany b.		*Johann Griesbach d.* Norman Macleod b. Wm. Geo. Ward b.	Marquess of Dalhousie b. Casimir Davaine b. *Richard Kirwan d.* Wm. Pengelly b. Albert Wigand b.	Sir Edward S. Creasy b. Giuseppe Ferrari b. *Christian Heyne d.* F. F. Kuhn b. Robt. G. Latham b. *Edmund Malone d.* Lady Schreiber b. *John Horne Tooke d.* Henri Wallon b.	Thos. G. Appleton b. Berthold Auerbach b. *Joel Barlow d.* Robt. Browning b. Hendrik Conscience b. Chas. Dickens b. John Forster b. Lady Georgiana Fullerton b. János Garay b. Ivan Goncharov b. Geraldine Jewsbury b. Victor de Laprade b. Edward Lear b. Henry Mayhew b. Saml. Smiles b. *John Walter d.*	Wm. J. Linton b. Théodore Rousseau b. *John Raphael Smith d.*	*Jan Dussek d.* Friedrich von Flotow b. Louis A. Jullien b. Sigismond Thalberg b.	Kaspar Hauser b.? A. W. N. Pugin b.
1813	Viscount Cardwell b. Stephen A. Douglas b. *Wm. Franklin d.* *Robt. Livingston d.* *Edmund Randolph d.* *Juan de Rozas d.* *Theodore Sedgwick d.* *Tecumseh d.* Allen G. Thurman b.	*J. B. Bessières d.* *Jas. Lawrence d.* *Jean Moreau d.* *Jos. Poniatowski d.* David D. Porter b. *Gerhard von Scharnhorst d.* John Sedgwick b.	Sir Henry Bessemer b. Sir Isaac Pitman b.	John C. Frémont b. Évariste Huc b. David Livingstone b. *Zebulon E. Pike d.* John Rae b.	Henry Ward Beecher b. Franz Delitzsch b. Julius Frauenstädt b. John Grote b. S. A. Kierkegaard b. *Philip Otterbein d.* A. F. Ozanam b. Daniel Schenkel b. Fredk. Scrivener b.	Claude Bernard b. Samuel Brown b. Wm. B. Carpenter b. Jas. D. Dana b. Baron Jozsef von Eötvös b. *Comte de La Grange d.* *Johann Reil d.* *Benj. Rush d.* Jas. Marion Sims b. Jean Stas b. Johannes Steenstrup b. *Benj. West d.* *Alexander Wilson d.*	Otto Jahn b. Franz von Miklosic b. Sir Wm. Smith b. Anna Swanwick b.	Wm. Aytoun b. Georg Büchner b. *St. J. de Crèvecœur d.* George Gilfillan b. Friedrich Hebbel b. Sir Arthur Helps b. *Karl T. Körner d.* J. B. Lippincott b. Danl. Macmillan b. Mark Pattison b. *Henry Pye d.* Henry T. Tuckermann b. Jones Very b. *C. M. Wieland d.*	Christopher P. Cranch b. Thomas Crawford b. Constant Troyon b.	*André Grétry d.* Sir Geo. A. Macfarren b. Giuseppe Verdi b. Richard Wagner b.	*Giambattista Bodoni d.* *Granville Sharp d.*

Year A.D.	Government and Law	Military and Naval Affairs	Industry Commerce Economics Finance Invention Labor	Travel and Exploration	Philosophy and Religion	Science and Medicine	Education Scholarship History	Literature	Painting and Sculpture	Music	Miscellaneous
1814	*Lord Wm. Auckland d.* *Edmond Dubois-Crancé d.* Pasha Fuad b. *Elbridge Gerry d.* *Empress Josephine d.* Louis XVIII (France) a. Duc de Nemours b. Edwin M. Stanton b. Saml. J. Tilden b. David Wilmot b. Wm. L. Yancey b.	*Sir Saml. Hood d.* Jos. Hooker b. *Viscount Howe d.* Philip Kearny b. *Prince de Ligne d.*	Mikhail Bakunin b. Saml. Colt b. *Thos. Spence d.*	*Matthew Flinders d.*	*Thos. Coke d.* J. W. Colenso b. F. W. Faber b. *J. G. Fichte d.* Jules Simon b. *Johanna Southcott d.* Eduard Zeller b.	John Goodsir b. August Grisebach b. Julius R. Mayer b. Sir Jas. Paget b. Sir Andrew Ramsay b. *Count Rumford d.* Jeffries Wyman b.	Ernst Curtius b. Edward B. Eastwick b. Wilhelm von Giesebrecht b. John L. Motley b. Jules Quicherat b.	Thos. Davis b. Aubrey De Vere b. Franz Dingelstadt b. W. H. G. Kingston b. Jos. S. LeFanu b. Mikhail Lermontov b. Chas. MacKay b. "Luise Muhlbach" b. Robt. Nicoll b. Geo. P. Putnam b. Chas. Reade b. *Marquis de Sade d.* *Bernardin de Saint-Pierre d.* Taras Sewchenko b. Benj. P. Shillaber b. *Mercy Warren d.* Mrs. Henry Wood b.	Henry Kirke Brown b. J. F. Millet b.	*Chas. Burney d.* *Chas. Dibdin d.* Stephen Heller b. *Abt Vogler d.*	*Philip Astley d.* Lady Burdett-Coutts b. Edward L. Davenport b. *Joseph Guillotin d.* Eugène Viollet-le-Duc b.
1815	Aali Pasha b. Prinz von Bismarck b. *Chevalier de Boufflers d.* Edward J. Eyre b. Sir Henry Frere b. Earl George of Granville b. Sir John Macdonald b. *Joachim Murat (Naples) d.* Sir Henry Parkes b. *John Sevier d.* Willem I (Holland) a.	*Louis F. Berthier d.* Anna Ella Carroll b. Henry Halleck b. Geo. G. Meade b. *Michel Ney d.* *Sir Thos. Picton d.* Louis Trochu b.	*Robt. Fulton d.*	Arnaud Abbadie b. *Karsten Niebuhr d.*	Wm. J. Conybeare b. *Andrew Fuller d.* Chas. Renouvier b. Arthur Penrhyn Stanley b. Konstantin von Tischendorf b.	Geo. Boole b. Warren De la Rue b. Edward Forbes b. Sir Wm. Jenner b. Crawford W. Long b. *Franz Mesmer d.* Robt. Remak b. Karl Weierstrass b. Horace Wells b.	Jas. Legge b. *David Ramsay d.*	*Richard Alsop d.* R. H. Dana, Jr. b. R. W. Griswold b. Johann Kinkel b. Eugène Labiche b. Edmond Schérer b. Anthony Trollope b.	Andreas Achenbach b. Hablôt K. Browne b. *John S. Copley d.* *Jas. Gillray d.* Jean Meissonier b. Adolph Menzel b.	Robert Franz b. *Johann Salomon d.* Karl Wilhelm b.	*Frances Abington d.* Grace Darling b. *Lady Emma Hamilton d.* Elizabeth Cady Stanton b.
1816	Sir Chas. G. Duffy b. Stephen J. Field b. Rudolf von Gneist b. *Gouverneur Morris d.* Johan Sverdrup b. Elihu B. Washburne b.	Nathaniel P. Banks b. Jubal A. Early b. August von Goeben b. *Viscount Hood d.* *Francisco Miranda d.* Geo. H. Thomas b.	August Belmont b. Edward Hargraves b. Philo Remington b. Russell Sage b. Werner von Siemens b.	Friedrich Gerstäcker b.	Francis Asbury d. *Adam Ferguson d.* *Johann Jahn d.* *Jean Maury d.*	Wm. Bowman b. Karl Gerhardt b. Karl Ludwig b. Sir Richard Quain b. Lewis M. Rutherfurd b. *Christian C. Sprengel d.* *Earl of Stanhope d.* Louis de Vilmorin b.	Saml. Allibone b. E. A. Duyckinck b. Fredk. A. Paley b. Sir Danl. Wilson b.	Grace Aguilar b. Philip Bailey b. Charlotte Brontë b. Chas. Brooks b. Philip P. Cooke b. Peter Cunningham b. *Gavrila Derzhávin d.* Gustav Freytag b. Comte de Gobineau b. Parke Godwin b. Friedrich von Hackländer b. *Elizabeth Hamilton d.* Sir Theodore Martin b. J. G. Saxe b. *R. B. Sheridan d.*	Emanuel Leutze b. Giovanni Morelli b. David H. Strother b.	*E.-N. Méhul d.* *Giovanni Paisello d.*	John Close b. Charlotte Cushman b. *Dorothea Jordan d.*

1817–1822 A.D.

Year A.D.	Government and Law	Military and Naval Affairs	Industry Commerce Economics Finance Invention Labor	Travel and Exploration	Philosophy and Religion	Science and Medicine	Education Scholarship History	Literature	Painting and Sculpture	Music	Miscellaneous
1817	John P. Curran d. Andrew G. Curtin b. Alexander J. Dallas d. Fredk. T. Frelinghuysen b. Pasquale Mancini b. Milos I (Serbia) a. Sir Theophilus Shepstone b. Graf von Toll d.	Archduke Albrecht (Austria) b. Wm. Bligh d. Braxton Bragg b. Thaddeus Kosciuszko d. André Massena d. Andrew Pickens d.	Geo. H. Corliss b. Pierre Du Pont de Nemours d. Wilhelm Roscher b.	Johann Burckhardt d.	Tomothy Dwight d. Warren Felt Evans b. Geo. J. Holyoake b. Rudolf Lotze b.	Chas. Brown-Séquard b. Jean Deluc d. Jos. D. Hooker b. Martin Klaproth d. Albrecht von Kölliker b. Hermann Kopp b. Fielding B. Meek b. Chas. Messier d. Karl von Nägeli b. Gustave Thuret b. Karl Vogt b. Abraham Werner d.	François Chabas b. Heinrich Grätz b. Benj. Jowett b. Pierre Larousse b. Sir Austin H. Layard b. Theodor Mommsen b. Heinrich von Sybel b.	Jane Austen d. John Bigelow b. Ramon de Campoamor b. John Cassell b. Richard L. Edgeworth d. Paul Féval b. Jas. T. Fields b. Georg Herwegh b. Jung-Stilling d. Geo. H. Lewes b. Denis F. MacCarthy b. Mme. de Staël d. Theodor Storm b. Tom Taylor b. H. D. Thoreau b. Edwin Waugh b. José Zorrilla b.	Charles Daubigny b. Giovanni Dupre b. Sir John Gilbert b. John Leech b. G. F. Watts b. Chas. A. Wurtz b.	Niels Gade b.	Fredk. Douglass b. Helena Faucit b. John B. Gough b.
1818	Charles XIII (Sweden) d. Charles XIV (Sweden) a. Ernst II (Saxe-Coburg-Gotha) b. Wm. E. Forster b. Wade Hampton b. Warren Hastings d. Earl of Iddesleigh b. Rudolf von Jhering b. Alexandre Pétion d. Chas. Robinson b. Sir Saml. Romilly d. Duke of Rutland b. Baron von Thugut d.	P. G. T. Beauregard b. B. F. Butler b. Sir Robt. Calder d. Arthur Görgei b. Henry Lee d. Irvin McDowell b. Count Platov d. Aloys von Reding d. Paul Revere d. Count Todleben b.	William G. Fargo b. Richard J. Gatling b. Karl Marx b. Marco Minghetti b.	Geo. Rogers Clark d.	Alexander Bain b.	Emil DuBois-Reymond b. Karl Fresenius b. August von Hofmann b. Jas. P. Joule b. Adolphe Kolbe b. John Le Conte b. Maria Mitchell b. Gaspard Monge d. Lewis H. Morgan b. E. Sainte-Claire Deville b. Pietro Secchi b. Ignaz Semmelweiss b. Friedrich Stein b. Caspar Wistar d.	Malcolm Laing d.	Gustave Aimard b. Emily Brontë b. Wm. E. Channing (Younger) b. Eliza Cook b. Baron De Geer b. Sir Philip Francis d. Jas. A. Froude b. Chas. Leconte de Lisle b. Matthew G. Lewis d. Alexander Macmillan b. Chas. E. Mudie b. John M. Neale b. Mayne Reid b. Henry W. Shaw b. Frank Smedley b. Ivan Turgeniev b.	John Foley b. Sir Francis Haden b. Jas. J. Jarves b. Alfred Stevens (sculptor) b.	C. F. Gounod b. Clara Novello b.	Abigail Adams d. Amelia Bloomer b. Lola Montez b. Lucy Stone b.
1819	Prince-Consort Albert b. J. Billaud Varenne d. Francesco Crispi b. Duc de Gramont b. Prinz von Hohenlohe-Schillingsfürst b. Kamehameha I (Hawaii) d. Sir Jas. McCulloch b. Marthinus Pretorius b.	Gebhard von Blücher d. Sir Wm. Cornwallis d. John W. Geary b. Oliver H. Perry d. Wm. S. Rosecrans b.	Pierre Bertin d. Cyrus W. Field b. Elias Howe b. Ernest C. Jones b. Gustave de Molinari b. Jas. Watt d.		Isaac T. Hecker b. Friederich Jacobi d. Philip Schaff b. Isaac M. Wise b.	Erik Acharius d. John Couch Adams b. Louis Figuier b. Jean Foucault b. J. Peter Lesley b. Wm. T. G. Morton b. John Playfair d. Danl. Rutherford d. Sir Geo. G. Stokes b. Geo. Wilson b.	Sir Wm. Muir b. H. A. J. Munro b. Bernhard Quaritch b. John C. Shairp b. Henry Stevens b. Chas. J. Stillé b.	Arthur H. Clough b. Chas. A. Dana b. "George Eliot" b. Thos. Dunn English b. J. G. Holland b. Julia Ward Howe b. Gottfried Keller b. Chas. Kingsley b. August von Kotzebue d. Jas. Russell Lowell b. John W. Marston b. Herman Melville b. Anna C. Mowatt b. Francisco de Nascimento d. "Peter Pindar" d. John Ruskin b. E. D. E. N. Southworth b. Graf F. zu Stolberg d. Susan B. Warner b. Walt Whitman b.	Gustave Courbet b. Wm. Frith b. Wm. Wetmore Story b. Sir Henry Tate b.	Franz Abt b. Sir Chas. Hallé b. Jenny Lind b. Jacques Offenbach b. Klara Schumann b.	Felice Orsini b. Allan Pinkerton b.

Year A.D.	Government and Law	Military and Naval Affairs	Industry Commerce Economics Finance Invention Labor	Travel and Exploration	Philosophy and Religion	Science and Medicine	Education Scholarship History	Literature	Painting and Sculpture	Music	Miscellaneous
1820	Susan B. Anthony b. Anson Burlingame b. Comte de Chambord b. *Henri Christophe (Haiti) d. Jos. Fouché d. George III (England) d.* George IV (England) a. *Henry Grattan d.* Pierre Nord Alexis b. Lord Strathcona b. *Jean Tallien d.* Francis Wharton b.	*Stephen Decatur d.* Georg Klapka b. John F. Reynolds b. *Prinz K. zu Schwarzenberg d.* Wm. T. Sherman b.	Jas. B. Eads b. Friedrich Engels b. I. C. Vidyasagar b. *Arthur Young d.*	*Daniel Boone d.* Robt. O'Hara Burke b. Elisha Kent Kane b. *Sir Alexander Mackenzie d.*	John Caird b. Fanny Crosby b. Lord Gifford b. Henry L. Mansel b. Herbert Spencer b. Jas. H. Stirling b. *Comte de Volney d.*	*Sir Jos. Banks d. Thos. Brown d.* Sir John W. Dawson b. Wm. M. Rankine b. Isaac Todhunter b. John Tyndall b.	John Bartlett b. Wilhelm Corrsen b. Georg Curtius b. Jas. O. Halliwell-Phillips b. *Danl. A. Wyttenbach d.* Sir Henry Yule b.	Guillaume Augier b. Dion Boucicault b. Anne Brontë b. lice Cary b. rd Dekker b. *Jos. Rodman Drake d. Wm. Drennan d.* Lucretia P. Hale b. *Wm. Hayley d.* Jean Ingelow b. Ebenezer Jones b. Aleksei Pisemski b. Margaret Preston b. Henry J. Raymond b. Anna Sewell b. Henry Vizetelly b.	Giovanni Cavalcaselle b. Eugene Fromentin b. Joseph Mánes b. Sir John Tenniel b. *Benj. West d.*	Sir Geo. Grove b. Geo. F. Root b. Franz von Suppé b. Henri Vieuxtemps b.	Florence Nightingale b. *Arthur Thistlewood d.* Harriet Tubman b. Lester Wallack b.
1821	John C. Breckinridge b. Duc Jacques de Broglie b. *Caroline of Brunswick d. José Carrera d.* Bartolomé Mitre b. *Napoleon I (Bonaparte) d.* Sir Chas. Tupper b.	N. B. Forrest b. Wm. Hodson b. Jas. Longstreet b. *Comte de Maistre d.* J. B. Topete b.	Jay Cooke b. C. P. Huntington b. Leone Levi b. Baron de Reuter b. Wm. H. Vanderbilt b.	Sir Saml. White Baker b. Heinrich Barth b. Sir Richard F. Burton b. Chas. F. Hall b.	Mary Baker Eddy b. Cornelis Opzoomer b. Fredk. Temple b. Sir Geo. Williams b.	*Franz Achard d. Franz Brünnow d.* Arthur Cayley b. Pafnuti Chebyshëv b. Jas. Croll b. *James Gregory (Later) d.* Hermann von Helmholtz b. Félix Lacaze-Dutheirs b. Franz Leydig b. Amédée Mouchez b. Fritz Müller b. Rudolf Virchow b. Edward L. Youmans b.	Elizabeth Blackwell b. Henry Thos. Buckle b. Mariano Paz Soldan b. Edward H. Plumptre b. Wm. F. Poole b. August Schleicher b. Edward Thring b. Jas. H. Trumbull b. Richard Grant White b.	Henri F. Amiel b. Charles Baudelaire b. "Champfleury" b. Fyodor Dostoievsky b. Lady Duff-Gordon b. Pierre Dupont b. Octave Feuillet b. Gustave Flaubert b. *Marquis de Fontanes d.* Moritz Hartmann b. *Elizabeth Inchbald d. John Keats d.* Frank Leslie b. F. Locker-Lampson b. Nikolai Nekrasov b. *Isabel Pagan d. Hester Thrale Piozzi d.* Chas. Scribner b. *Graf C. zu Stolberg d.* Jan Van Beers b. G. J. Whyte-Melville b.	Hercules Brabazon b. Ford Madox Brown b. *John Crome d.* Chas. Meryon b. Sir Jos. Paton b.	*John W. Callcott d.* Pauline Viardot-Garcia b.	Clara Barton b. Mary A. Livermore b. Rachel b.
1822	*Lord Castlereagh d. Prinz von Hardenberg d.* Rutherford B. Hayes b. Sir Henry Maine b. Midhat Pasha b. *Wm. Pinkney d. Duc de Richelieu d.*	U. S. Grant b. John Nicholson b. John Pope b. Fitz-John Porter b. *John Stark d. Thos. Truxton d.*	*Thos. Coutts d.* Abram S. Hewitt b.		Jas. Hinton b. Albrecht Ritschl b.	*Claude de Berthollet d.* Rudolf Clausius b. *Jean Delambre d.* Sir Francis Galton b. Oliver W. Gibbs b. *René Haüy d. Sir Wm. Herschel d.* Karl Leuckart b. Gregor Mendel b. Jacob Moleschott b. Louis Pasteur b.	Heinrich Schliemann b. *Roch Sicard d.*	Wm. Taylor Adams b. *John Aikin d.* Matthew Arnold b. *Sir Alexander Boswell d.* Louis Bouilhet b. Frances P. Cobbe b. Maxime Du Camp b. Émile Erckmann b. Paolo Ferrari b. Edmond de Goncourt b. Edward Everett Hale b. *E.T.W. Hoffmann d.* Thos. Hughes b. Eliza Lynn Linton b. David Masson b. Donald G. Mitchell b. Henry Morley b. Henri Murger b. Jas. Parton b. Thos. B. Read b. *P. B. Shelley d.*	Rosa Bonheur b. *Antonio Canova d. Jas. Sowerby d.*	Luigi Arditi b. César Franck b. Joseph J. Raff b.	Fredk. L. Olmsted b. Adelaide Ristori b.

1823–1829 A.D.

Year A.D.	Government and Law	Military and Naval Affairs	Industry Commerce Economics Finance Invention Labor	Travel and Exploration	Philosophy and Religion	Science and Medicine	Education Scholarship History	Literature	Painting and Sculpture	Music	Miscellaneous
1823	Count Andrássy (Sr.) b. *Marco Bozzaris d.* Gustave Cluseret b. Schuyler Colfax b. *Lord Erskine d.* Li Hung-Chang b. *Jean Pache d.* John Sherman b. Wm. M. Tweed b.	*L. N. M. Carnot d.* *Edmund Cartwright d.* Antoine Chanzy b. *Chas. Dumouriez d.* *Sir Wm. Jervis d.* *Viscount Keith d.* Thos. F. Meagher b. John Newton b. *Earl of St. Vincent d.*	John E. Cairnes b. John K. Ingram b. *David Ricardo d.* Jas. E. T. Rogers b. Sir Wm. Siemens b.	*Giovanni Belzoni d.*	Pope Leo XII a. *Pope Pius VII d.* Ernest Renan b. John Tulloch b.	*Matthew Baillie d.* Spencer F. Baird b. *Wm. Bartram d.* Friedrich von Esmarch b. Jean Fabre b. John R. Hind b. *Edward Jenner d.* Jos. LeConte b. Jos. Leidy b. *Nathanael Pringsheim d.* Alfred Russel Wallace b.	Gaston Boissier b. Edward A. Freeman b. Augustus Jessopp b. Max Muller b. Francis Parkman b. Reinhold Pauli b. Goldwin Smith b.	Théodore de Banville b. *Robt. Bloomfield d.* Geo. H. Boker b. *Friedrich Brockhaus d.* Sylvanus Cobb, Jr. b. *Wm. Combe d.* Wm. Cory b. Geo. H. Derby b. *Heinrich von Gerstenberg d.* T. W. Higginson b. Henry O. Houghton b. Edward Judson b. Alexander Ostrovsky b. Coventry Patmore b. Sandor Petöfi b. *Ann Radcliffe d.* *Friedrich Werner d.* *Chas. Wolfe d.* Charlotte M. Yonge b.	Chas. S. Keene b. *Jos. Nollekens d.* Louis Prang b. *Pierre Prud'hon d.* *Sir Henry Raeburn d.*	Edouard Lalo b.	*John Philip Kemble d.*
1824	*Jean de Cambacérès d.* Charles X (France) a. *Ercole Consalvi d.* *Jean Drouet d.* *Augustin de Iturbide d.* Sir Geo. Jessel b. Leopold II (Tuscany) a. A. Lobanov-Rostovski b. *Louis XVIII (France) d.* *Chas. Pinckney d.* Lord Rosmead b.	*Eugène de Beauharnais d.* A. E. Burnside b. Winfield S. Hancock b. "Stonewall" Jackson b. Franz Sigel b. Edmund Kirby Smith b. Wm. Farrar Smith b. Sir Donald Stewart b. Wm. Walker b.	Leland Stanford b.	Wm. Baikie b.	*Richard Brothers d.* Ludwig Büchner b. Kuno Fischer b. *Baronesse von Krudener d.* Moritz Lazarus b. *François Maine de Biran d.* Chas. B. Waite b.	Paul Broca b. Benj. A. Gould b. Johann Hittorf b. Wilhelm Hofmeister b. Sir Wm. Huggins b. Pierre Janssen b. Lord Kelvin b. Gustav Kirchoff b. *Jas. Parkinson d.* Louis de Pourtalès b. Alexander Williamson b. Alexander Winchell b.	*John Lempriere d.* *Friedrich August Wolf d.*	Wm. Allingham b. *Lord Byron d.* Phoebe Cary b. Wilkie Collins b. Geo. Wm. Curtis b. Sydney Dobell b. Alexandre Dumas, Fils b. M. M. S. Dutt b. *Rhijnvis Feith d.* *Jos. Joubert d.* Lucy Larcom b. Chas. G. Leland b. Geo. Macdonald b. Edward Maitland b. *Chas. R. Maturin d.* Ivan Nikitin b. Francis T. Palgrave b. *Jane Taylor d.* A. D. T. Whitney b.	Richard Doyle b. *Théodore Géricault d.* J. L. Gérôme b. Wm. M. Hunt b. Josef Israëls b. P. Puvis de Chavannes b. J. Valera y Alcalá Galiano b.	Anton Bruckner b. Karl Reinecke b. Bedrich Smetana b.	Charles Blondin b. Charles Fechter b. Saml. Plimsoll b. Geo. E. Street b.
1825	*Alexander I (Russia) d.* *Ferdinand IV (Naples) d.* L. Q. C. Lamar b. Ludwig I (Bavaria) a. *Maximilian I (Bavaria) d.* Thos. D'Arcy McGee b. Nicholas I (Russia) a. Emile Ollivier b. *Chas. C. Pinckney d.* *Danl. D. Tompkins d.*	Paul Krüger b. *Thos. Macdonough d.* John H. Morgan b. Geo. E. Pickett b. *Conde diSantarosa d.* *Danl. Shays d.* Danl. E. Sickles b. *Jas. Wilkinson d.*	Ferdinand Lassalle b. D. O. Mills b. *Comte de Saint-Simon d.* *Eli Whitney d.* Chas. Worth b.	*Wm. Moorcraft d.*	Theodor Keim b. B. F. Westcott b.	Henry W. Bates b. Jean Charcot b. Sir Edward Frankland b. Thos. H. Huxley b. *Comte de Lacépède d.* Ferdinand von Müller b. *Johann Pfaff d.* Max Schultze b. Wm. Spottiswoode b.	Francis J. Child b. John Conington b. Fredk. J. Furnivall b. Henry C. Lea b. Francis A. March b. John E. B. Mayor b. Julius Oppert b. *Saml. Parr d.* Percy Strangford b. Wm. Stubbs b.	*Anna Letitia Barbauld d.* *Lady Anne Barnard d.* R. D. Blackmore b. Henri de Blowitz b. *Thos. Bowdler d.* *Paul Courier d.* Mary J. Holmes b. Maurus Jokai b. Annie Keary b. Julian Klaczko b. Conrad Meyer b. Adelaide A. Procter b. *Jean Paul Richter d.* Paul de Saint-Victor b. Jas. B. Stephens b. R. H. Stoddard b. Bayard Taylor b. *Mason L. Weems d.*	Adolphe Bouguereau b. *Jacques David d.* Birket Foster b. *Henry Fuseli d.* Geo. Inness b. Wm. H. Rinehart b. Thos. Woolner b.	*Antonio Salieri d.* Johann Strauss (Younger) b.	*Pierre L'Enfant d.* Ainsworth R. Spofford b.

Year A.D.	Government and Law	Military and Naval Affairs	Industry Commerce Economics Finance Invention Labor	Travel and Exploration	Philosophy and Religion	Science and Medicine	Education Scholarship History	Literature	Painting and Sculpture	Music	Miscellaneous
1826	John Adams d. François Boissy-d'Anglas d. Marquess of Dufferin b. Empress Eugènie b. Thos. Jefferson d. Earl of Kimberley b. Sir Thos. Raffles d. Léon Say b. Wm. H. Waddington b.	Marquess of Hastings d. John A. Logan b. Louis Suchet d.	Matilda J. Gage b. Wilhelm Liebknecht d.	Alexander G. Laing d.	Elme Caro b. Reginald Heber d. Friedrich Überweg b.	Adolf Bastian b. Johann Bode d. Geo. P. Bond b. Stanislas Cannizzaro b. Giovanni Donati b. Josef von Fraunhofer d. Karl Gegenbaur b. Rene Laennec d. Jedidiah Morse d. Giuseppi Piazzi d. Philippe Pinel d. Jos. L. Proust d. Georg Riemann b. Hans Thomsen b.	Edward Cowell b. Léopold V. Delisle b. Lindley Murray d. Wm. G. Palgrave b. Hormuzd Rassam b.	Walter Bagehot b. Jens Baggesen d. Saml. Bowles b. Camillo Castello Bronco b. Alexandre Chatrian b. Dinah Mulock Craik b. John W. DeForest b. Wm. Gifford d. Nikolai Karamzin d. Josef von Scheffel b. Johann Voss d.	Fredk. E. Church b. Thos. Faed b. John Flaxman d. John Kay d. Karl von Piloty b.	Stephen Foster b. Mathilde Marchesi b. Carl Maria von Weber d.	Anthelme Brillat–Savarin d. Laura Keene b. Jean Laffite d. J. F. Oberlin d. E. A. Sothern b. François Talma d.
1827	Dominico Azuni d. Geo. Canning d. Manuel da Fonseca b. Friedrich Augustus I (Saxony) d. Sir Wm. V. Harcourt b. Rufus King d. Lord Loch b. Count Reventlow d. Marquess of Ripon b. Duke Fredk. Augustus of York d.	Christian von Massenbach d. Geo. B. McClellan b. Henry W. Slocum b.	Duc de Larochefoucauld-Liancourt d.	John H. Speke b.	Johann Eichhorn d. Edward B. Foote b. Chas. Loyson b.	Sir Fredk. Abel b. Marcellin Berthelot b. Friedrich Chladni d. Augustin Fresnel d. Marquis de Laplace d. Lord Lister b. St. George J. Mivart b. Alessandro Volta d.	Wm. Bleek b. Heinrich Brugsch b. Emily Howland b. Chas. Eliot Norton b. Johann Pestalozzi d. Wm. Rolfe b. Pasquale Villari b. Wm. Dwight Whitney b.	Ethel Lynn Beers b. Wm. Blake d. Archibald Constable d. Rose Terry Cooke b. Chas. de Coster b. Ugo Foscolo d. Jas. Hannay b. Wilhelm Hauff d. Geo. A. Lawrence b. Robt. Pollok d. "Mikhail Saltykov" b. Francisque Sarcey b. J. T. Trowbridge b. St. George Tucker d. Christian Vulpius d. Lew Wallace b.	José Alvarez d. Arnold Boecklin b. Jules Breton b. Jean Carpeaux b. Holman Hunt b. Chas. W. Peale d. Thos. Rowlandson d.	Ludwig van Beethoven d.	
1828	Thos. F. Bayard b. DeWitt Clinton d. Luke Hansard d. Giovanni Nicotera b.	Jacob D. Cox b. Jas. B. McPherson b. Mikhail Tchernaiev b. Prince Ypsilanti d.	Chas. H. Cramp b. John T. W. Mitchell b. Sir Jos. Swan b. David A. Wells b.		Abraham Kuenen b. F. A. Lange b. Dugald Stewart d.	Sir John Burdon–Sanderson b. Alexander R. Clarke b. Ferdinand Cohn b. Franz J. Gall d. Sir Benj. W. Richardson b. Balfour Stewart b. Karl P. Thunberg d. Wm. Hyde Wollaston d.	Pierre Lanfrey b. Gúdbrandr Vígfússon b.	Edmond About b. Nikolai Chernyshevski b. Martha F. Finley b. Alexander Gilchrist b. Anne Gilchrist b. Henrik Ibsen b. Gerald Massey b. Geo. Meredith b. Fitz-James O'Brien b. Margaret Oliphant b. Saml. Randall b. D. G. Rossetti b. A. V. Rydberg b. Geo. Augustus Sala b. Hippolyte Taine b. Geo. Thornbury b. Count Leo Tolstoy b. Jules Verne b. Wm. G. Wills b.	Paul Baudry b. Richard Bonington d. Élie Delaunay b. Francisco Goya d. J. A. Houdon d. Alfred Stevens (Painter) b. Wm. J. Stillman b. Gilbert Stuart d. Leonard W. Volk b.	Franz Peter Schubert d.	Theodore De Vinne b. Lady Caroline Lamb d. Andrew J. Still b.
1829	Lord Ampthill b. Comte de Barras d. Roscoe Conkling b. Geronimo b. B. A. Guzmán b. John Jay d. Eduard Lasker b. Johann von Miguel b. Timothy Pickering d. Carl Schurz b. Sir Jas. F. Stephen b. Marchese di Visconti-Venosta b.		Hinton R. Helper b.	Auguste Chouteau d.	Edward W. Benson b. Wm. Booth b. Pope Leo XII d. Henry P. Liddon b. Friedrich von Schlegel d.	Niels Henrik Abel d. Alfred Brehm b. Moritz Cantor b. Sir Humphry Davy d. Asaph Hall b. Friedrich Kekule b. Simon Schwendener b. Jas. Smithson d. Chas. W. Tuttle b. Louis Vauquelin d. Chas. Wachsmuth b. Thos. Young d.	Immanuel Deutsch b. Josef Dobrovsky d. Saml. R. Gardiner b. Jean de Lamarck d.	Geo. W. Childs b. Jane Croly b. Alexander Griboyedov d. S. Weir Mitchell b. Laurence Oliphant b. L. Prévost-Paradol b. W. M. Rossetti b. Henry Timrod b. Chas. Dudley Warner b.	Anselm Feuerbach b. Ludwig Knaus b. Sir John E. Millais b.	Louis Gottschalk b.	Laura Bridgman b. Wm. Burke d. Jos. Jefferson b. Thos. W. Robertson b. Tomasso Salvini b. Roger Tichborne b. Geo. Francis Train b.

1830–1835 A.D.

Year A.D.	Government and Law	Military and Naval Affairs	Industry Commerce Economics Finance Invention Labor	Travel and Exploration	Philosophy and Religion	Science and Medicine	Education Scholarship History	Literature	Painting and Sculpture	Music	Miscellaneous
1830	Chester A. Arthur b. Jas. G. Blaine b. *Simón Bolívar d.* Charles X (France) abd. *H. B. Constant de Rebecque d.* Porfirio Díaz b. *George IV (England) d.* *Wm. Huskisson d.* Louis Philippe (France) a. *Red Jacket d.* Marquis de Rochefort b. Marquess of Salisbury b. Kálmán Tisza b. William IV (England) a. Zobeir Rahama b.	O. O. Howard b. *Marquis de Saint-Cyr d.* *Antonio de Sucre d.* Gouverneur K. Warren b. *Graf von Yorck von Wartenburg d.*	Louise Michel b. *Wm. Murdock d.*	Sir Clements Markham b.	Henry Calderwood b. *Elias Hicks d.* Richard Lipsius b. Cornelis Tiele b. *Adam Weishaupt d.*	Abraham Jacobi b. *Ephraim McDowell d.* Julius L. Meyer b. Francois Raoult b. Jean J. Réclus b. *Saml. Sömmering d.* Sir Chas. W. Thomson b.	Numa Fustel de Coulanges b. *Henry Rutgers d.*	Thos. E. Brown b. John Esten Cooke b. João deDeus b. Emily Dickinson b. Marie von Ebner-Eschenbach b. *Mme. de Genlis d.* Jules de Goncourt b. Fredk. Greenwood b. Robt. Hamerling b. "Marion Harland" b. Paul H. Hayne b. *Wm. Hazlitt d.* Paul Heyse b. Helen Hunt Jackson b. Henry Kingsley b. *Károly Kisfaludy d.* Justin M'Carthy b. Frédéric Mistral b. Jas. Payn b. Christina Rossetti b. Alexander Smith b. *Johann Wyss d.*	Harriet Hosmer b. *Sir Thos. Lawrence d.* Lord Leighton b. John Q. A. Ward b.	Hans von Bülow b. Theodor Leschetizsky b. Ede Reményi b. Anton Rubinstein b.	Fanny Janauschek b. Belva Lockwood b. Alfred Waterhouse b.
1831	*Conde de Capo d'Istria d.* Graf von Caprivi de Capreda b. Carlo Alberto (Sardinia) a. Jos. Cowen b. Jas. A. Garfield b. Viscount Goschen b. *Henri Grégoire d.* Leopold I (Belgium) a. *Jas. Monroe d.* Pedro II (Brazil) a. *Baron vom und zu Stein d.* Heinrich von Stephan b.	*Karl von Clausewitz d.* Philip Colomb b. *Graf von Gneisenau d.* John B. Hood b. Sir Andrew Noble b. John M. Schofield b. Philip Sheridan b.	Geo. M. Pullman b. Wm. Whiteley b.	Paul Du Chaillu b.	Hiram Bingham, Jr. b. Helena Blavatsky b. Fredk. W. Farrar b. Pope Gregory XVI a. *G. W. F. Hegel d.* *Ismail Hadji Maulvi-Mohammed d.*	*John Abernethy d.* Heinrich de Bary b. Vandyke Carter b. O. C. Marsh b. Jas. Clerk Maxwell b. *J. L. Pons d.* Edward Routh b. Edward J. Stone b. Eduard Suess b. Peter G. Tait b.	B. L. Gildersleeve b. D. C. Gilman b. E. L. Godkin b. *Berthold Niebuhr d.* Justin Winsor b. *Sir Nathaniel Wraxall d.* Aldis Wright b.	Amelia E. Barr b. *Willem Bilderdijk d.* C. S. Calverley b. Rebecca Harding Davis b. Ignatius Donnelly b. Frederic Harrison b. *Friedrich von Klinger d.* Henry Labouchère b. Nikolai Leskov b. *Jose Macedo d.* *Henry Mackenzie d.* "Owen Meredith" b. *Wm. Roscoe d.* Franklin B. Sanborn b. Victorien Sardou b. *Isaiah Thomas d.* *John Trumbull d.* Wm. Hale White b. Edmund Yates b.	*Thos. Hope d.* Sho-Fu Kyōsai b. Constantin Meunier b. Albert J. Moore b. Camille Pissarro b.	Jos. Joachim b. *Ignatz Pleyel d.*	*Harmon Blennerhasset d.* Wm. J. Florence b. *Stephen Girard d.* Baron de Hirsch b. Richard N. Shaw b. *Sarah Siddons d.* *Nat Turner d.*
1832	*Chas. Carroll d.* Emilio Castelar b. Jos. H. Choate b. Lord Courtney b. Sir Jas. R. Dickson b. Jules Ferry b. *Friedrich von Gentz d.* *Graf von Haugwitz d.* *Sir Jas. Mackintosh d.* Otto (Greece) a. *Casimir Perier d.* *Duc de Reichstadt d.* Lord Russell of Killowen b.	John B. Gordon b. Osman Pasha b. Earl Roberts b. *Thos. Sumter d.*	*Jeremy Bentham d.* *Marquis de Jouffroy-d'Abbans d.* *J. B. Say d.*	Isaac I. Hayes b. Baron Nordenskjöld b. Karl Semper b. Armin Vambery b.	Moncure D. Conway b. Thos. Fowler b. *Karl Krause d.* Sir Leslie Stephen b. Thos. D. Talmage b. Herbert Vaughan b.	*Nicolas Carnot d.* *Jean Champollion d.* *Jean Chaptal d.* Sir Wm. Crookes b. *Baron de Cuvier d.* Gustav Jäger b. Karl R. König b. *Sir John Leslie d.* Karl Rudolphi d. Julius von Sachs b. *Antonio Scarpa d.* Sir Edward B. Tylor b. Andrew D. White b. Wilhelm Wundt b.	H. H. Bancroft b. *Andrew Bell d.* Theodor Gomperz b. John G. Nicolay b. *Rasmus Rask d.* *Jean P. Remusat d.* John H. Vincent b.	Louisa M. Alcott b. Horatio Alger b. Sir Edwin Arnold b. *Mary Berry d.* Bjornsterne Björnson b. Stopford A. Brooke b. "Lewis Carroll" b. *Geo. Crabbe d.* A. G. Droz b. José Echegaray b. *Philip Freneau d.* *J. W. von Goethe d.* G. A. Henty b. G. Nuñez de Arce b. *Sir Walter Scott d.* Mortimer Thomson b. Jules Vallés b. Theodore Watts-Dunton b.	Édouard Manet b. Sir Wm. Orchardson b.	*Muzio Clementi d.* Leopold Damrosch b. *Manuel García d.* Karl Goldmark b.	Chas. Peace b. *Johann Spurzheim d.*

Year A.D.	Government and Law	Military and Naval Affairs	Industry Commerce Economics Finance Invention Labor	Travel and Exploration	Philosophy and Religion	Science and Medicine	Education Scholarship History	Literature	Painting and Sculpture	Music	Miscellaneous
1833	8th Duke of Devonshire b. *Ferdinand VII (Spain) d.* *Paul von Feuerbach d.* Benj. Harrison b. Wayne Macveagh b. Mohammed Ali (Egypt) a. Thos. C. Platt b. M.S. Quay b. *John Randolph d.* Graf von Taafe b.	*Wm. Bainbridge d.* *Viscount Exmouth d.* *Lord Gambier d.* Chas. G. Gordon b. *J. B. Jourdan d.* Stephen D. Lee b. John S. Mosby b. *Jean Savary d.* Graf von Schlieffen b. J. E. B. Stuart b. *Sir Banistre Tarleton d.* Viscount Wolseley b.	Eugen Dühring b. Henry Fawcett b. *Friedrich König d.* Jas. Redpath b. *Richard Trevithick d.*		Chas. Bradlaugh b. *Rowland Hill d.* Robt. G. Ingersoll b. *Ram Mohan Roy d.*	*Pierre Latrielle d.* *Adrien Legendre d.* Stephen Perry b. Baron von Richthofen b. Sir Henry E. Roscoe b.	*Rawdon Brown d.* Sophus Bugge b. Richard Watson Dixon b. H. H. Furness b. Fredk. Seebohm b.	*Dominique Garat d.* Adam Lindsay Gordon b. *Arthur H. Hallam d.* Jonas Lie b. David R. Locke b. *Hannah More d.* Sir Lewis Morris b. John Nichol b. *John O'Keeffe d.* Ricardo Palma b. José de Pereda b. Edmund C. Stedman b. André Theuriet b. *Rahel Varnhagen von Ense d.*	E. Burne-Jones b. *P. G. Doré b.* *Raphael Morghen d.* Félicien Rops b.	Johannes Brahms b.	Edwin Booth b. *Marchese di Cagnola d.* *Kaspar Hauser d.* D. D. Home b. *Edmund Kean d.* Denman Thompson b. *Wm. Wilberforce d.*
1834	*Louis de Bourrienne d.* *Duc de Champagny d.* *Wm. H. Crawford d.* Chauncey M. Depew b. *Edmond Genêt d.* *Lord Grenville d.* *Marquis de Lafayette d.* *Wm. Wirt d.*	*Comte de Dessaix d.*	*Rudolf Ackermann d.* Marshall Field b. Hetty Green b. *Jos. Jacquard d.* Alfred Nobel b. *Alois Senfelder d.*	Richard Lander d. Gustav Nachtigal b. Wm. J. Wills b.	Cardinal Gibbons b. *Edward Irving d.* *Robt. Morrison d.* *Friedrich Schleiermacher d.* Chas. H. Spurgeon d. Thaddeus B. Wakeman b.	Sir Arthur Church b. Ernst Haeckel b. Jas. Hargreaves b. Rudolf Heidenhain b. Saml. P. Langley b. *Thos. Malthus d.* Dmitri Mendeléyev b. John W. Powell b. Georg H. Quincke b. Alexander Rollett b. *Thos. Say d.* Hermann Sprengel b. August Weismann b. Chas. A. Young b.	Lord Acton b. Chas. W. Eliot b. Robinson Ellis b. Heinrich von Treitschke b.	*Antoine-Vincent Arnault d.* Sabine Baring-Gould b. *Wm. Blackwood d.* Chas. Farrar Browne b. H. J. Byron b. *Alexander Chalmers d.* *S. T. Coleridge d.* Geo. Du Maurier b. Ludovic Halévy b. Augustus Hare b. *Chas. Lamb d.* Sir John Lubbock b. Wm. Morris b. Roden Noel b. *Thos. Pringle d.* Richard Realf b. Sir John Seeley b. J. Henry Shorthouse b. Frank R. Stockton b. Jas. Thomson ("B. V.") b.	Frédéric Bartholdi b. Sir Joseph Boehm b. *Conde di Cicognara d.* Edgar Degas b. *Thos. Stothard d.* Jas. A. M. Whistler b.	*François Boieldieu d.* Alexander Borodin b. Sir Chas. Santley b.	*John St. John Long d.*
1835	*Graf Christian von Bernstorff d.* Eugène Brisson b. Ferdinand I (Austria) a. Sir John E. Gorst b. Sir Thomas E. Holland b. Marquis Inouye b. *John Marshall d.* Prince Matsukata b. Richard Olney b. T. Estrada Palma b. Riaz Pasha b. Sir Julius Vogel b.	Fitzhugh Lee b. Wm. R. Shafter b. Sir Geo. S. White b.	Andrew Carnegie b. *Wm. Cobbett d.* Wm. S. Jevons b. *Comte de Roederer d.* *Sir John Sinclair d.*		Lyman Abbott b. Phillips Brooks b. Edward Caird b. Wm. T. Harris b. Alfred Weber b.	Johann von Baeyer b. Eugenio Beltrami b. Rudolf Fittig b. Sir Archibald Geikie b. Victor Hensen b. Simon Newcomb b. Louis Ranvier b. Giovanni Schiaparelli b. Johannes Wislicenus b.	Chas. K. Adams b. *Karl Böttiger d.* Geo. B. Hill b. *Wilhelm von Humboldt d.* W. W. Skeat b. *Thos. Taylor d.* Moses Coit Tyler b.	Alfred Austin b. Saml. Butler b. Giosuè Carducci b. Lord DeTabley b. Émile Gaboriau b. Richard Garnett b. *Felicia D. Hemans d.* *Jas. Hogg d.* Tom Hood b. Adah Isaacs Menken b. *Wm. Motherwell d.* Louise C. Moulton b. L. Sacher-Masoch b. Harriet E. Spofford b. "Mark Twain" b. Henry Villard b. Augusta E. Wilson b.	Jean Desbrosses b. *Baron de Gros d.* John LaFarge b. *Carle Vernet d.*	*Vincenzo Bellini d.* César Cui b. Modest Mussorgsky b. Nicholas Rubinstein b. Camille Saint-Saëns b. Theodore Thomas b. Henri Wieniawski b.	*Henry Hunt d.* *Wm. H. Ireland d.* *Chas. Mathews d.*

1836–1841 A.D.

Year A.D.	Government and Law	Military and Naval Affairs	Industry Commerce Economics Finance Invention Labor	Travel and Exploration	Philosophy and Religion	Science and Medicine	Education Scholarship History	Literature	Painting and Sculpture	Music	Miscellaneous
1836	Russell A. Alger b. *Aaron Burr d.* Sir Henry Campbell-Bannerman b. Jos. G. Cannon b. Jos. Chamberlain b. Lyman J. Gage b. *Edward Livingston d.* Cesare Lombroso b. *Jas. Madison d.* *Comte de Sieyès d.* *Lord Stowell d.*	*Lord de Saumarez d.* *John L. McAdam d.* Jos. Wheeler b.	Jay Gould b. *John L. McAdam d.*	*Stephen Austin d.* *Jas. Bowie d.* *David Crockett d.* Georg Schweinfurth b.	John Clifford b. Washington Gladden b. Thos. Hill Green b. Frances R. Havergal b. Chas. A. Watts b.	*André Ampère d.* *A. L. de Jussieu d.* Sir Norman Lockyer b. Henry Maudsley b. *John Pond d.*	Elizabeth Garrett Anderson b. *Jas. Mill d.* *François Raynouard d.* *Wm. Taylor d.*	Juliette Adam b. Henry M. Alden b. Thos. Bailey Aldrich b. Sir Walter Besant b. Sir Francis Burnand b. Sir W.S. Gilbert b. *Wm. Godwin d.* Bret Harte b. Marietta Holley b. Robt. H. Newell b. *C. Rouget de Lisle d.* *Marquise de Souza-Botelho d.* *Karl Tauchnitz d.* Celia Thaxter b. Wm. Winter b.	Sir Laurence Alma-Tadema b. Henri Fantin-Latour b. Winslow Homer b. Franz von Lenbach b. Homer D. Martin b. Alphonse de Neuville b. Sir Edward Poynter b. J. J. Tissot b. Alexander H. Wyant b.	Léo Delibes b. *Maria Malibran d.* E. Parepa-Rosa b.	*Geo. Colman (Younger) d.* Stuart Robson b. *Betsy Ross d.* Russell Sturgis b.
1837	Georges Boulanger b. Sadi Carnot b. Grover Cleveland b. M. A. Hanna b. Lord Herschell b. Friedrich von Holstein b. Count Itagaki b. *Nathaniel Macon d.* Whitelaw Reid b. Earl of St. Aldwyn b. Sitting Bull b. Prince Tokugawa b. Victoria (England) a. *William IV (England) d.*	Geo. Dewey b. *Sir Fredk. Ponsonby d.*	*Ludwig Börne d.* *François Fourier d.* J.P. Morgan, Sr. b.		Dwight L. Moody b. Alexander Whyte b.	John Burroughs b. Sir Wm. Dawkins b. Edward Divers b. W. W. Keen b. Willy Kühne b. Richard A. Proctor b. Johannes van der Waals b.	*Carlo Botta d.* *Henry T. Colebrooke d.* John R. Green b. François Lenormant b. Sir Jas. A. Murray b.	Alfred Ainger b. M. E. Braddon b. Oscar Browning b. *Georg Büchner d.* *Ivan Dmitriev d.* Georg Ebers b. Edward Eggleston b. *Thos. G. Fessenden d.* W. D. Howells b. Jorge Isaacs b. *Mariano de Larra d.* *Giacomo Leopardi d.* *Robt. Nicoll d.* Harrison G. Otis b. *Alexander Pushkin d.* Lady Ritchie b. Algernon Swinburne b.	Carolus-Duran b. *John Constable d.* *Baron de Gerard d.* Alphonse Legros b. Jacob Maris b.	Mily Balakirev b. François Dubois b. *John Field d.* *Johann Hummel d.* Benj. J. Lang b. *Jean Le Sueur d.* Cosima Wagner b. *Saml. Wesley d.* *Niccolo Zingarelli d.*	*Maria Fitzherbert d.* *Joseph Grimaldi d.* *Elijah Lovejoy d.* John McCullough b. Sir Chas. Wyndham b.
1838	*Black Hawk d.* *Earl of Eldon d.* Léon Gambetta b. John Hay b. Marquis Okuma b. *Osceola d.* Sir Sidney Shippard b. *Chas. de Talleyrand-Périgord d.*	*John Rodgers d.* Valeriano Weyler b. Sir Henry Wood b. Prince Yamagata b.	*John Stevens d.* John Wanamaker b. Graf von Zeppelin b.	*Wm. Clark d.* Karl Weyprecht b.	Julius A. Dresser b. Kesheb Chunder Sen b. *Johann Möhler d.* Saml. P. Putnam b. Henry Sidgwick b.	Cleveland Abbe b. *Nathaniel Bowditch d.* *Pierre Dulong d.* Alpheus Hyatt b. Camille Jordan b. Ernst Mach b. John Muir b. Sir Wm. H. Perkin b. Jacob Solis-Cohen b. Julius Wiesner b.	Henry Adams b. Viscount Bryce b. *Thos. Creevy d.* *Jos. Lancaster d.* W. E. H. Lecky b. Thos. R. Lounsbury b. Winwood Reade b. *Baron de Sacy d.* Sir Geo. Otto Trevelyan b.	*Adelbert von Chamisso d.* Mary Mapes Dodge b. Benj. L. Farjeon b. *Anne Grant d.* David Gray b. *Letitia E. Landon d.* Viscount Morley b. E. P. Roe b. Abram J. Ryan b. Margaret E. Sangster b. Horace E. Scudder b. F. Hopkinson Smith b. Albion W. Tourgée b. Villiers de l'Isle Adam b.	Jules Dalou b. Eduard von Gebhardt b. Anton Mauve b. Edward V. Valentine b.	Georges Bizet b. Max Bruch b. Edouard Colonne b.	Lawrence Barrett b. John Wilkes Booth b. Augustin Daly b. Chas. Forepaugh b. Octavia Hill b. Sir Henry Irving b. Henry H. Richardson b. Lord Rowton b. Victoria Woodhull b.

Year A.D.	Government and Law	Military and Naval Affairs	Industry Commerce Economics Finance Invention Labor	Travel and Exploration	Philosophy and Religion	Science and Medicine	Education Scholarship History	Literature	Painting and Sculpture	Music	Miscellaneous
1839	Abdul Mejid (Turkey) a. Christian VIII (Denmark) a. Mahmud II (Turkey) d. Ranjit Singh d. Thos. B. Reed b. Marchese di Rudini b. Count Speransky d. Stephen Van Rensselaer d.	Sir Redvers Buller b. Pascual Cervera b. Geo. A. Custer b. Sir Thos M. Hardy d. John McAnerney b. Nelson A. Miles b. Winfield S. Schley b.	Simon Bernard d. Henry George b. John D. Rockefeller, Sr. b. Benj. Waugh b.	René Caillé d. François Garnier b. Nikolai Prjevalsky b. Lady Hester Stanhope d. Alexandrine Tinné b.	Joseph Fesch d. Otto Pfleiderer b. John Williams d.	Julius Cohnheim b. Jas. Geikie b. Josiah W. Gibbs b. August Kundt b. Ludwig Mond b. Chas. S. Peirce b. Théodule Ribot b. Wm. Smith d.	Saml. C. Armstrong b. Sir John P. Mahaffy b. Gaston Paris b. Sir Spencer Walpole b.	Thos. H. Bayly d. Mathew Carey d. Wm. De Morgan b. John Galt d. Maurice de Guerin d. Jas. A. Herne b. Chas. Lloyd d. Joaquin Miller b. Mary L. Molesworth b. Karl A. Nicander d. "Ouida" b. Walter Pater b. W. M. Praed d. Jas. R. Randall b. Jas. Smith d. R. Sully-Prudhomme b.	Sir Wm. Beechey d. Paul Cézanne b.	Dudley Buck b. Antônio Gomes b. John K. Paine b.	Edmund Lodge d. Frances E. Willard b.
1840	Lucien Bonaparte d. Empress Carlotta b. Pierre Daunou d. Earl of Durham d. José Francia d. Friedrich Wilhelm III (Prussia) d. Friedrich Wilhelm IV (Prussia) a. Anton Thibault d. Édouard Vaillant b. Hugh Lawson White d. Willem I (Holland) abd. Willem II (Holland) a.	Piet Cronjé b. Alexandre Macdonald d. Alfred T. Mahan b. Wm. T. Sampson b. Sir Wm. Sidney Smith d.	August Bebel b. Thos. Cooper d. Sir Hiram Maxim b. Wm. Graham Sumner b. Carroll D. Wright b.	Eduard Schnitzer b. Edward Whymper b.	Father Damien b. Demetrius Gallitzin d. Fredk. L. Hosmer b. Richard Heber Newton b. Ira D. Sankey b.	Sir Robt. S. Ball b. Johann Blumenbach d. Edward D. Cope b. Anton Dohrn b. Jean Esquirol d. Alexander Goette b. Friedrich Kohlrausch b. Aleksandr Kovalevski b. Baron von Krafft—Ebing b. Gustave LeBon b. Heinrich Olbers d. S.—D. Poisson d. Constantine Rafinesque d.	Jeremiah Curtin b. Thos. Davidson b. Conte de Gubernatis b. J.J. Jacotot d. Sophia Jex-Blake b. Edward H. Palmer b. John C. Ridpath b. Geo. Smith b. Francis A. Walker b.	Wilfrid S. Blunt b. Rhoda Broughton b. Fanny Burney d. Rosa N. Carey b. Jules Clarétie b. Alphonse Daudet b. Austin Dobson b. Karl Follen d. Gerald Griffin d. Thos. Hardy b. Karl Immermann d. Rossiter Johnson b. N. Lemercier d. Marilla M. Ricker b. John A. Symonds b. Giovanni Verga b. Henry Watterson b. Richard Whiteing b. Émile Zola b.	Palmer Cox b. Thos. Hovenden b. Hans Makart b. Claude Monet b. Alexander Nasmyth d. Thos. Nast b. Auguste Rodin b. Alfred Sisley b. John Thomson d. J. G. Vibert b. Fredk. Walker b.	Franz Haberl b. Nicoló Paganini d. Peter Tschaikovsky b.	Beau Brummell d. Zerah Colburn d. Helena Modjeska b.
1841	Bertrand Barère de Vieuzac d. F. F. Faure b. Wm. Henry Harrison d. Oliver Wendell Holmes, Jr. b. Marquis Ito b. Sir Wilfrid Laurier b. Luigi Luzzatti b.	Lord John Fisher b. Claude Victor-Perrin d.	Benjamin Franklin Goodrich b. Lester F. Ward b.	Sir Henry M. Stanley b.	Franz Baader d. Thos. K. Cheyne b. J. F. Herbart d. Minot J. Savage b.	Jean Audouin d. Chas. Badham d. Augustin de Candolle d. Sir Astley Cooper d. Ignaz Döllinger d. Geo. Green d. John X. Merriman b. Eugen Warming b.	Sir Richard C. Jebb b. Hermann Von Holst b.	Isabella Alden b. Thos. Barnes d. Jacques Bertrand d. Wm. Black b. Mathilde Blind b. Sarah K. Bolton b. Robt. Buchanan b. Willis Gaylord Clark d. Thos. J. Dibdin d. Juliana H. Ewing b. Theodore Hook d. W. H. Hudson b. Mikhail Lermontov d. Catulle Mendès b. Clement Scott b. Edward R. Sill b. Eugene F. Ware b. Jos. Blanco White d.	Sir Francis Chantrey d. Johann von Dannecker d. Berthe Morisot b. Sir Geo. Reid b. P. A. Renoir b. Emily Sartain b. Sir David Wilkie d.	Alexis Chabrier b. Anton Dvořák b. Giovanni Sgambati b.	George Birkbeck d. Chas. F. Coghlan b. Benoît Coquelin b. Jean Mounet-Sully b.

1842–1845 A.D.

Year A.D.	Government and Law	Military and Naval Affairs	Industry Commerce Economics Finance Invention Labor	Travel and Exploration	Philosophy and Religion	Science and Medicine	Education Scholarship History	Literature	Painting and Sculpture	Music	Miscellaneous
1842	Giovanni Giolitti b. *Comte de Las Cases d.* *Bernardo O'Higgins d.* *Conde di Pozzo di Borgo d.* *Robt. Smith d.* *Marquess of Wellesley d.*	*Comte de Clausel d.* *Viscount Hill d.*	Millicent G. Fawcett b. Henry M. Hyndman b. Prince Kropotkin b. A. Leroy-Beaulieu b. John H. Logan b. Alfred Marshall b. M. G. Ranade b.	*Jules Dumont D'Urville d.*	Wm. E. Channing (Elder) d. John Fiske b. Eduard von Hartmann b. Wm. James b. *Théodore Jouffroy d.* Geo. Croom Robertson b. Augusta E. Stetson b.	*Sir Chas. Bell d.* Agnes M. Clerke b. Elliott Coues b. Sir Jas. Dewar b. Camille Flammarion b. Emil Hansen b. Mary Putnam Jacobi b. Clarence King b. Nicolaus Kleinenberg b. Geo. T. Ladd b. *Baron de Larrey d.* Marius Lie b. *Pierre Pelletier d.* August Rauber b. Lord Rayleigh b. Alphonse Renard b. Gustaf Retzius b. Sir Wm. Tilden b.	Thos. Arnold d. *Alexander Csoma de Körös d.* Ernest Lavisse b. *Jean de Sismondi d.* Albert Sorel b.	John Banim d. Ambrose Bierce b. *Jean Bouilly d.* Georg Brandes b. *Clemens Brentano d.* Ina Coolbrith b. François Coppée b. Gergely Csiky b. *Allan Cunningham d.* *José de Espronceda d.* John Habberton b. Alfred Hennequin b. Jose de Heredia b. *Wm. Hone d.* *Jos. Hopkinson d.* Bronson Howard b. Sidney Lanier b. *Wm. Maginn d.* Stephane Mallarmé b. Anthero de Quental b. *"Stendhal" d.* Henry D. Traill b. Jos. Widmann b. *Saml. Woodworth d.*	John S. Cotman d. Paul Rajon b. Vassili Vereshchagin b. *Mme. Vigée-Lebrun d.*	Arrigo Boïto b. *Luigi Cherubini d.* Clara L. Kellogg b. Jules Massenet b. Carl Rosa b. Sir Arthur Sullivan b.	*Grace Darling d.* Steele Mackaye b. Henry M. Taylor b. Edward Tuck b.
1843	Teófilo Braga b. Dhuleep Singh (Lahore) a. Sir Chas. W. Dilke b. Yves Guyot b. Isabella II (Spain) a. Jean de Lanessan b. *Hugh S. Legaré d.* Wm. McKinley b. *Sequoya d.* *K. Zachariae von Lingenthal d.*	*John Armstrong d.* Colmar von der Goltz b. *Baron Lynedoch d.* Mohammed Ahmed b. *David Porter d.* Mikhail Skobelev b.	P. Leroy-Beaulieu b. Gabriel Tarde b.	Chas. M. Doughty b.	*Richard Carlile d.* *Jakob Fries d.* F. W. H. Myers b. Wm. Sanday b. Jas. Ward b.	Richard Avenarius b. T. C. Chamberlin b. Theodor Eimer b. Theodor Engelmann b. Sir David Ferrier b. Walther Flemming b. *Saml. C. F. Hahnemann d.* Robt. Koch b.	Evelyn Abbott b. Mandell Creighton b. Wm. E. Griffis b. *Noah Webster d.*	"Carmen Sylva" b. *Jean Delavigne d.* Edward Dowden b. "Violet Fane" b. *John Foster d.* *Baron de la Motte Fouqué d.* Mrs. Burton Harrison b. *Friedrich Hölderlin d.* Laurence Hutton b. Henry James, Jr. b. *Francis Scott Key d.* *John Murray d.* Benito Pérez Galdós b. Jas. Rice b. *Robt. Southey d.* Chas. W. Stoddard b. Baronesse von Suttner b.	*Washington Allston d.* Hugo Salmson b. *John Trumbull d.* Chas. Van der Steppen b.	Edvard Grieg b. Christine Nilsson b. Adelina Patti b. Hans Richter b.	*Chas. J. Apperley d.*

Year A.D.	Government and Law	Military and Naval Affairs	Industry Commerce Economics Finance Invention Labor	Travel and Exploration	Philosophy and Religion	Science and Medicine	Education Scholarship History	Literature	Painting and Sculpture	Music	Miscellaneous
1844	*Joseph Bonaparte d.* *Sir Francis Burdett d.* *Charles XIV (Sweden) d.* Delphin M. Delmas b. Sanford B. Dole b. *Ernst I (Saxe-Coburg-Gotha) d.* Louis Riel b. *Viscount Sidmouth d.*	*Comte d'Erlon d.* *Sir Hudson Lowe d.*	Catherine Breshkovsky b. *Jacques Laffitte d.*	Geo. W. DeLong b. *Basil Hall d.* Noah Hayes b.	*John Abercrombie d.* Brother Joseph b. Friedrich Nietzsche b. *Edmund Rice d.* *Joseph Smith d.* *Robt. Taylor d.*	*Francis Baily d.* Ludwig Boltzmann b. *John Dalton d.* *E. Geoffroy Saint-Hilaire d.* Camillo Golgi b. *Karl Kielmeyer d.* Eduard Strasburger b.	Theodore W. Hunt b.	*Wm. Beckford d.* Robt. Bridges b. Geo. W. Cable b. *Lady Callcott d.* *Thos. Campbell d.* Edward Carpenter b. *Henry F. Cary d.* *Karl F. Dahlgren d.* Anatole France b. R. W. Gilder b. *Jónas Hallgrímsson d.* Gerard Manley Hopkins b. *Sándor Kisfaludy d.* *Ivan Krylov d.* Andrew Lang b. Baron von Liliencron b. *Charles Nodier d.* John Boyle O'Reilly b. Arthur O'Shaughnessy b. W. Stewart Ross b. Wm. Clark Russell b. "Margaret Sidney" b. *John Sterling d.* Paul Verlaine b. Elizabeth S. P. Ward b.	Thos. Eakins b. Moses J. Ezekiel b. Sir Luke Fildes b. Mihály von Munkácsy b. Henri Rousseau b. Edward L. Sambourne b. *Bertel Thorwaldsen d.*	*Henri Berton d.* Nikolai Rimsky-Korsakov b. Pablo de Sarasate b. Charles Widor b.	Sarah Bernhardt b. *Chas. Bulfinch d.* Richard D'Oyly Carte b. Anthony Comstock b. Karl Hagenbeck b.
1845	*Earl Charles Grey d.* Jan H. Hofmeyr b. *Andrew Jackson d.* Marquess (Chas.) Lansdowne b. Frédéric de Martens b. Earl of Minto b. Count Muraviev b. Elihu Root b. *Joseph Story d.*	Arthur MacArthur b. *Sir Robt. Sale d.* Chas. D. Sigsbee b.	Jules Guesde b. Theodore N. Vail b.		W. K. Clifford b. *P. Royer-Collard d.* *Henrik Steffens d.*	*Sir W. H. M. Christie b.* *John F. Daniell d.* Sir Geo. Darwin b. Hermann Fol b. Alphonse Laveran b. Chas. McBurney b. Élie Metchnikoff b. Wilhelm Pfeffer b. Wilhelm von Röntgen b. *Nicolas de Saussure d.* Sir Thos. Thorpe b. François Tisserand b. Edouard Van Beneden b. Karl Weigert b.	*John Adolphus d.* A. H. Sayce b. Anne H. Wharton b.	*Janos Bacsányi d.* *Richard Barham d.* *Nicolaus Becker d.* *Maria G. Brooke d.* Will Carleton b. Sir Sidney Colvin b. *Thos. Davis d.* *Thomas Hood d.* *Wm. Minto b.* *Lady Nairne d.* J. de Oliveira Martins b. Thos. S. Perry b. *Regina M. Roche d.* *August Wilhelm von Schlegel d.* George Saintsbury b. *Sydney Smith d.* Carl Spitteler b. Joseph M. Stoddart b. Moorfield Storey b. John B. Tabb b. E. von Wildenbruch b.	Mary Cassatt b. B. J. J. Constant b. Walter Crane b. Frank Holl b.	Leopold Auer b. Gabriel Fauré b.	Thos. J. Barnardo b. Wm. H. Crane b. "Deadwood Dick" b. *Elizabeth Fry d.* *Karl Naundorff d.*

1846–1851 A.D.

Year A.D.	Government and Law	Military and Naval Affairs	Industry Commerce Economics Finance Invention Labor	Travel and Exploration	Philosophy and Religion	Science and Medicine	Education Scholarship History	Literature	Visual Arts	Music	Miscellaneous
1846	Louis Bonaparte d. Michael Davitt b. Jos. B. Foraker b. Sir Geo. Goldie b. Chas. S. Parnell b. Nicholas Pasic b. V. Plehve b. P. Waldeck-Rousseau b.	Comte de Bourmont d.	Elbert H. Gary b. Laurence Gronlund b. Friedrich List d. Johann Most b. Geo. Westinghouse b.	Otto von Kotzebue d. Sir Henry Wickham b.	Francis H. Bradley b. Rudolph Eucken b. Pasquale Galluppi d. Pope Gregory XVI d. Richard L. Nettleship b. Friedrich Paulsen b. Pope Pius IX a.	Friedrich Bessel d. Max Fürbringer b. Alfred Giard b. G. Stanley Hall b. Christian Ideler d. Rodolfo Lanciani b. Edward C. Pickering b. Ira Remsen b.	Gaston Maspero b. Henry F. Pelham b. John Pickering d. Wm. Robertson Smith b.	Edmondo de Amicis b. Katharine H. Bradley b. Marcus A. H. Clarke b. Geo. Darley d. Paul Déroulède b. Holger Drachmann b. John H. Frere d. Anna Katharine Greene b. Julian Hawthorne b. H. W. Mabie b. Standish J. O'Grady b. Étienne de Sénancour d. Henryk Sienkiewicz Flora Annie Steel b. Esaias Tegnér d. Rodolphe Töpffer d. Christopher Wordsworth (Elder) d.	Kate Greenaway b. Benj. R. Haydon d. Henry Inman d. Francis D. Millet b. Albert P. Ryder b.	Italo Campanini b.	Camille Blanc b. Tennessee Claflin b. Thos. Clarkson d. Wm. F. Cody b.
1847	John P. Altgeld b. J. P. Casimir-Perier b. Prinz zu Eulenberg-Hertefeld b. Paul von Hindenberg b. Jas. Kent d. Empress Marie Louise d. Danl. O'Connell d. Prince de Polignac d. Earl of Rosebery b. Barone di Sonnino b. Benj. R. Tillman b.	Jacobus De la Rey b. Marquis de Grouchy d. Archduke Karl Ludwig d. José de Palafox y Mezi d. Radomir Putnik b. Count Togo b.	Alexander Graham Bell b. Thomas A. Edison b. Henry Demarest Lloyd b. Jacob Schiff b.	Sir John Franklin d.	Annie Besant b. Thos. Chalmers d. John A. Dowie b. Jas. Hannington b. Hugh O. Pentecost b. Georg Rapp d. Katherine Tingley b. Alexandre Vinet d.	Wm. E. Ayrton b. Alexandre Brongniart d. Andrew Combe d. Sir George Greenhill b. Edmund Gurney b. Christine Ladd-Franklin b. Sir E. Ray Lankester b.	Thos. F. Dibdin d. Erik Geijer d. Sharon Turner d.	Grace Aguilar d. Pierre Ballanche d. Mary H. Catherwood b. Chas. H. Clark b. "Hugh Conway" b. Alexander H. Everett d. Émile Faguet b. Jens Jacobsen b. Mary Lamb d. José de Olmedo d. Joseph Pulitzer b. Jas. J. Roche b. Geo. R. Sims b. E. Noyes Westcott b. Richard Henry Wilde d.	Wm. Collins d. Chas. F. McKim b. Wm. Simson d.	Wm. Crotch d. Adolph von Hildebrand b. Felix Mendelssohn-Bartholdy d. Sir Paolo Tosti b.	George Grossmith b. Jos. Gurney d. Jesse James b. Anna Howard Shaw b.
1848	Abbas I (Egypt) a. John Quincy Adams d. Lord Ashburton d. Arthur James Balfour b. Lord Bentinck d. Don Carlos b. Christian VIII (Denmark) d. Ferdinand I (Austria) abd. Franz Josef (Austro-Hungary) a. Keokuk d. Louis Philippe (France) dep. Ludwig I (Bavaria) abd. Maximilian II (Bavaria) a. Viscount Melbourne d. Nasr-el-Dīn (Persia) a. T. P. O'Connor b. Henry Wheaton d.	Ibrahim Pasha d. Alexei Kuropatkin b. Helmuth von Moltke b.	John Jacob Astor d. E. H. Harriman b. Otto Lilienthal b. Albert R. Parsons b. Conde di Rossi d. Geo. Stephenson d. Melville E. Stone b.		Bernhard Bolzano d. Bernard Bosanquet b. John E. Remsburg b.	J. J. Berzelius d. Otto Bütschli b. Baron Roland von Eötvös b. Caroline Herschel d. Victor Meyer b. Flora W. Patterson b. Jas. C. Prichard d. G. J. Romanes b. Henry A. Rowland b. Sir Arthur Rücker b. Horace Wells d. Robt. Wiedersheim b.	Heinrich Delbrueck b. Arthur Giry b. Sir Geo. Prothero b.	Grant Allen b. Wm. Waldorf Astor b. Emily Brontë d. François de Chateaubriand d. John C. Collins b. John R. Coryell b. Isaac D'Israeli d. Digby Dolben b. Annette von Droste-Hülshoff d. R. C. Dutt b. Josef von Görres d. Francis Grierson b. Sydney Grundy b. Eugénie de Guérin d. Joel C. Harris b. J. K. Huysmans b. Richard Jefferies b. Fredk. Marryat d. Georges Ohnet b. Alessandro Poerio d. Wm. Tennant d. Wm. Thom d. Comte de Vogüé b. Constance F. Woolson b.	Jules Bastien Lepage b. Paul Gauguin b. Augustus Saint-Gaudens b. Ludwig Schwanthaler d.	Gaetano Donizetti d. Lili Lehmann b. Vladimir de Pachmann b. Sir Chas. Parry b.	Wm. G. Grace b. Adelaide Neilson b. Sol Smith Russell b. Nathan Strauss b. Ellen Terry b.

Year A.D.	Government and Law	Military, Naval, and Aviation Affairs	Industry Commerce Economics Finance Invention Labor	Philosophy and Religion	Science, Technology, and Medicine	Education Scholarship History	Literature and Journalism	Visual Arts	Music	Miscellaneous
1849	Lord Geo. Auckland d. Carlo Alberto (Sardinia) d. Lord Randolph Churchill b. Dhuleep Singh (Lahore) dep. Faustin I (Haiti) a. Albert Gallatin d. Lalmohun Ghose b. Mohammed Ali (Egypt) d. Jas. K. Polk d. Willem II (Holland) d. Willem III (Holland) a. Count Witte b. Yakub Khan b.	Count Batthyányi d. Friederich von Bernhardi b. Sir Benj. D'Urban d. Joseph S. Gallieni d. August von Mackensen b. Alfred von Tirpitz b. Edmund Zalinski b.	Wm. Cunningham b. H. C. Frick b. Louis F. Post b. Jacob Riis b.	John B. Crozier b. Wilhelm De Wette d. Wm. Miller d. Cyrus R. Teed b.	Luther Burbank b. John H. Comstock b. Geo. M. Dawson b. Johann Dobereiner d. Stephan Endlicher d. George B. Grinnell b. Oskar Hertwig b. John Hopkinson b. Aletta Jacobs b. Sir Wm. Osler b. Ivan Pavlov b.	Jas. Darmesteter b. Wm. G. Hale b. Mary Lyon d. Giuseppi Mezzofanti d. Patrick F. Tytler d. Talcott Williams b. Karl Zumpt d.	Jas. Lane Allen b. Daniel Appleton d. Bernard Barton d. Thos. L. Beddoes d. Countess of Blessington d. Anne Brontë d. Ferdinand Brunetière b. Frances Hodgson Burnett b. Hartley Coleridge d. Maria Edgeworth d. Anne Edgren-Leffler b. Ebenezer Elliott d. Ernst von Feuchtersleben d. Sir Edmund Gosse b. Wm. E. Henley b. Thos. A. Janvier b. Sarah Orne Jewett b. Emma Lazarus b. Wm. H. Mallock b. Jas. C. Mangan d. Alice Meynell b. Max Nordau b. Sandor Petöfi d. E. A. Poe d. Jean Richepin b. Jas. Whitcomb Riley b. Horace Smith d. Wm. T. Stead b. August Strindberg b. Ruth McE. Stuart b.	Eugenè Carrière b. Wm. M. Chase b. Emile Claus b. Wm. Etty d. François Granet d. Sir Hubert von Herkimer b. Carl Hill b. Katsuhika Hokusai d. David Scott d. Abbott Thayer b. Peter de Wint d.	Emma Abbott b. Angelica Catalani d. Frédéric Chopin d. Benj. Godard b. Karl Otto Nicolaï d. Johann Strauss (Elder) d.	Pierce Egan d. Jéanne Récamier d.
1850	Jean Pierre Boyer d. John C. Calhoun d. Champ Clark b. Henry Cabot Lodge b. Seth Low b. Fredk. W. Maitland b. Thomas Masaryk b. Sir Robt. Peel d. José de San Martin d. Zachary Taylor d.	Conde di Cadorna b. Lord Kitchener b.	Frédéric Bastiat d. Edward Bellamy b. Eduard Bernstein b. F.-X. Droz d. Saml. Gompers b. Henry E. Huntington b. Nikolai Tschaikovsky b. Sir Basil Zaharofi b.	Adoniram Judson d. Leonard Darwin b. Johann Neander d.	Henri Blainville d. J. Walter Fewkes b. Karl Gärtner d. J. L. Gay-Lussac d. Oliver Heaviside b. Sofya Kovalevski b. Alford Nathorst b. August Pauly b. Wm. Prout d. Charles Richet b. John S. Rickard b. Augusto Righi b. Wilhelm Roux b. Wm. E. Story b. Gerard Troost d. Chas. D. Walcott b.	Herbert B. Adams b. Jane Harrison b. Fredk. York Powell b.	Honoré de Balzac d. Arlo Bates b. Augustine Birrell b. Wm. L. Bowles d. Philip P. Cooke d. "Charles Egbert Craddock" b. Eugene Field b. Margaret Fuller d. Giuseppe Giusti d. Lafcadio Hearn b. Lord Jeffrey d. "Pierre Loti" b. "Ian Maclaren" b. Philip B. Marston b. Guy de Maupassant b. Octave Mirbeau b. Kirk Munroe b. Bill Nye b. Adam Oehlenschlager d. Jane Porter d. Laura E. Richards b. G. de Porto-Riche b. R. L. Stevenson b. "Octave Thanet" b. Rose Hartwicke Thorpe b. Ella Wheeler Wilcox b. Wm. Wordworth d.	Sir Wm. Allan d. Edward J. Gregory b. Johann Schadow d. Sir Wm. H. Thornycroft b.	John Collier b. Jean de Reszke b. Anton Seidl b.	Daniel Carter Beard b. Fanny Davenport b. Wyatt Earp b. Sir Thomas Lipton b. Marie Tussaud d.
1851	John Dillon b. Manuel de Godoy d. Geo. McDuffie d. Lord Moncrieff d. Basil Montagu d. Richard L. Sheil d.	Ferdinand Foch b. Nicolas Soult d.	Robert Blatchford b. Louis Daguerre d. Sir Horace Darwin b. Viscount Leverhulme b.	Felix Adler b. Francis E. Clark b. Thos. W. Doane b. Cardinal Mercier b. Heinrich Paulus d. Chas. Wagner b.	J. J. Audubon d. Francis Maitland Balfour b. Emile Berliner b. Wm. Brewster b. John M. Coulter b. Geo. F. Fitzgerald b. Karl Jacobi d. David Starr Jordan b. Jacobus C. Kapteyn b. Sir Oliver Lodge b. Lillien J. Martin b. David Moir d. Hans Christian Oersted d. Lorenz Oken d. Walter Reed b.	E. A. Alderman b. George Crabb d. Melvil Dewey b. Gábor Döbrentei d. Heinrich Friedjung b. Thos. H. Gallaudet d. Karl Lachmann d. John Lingard d. Arthur Verrall b.	Joanna Baillie d. Kate Chopin b. Wells Drury b. Jas. Fenimore Cooper d. Henry Drummond b. Henry Arthur Jones b. M. M. Noah d. Emilia Pardo Bazán b. Edward Quillinan d. Fredk. C. Selous b. Mary W. Shelley d. Mary M. Sherwood d. Mrs. Humphry Ward b.	A. B. Frost b. Wilhelm Trübner b. J. M. W. Turner d.	Vincent D'Indy b. Gasparo Spontini d. Arthur Goring Thomas b. Geo. Thomson d.	Carl Lumholtz b. Frederick Warde b.

1852–1857 A.D.

Year A.D.	Government and Law	Military, Naval, and Aviation Affairs	Industry Commerce Economics Finance Invention Labor	Philosophy and Religion	Science, Technology, and Medicine	Education Scholarship History	Literature and Journalism		Visual Arts	Music	Miscellaneous
1852	Victor Adler b. Herbert Asquith b. *Henry Clay d.* Théophile Delcassé b. Napoleon III (France) a. Wm. O'Brien b. Alton B. Parker b. *Prinz F. zu Schwarzenberg d. Danl. Webster d.*	Viscount French b. *Comte de Gérard d.* F. Conrad von Hötzendorf b. J. J. C. Joffre b. Chas. Lanrezac b. *Duke of Wellington d.*	Barnett Barnato b. Sir Ernest J. Cassel b. "Stepniak" b. Arnold Toynbee b. F. W. Woolworth b. *Frances Wright d.*	Robt. Adamson b. Paul Carus b. *Adam Eschenmayer d. Vincenzo Gioberti d.*	Richard Altmann b. Antoine H. Becquerel b. Emil Fischer b. Wm. S. Halsted b. Friedrich Löffler b. Edward W. Maunder b. Albert A. Michelson b. Chas. S. Minot b. Henri Moissan b. John H. Poynting b. Santiago Ramón y Cajal b. Sir Wm. Ramsay b. Chas. Sajous b. Jacobus Van't Hoff b. Saml. W. Williston b. *David Young d.*	*Friedrich Froebel d. Friedrich Jahn d.* Walter Leaf b. J. B. McMaster b.	*Sara Coleridge d.* Nathan Haskell Dole b. Mary E. Wilkins Freeman b. *Nikolai Gogol d.* Robert Grant b. Lady Gregory b. "Lucas Malet" b. Edwin Markham b. Brander Matthews b.	Wilfred Meynell b. George Moore b. *Thos. Moore d. John Howard Payne d.* Opie Read b. Henry VanDyke b. C. E. S. Wood b. *Vasili Zhukovsky d.*	Edwin A. Abbey b. *Horatio Greenough d.* August Hagborg b. Ernst Josephson b. *Saml. Prout d. John Vanderlyn d.*	Rafael Joseffy b. Sir Chas. Stanford b.	*Junius Brutus Booth d.* Comte de Brazza b. *Count D'Orsay d.* Lillie Langtry b. *A. W. N. Pugin d. Thos. G. Wainewright d.*
1853	Sir Leander S. Jameson b. Philander C. Knox b. *Josef von Radowitz d.* Cecil Rhodes b.	Tasker H. Bliss b. *Baron von Haynau d. Sir Chas. Napier d. Andres Pretorius d.* Stepan Stepanovitch b.	Hudson Maxim b.	*A. F. Ozanam d.* Vladimir Soloviev b.	*François Arago d.* Alphonse Bertillon b. *Leopold von Buch d. Christian Doppler d.* Angelo Heilprin b. Heike Kamerlingh-Onnes b. *Auguste Laurent d.* Hendrick Lorentz b. Wilhelm Ostwald b. Sir W. M. Flinders Petrie b. Karl Rabl b. *Hugh E. Strickland d.* Sir Fredk. Treves b.	*Cesare Balboa d.* E. F. Fenellosa b. *Georg Grotefend d.* Lucy M. Salmon b.	René Bazin b. Sir Hall Caine b. *János Garay d.* Jacob Gordin b. E. W. Howe b. Robt. Underwood Johnson b. Vladimir Korolenko b.	Jules Lemaître b. *Amelia Opie d.* Thos. Nelson Page b. Irwin Russell b. *Ludwig Tieck d.*	Edward H. Garrett b. Ferdinand Hodler b. Howard Pyle b. Vincent Van Gogh b.	Teresa Carreño b.	Mrs. O. H. P. Belmont b. Rose Coghlan b. John Drew b. Billy Emerson b. J. Forbes-Robertson b. Sir H. Beerbohm Tree b. Stanford White b.
1854	*Abbas I (Egypt) d. Lord Cockburn d. Myron T. Herrick b.* Kamehameha IV (Hawaii) a. Viscount Milner b. *Lord Plunket d.* Stefan Stambolov b. *Comte de Villèle d.*	*Viscount Beresford d. Jos. Chlopicki d.* Christian de Wet b. L. H. Lyautey b. *Jacques de Saint-Arnaud d.*	Ernest Belfort Bax b. Richard Ely b. Andrew Furuseth b. Karl Kautsky b. Ottmar Mergenthaler b. *Francis Place d.*	*Friedrich Beneke d. Johann Gieseler d. Friedrich von Schelling d.*	Emil von Behring b. Yves Delage b. Paul Ehrlich b. *Edward Forbes d.* Sir James G. Frazer b. Sir Patrick Geddes b. Wm. C. Gorgas b. Giovanni Grassi b. Wm. T. Hornaday b. *Macedonio Melloni d. Chas. Mirbel d. Georg Ohm d.* Jules Poincare b. Jokichi Takamine b.	Albert Bushnell Hart b. Arthur A. Macdonnell b. Sir Paul Vinogradov b. Benj. Ide Wheeler b.	Isaak Babel b. *Robt. M. Bird d.* F. Marion Crawford b. Wm. Henry Drummond b. *Johann Eckermann d. Susan E. Ferrier d. João d'Almeida Garret d.* Frank Harris b. Jos. Jacobs b. *Robert de Lamennais d.*	*J. G. Lockhart d. Jas. Montgomery d.* Frank A. Munsey b. *Silvio Pellico d.* Arthur Rimbaud b. *José Rivera d. Anne Royall d.* E. W. Scripps b. *Emile Souvestre d. Sir Thos. Talfourd d.* Edith M. Thomas b. Oscar Wilde b. *John Wilson d.*	*John Martin d.*	Alfredo Catalani b. Philip Hale b. Engelbert Humperdinck b. Leoš Janáček b. Moritz Moszkowski b. Pol Plançon b. John Philip Sousa b.	S. A. Andrée b. George Eastman b. *Chas. Kemble d.* Richard Mansfield b. Robert Mantell b. *Roger Tichborne d.* Francis Wilson b.

Year A.D.	Government and Law	Military, Naval, and Aviation Affairs	Industry Commerce Economics Finance Invention Labor	Philosophy and Religion	Science, Technology, and Medicine	Education Scholarship History	Literature and Journalism		Visual Arts	Music	Miscellaneous
1855	Alexander II (Russia) a. J.J. Jusserand b. Marquis Komura b. Robt. M. La Follette b. *Nicholas I (Russia) d.* Walter Hines Page b.	*Guglielmo Pepe d. Lord Raglan d.*	Eugene V. Debs b. *Abbott Lawrence d.* Andrew H. Mellon b. *Feargus O'Connor d.*	Wm. Montgomery Brown b. *S. A. Kierkegaard d.* Eugene M. Macdonald b. *A. Rosmini-Serbati d.* Josiah Royce b.	*Sir Henry De la Beche d. Karl F. Gauss d. J. F. W. Johnston d.* Arnold Lang b. Edwin Linton b. Percival Lowell b. *François Magendie d.* C. Hart Merriam b. Albert Neisser b. *Jacques Sturm d.* L. Teisserenc de Bort b. David Todd b.	*Jean Lacretelle d.* Alice Freeman Palmer b. Barrett Wendell b.	Wm. C. Brann b. H. C. Bunner b. Houston Stewart Chamberlain b. Marie Corelli b. Adolf Frey b. *Delphine de Girardin d. Adam Mickiewicz d. Mary R. Mitford d. Robt. Montgomery d. "Gérard de Nerval" d.* Giovanni Pascoli b.	Sir Arthur Pinero b. *Saml. Rogers d.* Edgar Saltus b. Olive Schreiner b. Wm. Sharp b. Émile Verhaeren b. *Mihaly Vörösmarty d.* Arthur B. Walkley b. Stanley J. Weyman b. *Dorothy Wordsworth d.* Juan Zorilla b.	George deForest Brush b. *Jean Isabey d. François Rude d.*	*Sir Henry Bishop d.* Anatol Liadov b. Emil Mollenhauer b. Artur Nikisch b.	*Jacques Arago d.* Wm. Gillette b. *Sir Wm. Parry d.* Dmitri Trepov b.
1856	Theobald von Bethmann–Hollweg b. Louis D. Brandeis b. Alfred Deakin b. *Samuel Hoar d.* Aleksandr Izvolski b. Frank B. Kellogg b. Henri–Philippe Pétain b. John Redmond b. Joseph Reinach b. Woodrow Wilson b.	*Viscount Hardinge d.* Robert Nivelle b. *Ivan Paskevich d.*	*Étienne Cabet d.* Ernest H. Crosby b. E.L. Doheny b. Jas. Keir Hardie b. Viscount Rhondda b. *Robt. L. Stevens d. Max Stirner d.* B.G. Tilak b.	Bramwell Booth b. Frank W. Gunsaulus b. Viscount Haldane b. *Sir Wm. Hamilton d. Immanuel Ilmoni d. Father Mathew d.* Reuben A. Torrey b.	Edward D. Acheson b. *Amerigo Avogadro d. Samuel Brown d. Wm. Buckland d.* Francis X. Dercum b. Sigmund Freud b. *Karl Gerhardt d. Nikolai Lobachevsky d. Hugh Miller d. Jas. G. Percival d. Chas. G. W. St. John d.* Nikola Tesla b. Sir Jos. J. Thomson b. *John Collins Warren d. Wm. Yarnell d.*	Wm. R. Harper b. A. Lawrence Lowell b. Harry Thurston Peck b. Henry Osborn Taylor b. *Jacques Thierry d.* Booker T. Washington b. *Johann Zeuss d.*	*Gilbert a Beckett d.* "F. Anstey" b. Wm. Archer b. Harold Frederic b. Sir Rider Haggard b. *Heinrich Heine d.* Elbert Hubbard b. "Vernon Lee" b. Jean Moréas b.	H. W. Nevinson b. Fremont Older b. Matilda Serao b. George Bernard Shaw b. Kate Douglas Wiggins b. "John Strange Winter" b.	Hans von Bartels b. Reginald B. Birch b. Kenyon Cox b. *David d'Angers d. Paul Delaroche d.* Sir John Lavery b. John S. Sargent b. *Sir Richard Westmacott d.*	*John Braham d.* Felix Mottl b. Édouard de Reszke b. *Robert Schumann d.* Christian Sinding b.	Robert B. Peary b. Karl Peters b. *Sir John Ross d. Lucia Vestris d. Charles Mayne Young d.*
1857	*Jas. G. Birney d.* Alice Stone Blackwell b. Clarence Darrow b. *Daniele Manin d.* Stojan Protić b. Martinus Steyn b. Wm. H. Taft b.	*Louis Cavaignac d. Sir Henry Havelock d. Sir Henry M. Lawrence d. John Nicholson d.*	Maffeo Pantaleoni b. Georgy Plekhanov b. Filippo Turati b. Thorstein Veblen b. Clara Zetkin b.	*Auguste Comte d. Wm. J. Conybeare d.* Émile Coué b. Alfred Loisy b. Chas. M. Sheldon b.	John J. Abel b. Alfred Binet b. *Baron de Cauchy d.* Giacomo Ciamician b. *Wm. D. Conybeare d. Marshall Hall d.* Heinrich Hertz b. Sir Victor Horsley b. Jas. E. Keeler b. Alexander Liapunov b. John B. Murphy b. Henry Fairfield Osborn b. Sir Roland Ross b. *Louis Thénard d.* Julius Wagner-Jauregg b.	*François Isambert d. John M. Kemble d.* Ida M. Tarbell b.	Gertrude Atherton b. Hermann J. Bang b. *Pierre de Béranger d.* Alice Brown b. Arthur H. Bullen b. Jos. Conrad b. *John W. Croker d.* John Davidson b. Margaret Deland b. Geo. Gissing b. Karl Gjellerup b. *R. W. Griswold d.* Paul Hervieu b.	Emerson Hough b. *Douglas Jerrold d.* S.S. McClure b. *Danl. Macmillan d.* Axel Munthe b. *Alfred de Musset d.* Hendrik Pontoppidan b. *Manuel Quintana d.* Édouard Rod b. Clement K. Shorter b. Hermann Sudermann b. *Eugène Sue d.*	Robt. F. Blum b. *Thos. Crawford d.* F. B. Opper b. Joseph Pennell b. *Christian Rauch d.*	*Karl Czerny d.* Sir Edward Elgar b. *Mikhail Glinka d.*	Lord Robt. Baden–Powell b. Maggie Cline b. Ben Greet b. *Elisha Kent Kane d. Princess Liewen d.* Emmeline Pankhurst b. Gabrielle Réjane b. *Wm. Scoresby d. François Vidocq d.*

1858-1862 A.D.

Year A.D.	Government and Law	Military, Naval, and Aviation Affairs	Industry Commerce Economics Finance Invention Labor	Philosophy and Religion	Science, Technology, and Medicine	Education Scholarship History	Literature and Journalism		Visual Arts	Music	Miscellaneous
1858	Thos. H. Benton d. Jas. Gadsden d. E. M. House b. A. Bonar Law b. Theodore Roosevelt b. Prinz Rudolf von Hapsburg b.	G. W. Goethals b. Wm. Hodson d. Baron de Jacques b. Matthew Perry d. Count Radetzky d. Mahmoud Shevket b.	Rudolf Diesel b. Benj. Kidd b. Julia Lathrop b. Kokichi Mikimoto b. Adolph Ochs b. Robt. Owen d. Thos. Tooke d. Graham Wallas b. Beatrice Webb b. Baron von Welsbach b. Havelock Wilson b.	Mary Katherine Drexel b. Georg Simmel b.	Franz Boas b. Aimé Bonpland d. Sir J. C. Bose b. Richard Bright d. Robt. Brown d. Jonathan Dwight b. Alfred Lehmann b. Johannes P. Müller d. Christian Nees von Esenbeck d. Wm. H. Pickering b. Max Planck b. Michael Pupin b. Charles Schuchert b. Wm. Berryman Scott b. Frederick Starr b. Fredk. W. True b. Sir Bertram Windle b.	Friedrich Creuzer d. Charles M. Gayley b. Salomon Reinach b. Paul Sabatier b. Felix E. Schelling b.	Eugene Brieux b. Gaston Calmette b. Charles W. Chestnutt b. Thos. H. Chivers d. Sam Walter Foss b. Iwan Gilkin b. Remy de Gourmont b. K'ang Yu-wei b.	Selma Lagerlöf b. "Maarten Maartens" b. Jane Marcet d. Aylmer Maude b. Edith Nesbit b. C. B. Palleri b. Albert Samain b. Horace Traubel b. Karl Varnhagen von Ense d. Sir Wm. Watson b.	Julius Rolshoven b. Ary Scheffer d. Giovanni Segantini b.	Emma Calvé b. Johann Cramer d. Ruggiero Leoncavallo b. Giacomo Puccini b. Marcella Sembrich b. Dame Ethel M. Smyth b. Frank Van der Stucken b. Eugène Ysaÿe b.	George Combe d. De Wolfe Hopper b. Sir Harry H. Johnston b. Hans Meyer b. Felice Orsini d. Ida Pfeiffer d. Rachel d. Alexis Soyer d. Otis Skinner b. Joseph Thomson b. Eleazar Williams d.
1859	John Austin d. Venustiano Carranza b. Charles XV (Sweden) a. Rufus Choate d. Geo. N. Curzon b. Lord Elphinstone d. Faustin I (Haiti) dep. Wm. Travers Jerome b. Takaakiro Kato b. Prinz von Metternich d. Alexandre Millerand b. Richard Rush d. Sir Cecil Spring-Rice b. Yuan Shih-K'ai b.	Alexander Samsonov b.	Samuel Insull b. Jean Jaurès b. Florence Kelley b. Geo. Lansbury b. Robt. Stephenson d. Sidney Webb (Lord Passfield) b.	Henri Bergson b.	Carl Agardh d. Svante Arrhenius b. William Bond d. Wm. H. Bristol b. Pierre Curie b. Havelock Ellis b. Baron von Humboldt d. Jas. F. Kemp b. Chas. C. de Latour d. Jacques Loeb b. Thos. Nuttall d. Karl Ritter d. Richard Semon b. Jan Tschakste b. Geo. Wilson d.	John Dewey b. Francisco Ferrer b. Wilhelm Grimm d. Henry Hallam d. Horace Mann d. Wm. H. Prescott d. L. L. Zamenhof b.	Sergei Aksakov d. Bettina von Arnim d. Irving Bacheller b. Katherine Lee Bates b. Thos. DeQuincey d. Sir A. Conan Doyle b. J. Bruce Glazier b. Kenneth Grahame b. Knut Hamsun b. Werner von Heidenstam b. Horace E. Hooper b. A. E. Housman b. Leigh Hunt d. Washington Irving d.	J. K. Jerome b. Basil King b. Dionysius Lardner d. Sir Sidney Lee b. Chas. F. Lummis b. Thos. B. Macaulay d. Lady Sydney Morgan d. S Gabriele Reuter b. Sir Jas. Stephen d. Jas. K. Stephen b. Wm. R. Thayer b. Francis Thompson b. A. de Tocqueville d. A. de Tocqueville d.	David Cox d. Childe Hassam b. Edmund Osthaus b. Georges Seurat b. C. Traviès de Villers d.	Mary Anderson b. Reginald DeKoven b. Victor Herbert b. Lillian Nordica b. Louis Spohr d.	Delia Bacon d. Karl Baedeker d. "Billy the Kid" (Wm. H. Bonney) b. John Brown d. Alfred Dreyfus b. Eleonora Duse b. Cass Gilbert b.
1860	Earl of Aberdeen d. Jerôme Bonaparte d. Karl Branting b. Wm. J. Bryan b. Baron von Bunsen d. Charles Curtis b. Élie Decazes d. Fernand Labori b. Leopold II (Tuscany) abd. Prinz von Lichnowsky b. Milos I (Serbia) d. Vittorio Emanuele Orlando b. Raymond Poincaré b. Count Szecheny d. Saad Zaghlul b.	Earl of Dundonald d. Sir Wm. Napier d. John J. Pershing b. Sir Harry G. W. Smith d. Wm. Walker d. Leonard Wood b.	Victor Berger b. E. A. Filene b. Chas. Goodyear d. Émile Pathé b. Elmer A. Sperry b.	Ferdinand Baur d. Sir Chas. Fellows d. Israel Hwasser d. Wm. R. Inge b. Theodore Parker d. Arthur Schopenhauer d.	Thos. Addison d. Sir Wm. Bayliss b. Sir Thos. Brisbane d. Eduard Buchner b. Jas. McKeen Cattell b. Marquess of Dalhousie d. Félix Dujardin d. Niels R. Finsen b. J. S. Haldane b. Hans Hoebiger b. Martin Rathke d. Anders Retzius d. Per Alex Rydberg b. Louis de Vilmorin d.	Friedrich Dahlmann d. Douglas Hyde b. Otto Jesperson b. Théodore Reinach b.	Ernst Arndt d. Sir James Barrie b. Marie Bashkirtsev b. Horatio Bottomley b. Abraham Cahan b. Anton Chekhov b. "Ralph Connor" b. Saml. R. Crockett b. Geo. Croly d. Isaac Da Costa d. Ellen Thorneycroft Fowler b. Hamlin Garland b. S. G. Goodrich d. Johann L. Heiberg d.	J. G. Huneker b. Leonard Huxley b. G. P. R. James d. Anna B. Jameson d. Ebenezer Jones d. Jules LaForgue b. Paul Margueritte b. Jas. Kirke Paulding d. Sir Chas. G. D. Roberts b. Clinton Scollard b. Ernest Thompson Seton b. J. St. Loe Starchey b. Owen Wister b. John Younger d.	Alexandre Decamps d. "Grandma" Moses b. Rembrandt Peale d. Lorado Taft b. Anders Zorn b.	Isaac Albéniz b. Louis A. Jullien d. Gustav Mahler b. Ignace J. Paderewski b. Hugo Wolf b.	Jane Addams b. Lizzie Borden b. Michel Fokine b. Chas. Frohman b. Theodor Herzl b. Évariste Huc d. Chauncey Olcott b. Ada Rehan b.

Year A.D.	Government and Law	Military, Naval, and Aviation Affairs	Industry Commerce Economics Finance Invention Labor	Philosophy and Religion	Science, Technology, and Medicine	Education Scholarship History	Literature and Journalism		Visual Arts	Music	Miscellaneous
1861	Abdul Aziz (Turkey) a. *Abdul Mejid (Turkey) d.* Prince-Consort *Albert d.* Alexander Cuza (Rumania) a. *Camillo di Cavour d.* *Prince Czartoryski d.* *Stephen A. Douglas d.* *Friedrich Wilhelm IV (Prussia) d.* *Sir Jas. Graham d.* *Wm. L. Mackenzie d.* George W. Norris b. Jose Rizal b. *Karl von Savigny d.* *Friedrich Stahl d.* Victor Emmanuel II (Italy) a.	Viscount Allenby b. Carl Legien b. Eric von Falkenhayn b. Earl Haig b. *Saml. C. Reid d.* Sir Chas. Townsend b. Sir Francis Wingate b.	*MacGregor Laird d.* Carl Legien b. *Richard Oastler d.* Wm. Wrigley b.	*Edward Cardwell d.* *J. B. Lacordaire d.* Benj. Purnell b. Rudolf Steiner b. Geo. Tyrrell b.	Wm. Bateson b. *Sir John Forbes d.* Fredk. G. Hopkins b. Sir Halford J. McKinder b. Wm. Patten b. Sir Arthur E. Shipley b. Eugen Steinach b. Alfred North Whitehead b.	*August Gfrörer d.* J. G. Hibben b. Morris Jastrow b.	Wm. E. Barton b. *Elizabeth Barrett Browning d.* William Wilfred Campbell b. Bliss Carman b. *Arthur H. Clough d.* Frank Crane b. "Alan Dale" b. *Geo. H. Derby d.* *Alexander Gilchrist d.* *David Gray d.* Maximilian Harden b. Henry Harland b. Maurice Hewlett b. Harriet Monroe b.	*Henri Murger d.* *Ivan Nikitin d.* *Sir Francis Palgrave d.* Herbert Quick b. Sir Walter Raleigh b. Morgan Robertson b. *Augustin Scribe d.* Sir Owen Seaman b. *T. Sewchenko d.* Edith O. Somerville b. Italo Svevo b. Rabindranath Tagore b. Katharine Tynan b.	Cyrus E. Dallin b. *Karl W. von Heidegger d.* E. W. Kemble b. Frederic Remington b.	Anton Arenski b. Cécile Chaminade b. *Anthony P. Heinrich d.* Edward A. MacDowell b. Nellie Melba b. *Vincent Novello d.* Ernestine Schumann–Heink b.	*Robt. O'Hara Burke d.* Wm. J. Burns b. Albert Chevalier b. Dan Leno b. *Lola Montez d.* Fridtjof Nansen b. Theodore Roberts b. *Wm. J. Wills d.*
1862	Count Andrássy (Jr.) b. Aristide Briand b. Viscount Byng b. *Earl of Canning d.* *Hans Hassenpflug d.* Chas. Evans Hughes b. *Otto (Greece) d.* *John Tyler d.* Oscar W. Underwood b. *Martin Van Buren d.* *Edward G. Wakefield d.*	Graf Johann von Bernstorff b. Louis Botha b. *Albert Sidney Johnston d.* *Philip Kearny d.* Nikolai Yudenitch b.	Ella Reeve Bloor b. *Saml. Colt d.* Geo. D. Herron b. Chas. M. Schwab b.	Billy Sunday b.	*Jean Biot d.* Theodor Bovén b. Sir Wm. H. Bragg b. W. W. Campbell b. Prince Golitsyn b. Edward A. Westermarck b.	*Henry Thos. Buckle d.* Nicholas Murray Butler b. David Hogarth b.	Paul Adam b. Francis W. L. Adams b. John Kendrick Bangs b. Maurice Barrès b. A. C. Benson b. Hayden Carruth b. Edith E. Cooper b. G. Lowes Dickinson b. F. N. Doubleday b. "Sarah Grand" b. Gerhart Hauptmann b "O. Henry" b. *T. J. Hogg d.* *Justinus Kerner d.*	*J.S. Knowles d.* Oscar Levertin b. Maurice Maeterlinck b. Lee Meriwether b. "H.S. Merriman" b. Semion Nadson b. *Fitz–James O'Brien d.* Sir Gilbert Parker b. Eden Phillpotts b. Marcel Prévost b. Morris Rosenfeld b. "Martin Ross" b. Arthur Schnitzler b. Don C. Seitz b. May Sinclair b. ? *H. D. Thoreau d.* *Johann Uhland d.* Edith Wharton b. *Chas. Whitehead d.* Casper Whitney b. *Josef von Zedlitz d.*	Arthur B. Davies b. Chas. Grafly b. John Huffington b. *Friedrich Schadow d.* Eugene Zimmermann b	Jos. Adamowski b. Carrie Jacobs Bond b. Walter Damrosch b. Claude Debussy b. Frederick Delius b. Nathan Franko b. *Jacques F. Halévy d.* Emma Nevada b. Ethelbert Nevin b. Moriz Rosenthal b.	May Irwin b. Mary Kingsley b. Wilton Lackaye b. "Connie Mack" b. Cyril Maude b. Julius Rosenwald b.

1863–1867 A.D.

Year A.D.	Government and Law	Military, Naval, and Aviation Affairs	Industry Commerce Economics Finance Invention Labor	Philosophy and Religion	Science, Technology, and Medicine	Education Scholarship History	Literature and Journalism		Visual Arts	Music	Miscellaneous
1863	Joseph Cailloux b. *Lord Campbell d.* Christian IX (Denmark) a. *John J. Crittenden d.* *Khan Dost Mohammed d.* Archduke Franz Ferdinand b. George I (Greece) a. Ismail (Egypt) a. *Kamehameha IV (Hawaii) d.* *Kamehameha V (Hawaii) a.* *Sir Geo. Cornewall Lewis d.* David Lloyd-George b. *Lord Lyndhurst d.* Milovan Milovanović b. *Baron von Stockmar d.* Peter Stolypin b. Baron Tanaka b. René Viviani b. Geo. Wyndham b. *Wm. L. Yancey d.*	*Lord Clyde d.* *"Stonewall" Jackson d.* *John F. Reynolds d.* *Edwin V. Sumner d.*	Henry Ford b. Hugo Haase b. Wm. Randolph Hearst b. Samuel H. Kress b. Werner Sombart b.	*Lyman Beecher d.* *F. W. Faber d.* Rufus M. Jones b. Shailer Mathews b. George Santayana b. *Richard Whately d.*	Stefan Apathy b. Henry Balfour b. Mary W. Calkins b. Annie J. Cannon b. Edwin G. Conklin b. *Ebenezer Emmons d.* Simon Flexner b. Joseph Jastrow b. Geo. Grant MacCurdy b. *Eilhardt Mitscherlich d.* Hugo Munsterberg b. Max Verworn b.	*Jakob Grimm d.* Alfred E. Newton b. *Johannes Voigt d.*	Edward W. Bok b. Gamaliel Bradford b. William A. Brady b. Constantine Cavafy b. Louis Couperus b. Gabriele D'Annunzio b. Adolfo DeBosis b. John Fox b. Gustav Frenssen b. *Friedrich Hebbel d.* Wm. Heinemann b. Arno Holz b. "Anthony Hope" b. W. W. Jacobs b. Edgar Jepson b. Wm. J. Locke b. Arthur Machen b.	*Clement C. Moore d.* A. T. Quiller-Couch b. Amélie Rives b. "Feodor Sologub" Lionel Strachey b. *W. M. Thackeray d.* Louis Tracy b. *Frances Trollope d.* *Iancu Vacarescu d.* *Alfred de Vigny d.*	Geo. Gray Barnard b. Cecilia Beaux b. *Eugène Delacroix d.* J. L. G. Ferris b. Frederick MacMonnies b. *Wm. Mulready d.* Richard F. Outcault b. Joaquin Sorolla b. Franz von Stuck b. *Horace Vernet d.*	Pietro Mascagnoi b. Horatio W. Parker b. Felix Weingartner b.	Ralph Adams Cram b. *Sam Houston d.* Jesse Pomeroy b.
1864	Ion Bratianu b. Roger Casement b. *Joshua R. Giddings d.* Franklin K. Lane b. Robt. Lansing b. Li Yuan-Hung b. Ludwig II (Bavaria) a. Sir Fredk. Maude b. *Maximilian (Mexico) a.* *Maximilian II (Bavaria) d.* *Wm. Smith O'Brien d.* Rushdi Pasha b. Satyendro Sinha b. *Roger Taney d.* Eleutherios Venizelos b.	Reginald Dyer b. *Jas. B. McPherson d.* *John H. Morgan d.* *Leonidas Polk d.* *John Sedgwick d.* *J. E. B. Stuart d.* Sir Henry H. Wilson b.	*Barthélemy Enfantin d.* *Ferdinand Lassalle d.* *Nassau Senior d.* Philip Snowden b. *Platt R. Spencer d.* *Robt. Torrens d.* Max Weber b.	*Jas. F. Ferrier d.* *Theodor Fliedner d.*	Vernon Bailey b. *George Boole d.* George W. Carver b. George W. Crile b. *Edward Hitchcock d.* W. H. Nernst b. Wm. H. R. Rivers b. *Benj. Silliman d.* *Friedrich von Struve d.* Henry D. Thompson b. *Ludolph Treviranus d.* *Rudolf Wagner d.* Wilhelm Wien b. Sir Arthur Smith Woodward b.	Lord Charnwood b. *Wm. Cureton d.* Ellen Fitz Pendleton b. *Josiah Quincy d.* *Karl Christian Rafn d.* *Henry R. Schoolcraft d.* Frank H. Vizetelly b.	*Lucy Aikin d.* *Park Benjamin d.* Arthur Brisbane b. *John Clare d.* Richard Harding Davis b. *Chas. W. Dilke d.* Thos. Dixon b. *Andras Fáy d.* Elinor Glyn b. *Louis Hachette d.* Geo. B. Harvey b. *Nathaniel Hawthorne d.* Richard Hovey b. M. A. De Wolfe Howe b. Ricarda Huch b. *Jacques Jasmin d.*	*V. S. Karajich d.* *Walter Savage Landor d.* Wm. Le Queux b. Leonard Merrick b. Paul Elmer More b. Neil Munro b. *Adelaide A. Procter d.* Henri de Regnier b. *Frank Smedley d.* *Robt. Surtees d.* Miguel de Unamuno b. Francis Viele-Griffin b. *A. A. Watts d.* Frank Wedekind b. Israel Zangwill b. Stephen Zeromski b.	*Wm. Dyce d.* Louis Eilshemius b. *Sir John W. Gordon d.* Henri de Lautrec-Toulouse b. *John Leech d.* Phil May b. Alfred Stieglitz b.	*Stephen Foster d.* *Giacomo Meyerbeer d.* Richard Strauss b. Leslie Stuart b.	*Wm. Baikie d.* *John H. Speke d.* Vesta Tilley b.

Year A.D.	Government and Law	Military, Naval, and Aviation Affairs	Industry Commerce Economics Finance Invention Labor	Philosophy and Religion	Science, Technology, and Medicine	Education Scholarship History	Literature and Journalism	Visual Arts	Music	Miscellaneous
1865	Pierre de Chambrun b. Charles C. Dawes b. *Edward Everett d.* Warren G. Harding b. *L. Lajpat Rai b. Leopold I (Belgium) d. Leopold II (Belgium) a. Abraham Lincoln d. Prince Mavrokordatos d. Duc de Morny d. Viscount Palmerston d.* Gifford Pinchot b. Philipp Scheidemann b.	Fredk. Funston b. Erich Ludendorff b.	*Richard Cobden d. Sir Saml. Cunard d.* Sir Henri Deterding b. Lincoln Filene b. *P.J. Proudhon d.*	Irving Babbitt b. Evangeline Booth b. Sir Wilfred T. Grenfell b. Rafael Merry del Val b. *Alonzo Potter d. Isaac Williams d. Cardinal Wiseman d.*	Geo. P. Bond d. Henry Christy d. Johann Encke d. Hugh Falconer d. Robt. Fitzroy d. Sir Wm. Rowan Hamilton d. Edgar L. Hewett b. Sir Wm. Hooker d. John Lindley d. Henrich Pander d. John S. Plaskett b. Robt. Remak d. Ignaz Semmelweiss d. Chas. P. Steinmetz b. Wm. Morton Wheeler b. Richard Zsigmondy b.	*Richard Hildreth d. Henri Ollendorff d. Chas. Richardson d. Joseph E. Worcester d.*	Wm. Aytoun d. Otto Birbaum b. *Fredrika Bremer d. Charlotte Brontë d. John Cassell d.* Madison Cawein b. Robert W. Chambers b. Frank M. Colby b. Holman F. Day b. Clyde Fitch b. Laurence Housman b. Paul Leicester Ford b. *Elizabeth C. Gaskell d.* Wm. Gay b. *Fulke Greville d.* Thos. C. Haliburton d. Rudyard Kipling b. A.E.W. Mason b. Dmitri S. Merezhkovski b. Baroness Orczy b. Barry Pain b. Wm. Lyon Phelps b. *Duc de Rivas d. Lydia H. Sigourney d.* Logan Pearsall Smith b. Arthur Symons b. *Isaac Taylor d.* Fredk. H. Trench b. Wm. Butler Yeats b.	Bernard Berenson b. *Sir Chas. L. Eastlake d.* Robert Henri b. *Constant Troyon d. Antoine Wiertz d.*	Anton Beer-Walbrunn b. H.C. Chatfield-Taylor b. Emma Eames b. Franz Kneisel b. Jean Sibelius b.	*Heinrich Barth d. John Wilkes Booth d.* Edith Cavell b. Fredk. A. Cook b. Minnie Maddern Fiske b. Yvette Guilbert b. *Sir Jos. Paxton d. Sir John Richardson d.* Fay Templeton b.
1866	Alexander Cuza (Rumania) abd. *Lewis Cass d. Luigi Farini d.* G.J. Gokhale b. Maud Gonne b. J. Ramsey MacDonald b. *Don Miguel d. John Ross d.* Sergei Sazonov b. Sun Yat-Sen b.	*Winfield Scott d. Robt. F. Stockton d.*	Voltairine DeCleyre b. Emile Vandervelde b.	*Christoffer Boström d. Alexander Campbell d.* Benedetto Croce b. *John Keble d. Phineas Quimby d.*	Earl of Carnarvon b. Harrison G. Dyar b. Emil Holmgren b. Smith Ely Jelliffe b. Peter Lebedev b. Graham Lusk b. Robt. MacDougall b. Thos. Hunt Morgan b. *Alexander von Nordmann d. Georg Riemann d.* Ernest Starling b. Serge Voronoff b. August von Wassermann b. Alfred Werner b. *Wm. Whewell d.*	Archibald Coolidge b. Abraham Flexner b. Anne Sullivan Macy b. *Jared Sparks d.* Alfredo Trombetti b.	George Ade b. *Karl Almqvist d.* Jacinto Benavente y Martínez b. Claude F. Bragden b. George Cosbuc b. Gergely Czuczor b. David Edelstadt b. "Elizabeth" b. Richard Le Gallienne b. *Francis S. Mahony d.* Geo. Barr McCutcheon b. Thos. L. Masson b. W.B. Maxwell b. *John M. Neale d.* Meredith Nicholson b. E. Phillips Oppenheim b. *Thos. Love Peacock d. John Pierpont d.* Romain Rolland b. *Friedrich Rückert d.* Dora Sigerson b. Lincoln Steffens b. *Ann Taylor d.* H.G. Wells b.	Leon Bakst b. *"Paul Gavarni" d. John Gibson d. Clarkson Stanfield d.* Art Young b.	Ferruccio Busoni b. Andreas Dippel b. Erik Satie b. Antonio Scotti b.	Maclyn Arbuckle b. John Ringling b.
1867	Stanley Baldwin b. Kurt Eisner b. *Maximilian (Mexico) d. Mutsuhito (Japan) a.* Joseph Pilsudski b. Henry L. Stimson b.	Carl Gustav Mannerheim b. *Thos. F. Meagher d.* Alexander Protoguerov b. Maxime Weygand b.	Irving Fisher b. Simon Guggenheim b. *Elias Howe d.* Sebastian Kresge b. J. Pierpont Morgan, Jr., b. Wm. Z. Ripley b. Lillian Wald b. Wilbur Wright b.	*Alexander D. Bache d. Victor Cousin d. Richard Rothe d.*	Thos. Clarks d. Marie Curie b. Hans A. Driesch b. *Michael Faraday d. Jean Flourens d. John Goodsir d. Earl of Rosse d.* Edward B. Titchener b. *Lord Wrottesley d.*	*Sir Archibald Alison d. Chas. Anthon d. Franz Bopp d.* Edith Hamilton b. Robt. R. Moton b. Sir Bernard Pares b.	Emily G. Balch b. *Charles Baudelaire d. Robt. Bell d.* Julien Benda b. Arnold Bennett b. E.F. Benson b. "Nellie Bly" b. *Chas. Farrar Browne d.* Rubén Dario b. Léon Daudet b. *Digby Dolben d.* Ernest Dowson b. *Lady Dufferin d.* Finley P. Dunne b. John Galsworthy b. *Fitz-Greene Halleck d.* "John Oliver Hobbes" b. V. Blasco Ibanez b. Lionel Johnson b. Chas. E. Montague b. David Graham Phillips b. Luigi Pirandello b. Wladyslas Reymont b. *Henry Crabb Robinson d.* Geo. W. Russell b. *Catherine Sedgwick d. Alexander Smith d. Henry Timrod d.* Marie Van Vorst b. Laura Ingalls Wilder b. *N.P. Willis d.* Harry Leon Wilson b.	Frank Brangwyn b. *Peter von Cornelius d.* Chas. Dana Gibson b. *Dominique Ingres d. Horatio McCulloch d.* Julius Meier-Graefe b. Emil Nolde b. Arthur Rackham b. *Théodore Rousseau d.*	Harry T. Burleigh b. *Edmond Clément d.* Patrick Conway b. Umberto Giordano b. Enrique Granados b. Edmond Clement b. Arturo Toscanini b.	Mrs. Patrick Campbell b. Jean Charcot b.

1868–1873 A.D.

Year A.D.	Government and Law	Military, Naval, and Aviation Affairs	Industry Commerce Economics Finance Invention Labor	Philosophy and Religion	Science, Technology, and Medicine	Education Scholarship History	Literature and Journalism		Visual Arts	Music	Miscellaneous
1868	Sir Jas. Brooke d. / Lord Brougham d. / Jas. Buchanan d. / Chulalongkorn (Siam) a. / John Nance Garner b. / Nicholas Horthy de Nagybánya b. / Thos. D'Arcy McGee d. / Gustav Noske b. / Thaddeus Stevens d. / Comte de Walewski d. / David Wilmot d.		Harvey S. Firestone b. / Lord Rothermere (Harold Harmsworth) b.		Emil Bose b. / Sir David Brewster d. / Robt. K. Duncan b. / Sir Frank Dyson b. / Jas. D. Forbes d. / Jean Foucault d. / Eleanor A.M. Gamble b. / Fritz Haber b. / George Ellery Hale b. / Herbert S. Jennings b. / Robert A. Millikan b. / August Möbius d. / Wm. T. Morton d. / Julius Plücker d. / Theodore Richards b. / Antoine Serres d. / Wilhelm Stekel b.	Wm. Allen d. / J. Boucher de Crèvecoeur d. / John Elliotson d. / Henry H. Milman d. / August Schleicher d. / Matthew Vassar d.	Mary Austin b. / Paul Claudel b. / Norman Douglas b. / W.E.B. Dubois b. / Friedrich Forster d. / Edward Garnett b. / Maxim Gorky b. / Norman Hapgood b. / Robt. Herrick b. / Francis Jammes b. / Jacob van Lennep d. / G.H. Lorimer b.	Saml. Lover d. / Marie Belloc Lowndes b. / Edgar Lee Masters b. / Adah Isaacs Menken d. / Stephen Phillips b. / Edmond Rostand b. / Seba Smith d. / Wm. Allen White b.	F. McKinney Hubbard b. / Emanuel Leutze d. / Chas. Meryon d.	Henry F. Gilbert b. / Louis F. Gottschalk b. / Marcel Journet b. / Hamish Maccunn b. / Maud Powell b. / Gioachino Rossini d. / Oscar Saenger b. / Ellen Beach Yaw b.	George Arliss b. / Gertrude Bell b. / Kit Carson d. / Chas. John Kean d. / Robert Scott b.
1869	Abdur Rahman Khan (Afganistan) a. / Emilio Aguinaldo b. / Neville Chamberlain b. / Earl of Derby d. / Wm. Pitt Fessenden d. / Ben B. Lindsey b. / Kenneth D. McKellar b. / Fuad Pasha d. / Franklin Pierce d. / Edwin M. Stanton d. / Robt. J. Walker d.	Viscount Gough d. / Adolphe Niel d.	Francisco Largo Caballero b. / J. Frank Duryea b. / Emma Goldman b. / Wm. D. Haywood b. / Karl Haushofer b. / Morris Hillquit b. / Ernest C. Jones d. / John A. Roebling d. / Claudio Treves b.	Hiram Bingham, Sr. d. / Mohandas K. Gandhi b. / Woodbridge Riley b.	Aristides Agramonte b. / Karl Carus d. / Harvey W. Cushing b. / Otto Erdmann d. / Thos. Graham d. / John W. Harshberger b. / Aleš Hrdlička b. / Jos. B. Jukes d. / John C. Merriam b. / Johannes Purkinje d. / Baron von Reichenbach d. / James Rush d. / Michael Sars d.	John Conington d. / Alexander Dyce d. / Otto John d. / Christian L. Lange b. / P.M. Roget d. / Percy Strangford d.	Laurence Binyon b. / Algernon Blackwood b. / Louis Bouilhet d. / Geo. Douglas Brown b. / Wm. Carleton d. / Herbert Croly b. / Peter Cunningham d. / Lady Duff-Gordon d. / André Gide b. / Jas. Harper d. / John Cam Hobhouse d. / Alphonse de Lamartine d. / Stephen Leacock b. / Wm. Vaughn Moody b. / Fredk. O'Brien b. / S. Przybyszewski b.	Henry J. Raymond d. / Eugene Manlove Rhodes b. / Jessie B. Rittenhouse b. / E.A. Robinson b. / C.A. Sainte-Beuve d. / Felix Salten b. / George Sterling b. / Booth Tarkington b. / R.A.J. Walling b. / Brand Whitlock b. / Josiah Flint Willard b.	Henri Matisse b. / Friedrich Overbeck d. / Frank Lloyd Wright b. / Stanislaw Wyspianski b.	Julien Aguirre b. / Hector Berlioz d. / Will Marion Cook b. / Louis Gottschalk d. / Giulia Grisi d. / Gottfried Loewe d. / Siegfried Wagner b.	Otto Nordenskjold b. / Geo. Peabody d. / Tyrone Power b. / Charles Sturt d. / Howard Thurston b. / Alexandrine Tinne d. / Wayne B. Wheeler b. / Florenz Ziegfeld b.
1870	Amadeus I (Spain) a. / Armand Barbès d. / Duc Achille de Broglie d. / Anson Burlingame d. / Benjamin N. Cardozo b. / Jas. Connolly b. / C.R. Das b. / Friedrich Ebert b. / Isabella II (Spain) abd. / Leonid Krassin b. / Napoleon II (France) dep. / Sir Jonathan Pollack d. / Jan Smuts b.	John A. Dahlgren d. / David C. Farragut d. / Richmond P. Hobson b. / Lavr Kornilov b. / Robt. E. Lee d. / Geo. H. Thomas d.	Bernard M. Baruch b. / Alexander Berkman b. / Amadeo P. Giannini b. / Alexander Herzen d. / Thomas W. Lamont b. / Nikolai Lenin b. / Rosa Luxemburg b. / John Mitchell b. / Helena Rubenstein b.	Daisetz T. Suzuki b.	Alfred Adler b. / Clarence E. McClung b. / Heinrich Magnus d. / Sir Jas. Y. Simpson d. / Jas. Syme d. / Franz Unger d. / Wm. Alanson White b. / Clark Wissler b.	Paul Botta d. / Burton J. Hendrick b. / Comte de Montalembert d. / Maria Montessori b. / Emma Willard d.	Saml. Bailey d. / Hilaire Belloc b. / Ray Stannard Baker b. / Solomon Bloomgarden b. / Ivan Bunin b. / Hubert Crackanthorpe b. / Charles Dickens d. / Lord Alfred Douglas b. / Alexandre Dumas, Pére d. / Pierre Dupont d. / Jules de Goncourt d. / Adam Lindsay Gordon d.	Henrik Hertz d. / John P. Kennedy d. / Alexander Kuprin b. / Mark Lemon d. / Jos. C. Lincoln b. / Prosper Mérimée d. / Charlotte Mew b. / Anna C. Mowatt d. / H.H. Munro b. / Ada Negri b. / Frank Norris b. / Roscoe Pound b. / L.Prévost-Paradol d. / Alice Hegan Rice b. / Wm. J. Simms d. / G.C. Verplanck d.	Alexander Stirling Calder b. / Wm. J. Glackens b. / Jean Charles Langlois d. / Danl. Maclise d. / Maxfield Parrish b. / Ignazio Zuloaga b.	Michael W. Balfe d. / Alessandro Bonci b. / Leopold Godowsky b. / Franz Lehar b. / Arthur Pryor b. / Oskar Straus b. / Sir Henry Wood b.	Henrietta Crossman b. / Dorothy Dix b. / Trixie Friganza b. / Burton Holmes b. / Henry B. Irving b. / Marie Lloyd b. / Olga Nethersole b. / Baron von Wrangel d.

Year A.D.	Government and Law	Military, Naval, and Aviation Affairs	Industry Commerce Economics Finance Invention Labor	Philosophy and Religion	Science, Technology, and Medicine	Education Scholarship History	Literature and Journalism		Visual Arts	Music	Miscellaneous
1871	Aali Pasha d. Earl of Ellenborough d. Cordell Hull b. Jas. M. Mason d. Louis J. Papineau d. Stjepan Radić b. John Slidell d. Wilhelm I (Germany) a.	Pietro Badoglio b. John B. Magruder d.	Louis Delescluze d. Pierre Leroux d. Karl Liebknecht b. Melville D. Post b. Orville Wright b.	Henry Alford d. Sherwood Eddy b. Henry L. Mansel d. Friedrich Uberweg d.	Chas. Babbage d. Walter B. Cannon b. Augustus De Morgan d. Baron Jozsef von Eötvös d. Sir John Herschel d. Alexander K. Johnston d. Wm. Lonsdale d. Sir Roderick Murchison d. Lord Rutherford b. Florence Sabin b. Albert E. Wiggam b.	Wm. F. Badé b. Guglielmo Ferrero b. George Grote d.	S. Alvarez Quintero b. Leonid Andreev b. Henri Barbusse b. Herbert Bashford b. Alice Cary d. Phoebe Cary d. Robt. Chambers d. Winston Churchill b. Stephen Crane b. W.H. Davies b. Emile Deschamps d. Theodore Dreiser b. Arthur Guiterman b. Wilhelm Häring d.	Jas. Weldon Johnson b. Paul de Kock d. Harold MacGrath b. Heinrich Mann b. Marcel Proust b. Chas. Scribner d. Wickham H. Steed b. John M. Synge b. Geo. Ticknor d. Henry T. Tuckermann d. Paul Valéry b. Jesse Lynch Williams b.	Gutzon Borglum b. Lyonel Feininger b. Joseph Mánes d. Georges Rouault b. Moritz von Schwind d. John Sloan b.	Danl. Auber d. Henry Hadley b. Louise Homer b. Sigismond Thalberg d.	Winthrop Ames b. Chas. F. Hall d. J.E.R. Houdin d. Laurence Irving b. Elizabeth Kingsley b. Grigor Rasputin b. Blanche Ring b. Thos. W. Robertson d.
1872	Leon Blum b. Charles XV (Sweden) d. Calvin Coolidge b. Arthur Griffith b. Learned Hand b. Eduard Herriot b. Benito Juárez d. Kamehameha V (Hawaii) d. Alexandra Kollontay b. Giuseppe Mazzini d. Oscar II (Sweden) a. Wm. H. Seward d. Wm. C. Wentworth d.	Maurice Gamelin b. Geo. G. Meade d. Henry Halleck d. Tseng Kuo-Fan d.	Francis Lieber d. Saml. F.B. Morse d. Gerard Swope b.	Jean d'Aubigné d. Peter Cartwright d. Ludwig Feuerbach d. Inayat Khan b. Norman Macleod d. F.D. Maurice d. Alexander Meiklejohn b. José Rodó b. Bertrand Russell b. Friedrich Trendelenburg d.	Geo. Catlin d. J.E. Coover b. Francis Lieber d. Hugo von Mohl d. Félix Pouchet d. Wm. M. Rankine d. Maynard Shipley b. Mary Somerville d. Henshaw Ward b.	Gustavus Myers b. Louise Pound b.	Pio Baroja y Nessi b. Max Beerbohm b. Jas. Gordon Bennett d. Holbrook Blinn b. Sir John Bowring d. Paul Laurence Dunbar b. Théophile Gautier d. Horace Greeley d. Franz Grillparzer d. Nikolai Grundtvig d. Louise Closser Hale b. Moritz Hartmann d. Johannes C. Hauch d.	Rupert Hughes b. Chas. Jas. Lever d. Karin Michaëlis b. Sara Parton d. Geo. P. Putnam d. Thos. B. Read d. Emily Post b. Leonora Speyer b. Albert Payson Terhune b. Oswald Garrison Villard b. Carolyn Wells b. ? Harold Bell Wright b.	Albert C. Barnes b. Aubrey Beardsley b. J. Schnorr von Karolsfeld d. Winsor McCay b. John Marin b. Sir Wm. Rothenstein b. Thos. Sully d. Joseph Urban b.	Olive Fremstad b. Johanna Gadski b. Alfred Hertz b. John A. Lomax b. Lowell Mason d. Alexander Scriabin b. Frederick A. Stock b. Ralph Vaughan Williams b.	Maude Adams b. Roald Amundsen b. Francis R. Chesney d. Serge Diaghiliev b. Edwin Forrest d. Friedrich Gerstäcker d. William S. Hart b. "Little Egypt" b. J. Mylius-Erichsen b.
1873	Amadeus I (Spain) abd. Salmon P. Chase d. John W. Davis b. Joseph Howe d. Francisco Madero b. Dwight Morrow b. Abdel Sarwat Pasha b. Alfred E. Smith b. Lord Westbury d.	Sir Richard Church d. John W. Geary d.	Sir Norman Angell b. William Green b. Albert Santos-Dumont b.	John Stuart Mill d. G.E. Moore b. Harry F. Ward b. Saml. Wilberforce d.	Louis Agassiz d. Alexis Carrel b. Lee De Forest b. Auguste De La Rive d. Giovanni Donati d. Victor Lenher b. Yandell Henderson b. Baron von Liebig d. Matthew F. Maury d. Moritz Romberg d. Adam Sedgwick d. Wm. S. Sullivant d. John Torrey d. Franz Weidenreich b.	Immanuel Deutsch d. Julius Fürst d. Stanislas Julien d. Wm. H. McGuffey d. Friedrich Raumer d.	J. Alvarez Quintero b. Henri Barbusse b. John D. Beresford b. Valeri Bryusov b. E.G. Bulwer-Lytton d. Willa Cather b. S.G. Collette b. Walter de la Mare b. Lewis Gaylord Clark d. M.M.S. Dutt d. Ford Maddox Ford b. Emile Gaboriau d. Francesco Guerrazzi d. Jas. Hannay d.	Will Irwin b. Chas. Knight d. Joseph S. Le Fanu d. Alessandro Manzoni d. "Luise Muhlbach" d. Oliver Onions b. Charles Péguy b. Anne Douglas Sedgwick b. Fyodor Tyutchev d. Jakob Wasserman b. Stewart Edward White b.	Elie Faure b. Sir Edwin Landseer d. Hiram Powers d. Eliel Saarinen b. Janet Scudder b. Hugo Sunberg b.	Clara Butt b. Enrico Caruso b. Feodor Chaliapin b. W.C. Handy b. Sergei Rachmaninoff b. Max Reger b. Harry Von Tilzer b. Karl Wilhelm d. Herbert Witherspoon b.	Marie Dressler b. Sir Gerald Du Maurier b. François Garnier d. Percy Hammond b. Laura Keene d. David Livingstone d. Sir Robt. McClure d. Wm. Chas. Macready d. Burns Mantle b. Max Reinhardt b. Vesta Victoria b.

1874–1879 A.D.

Year A.D.	Government and Law	Military, Naval, and Aviation Affairs	Industry Commerce Economics Finance Invention Labor	Philosophy and Religion	Science, Technology, and Medicine	Education Scholarship History	Literature and Journalism		Visual Arts	Music	Miscellaneous
1874	Alfonso XII (Spain) a. Sir Winston Churchill b. E.H. Crump b. Luigi Einaudi b. Millard Filmore d. Ilya Garashanin d. Herbert Hoover b. Harold Ickes b. Kalakaua (Hawaii) a. MacKenzie King b. Daniel François Malan b. A. Ledru-Rollin d. Chas. Sumner d. Chaim Weizmann b.	Aleksandr Kolchak b.	Robert Hunter b. John D. Rockefeller, Jr. b. Thomas J. Watson, Sr. b. Owen D. Young b.	Nikolai Berdyaev b. A.A. Brill b. "Father Divine" b. David Strauss d. Stephen S. Wise b.	Jean de Beaumont d. Jean Cruveilhier d. Joseph Goldberger b. Peter A. Hansen d. Guglielmo Marconi b. Adolphe Quetelet d. Max Schultze d. Edward L. Thorndike b. Konstantin von Tischendorf d. Jeffries Wyman d.	Chas. A. Beard b. Ezra Cornell d. Henry W.C. Davis b. Hans von der Gabelentz d. François Guizot d. Alvin Johnson b. Herman Merivale d. Jules Michelet d. Agnes Strickland d.	Michael Banim d. Maurice Baring b. Adam Black d. Charles Brooks d. Gilbert K. Chesterton b. Owen Davis b. Sydney Dobell d. Robert Frost b. Zona Gale b. Ellen Glasgow b. August Hoffmann d. Hugo von Hofmannsthal b.	Tom Hood d. Holbrook Jackson b. Amy Lowell b. W. Somerset Maugham b. Samuel Merwin b. Alice Duer Miller b. Josephine Preston Peabody b. Bryan Waller Procter d. Fritz Reuter d. Robert W. Service b. Gertrude Stein b. Mark Sullivan b. Eugene Walter b.	John Foley d. Louis A. Fuertes b. Wilhelm von Kaulbach d. John Pye d. Wm. H. Rinehart d. Nicholas Roerich b.	Lina Cavalieri b. Charles Ives b. Serge Koussevitzky b. Josef Lhévinne b. E. Parepa-Rosa d. Arnold Schönberg b. Luisa Tetrazzini b.	Henry Betty d. Raymond Duncan b. Edna Wallace Hopper b. James Eads How b. H. Karl Kumm b. Nance O'Neil b. Sir Ernest Shackleton b. Gerrit Smith d. Harry Thurston d. Honus Wagner b.
1875	Hiram Bingham b. John C. Breckinridge d. Matthias Erzberger b. Duff Green d. Andrew Johnson d. Mikhail Kalinin b. John Mitchel d. Syngman Rhee b. Owen J. Roberts b.	Wm. D. Leahy b. Geo. E. Pickett d. Karl von Rundstedt b.	Roger Babson b. John E. Cairnes d. Charles S. Mott b. James Cash Penney b. Johann K. Rodbertus d. Lee Shubert b. ? Alfred P. Sloan b. Amasa Walker d.	Georg Ewald d. Chas. G. Finney d. Jas. Hinton d. Carl G. Jung b. Anton Lang b. F.A. Lange d. John Roach Straton b. Evelyn Underhill b.	Friedrich Argelander d. Gerard Deshayes d. Guillaume Duchenne d. Charles Fort b. John E. Gray d. Christopher Hansteen d. Gilbert N. Lewis b. Sir Chas. Lyell d. Elsie Clews Parsons b. Henry C. Plummer b. Albert Schweitzer b. Vesto M. Slipher b. ? Gustave Thuret d. Sir Chas. Wheatstone d.	Mary McLeod Bethune b. Wm. Bleek d. Wilhelm Corssen d. Geo. Finlay d. Pierre Larousse d. Winwood Reade d. Earl Philip of Stanhope d. Connop Thirlwall d. Sir John Wilkinson d.	Hans Christian Andersen d. John Buchan b. Edgar Rice Burroughs b. Antonio Castilho d. Grazia Deledda b. Zane Grey b. Robt S. Hawker d. Sir Arthur Helps d. Georg Herwegh d. Wallace Irwin b. Chas. Kingsley d. Percy MacKaye b. Thomas Mann b.	Jacques Migne d. Harry A. Overstreet b. M.W. Pickthall b. T.F. Powys b. Edgar Quinet d. Rainer Maria Rilke b. Rafael Sabatini b. Mortimer Thomson d. Arthur Train b. Thomas Wade d. Edgar Wallace b.	Antoine Barye d. Jean Carpeaux d. Jean Corot d. Rollin Kirby b. Carl Milles b. J. F. Millet d. Alfred Stevens (sculptor) d. Fredk. Walker d.	Georges Bizet d. Fritz Kreisler b. Pierre Monteux b. Maurice Ravel b. Leo Slezak b. Saml. Coleridge Taylor b.	Arnold Daly b. "Beatrice Fairfax" b. David Wark Griffith b. James J. Jeffries b. Napoleon Lajoie b. Mistinguett b.
1876	Konrad Adenauer b. Abdul Aziz (Turkey) d. Abdul Hamid II (Turkey) a. George Creel b. Ferencs Deák d. Frank Hague b. Reverdy Johnson d. Maxim Litvinov b. Pat McCarran b. Countess Markievicz b. Paul Reynaud b.	Braxton Bragg d. Geo. A. Custer d. Manuel Enceladus d. A.L. de Santa-Anna d. Henry A. Wise d.	Mikhail Bakunin d. Irénée DuPont b. Frank E. Gannett b. Harry F. Sinclair b. Thomas M. Storke b. A.T. Stewart d. H.B. Warner d. Louis Wolowski d.	Orestes A. Brownson d. Horace Bushnell d.	Karl von Baer d. Robt. Briffault b. Adolphe Brongniart d. Raymond L. Ditmars b. Christian Ehrenberg d. Vladimir Karapetoff b. Charles F. Kettering b. A.L. Kroeber b. Fielding B. Meek d. Danl. W. Morehouse b. Hideyo Noguchi b. E.E. Southard b. August Vollmer b.	Mary G. Beard b. Friedrich Diez d. Giuseppe Ferrari d. Saml. Gridley Howe d. Edward W. Lane d. Christian Lassen d. Frantisek Palacký d. Friedrich Ritschl d. Karl Simrock d. Geo. Smith d.	Comtesse d'Agoult d. Thos. Aird d. Sherwood Anderson b. Henry Bernstein b. Sarah N. Cleghorn b. Irvin S. Cobb b. Catherine S. Crowe d. Olav Duun b. John Forster d. Ferdinand Freiligrath d. James M. Hopper b. Henry Kingsley d. Geo. A. Laurence d. Wm. Ellery Leonard b.	Jack London b. Isaac F. Marcosson b. Filippo T. Marinetti b. Harriet Martineau d. Wilson Mizner b. Harvey O'Higgins b. Frederik Paludan-Muller d. Mary Roberts Rinehart b. Ole Rölvaag b. "George Sand" d. Geo. Thornbury d.	Constantin Brancusi b. Narcisse de la Peña Diaz d. "Ding Darling" b. James Earle Fraser b. Eugene Fromentin d. Sir Geo. Harvey d. Anna Hyatt Huntington b. Jo Mora b. José Maria Sert b. Maurice de Vlaminck b.	John Alden Carpenter b. Pablo Casals b. Félicien David d. Manuel DeFalla b. Alice Nielson b. Ernest H. Schelling b. Oley Speaks b. Bruno Walter b. Saml. Sebastian Wesley d. Ermanno Wolf-Ferrari b.	Margaret Anglin b. Charlotte Cushman d. Jas. Lick d. John S. Sumner b.

Year A.D.	Government and Law	Military, Naval, and Aviation Affairs	Industry Commerce Economics Finance Invention Labor	Philosophy and Religion	Science, Technology, and Medicine	Education Scholarship History	Literature and Journalism		Visual Arts	Music	Miscellaneous
1877	Aga Khan III (Ismailians) b. Alben W. Barkley b. *Wm. G. Brownlow d.* Plutarco Elias Calles b. Tom Connally b. Feliks Dzerzhinski b. Ruth Sears (Baker)Pratt b. *Juan de Rosas d.* Hjalmar Schacht b. *Louis Thiers d.* Leon Trotsky b. *David Urquhart d.* Robert Wagner, Sr. b.	*N.B. Forrest d.* Adolfo de la Huerta b. *Raphael Semmes d.* *Karl von Steinmetz d.* Pancho Villa b. *Chas. Wilkes d.* *Graf von Wrangel d.*	*Robt. Dale Owen d.* M.L. Schiff b. *Wm. H.F. Talbot d.* *Cornelius Vanderbilt d.* Wm. English Walling b.	*Wm. A. Muhlenberg d.* *Friedrich Tholuck d.* *Brigham Young d.*	William Beebe b. *Alexander Braun d.* *Vandyke Carter d.* *Antoine Cournot d.* Jos. Grinnell b. *Wilhelm Hofmeister d.* Sir James Jeans b. *Urbain Leverrier d.* Hugo Obermaier b. *Johann Poggendorf d.* Béla Schick b. *Alfred Volkmann d.*	*Ernst Ettmüller d.* Frederick Soddy b. *A. Herculano Carvalho d.* *Pierre Lanfrey d.* *John L. Motley d.* Virginia Gildersleeve b. Angelo Patri b. Fredk. Logan Paxson b. *Thos. Wright d.*	*John C.S. Abbott d.* *Walter Bagehot d.* Rex Beach b. *Chas. Cowden Clarke d.* Sir Philip Gibbs b. Montague Glass b. H.G. Granville-Barker b. *Friedrich von Hackländer d.* Archibald Henderson b. Hermann Hesse b.	Elizabeth Jordan b. John Macy b. *Nikolai Nekrasov d.* *Caroline Norton d.* Ameen Rihani b. *J.L. Runeberg d.* Alice B. Toklas b. Richd. Walton Tully b. *Saml. Warren d.* Michael Williams b.	*Gustave Courbet d.* T.A. Dorgan b. Raoul Dufy b. Harrison Fisher b. James Montgomery Flagg b. Marsden Hartley b.	Artur Bodanzky b. Alfred Cortot b. Mary Garden b. *Ludwig von Köchel d.* Wanda Landowska b. Titta Ruffo b.	*Edward L. Davenport d.*
1878	*Lord Chelmsford d.* *Franz Karl (Austria) d.* Walter F. George b. Humbert I (Italy) a. Herbert H. Lehman b. Manuel Quezon y Molina b. *Earl Russell d.* Gustav Stresemann b. *Wm. M. Tweed d.* *Victor Emmanuel II (Italy) d.* *Benj. F. Wade d.*	Baron Pyotr Wrangel b.	André Citroen b. Glenn Curtiss b.	*Alexander Duff d.* Harry Emerson Fosdick b. *Chas. Hodge d.* *Theodor Keim d.* Pope Leo XIII a. *Julius Müller d.* *Pope Pius IX d.* Agnes Maude Royden b.	*Antoine C. Becquerel d.* *Claude Bernard d.* *Elias Fries d.* Lawrence J. Henderson b. *Joseph Henry d.* *Crawford W. Long d.* *Julius R. von Mayer d.* Lise Meitner b. *François Raspail d.* *H.V. Regnault d.* *Carl Rokitansky d.* *Pietro Secchi d.* John B. Watson b. *Ernst H. Weber d.* Hans Zinsser b.	Jas. Truslow Adams b. *Catherine Beecher d.* Claude G. Bowers b. *Sir Edward S. Creasy d.* *E.A. Duyckinck d.* Christian Gauss b. *David Laing d.* *Karl Lehrs d.* *Heinrich Leo d.*	Mikhail Artzybashev b. Rudolph Besier b. *Saml. Bowles d.* Wm. S.B. Braithwaite b. *Wm. Cullen Bryant d.* Henry Seidel Canby b. Adelaide Crapsey b. Lord Dunsany b. Jeffery Farnol b. *Geo. Gilfillan d.* *L.A. Godey d.* Oliver St. John Gogarty b. *Karl F. Gutzkow d.* Georg Kaiser b.	*Geo. H. Lewes d.* Don Marquis b. John Masefield b. *Chas. Jas. Mathews d.* Ferenc Molnar b. Sarojini Naidu b. *Richard Realf d.* Carl Sandburg b. *Anna Sewell d.* *Bayard Taylor d.* Edward Thomas b. *G.J. Whyte-Melville d.*	*Geo. Cruikshank d.* *Charles Daubigny d.* Augustus John b. Ambrose McEvoy b. Maurice Sterne b. Gertrude Vanderbilt Whitney b.	Pasquale Amato b. Emmy Destinn b. Ossip Gabrilowitsch b. *Franz Schubert (later) d.*	*Sir George Back d.* Lionel Barrymore b. George M. Cohan b. Constance Collier b. Isadora Duncan b. Bill Robinson (Bojangles) b. Ruth St. Denis b. Fritzi Scheff b. *Sir Geo. Gilbert Scott d.* *George Selwyn d.*
1879	Sir William Beveridge b. James F. Byrnes b. *Caleb Cushing d.* *Baldomero Espartero d.* *William Lloyd Garrison d.* Will H. Hays b. *Ismail (Egypt) dep.* *Lord Lawrence d.* Franz von Papen b. Patrick Pearse b. *Jón Sigurdsson d.* Joseph Stalin b. Alexander Stambolisky b. Tewfik Pasha (Egypt) a. Joseph P. Tumulty b.	*John A. Dix d.* *John B. Hood d.* *Joseph Hooker d.* William Mitchell b. *Graf von Roon d.*	Lord Beaverbrook b. Howard C. Candler b. *Henry C. Carey d.* Sid Grauman b. *Sir Rowland Hill d.* Rose Pastor Stokes b.	*W.K. Clifford d.* *Juilius Frauenstädt d.* *Frances R. Havergal d.* John Haynes Holmes b. *Karl Rosenkranz d.*	*Bernhard von Cotta d.* *Heinrich Dove d.* Edward M. East b. Albert Einstein b. *August Grisebach d.* *Johann von Lamont d.* *Jas. Clerk Maxwell d.* Raymond A. Pearl b.	*John S. Brewer d.* *Elihu Burritt d.* *George Long d.* *Sir Anthony Panizzi d.*	*Jacob Abbott d.* *Ethel Lynn Beers d.* *Chas. de Coster d.* *R.H. Dana, Sr. d.* John Erskine b. Mazo De la Roche b. Dorothy Canfield Fisher b. E.M. Forster b. Katharine Fullerton Gerould b. *Sarah J. Hale d.* "Cosmo Hamilton" b. *Wm. Howitt d.* Vachel Lindsay b.	Harold Monro b. *Marie Roch Reybaud d.* Will Rogers b. *Irwin Russell d.* Elsie Singmaster b. Wallace Stevens b. Hannen Swaffer b. *Chas. Tennyson Turner d.* Louis Joseph Vance b. *Chas. J. Wells d.*	*Honoré Daumier d.* *Wm. M. Hunt d.* Paul Klee b. Edward Steichen b.	Sir Thomas Beecham b. Rudolf Friml b. Otterino Respighi b.	Ethel Barrymore b. Sydney Greenstreet b. *Chas. Fechter d.* Walter Hampden b. Alla Nazimova b. *Charles Peace d.* Paul Poiret b. Knud Rasmussen b. Vilhjalmur Stefansson b. Ernest Torrence b. *Eugène Viollet-le-Duc d.*

1880–1885 A.D.

Year A.D.	Government and Law	Military, Naval, and Aviation Affairs	Industry Commerce Economics Finance Invention Labor	Philosophy and Religion	Science, Technology, and Medicine	Education Scholarship History	Literature and Journalism		Visual Arts	Music	Miscellaneous
1880	Manuel Azaña b. *Sir Alexander Cockburn d.* *Adolphe Crémieux d.* *Jules Favre d.* *Duc de Gramont d.* Joseph C. Grew b. Alvaro Obregón b. Jeannette Rankin b. *Viscount Stratford de Redcliffe d.*	Douglas MacArthur b. *August von Goeben d.* George C. Marshall b.	Henry Pratt Fairchild b. Ivar Kreuger b. John L. Lewis b. Robert R. McCormick b. Christabel Pankhurst b. Jacob J. Shubert b. Josiah Stamp b. Matthew Woll b.	Morris R. Cohen b. Graf Hermann von Keyserling b. *Arnold Ruge d.*	*Thos. Bell d.* *Paul Broca d.* Peter H. Buck b. *Michel Chasles d.* Ralph H. Curtiss b. Arnold Gesell b. *Wm. Lassell d.* *Benj. Peirce d.* *Louis de Pourtales d.* Marie C. Stopes b. Leonard Woolley b.	Everett Dean Martin b. Albert L. Guérard b. Preserved Smith b. Lytton Strachey b. Leonard Woolf b.	Guillaume Apollinaire b. Sholem Asch b. Aleksander Blok b. *Lydia M. Child d.* *"George Eliot" d.* *Gustave Flaubert d.* John Freeman b. Louis Hémon b. Joseph Hergesheimer b. Robt. Cortes Holliday b. *Geraldine Jewsbury d.* Sophie Kerr b. *W.H.O. Kingston d.* *Frank Leslie d.*	H.L. Mencken b. Alfred Noyes b. Sean O'Casey b. *Arthur O'Shaughnessy d.* Julia Peterkin b. Channing Pollock b. Ernest Poole b. Max Radin b. Grantland Rice b. "H.H. Richardson" b. *George Ripley d.* Oswald Spengler b. *Tom Taylor d.* Carl Van Vechten b. *Jones Very d.*	André Derain b. Arthur G. Dove b. Jacob Epstein b. *Anselm Feuerbach d.* Hans Hoffman b. John La Farge b. Jonas Lie b. Jan Stursa b.	Ernest Bloch b. *Ole Bull d.* Alfred Einstein b. Sir Hamilton Harty b. Jerome Kern b. Jan Kubelik b. *Jacques Offenbach d.* Homer Rodeheaver b. Jacques Thibaud b. *Henri Wieniawski d.*	Monte Blue b. Leo Carrillo b. Lincoln Ellsworth b. W.C. Fields b. Michel Fokine b. Duncan Hines b. Helen Keller b. Tom Mix b. *Lucretia Mott d.* *Jas. R. Planché d.*
1881	*Aga Khan I (Bombay) d.* *Alexander II (Russia) d.* Alexander III (Russia) a. Ernest Bevin b. *Johann Bluntschli d.* Charles I (Rumania) a. *Benjamin Disraeli d.* *Jules Dufaure d.* Enver Pasha b. *Jas. A. Garfield d.* Alcide de Gasperi b. Earl of Halifax (Edward Wood) b. Kemal Atatürk b. Alexander Kerenski b. Klementii E. Voroshilov b.	*A.E. Burnside d.* Jean Darlan b. Sir John Dill b. *Friedrich Hecker d.* Paul Ludwig von Kleist b. Henry Maitland Wilson b.	*Louis Blanqui d.* Cecil B. DeMille b. *William G. Fargo d.* William Z. Foster b. Arthur Garfield Hays b. R.S. Reynolds, Sr. b.	Augustin Cardinal Bea b. "Daddy" Grace b. ? *Maximilien Littré d.* *Rudolf Lotze d.* Giovanni Papini b. *Arthur Penrhyn Stanley d.* Pierre Teilhard de Chardin b.	*E. Ste.-Claire Deville d.* Hans Fischer b. Alexander Fleming b. Walter R. Hess b. Irving Langmuir b. *Lewis H. Morgan d.* Abraham Myerson b. *Matthias Schleiden d.* Richard C. Tolman b. *Chas. W. Tuttle d.*	*Theodore Benfey d.* *John Hill Burton d.* Charles E. Funk b. Sidonie M. Gruenberg b. *F.F. Kuhn d.* *Jas. Spedding d.*	Achmed Abdullah b. Lascelles Abercrombie b. Franklin P. Adams b. *Henri F. Amiel d.* Daisy Ashford b. Octave Aubry b. Leonard Bacon b. *George Borrow d.* *Thomas Carlyle d.* Richard Washburn Child b. *Marcus A.H. Clarke d.* *Franz Dingelstadt d.* *Fyodor Dostoievsky d.* *James T. Fields d.* *Emile de Girardin d.* Edgar A. Guest b. Clayton Hamilton b. *J.G. Holland d.*	Juan Ramón Jiménez b. Clarence Budington Kelland b. Sidney Lanier d. Frederick Lonsdale b. Amy Loveman b. "Lu Hsün" b. Emil Ludwig b. Wm. McFee b. Gregorio Martinez Sierra b. Charles G. Norris b. *J.G. Palfrey d.* *Aleksei Pisemski d.* *Paul de Saint-Victor d.* Stuart P. Sherman b. *E.J. Trelawny d.* Guido da Verona b. Mary Webb b. Stark Young b. Stefan Zweig b.	*Solomon Hart d.* Fernand Léger b. Pablo Picasso b. *Eugène Verboeckhoven d.*	Béla Bartok b. Chas. Wakefield Cadman b. *Modest Mussorgsky d.* *Nicholas Rubinstein d.* *Henri Vieuxtemps d.*	"Billy the Kid" (Wm. H. Bonney) d. *Geo. W. DeLong d.* *Isaac J. Hayes d.* Margaret Illington b. Mikhail Mordkin b. Louella Parsons b. Harry Price b. Branch Rickey b. Nicholas M. Schenck b. Eleanora Sears b. E.A. Sothern d. *George E. Street d.* *Karl Weyprecht d.*
1882	Giovanni Amendola b. Giorgi Dimitrov b. Felix Frankfurter b. *Léon Gambetta d.* *Giuseppe Garibaldi d.* Gustave VI Adolf b. Fiorello H. LaGuardia b. Dudley Field Malone b. Sam Rayburn b. Franklin D. Roosevelt b. Louis S. St. Laurent b.	Wm. F. Halsey b. *Mikhail Skobelev d.* *Gouverneur K. Warren d.*	Sosthenes Behn b. *Louis Blanc d.* René Coty b. Louis Dublin b. *Wm. S. Jevons d.* Henry J. Kaiser b. *Pierre LePlay d.* E. Sylvia Pankhurst b. Frances Perkins b. William E. Scripps b.	*Bruno Bauer d.* *Thos. Hill Green d.* *Henry James, Sr. d.* Jacques Maritain b. Edward B. Pusey d. *Archibald C. Tait d.* *Wm. Geo. Ward d.*	*Francis Maitland Balfour d.* *Theodor Bischoff d.* Max Born b. *Jas. Challis d.* *Chas. Darwin d.* *Casimir Davaine d.* *John W. Draper d.* Sir Arthur S. Eddington b. *Theodor Schwann d.* *Sir Chas. W. Thomson d.* *Friedrich Wöhler d.*	Benj. G. Brawley b. *François Chabas d.* *Johan Madvig d.* *Edward H. Palmer d.* *Reinhold Pauli d.* *Jules Quicherat d.*	*Wm. H. Ainsworth d.* *Berthold Auerbach d.* Konrad Bercovici b. *John Brown d.* R.H. Dana, Jr. d. John Drinkwater b. *Karl Ebert d.* *R.W. Emerson d.* W.L. George b. Jean Giraudoux b. Susan Glaspell b. *Comte de Gobineau d.* Jackson Gregory b. Herman Hagedorn b. Paul Hanna b. Avery Hopwood b. James Joyce b. *Annie Keary d.* *Johann Kinkel d.* *H.W. Longfellow d.*	*Denis F. MacCarthy d.* Richard Middleton b. A.A. Milne b. George Jean Nathan b. James Oppenheim b. Olive Prouty b. *James Rice d.* *D.G. Rossetti d.* James Stephens b. Herbert Bayard Swope b. *Jas. Thomson ("B.V.") d.* Alexei Tolstoy b. *Anthony Trollope d.* Sigrid Undset b. Henrik Willem Van Loon b. *Thurlow Weed d.* Virginia Woolf b.	Geo. Bellows b. Georges Braque b. *Hablôt K. Browne d.* *Giovanni Dupre d.* Samuel Goldwyn b. Edward Hopper b. Rockwell Kent b. Gaston LaChaise b. *John Linnell d.* Willy Pogany b.	Geraldine Farrar b. Zoltán Kodály b. *Joseph J. Raff d.* *John W. Griffiths d.* Olga Samaroff b. Artur Schnabel b. Igor Stravinski b.	John Barrymore b. Frank Buck b. Louise Dresser b. *John W. Griffiths d.* *Jesse James d.* Douglas Mawson b. Tony Sarg b. Lou Tellegen b.

Year A.D.	Government and Law	Military, Naval, and Aviation Affairs	Industry Commerce Economics Finance Invention Labor	Philosophy and Religion	Science, Technology, and Medicine	Education Scholarship History	Literature and Journalism		Visual Arts	Music	Miscellaneous
1883	Clement Attlee b. Comte de Chambord d. William J. Donovan b. Sir Geo. Jessel d. Edouard Laboulaye d. Pierre Laval b. Lewis E. Lawes b. Benito Mussolini b. Alexander H. Stephens d. Andrei Vishinski b.	Antoine Chanzy d. Jos. W. Stilwell b. Archibald Wavell b.	Peter Cooper d. "Coco" Chanel b. Stuyvesant Fish b. Clifford M. Holland b. Roy W. Howard b. John Maynard Keynes b. Karl Marx d. Chas. E. Ruthenberg b. F. Schulze-Delitzsch d. Sir William Siemens d. Walter Dorwin Teague b. Arnold Toynbee d. James Young d.	Cardinal Amleto Cicognani b. J. W. Colenso d. Thos. E. Hulme b. Karl Jaspers b. Bob Jones, Sr. b. Paul Radin b.	Eric T. Bell b. Oswald Heer d. Jos. Plateau d. Karl Reichert d. Sir Edward Sabine d. Margaret Sanger b. Jas. Marion Sims d. Wm. Spottiswoode d. Friedrich Stannius d. Otto H. Warburg b.	Lorenz Diefenbach d. Edward B. Eastwick d. John R. Green d. François Lenormant d. Alexander S. Neill b.	Gustave Aimard d. Lincoln Colcord b. Hendrik Conscience d. Max Eastman b. St. John Ervine b. Caradoc Evans b. Arthur Davison Ficke b. Edward Fitzgerald d. Martin Flavin b. Francis Hackett b.	Franz Kafka b. Harry Kemp b. Victor de Laprade d. Ludwig Lewisohn b. Compton MacKenzie b. Mary MacLane b. Mayne Reid d. Lola Ridge b. Arthur Somers Roche b. Jules Sandeau d. Ivan Turgeniev d. William Carlos Williams b.	Jo Davidson b. P.G. Doré d. Richard Doyle d. Will Dyson b. Rube Goldberg b. Walter Gropius b. Edouard Manet d. Ivan Mestrovic b. José Orozco b. Charles Sheeler b. Maurice Utrillo b.	Ernest Ansermet b. Friedrich von Flotow d. Giuseppe Mario d. Richard Wagner d.	Douglas Fairbanks, Sr. b. Elsa Maxwell b.
1884	Lord Ampthill d. Eduard Beneš b. Judah P. Benjamin d. Edouard Daladier b. Sir Henry Frere d. Theodor Heuss b. Ismet Inönü b. Eduard Lasker d. Midhat Pasha d. Eleanor Roosevelt b. Hideki Tojo b. Harry S. Truman b. Arthur H. Vandenberg b.	Count Todleben d.	Elizabeth Arden b. Henry Fawcett d. Cyrus H. McCormick d. Norman Thomas b. Alexander Trachtenberg b.	Kesheb Chunder Sen d. Charles H. Dodd b. Eli Stanley Jones b. Cardinal Achille Lienart b. Hans Martensen d. Wendell Phillips d. Clarence E. Pickett b. Daniel A. Poling b. Eugène Cardinal Tisserant b. Hermann Ulrici d.	Roy Chapman Andrews b. Alfred Brehm d. Logan Clendening b. Julius Cohnheim d. Jean Dumas d. Hugo Gernsback b. Arnold Guyot d. Adolphe Kolbe d. Bronislaw K. Malinowski b. Gregor Mendel d. Karl F. Meyer b. Jean F. Piccard b. Otto Rank b. Isaac Todhunter d. Adriaan Van Maanen b. Sir Erasmus Wilson d.	Sanford Bates b. Johann Droysen d. Karl Lepsius d. Elias Lönnrot d. François Mignet d. George Sarton b.	Thos. G. Appleton d. Marie Bashkirstev d. Earl Derr Biggers b. H.J. Byron d. C.S. Calverley d. Will Cuppy b. Georges Duhamel b. Walter Duranty b. Lion Feuchtwanger b. Jas. E. Flecker b. Gilbert Frankau b. Abraham Hayward d. Chas. F. Hoffman d. Richard Hengist Horne d.	Heinrich Laube d. Wyndham Lewis b. Cornelia L. Meigs b. Mark Pattison d. Guy de Pourtalès b. Llewellyn Powys b. Keith Preston b. Charles Reade d. Panteleimon Romanov b. Damon Runyon b. John C. Squire b. Eunice Tietjens b. Sir Hugh Walpole b.	Jules Bastien-Lepage d. Guy Pène Du Bois b. Hans Makart d. Amadeo Modigliani b. Clive Weed b. Chas. A. Wurtz d.	Wilhelm Backhaus b. Alma Gluck b. Chas. T. Griffes b. John McCormack b. Bedrich Smetana d. Heitor Villa-Lobos b.	Ruth Draper b. Fanny Elssler d. Robert Flaherty b. Texas Guinan b. Walter Huston b. Bela Lugosi b. Allan Pinkerton d. Mack Sennett b. Maria Taglioni d. Laurette Taylor b. Sophie Tucker b. Charles Winninger b. Margaret Wycherly b.
1885	Alfonso XII (Spain) d. Alfonso XIII (Spain) a. Schuyler Colfax d. Fredk. T. Frelinghuysen d. Louis Riel d. Chas. Rogier d.	Mikhail Frunze b. Chas. G. Gordon d. U.S. Grant d. Geo. B. McClellan d. Irvin McDowell d. Mohammed Ahmed d. Chester W. Nimitz b. George S. Patton b. Francisco Serrano d. Lord Strathnairn d. Robt. Toombs d. J.B. Topete d.	Raoul Fleischmann b. Alfred C. Fuller b. Bernard F. Gimbel b. György Lukács b. Louis B. Mayer b. Tom Mooney b. A.J. Muste b. Joseph Pulitzer, Jr. b. Anna Louise Strong b. Wm. H. Vanderbilt d.	Thos. W. Doane d. Jas. Hannington d. David de Sola Pool b. Daniel Schenkel d.	Niels Bohr b. William B. Carpenter d. Jakob Henle d. Karen Horney b. Henri Milne-Edwards d. Cesar Searchinger b. Harlow Shapley b. Karl von Siebold d. Friedrich Stein d. Sir Henry Tizard b.	Georg Curtius d. Andrew Findlater d. Henri Martin d. H.A.J. Munro d. John C. Shairp d. Wm. J. Thoms d. Richard Grant White d.	Edmond About d. T.S. Arthur d. "Hugh Conway" d. Thomas B. Costain b. Ashley Dukes b. Juliana H. Ewing d. Lady Georgiana Fullerton d. Anne Gilchrist d. DuBose Heyward b. Lord Houghton d. Victor Hugo d. Helen Hunt Jackson d. Jens Jacobsen d. Nikos Kazantzakis b. Frances Parkinson Keyes b.	Ring Lardner b. D.H. Lawrence b. Sinclair Lewis b. François Mauriac b. Andre Maurois b. Graf von Platen d. Ezra Pound b. Kenneth Roberts b. Jules Romains b. Constance Rourke b. Henry W. Shaw d. Jules Vallès d. Susan B. Warner d. Humbert Wolfe b. Christopher Wordsworth (Younger) d. Percival C. Wren b. Elinor Wylie b.	Marie Laurencin b. Paul Manship b. Alphonse de Neuville d. H.T. Webster b.	Franz Abt d. Sir Julius Benedict d. Alban Berg b. Leopold Damrosch d. Otto Klemperer b. Giovanni Martinelli b. Clare Sheridan b. Sigmund Spaeth b. Deems Taylor b. Edgar Varese b.	Mary Boland b. Billie Burke b. Francis X. Bushman b. Sidney Chaplin b. Elsie Ferguson b. Pauline Frederick b. Bert Lytell b. John E. McCullough d. Sir Moses Montefiore d. Gustav Nachtigal d. Evelyn Nesbit b. Anna Pavlova b. Erich Von Stroheim b.

1886–1891 A.D.

Year A.D.	Government and Law	Military, Naval, and Aviation Affairs	Industry Commerce Economics Finance Invention Labor	Philosophy and Religion	Science, Technology, and Medicine	Education Scholarship History	Literature and Journalism		Visual Arts	Music	Miscellaneous
1886	Charles F. Adams d. Chester A. Arthur d. David Ben-Gurion b. Francis Biddle b. Hugo L. Black b. Viscount Cardwell d. Wm. E. Forster d. Ludwig II (Bavaria) d. Jan Masaryk b. Harold Nicolson b. Horatio Seymour d. Saml. J. Tilden d.	Winfield S. Hancock d. John A. Logan d.	Stephen Pearl Andrews d. Bruce Barton b. Clarence Birdseye b. Richard M. Hoe d. Glenn Martin b. Marco Minghetti d. Philip Murray b. John H. Noyes d. J. David Stern b. Ernest Thaelmann b.	Karl Barth b. Msgr. Edw. J. Flanagan b. John Grote d. Paul J. Tillich b. John Tulloch d.	Edward Kendall b. Sister Elizabeth Kenny b. Isaac Lea d. Paul Dudley White b. Albert Wigand d.	Vicomte de Falloux d. Douglas Southall Freeman b. Leopold von Ranke d. Mariano Paz Soldan d. Henry Stevens d.	Zoë Akins b. Wm. Barnes d. Wm. Rose Benét b. Edouard Bourdet b. Randolph Bourne b. Hermann Broch b. Van Wyck Brooks b. Thomas Burke b. John Esten Cooke d. Emily Dickinson d. Hilda Doolittle b. Sir Samuel Ferguson d. Ronald Firbank b. John Gould Fletcher b. Alain Fournier b. Paul H. Hayne d. Vyvyan Holland b. Edward Judson d. Joyce Kilmer b.	Alain Locke b. Hugh Lofting b. Alexander Ostravsky d. Elizabeth Madox Roberts b. Sax Rohmer b. Abram J. Ryan d. Siegfried Sassoon b. Josef von Scheffel d. Wm. B. Seabrook b. Edward B. Sheldon b. Vincent Starrett b. Wilbur D. Steele b. Sir Henry Taylor d. Richard Chenevix Trench d. Francis Yeats-Brown b.	Arthur("Bugs") Baer b. Paul Baudry d. Henry Kirke Brown d. Bernard Karfiol b. Ludwig Mies van der Rohe b. Karl von Piloty d. Diego Rivera b. Russ Westover b.	Olin Downes b. Marcel Dupré b. Wilhelm Furtwängler b. Jenny Lind d. Franz Liszt d.	Ty Cobb b. John B. Gough d. D.D. Home d. Al Jolson b. Victor McLaglen b. Henry H. Richardson d. Grover A. Whalen b. Mary Wigman b. Ed. Wynn b.
1887	Hitoshi Ashida b. Ferdinand I (Bulgaria) a. Ramon Grau San Martin b. Theodore Francis Green b. Ernest Gruening b. Earl of Iddesleigh d. Vidkun Quisling b. Elihu B. Washburne d.	Albert Kesselring b. Erich von Manstein b. Sgt. Alvin C. York b.	Jas. B. Eads d. Sidney Hillman b. Alfred Krupp d. Agnes E. Meyer b. Albert R. Parsons d.	Henry Ward Beecher d. Elme Caro d. Geoffrey Frances Fisher b. Lord Gifford d.	Spencer F. Baird d. Ruth F. Benedict b. Karl T. Compton b. Gustav Fechner d. Karl Fresenius d. Earnest Albert Hooton b. Gustav Kirchoff d. Henry G. Moseley b. Balfour Stewart d. Adrian Stokes b. James B. Sumner b. Edward L. Youmans d.	Glen Frank b. Mark Hopkins d. August Pott d. Edward Thring d.	Leonard Bacon b. Henry Bedford-Jones b. Ernest Boyd b. Rupert Brooke b. Mary Ellen Chase b. Sylvanus Cobb, Jr. d. Dinah Mulock Craik d. Eduard Dekker d. Floyd Dell b. Alfred Domett d. Edna Ferber b. Paul Féval d. Bruno Frank b. James Norman Hall b. Zsolt de Harsányi b. Alfred Hennequin d. Richard Jeffries d.	Robinson Jeffers b. Orrick Johns b. Sheila Kaye-Smith b. George E. Kelly b. Arthur Krock b. Jules La forgue d. Emma Lazarus d. J.B. Lippincott d. Philip B. Marston d. Henry Mayhew d. Marianne Moore b. Edwin Muir b. Chas. B. Nordhoff b. Hesketh Pearson b. John Reed b. J.G. Saxe d. Edward R. Sill d. Mrs. Henry Wood d. Alexander Woollcott b.	Alexander Archipenko b. Marcel Duchamp b. Hendrik Glintenkamp b. "Le Corbusier" b. August Macke b. Friedrich Vischer d. William Zorach b.	Alexander Borodin d. Sir Geo. A. Macfarren d. Louis Persinger b. Sigmund Romberg b.	"Fatty" Arbuckle b. Dorothea Dix d. Marcus Garvey b. Willie (Wm. F.) Hoppe b. Edward Everett Horton b. Boris Karloff b. Raymond Swing b. Felix Youssoupoff b.
1888	L.H. Carnot d. Roscoe Conkling d. John Foster Dulles b. Friedrich III (Germany) a. and d. Carl C. Hall d. Sir Henry Maine d. Pasquale Mancini d. George Papandreou b. Domingo Sarmiento d. Henry A. Wallace b. Wilhelm I (Germany) d. Wilhelm II (Germany) a.	Achille Bazaine d. T.E. Lawrence b. Philip Sheridan d.	Dale Carnegie b. Geo. H. Corliss d. Pascal Covici b. John C. Garand b. Benjamin Franklin Goodrich d. Leone Levi d. Malcolm Lockheed b. Lord Arthur Rank b. Bartolomeo Vanzetti b.	Bronson Alcott d. Isaac T. Hecker d. Asa Gray d. Msgr. Ronald Knox b.	Heinrich de Bary d. Rudolf Clausius d. Asa Gray d. Grey Owl b. Edmund Gurney d. John Hays Hammond, Jr. b. Richard A. Proctor d. Theodor Reik b. Selman A. Waksman b. Geo. Waterhouse d.	Robt. G. Latham d. Lewis B. Namier b. Fredk. A. Paley d. Wm. G. Palgrave d.	S.Y. Agnon b. Anna Akhmatova b. Louisa M. Alcott d. Maxwell Anderson b. Matthew Arnold d. Vicki Baum b. Georges Bernanos b. James Boyd b. Heywood Broun b. Joyce Cary b. Raymond Chandler b. Jas. Freeman Clarke d. J. Frank Dobie b. Sir Francis H. Doyle d. T.S. Eliot b. A. Hamilton Gibbs b. Mary Howitt d.	Eugène Labiche d. David Lawrence b. Edward Lear d. David R. Locke d. Katherine Mansfield b. Frances Newman b. Laurence Oliphant d. Eugene O'Neill b. Nina Wilcox Putnam b. John Crowe Ransom b. E.P. Roe d. Michael Sadleir b. Alan Seeger b. Franz Sillanpää b. Theodor Storm d. Jan Van Beers d. Clement Wood b. Willard Huntington Wright b.	Bruce Bairnsfather b. Frank Holl d. Jas. J. Jarves d. Anton Mauve d. Henry Varnum Poor b. Paul Rajon d. Richard Redgrave d. David H. Strother d. J.R. Williams b.	Lucrezia Bori b. Stephen Heller d.	Henry Bergh d. Richard E. Byrd b. Maurice Chevalier b. Chester Conklin b. Gladys Cooper b. Barry Fitzgerald b. Sol Hurok b. Nikolai Prjevalsky d. Knute Rockne b. Jim Thorpe b. Lester Wallack d. Sir Hubert Wilkins b.

Year A.D.	Government and Law	Military, Naval, and Aviation Affairs	Industry Commerce Economics Finance Invention Labor	Philosophy and Religion	Science, Technology, and Medicine	Education Scholarship History	Literature and Journalism	Visual Arts	Music	Miscellaneous
1889	Alexander (Serbia) a. Georges Bonnet b. *John Bright d.* Carlos I (Portugal) a. Stafford Cripps b. *Jefferson Davis d.* Adolf Hitler b. Menelik II (Abyssinia) a. Jawarlahal Nehru b. Pedro II (Brazil) dep. *Prinz Rudolf von Hapsburg d.* Antonio Salazar b. Robert A. Taft b. *Francis Wharton d.*	Hanford MacNider b.	*John Ericsson d.* H.L. Hunt b. Lucien Lelong b. *Félix Pyat d.* *Philo Remington d.* Igor Sikorsky b.	*Father Damien d.* *Warren Felt Evans d.* *Alessandro Gavazzi d.* Gabriel Marcel b. *Albrecht Ritschl d.* Francis Cardinal Spellman b. Ludwig Wittgenstein b.	*Warren De la Rue d.* *Jas. P. Joule d.* *Maria Mitchell d.* *Stephen Perry d.*	*Saml. Allibone d.* *Fredk. A. P. Barnard d.* *Numa Fustel de Coulanges d.* *Wilhelm von Giesebrecht d.* Philip Guedalla b. *Jas. O. Halliwell-Phillips d.* C.K. Ogden b. *Gudbrandr Vigfusson d.* *Theodore Dwight Woolsey d.* *Sir Henry Yule d.*	Conrad P. Aiken b. Hervey Allen b. *Wm. Allingham d.* *Guillaume Augier d.* *Jules Barbey d'Aurevilly d.* Thomas Beer b. Robt. Benchley b. Herschel Brickell b. *Robt. Browning d.* Donn Byrne b. *"Champfleury" d.* *Nikolai Chernyshevski d.* Jean Cocteau b. *Wilkie Collins d.* *Eliza Cook d.* Bruce Cummings b. *Paolo Ferrari d.* Waldo Frank b. Erle Stanley Gardner b. *Robt. Hamerling d.* *Chas. B. Hawes d.* Elisabeth Sanxay Holding b. / *Gerard Manley Hopkins d.* Helen Hull b. Fannie Hurst b. George S. Kaufman b. "Hugh Kingsmill" b. *Fanny Lewald d.* Howard Lindsay b. Walter Lippmann b. Rose Macaulay b. *Chas. MacKay d.* Sarah Gertrude Millin b. Gabriela Mistral b. *Semion Nadson d.* "Mikhail Saltykov" d. *Edmond Scherer d.* Howard Spring b. *Martin F. Tupper d.* *Villiers de l'Isle-Adam d.* Arthur Waley b. Ben Ames Williams b.	*Jules Dupré d.* Don Herold b. *Sho-Fu Kyōsai d.* *Robt. Weir d.*	Amelita Galli-Curci b. *Carl Rosa d.* E. Robert Schmitz b. Alexander Smallens b.	*Laura Bridgman d.* Hattie Carnegie b. Joe Gould b. Elsie Janis b. Mae Murray b. Claude Rains b. Marjorie Rambeau b.
1890	*Count Andrássy d.* Michael Collins b. Charles De Gaulle b. Maurice Duplessis b. Dwight David Eisenhower b. Harry L. Hopkins b. Stewart G. Menzies b. Wm. O'Dwyer b. *Sitting Bull d.* Kotaro Tanaka b. Fred Vinson b. Joseph N. Welch b. *Willem III (Holland) d.*	Claire L. Chennault b. *Lord Napier of Magdala d.*	*August Belmont d.* Arthur Deakin b. Elizabeth Gurley Flynn b. *Jas. Nasmyth d.* Eddie Rickenbacker b. *Jas. E.T. Rogers d.* Elsa Schiaparelli b. ? Harold Vance b.	*Franz Delitzsch d.* *Johann von Döllinger d.* *Henry P. Liddon d.* Aimee Semple McPherson b. *Cardinal Newman d.*	Vannevar Bush b. *Jas. Croll d.* Paul De Kruif b. Hermann J. Muller b. Gregory Zilboorg b.	Allan Nevins b. Edward J. O'Brien b. *Heinrich Schliemann d.*	*Geo. H. Baker d.* *Dion Boucicault d.* *C. Castello Branco d.* Karel Capek b. Leonard Cline b. Elmer Davis b. "E.M. Delafield" b. *Octave Feuillet d.* Gene Fowler b. Saml. Hoffenstein b. *Jean Karr d.* *Gottfried Keller d.* *John W. Marston d.* Claude McKay b. / Christopher Morley b. *Chas. E. Mudie d.* John Boyle O'Reilly d. Boris L. Pasternak b. *Saml. Randall d.* Conrad Richter b. *Wm. Bell Scott d.* *Benj. P. Shillaber d.* Michael Strange b. Angela Thirkell b. B. Traven b. ? *Edwin Waugh d.* Franz Werfel b. Harry C. Witwer b.	*Sir Joseph Boehm d.* *Chas. W. Cope d.* *Vincent Van Gogh d.*	*César Franck d.* *Niels Gade d.* Beniamino Gigli b. Lauritz Melchior b. Paul Rosenfeld b. Tito Schipa b.	Theda Bara b. Floyd Bennett b. *Sir Richard F. Burton d.* *John C. Frémont d.* Sessue Hayakawa b. Hedda Hopper b. Duke Kahanamoku b. Stan Laurel b. Adolphe Menjou b. *Adelaide Neilson d.* Waslaw Nijinsky b. Carl von Ossietzky b.
1891	Thurman W. Arnold b. *Georges Boulanger d.* Earl Browder b. William C. Bullitt b. *Earl George of Granville d.* *Jules Grévy d.* *Hannibal Hamlin d.* *Kalakaua (Hawaii) d.* Liliuokalani a. *Sir John Macdonald d.* *Chas. S. Parnell d.* T.V. Soong b. Rafael Leonidas Trujillo Molina b. Earl Warren b.	Harold R.L. Alexander b. *Joseph E. Johnston d.* *Graf von Moltke d.* *David D. Porter d.* Erwin Rommel b. *Wm. T. Sherman d.* General Carl Spaatz b.	Louis Budenz b. *Edward Hargraves d.* *Baron de Haussmann d.* Paul G. Hoffman b. Willard M. Kiplinger b. *Jas. Redpath d.* Nicola Sacco b. Arthur Hays Sulzberger b. *I.C. Vidyasagar d.*	*Helena Blavatsky d.* *Chas. Bradlaugh d.* *Saml. A. Crowther d.* *Abraham Kuenen d.* G. Bromley Oxnam b. *Fredk. Scrivener d.*	Sir Fredk. G. Banting b. *Franz Brünnow d.* Sir James Chadwick b. *Sofya Kovalevski d.* *John LeConte d.* *Joseph Leidy d.* *Karl von Nägeli d.* *F. Poey y Aloy d.* Sir Andrew Ramsay d. *Jean Stas d.* *Wilhelm Weber d.* *Alexander Winchell d.*	*Geo. Bancroft d.* Hans Kohn b. *Heinrich Grätz d.* Samuel Flagg Bemis b. Lloyd Lewis b. *Franz von Miklošič d.* *Edward H. Plumptre d.*	Herbert Asbury b. *Théodore de Banville d.* Wm. Bolitho b. Octavus Roy Cohen b. *Gergely Csiky d.* Ilya Ehrenberg b. Lewis Gannett b. *Ivan Goncharov d.* Maurice Hindus b. Sidney Howard b. Cyril E. Joad b. *A.W. Kinglake d.* Pär Fabian Lagerkvist b. *Jas. Russell Lowell d.* Osip Mandelstam b. / *Herman Melville d.* *"Owen Meredith" d.* Anne Nichols b. *James Parton d.* Elliott Paul b. *Albert Pike d.* *Anthero de Quental d.* *Arthur Rimbaud d.* Nelly Sachs b. Harold E. Stearns b. *William G. Wills d.* Romer Wilson b.	Ralph Barton b. Percy L. Crosby b. *Elie Delaunay d.* Henri Gaudier-Brzeska b. *Chas. S. Keene d.* Jacques Lipchitz b. David Low b. *Jean Meissonier d.* *Giovanni Morelli d.* *Georges Seurat d.* *Sir John Steel d.*	*Emma Abbott d.* *Léo Delibes d.* Charles Münch b. Serge Prokofiev b. Erno Rapee b. John Charles Thomas b. ? Paul Whiteman b.	*P.T. Barnum d.* *Lawrence Barrett d.* Fanny Brice b. *John Close d.* Ronald Colman b. *Mischa Elman b.* *Wm. J. Florence d.* Harold Loeb b. Ted Shawn b. Clara Kimball Young b.

1892–1897 A.D.

Year A.D.	Government and Law	Military, Naval, and Aviation Affairs	Industry Commerce Economics Finance Invention Labor	Philosophy and Religion	Science, Technology, and Medicine	Education Scholarship History	Literature and Journalism	Visual Arts	Music	Miscellaneous
1892	Engelbert Dollfuss b. *Manuel da Fonseca d.* Robert Jackson b. *Rudolf von Jhering d.* *Juan Negrín b.* Kevin O'Higgins b. A. Roxas y Manuel b. *Viscount Sherbrook d.* *Johan Sverdrup d.* *Tewfik Pasha (Egypt) d.* Sumner Welles b. Wendell L. Wilkie b.	Wladyslaw Anders b. *Georg Klapka d.* *John Pope d.*	Julius Ochs Adler b. *Cyrus W. Field d.* *Jay Gould d.* Robt. S. Lynd b. *Edward V. Neale d.* *Ernestine Rose d.* *Werner von Siemens d.*	*Richard Lipsius d.* *Henry E. Manning d.* *Richard L. Nettleship d.* Reinhold Niebuhr b. *Cornelis Opzoomer d.* *Ernest Renan d.* *Geo. Croom Robertson d.* *Chas. H. Spurgeon d.*	*John Couch Adams d.* *Sir George Airy d.* *Henry W. Bates d.* *Henry I. Bowditch d.* *Wm. Bowman d.* Arthur H. Compton b. *Hermann Fol d.* J.B.S. Haldane b. *August von Hofmann d.* *Hermann Kopp d.* *Amedée Mouchez d.* *Sir Richard Owen d.* Thomas Parran b. *J. deQuatrefages de Breau d.* Hans Rademacher b. *Lewis M. Rutherfurd d.*	*Eduard A. Freeman d.* *Wm. F. Skene d.* Newman I. White b. *Sir Daniel Wilson d.*	Stella Benson b. John Peale Bishop b. "Max Brand" b. Pearl S. Buck b. Robert P.T. Coffin b. Ivy Compton-Burnett b. *Rose Terry Cooke d.* *Thos. Cooper d.* *Wm. Cory d.* *Geo. Wm. Curtis d.* *David Edelstadt d.* *Anne Edgren-Leffler d.* Alice Tisdale Hobart b. Jack Kerouac b. Edna St. Vincent Millay b. — *A.R. Rangabé d.* Burton Rascoe b. Elmer L. Rice b. Harold Ross b. Victoria Sackville-West b. *Franz Schoenberner b.* Frank Scully b. Osbert Sitwell b. *Jas. K. Stephen d.* James F. Stevens b. *Lord Tennyson d.* J.R.R. Tolkien b. *Thos. Adolphus Trollope d.* *Walt Whitman d.* *J.G. Whittier d.*	*Christopher P. Cranch d.* Will James b. Grant Wood b. *Thomas Woolner d.* *Alexander H. Wyant d.*	Sophie Braslau b. *Robert Franz d.* Ferde (von) Grofé b. Arthur Honegger b. *Edouard Lalo d.* Darius Milhaud b. Ezio Pinza b. Joseph Szigeti b. *Arthur Goring Thomas d.*	Juan Belmonte b. Eddie Cantor b. *Thomas Cook d.* Jennie Grossinger b. Walter C. Hagen b. Oliver Hardy b. Ted Lewis b. Basil O'Connor b. Basil Rathbone b. Dame Margaret Rutherford b. *Eduard Schnitzer d.* Lenore Ulric b.
1893	Dean Acheson b. *Jas. G. Blaine d.* *Ernst II (Saxe-Coburg-Gotha) d.* *Jules Ferry d.* *Hamilton Fish d.* *Rutherford B. Hayes d.* Leslie Hore-Belisha b. Haj Amin el-Husseini b. Liliuokalani dep. *Sir Jas. McCulloch d.* *Sir Theophilus Shepstone d.* Walter Ulbricht b.	*P.G.T. Beauregard d.* *B.F. Butler d.* *Comte de MacMahon d.* *Edmund Kirby Smith d.*	Warren K. Billings b. *Victor Considérant d.* Marshall Field, Jr. b. Victor Gollancz b. Harold Laski b. Spyros Skouras b. *Leland Stanford d.* Palmiro Togliatti b.	*Phillips Brooks d.* *Julius A. Dresser d.* *Philip Schaff d.* Abba Hillel Silver b.	*Jean Charcot d.* *Jacob Moleschott d.* *Chas. Pritchard d.* *John Tyndall d.*	*Samuel C. Armstrong d.* *Benj. Jowett d.* *Chas. Merivale d.* *Francis Parkman d.* *Sir Wm. Smith d.*	*Francis W.L. Adams d.* S.N. Behrman b. Maxwell Bodenheim b. "Hans Fallada" b. Stewart H. Holbrook b. *H.P. Holst d.* Vicente Huidobro b. *Lucy Larcom d.* Lois Lenski b. John P. Marquand b. *Guy de Maupassant d.* — Vladimir Mayakovsky b. *Wm. Minto d.* Fulton Oursler b. Wilford Owen b. Margaret Pulitzer b. Dorothy Parker b. Herbert Read b. Gilbert Seldes b. *John Addington Symonds d.* *Hippolyte Taine d.* Ernst Toller b. *José Zorrilla d.*	*Ford Madox Brown d.* Georg Grosz b.	*Alfredo Catalani d.* Eugene Goosens b. *C.F. Gounod d.* Hans Kindler b. Cole Porter b. Rosa Raisa b. *Peter Ilyich Tschaikovsky d.*	*Arnaud Abbadie d.* *Sir Saml. Baker d.* Norman Bel Geddes b. *Edwin Booth d.* Frank Borzage b. Spring Byington b. Ruth Chatterton b. Katharine Cornell b. Ely Culbertson b. Sir Cedric Hardwicke b. Peggy Hopkins Joyce b. *Fanny Kemble d.* Alexander Korda b. Harpo Marx b. Ivor Novello b. Francis Ouimet b. *John Rae d.* Robert Ripley b. E. G. Robinson b. *Karl Semper d.* *Lucy Stone d.*
1894	*Alexander III (Russia) d.* Oswaldo Aranha b. *Sadi Carnot d.* *Andrew G. Curtin d.* *Geo. T. Curtis d.* Herbert V. Evatt b. *David Dudley Field d.* *Earl Henry Grey d.* Ho Chi Minh b. Nikita S. Khrushchev b. *Louis Kossuth d.* *Ferdinand de Lesseps d.* Nicholas II (Russia) a. *Giovanni Nicotera d.* *Chas. Robinson d.* Moshe Sharett b. *Sir Jas. Stephen d.* *Wm. H. Waddington d.* *Robt. C. Winthrop d.*	*Nathaniel P. Banks d.* *Anna Ella Carroll d.* *Jubal A. Early d.* *Henry W. Slocum d.*	Blanche Wolf Knopf b. Edward H. Molyneux b. *Wilhelm Roscher d.* Beardsley Ruml b.	*Jas. McCosh d.*	*Chas. Brown-Séquard d.* *Pafnuti Chebyshëv d.* *Louis Figuier d.* *Hermann von Helmholtz d.* *Heinrich Hertz d.* Alfred C. Kinsey b. *August Kundt d.* *Wm. Pengelly d.* *Nathanael Pringsheim d.* *G.J. Romanes d.* Norbert Wiener b.	*Heinrich Brugsch d.* *Jas. Darmesteter d.* *Jean Duruy d.* *Wilhelm Freund d.* *Sir Austin H. Layard d.* *Elizabeth Peabody d.* *Wm. F. Poole d.* *Wm. Robertson Smith d.* *Wm. Dwight Whitney d.*	*Henry G. Bohn d.* Louis-Ferdinand Céline b. *Geo. W. Childs d.* E.E. Cummings b. *Maxime Du Camp d.* Rachel Field b. *Jas. A. Froude d.* Michael Gold b. Dashiell Hammett b. Ben Hecht b. *O.W. Holmes (Sr.) d.* Aldous Huxley b. Eugene Jolas b. *Chas. Leconte de Lisle d.* D.B. Wyndham Lewis b. *John Nichol d.* *Roden Noel d.* *J. de Oliveira Martins d.* — *Walter Pater d.* Westbrook Pegler b. *Christina Rossetti d.* Laurence Stallings b. *Robt. Lewis Stevenson d.* Genevieve Taggard b. *Celia Thaxter d.* Dorothy Thompson b. James Thurber b. Mark Van Doren b. *Henry Vizetelly d.* *Constance F. Woolson d.* *Edmund Yates d.*	Stuart Davis b. *Geo. Inness d.* *Hugo Salmson d.*	*Hans von Bülow d.* *Alexis Chabrier d.* *Anton Rubinstein d.* Artur Rodzinski b.	Fred Allen b. Charles Atlas b. Jack Benny b. Amelia Bloomer d. Alexander De Seversky b. Osa Johnson b. *Steele Mackaye d.* Tommy Manville b. Edison Marshall b. *Framjee Patel d.* Joseph von Sternberg b. Walter Wanger b.

Year A.D.	Government and Law	Military, Naval, and Aviation Affairs	Industry Commerce Economics Finance Invention Labor	Philosophy and Religion	Science, Technology, and Medicine	Education Scholarship History	Literature and Journalism		Visual Arts	Music	Miscellaneous
1895	Adolf A. Berle b. Count Folke Bernadotte b. Lázaro Cárdenas b. *Lord Randolph Churchill d.* Josephus Daniels, Jr. b. *Rudolf von Gneist d.* J. Edgar Hoover b. Liaquat Ali Khan b. Robt. M. La Follette, Jr. b. Maury Maverick b. Juan Perón b. *Earl of Selborne d. Stefan Stambolov d. Graf von Taafe d. Allen G. Thurman d.*	*Archduke Albrecht (Austria) d. Philip St. G. Cooke d.* B. H. Liddell Hart b. *John Newton d.*	*Friedrich Engels d.* Ragnar Frisch b. Laurens Hammond b. *John T. W. Mitchell d. "Stepniak" d.* Max Valier b. *Chas. Worth d.*	Richard Cushing b.	*Arthur Cayley d. Jas. D. Dana d. John R. Hind d. Thos. H. Huxley d. S. L. Lovén d. Karl Ludwig d.* Finn Malmgren b. *Julius L. Meyer d. Franz Neumann d. Louis Pasteur d.* Artturi I. Virtanen b. *Karl Vogt d.*	*C. E. A. Gayarré d. Sir Henry C. Rawlinson d. Lady Schreiber d. Heinrich von Sybel d.*	Michael Arlen b. Antonin Artaud b. *John S. Blackie d. Cesare Cantù d. Lord De Tabley d. A. G. Droz d. Alexandre Dumas, Fils, d.* Eugene Field b. Vardis Fisher b. *Gustav Freytag d.* Louis Golding b. *Thos. G. Hake d.* L. P. Hartley b. Robert Hillyer b. *Henry O. Houghton d. Jorge Isaacs d. Nikolai Leskov d.*	*F. Locker-Lampson d.* Charles MacArthur b. Archibald G. McDonnell b. Marcel Pagnol b. *A. V. Rydberg d. L. Sacher-Masoch d. Geo. Augustus Sala d. Sir John Seeley d. Saml. F. Smith d.* Hans Otto Storm b. Edmund Wilson b. Sergei Yessenin b.	Adolf Dehn b. Milt Gross b. *Thos. Hovenden d. Berthe Morisot d. Wm. Wetmore Story d. Leonard W. Volk d.*	Kirsten Flagstad b. Walter Gieseking b. *Benj. Godard d. Sir Chas. Hallé d.* Oscar Hammerstein, II b. Paul Hindemith b. *Geo. F. Root d.* Harry Ruby b. *Franz von Suppe d.*	Louis Calhern b. *Fredk. Douglass d.* Louise Fazenda b. John Ford b. Doris Humphrey b. Bert Lahr b. Paul Lukas b. Mae Marsh b. Florence Mills b. Paul Muni b. Babe (Geo. Herman) Ruth b. Joseph Schildkraut b. *Joseph Thomson d.*
1896	Trygve Lie b. *A. Lobanov-Rostovski d.* Muzaffar-ed-Din (Persia) a. *Nasr-el-Din (Persia) d. Duc de Nemours d. Sir Henry Parkes d. José Rizal d.* Samuel I. Rosenman b. *Léon Say d.*	Evans F. Carlson b. Arthur (Wm.) Radford b. Lewis Strauss b. *Louis Trochu d.* Marshall Georgi Zhukov b.	*Otto Lilienthal d. Alfred Nobel d.*	*Edward W. Benson d.* Irwin Edman b. R. DeRoussy deSales b. *Saml. P. Putnam d. Jules Simon d.*	*Richard Avenarius d. Ernst Curtius d. Emil Dubois-Reymond d. Benj. A. Gould d. Sir Wm. Grove d.* Leslie Groves b. *Friedrich Kekule d. Nicolaus Kleinenberg d. Ferdinand von Müller d. Sir Benj. W. Richardson d. François Tisserand d. Chas. Wachsmuth d.*	*Francis J. Child d.* James Muilenburg b. *Henrich von Treitschke d.*	Philip Barry b. *Mathilde Blind d.* Roark Bradford b. Louis Bromfield b. *H. C. Bunner d. Hubert Crackanthorpe d. João de Deus d. Baron De Geer d.* John Dos Passos b. *Geo. Du Maurier d.* F. Scott Fitzgerald b. *Edmond de Goncourt d.*	*Thos. Hughes d.* Giuseppi Tomasi di Lampedusa b. Frances Lockridge b. *Alexander Macmillan d. Wm. Morris d. Bill Nye d. Coventry Patmore d.* Marjorie Kinnan Rawlings b. Robert E. Sherwood b. *Harriet Beecher Stowe d. Paul Verlaine d.*	*Lord Leighton d. Sir John E. Millais d. Albert J. Moore d.* David Siqueiros b.	*Anton Bruckner d. Italo Campanini d. Antônio Gomes d. Klara Schumann d. Ambroise Thomas d.* Lawrence Tibbett b.	Luis Angel Firpo b. *Baron de Hirsch d.* Rex Ingram b. Buster Keaton b. *Enoch Pratt d.*
1897	Aneurin Bevan b. Gerhart Eisler b. V. K. Krishna Menon b. Michael A. Musmanno b. Lester B. Pearson b. *Lord Rosmead d. Heinrich von Stephan d.*		*Barnett Barnato d. Henry George d.* Harold Harmsworth b. Seymour Harris b. *Sir Isaac Pitman d. Geo. M. Pullman d.* Robert E. Ringling b. *Sir Travers Twiss d.*	Henry Calderwood d.	*Edward D. Cope d. Rudolf Heidenhain d.* Irène Joliot-Curie b. Louis S. Katz b. *Victor Meyer d. Fritz Müller d.* Wilhelm Reich b. *Julius von Sachs d. Johannes Steenstrup d. Edward J. Stone d. Karl Weierstrass d.*	*Jas Legge d. Francis Newman, d. Jas. H. Trumbull d. Francis A. Walker d. Justin Winsor d.*	*Wm. Taylor Adams d. Thos. E. Brown d.* Lewis Browne b. *Chas. A. Dana d. Alphonse Daudet d.* Bernard De Voto b. *Henry Drummond d.* William Faulkner b. William Gay b. Josephine Herbst b. Ilya Ilf b.	*Jean Ingelow d.* Eric Knight b. Christopher La Farge b. *Edward Maitland d. Margaret Oliphant d.* Drew Pearson b. Dawn Powell b. Fletcher Pratt b. *Margaret Preston d.* Lillian Smith b.	*Giovanni Cavalcaselle d.* John Stewart Curry b. *Sir John Gilbert d.* William Gropper b. *Wm. J. Linton d. Homer D. Martin d. John Sartain d.*	*Johannes Brahms d.*	*Antoine Abbadie d. S. A. Andrée d.* Richard Barthelmess b. *Charles Blondin d. Neal Dow d.* Charles ("Lucky") Luciano b. Paavo J. Nurmi b. Gregory Ratoff b. Norma Talmadge b. Walter Winchell b.

1898–1903 A.D.

Year A.D.	Government and Law	Military, Naval, and Aviation Affairs	Industry Commerce Economics Finance Invention Labor	Philosophy and Religion	Science, Technology, and Medicine	Education Scholarship History	Literature and Journalism	Visual Arts	Music	Miscellaneous
1898	Thos. E. Bayard d. Prinz von Bismarck d. Wm. E. Gladstone d. Sir Geo. Grey d. Liu Shao-Chi b. Chas. P. Villiers d. Wilhelmina (Netherlands) a.	Marie Pierre Koenig b. Wm. S. Rosecrans d. Mikhail Tchernaiev d. Matvei Zakharov b.	Edward Bellamy d. Sir Henry Bessemer d. Matilda J. Gage d. Daniel Gerber b. Henry R. Luce b. Albert John Luthuli b. David A. Wells d.	John Caird d.	Ferdinand Cohn d. Theodor Eimer d. Eleanor Glueck b. Jas. Hall d. John Hopkinson d. Sir Wm. Jenner d. Karl Leuckart d. Charles W. Mayo d. Sir Richard Quain d. Leo Szilard b. Karl Ziegler b.	Crane Brinton b. H. G. Liddell d.	Ludwig Bemelmans b. Stephan Vincent Benét b. Wm. Black d. Thomas Boyd b. Wm. C. Brann d. "Lewis Carroll" d. Bennett A. Cerf b. Georg Ebers d. Harold Frederic d. F. Garcia Lorca b. / C. S. Lewis b. Eliza Lynn Linton d. Stephane Mallarmé d. James Payn d. Donald Culross Peattie b. Eric Maria Remarque b. Fredk. Tennyson d. E. Noyes Westcott d.	Aubrey Beardsley d. Beniamino Bufano b. E. Burne-Jones d. Jimmy Hatlo b. Reginald Marsh b. P. Puvis de Chavannes d. Fèlicien Rops d. Ben Shahn b. Pavel Tchelitchew b.	George Gershwin b. Mischa Levitzki b. Ede Reményi d. Anton Seidl d. Vincent Youmans b.	Fanny Davenport d. Sergei Eisenstein b. Helena Faucit d. Dorothy Gish b. Alan Guttmacher b. Hattie McDaniel b. Saml. Plimsoll d. Earl Sande b. Frances E. Willard d.
1899	Marshall Mohammad Ayub Khan b. Lavrenti Beria b. Graf von Caprivi de Capreda d. Emilio Castelar d. F. F. Faure d. Stephen J. Field d. B. A. Guzman d. Lord Herschell d. Graf von Rechberg-Rothenlowen d. Paul-Henri Spaak b. Hoyt Vandenberg b. Sir Julius Vogel d.	Philip Colomb d.	Giuseppe Amato b. Norman Chandler b. Laurence Gronlund d. Ottmar Mergenthaler d. Baron de Reuter d.	Ludwig Büchner d. Robt. G. Ingersoll d. Dwight L. Moody d.	Bernt Balchen b. Robt. von Bunsen d. Elliott Coues d. Sir John W. Dawson d. Sir Edward Frankland d. O. C. Marsh d. Wm. Menninger b. Sir Jas. Paget d.	Arthur Giry d. Bernard Quaritch d. Chas J. Stillé d. Anna Swanwick d.	Louis Adamic b. Horatio Alger d. Grant Allen d. Miguel Asturias b. Elizabeth Bowen b. Whit Burnett b. Humphrey Cobb b. Sir Noel Coward b. Hart Crane b. Emile Erckmann d. / C. S. Forester b. Ernest Hemingway b. Erich Kästner b. Yasunari Kawabata b. Francisque Sarcey d. "Nevil Shute" b. E. D. E. N. Southworth d. Samuel Spewack b.	Eugene Berman b. Rosa Bonheur d. Birket Foster d. Jacob Maris d. Giovanni Segantini d. Alfred Sisley d. Sir Henry Tate d.	John Barbirolli b. Robert Casadesus b. Duke Ellington b. Johann Strauss (Younger) d.	Humphrey Bogart b. Chas. F. Coghlan d. Augustin Daly d. Charles Laughton b. Billy Rose b.
1900	Gustave Cluseret d. Joseph Cowen d. Heinrich Himmler b. Humbert I (Italy) d. Lord Loch d. Wayne Morse b. Karl Mundt b. Count Muraviëv d. Elmo Roper b. Lord Russell of Killowen d. John Sherman d. Adlai Stevenson b. Victor Emmanuel III (Italy) a.	Jacob D. Cox d. Osman Pasha d. Rabah Zobeir d. Sir Donald Stewart d.	C. P. Huntington d. Wilhelm Liebknecht d. Maurice Thorez b.	Jas. Martineau d. Friedrich Nietzsche d. Henry Sidgwick d. Vladimir Soloviev d. Isaac M. Wise d.	Eugenio Beltrami d. Frédéric Joliot-Curie b. Jas. E. Keeler d. Willy Kuhne d. Marius Lie d. St. George J. Mivart d. Ludwig Mond d. Wolfgang Pauli b.	Howard Aiken b. William B. Benton b. Henry Barnard d. Sir Denis Brogan b. Thos. Davidson d. Moses Hadas b. Max Müller d. John C. Ridpath d. Moses Coit Tyler d.	R.D. Blackmore d. John Mason Brown b. Paul Vincent Carroll b. Stephen Crane d. Richard Watson Dixon d. Ernest Dowson d. Guy Endore b. Lucretia P. Hale d. James Hilton b. Richard Hovey d. Alexander King b. Margaret Mitchell b. / Stephen Potter b. John Ruskin d. Albert Samain d. Antoine de St. Exupéry b. Giorgos Seferis b. Henry D. Traill d. Henry Villard d. Chas. Dudley Warner d. Albert R. Wetjen b. Oscar Wilde d. Thomas Wolfe b.	Fredk. E. Church d. Thos. Faed d. Mihaly von Munkacsy d. Sir Joseph Paton d.	George Antheil b. Louis ("Satchmo") Armstrong b. Eduard van Beinum b. Sir Geo. Grove d. Sir Arthur Sullivan d. Kurt Weill b.	Mady Christians b. Marion Davies b. Richard Halliburton b. Mary Kingsley d. Clementine Paddleford b. ZaSu Pitts b. Spencer Tracy b.

Year A.D.	Government and Law	Military, Naval, and Aviation Affairs	Industry Commerce Economics Finance Invention Labor	Philosophy and Religion	Science, Technology, and Medicine	Education Scholarship History	Literature and Journalism		Visual Arts	Music	Miscellaneous
1901	Abdur Rahman Khan (Afghanistan) d. Fulgencio Batista y Zaldivar b. Duc Jacques de Broglie d. Francesco Crispi d. Sir Jas. R. Dickson d. Ngo Dinh Diem b. Martin Dies b. Edward VII (England) a. Edward J. Eyre d. Benj. Harrison d. Prinz von Hohenlohe-Schillingsfürst d. Ibn Saud (Saudi Arabia) a. Li Hung-Chang d. Wm. McKinley d. Johann von Miquel d. Sir Leslie Munro b. Marthinus Pretorius d. Sukarno b. Henrik Verwoerd b. Victoria (England) d. Charles Whittaker b.	Fritz-John Porter d.	John M. Lewis b. Homer Martin b. M. G. Ranade d. Evelyn John Strachey b.	John Fiske d. Samuel Hepburn b. F. W. H. Myers d. B. F. Westcott d.	Richard Altmann d. Geo. M. Dawson d. Enrico Fermi b. Geo. F. Fitzgerald d. Clarence King d. Karl R. König d. Aleksandr Kovalevski d. Felix Lacaze-Duthiers d. Ernest O. Lawrence b. Joseph Le Conte d. François Raoult d. Henry A. Rowland d. John T. Scopes b. Peter G. Tait d.	Evelyn Abbott d. Herbert B. Adams d. Mandell Creighton d. John G. Nicolay d. Wm. Stubbs d.	Sir Walter Besant d. Robt. Buchanan d. Ramón de Campoamor d. Whittaker Chambers b. Wm. E. Channing (Younger) d. Jane Croly d. Ignatius Donnelly d. Dudley Fitts b. John Gunther b.	Jas. A. Herne d. Zora N. Hurston b. Oliver La. Farge b. Max Miller b. Robt. H. Newell d. Salvatore Quasimodo b. Mari Sandoz b. John Van Druten b. Charlotte M. Yonge d.	Arnold Boecklin d. Walt Disney b. Philip Evergood b. Alberto Giacometti b. Kate Greenaway d. Louis I. Kahn b. Wm. J. Stillman d. Henri de Toulouse-Lautrec d.	Nelson Eddy b. Grace Moore b. Ethelbert Nevin d. Harry Partch b. Giuseppe Verdi d.	Richard D'Oyly Carte d. Sir Frances Chichester b. Gary Cooper b. Bebe Daniels b. Clark Gable b. Helen Menken b. Chester Morris b. Baron Nordenskjöld d. Ernie Pyle b.
1902	John P. Altgeld d. Thomas E. Dewey b. Wade Hampton d. Earl of Kimberley d. Thos. B. Reed d. Cecil Rhodes d. Sir Sidney Shippard d. Kálmán Tisza d.	Admiral Nikolai Kuznetsov b. Charles Lindbergh b. Wm. T. Sampson d. Franz Sigel d.	Eugen Dühring d. David O. Selznik b. Chas. Tiffany d.	Robert Adamson d. Maurice Eisendrath b. Thos. D. Talmage d. Fredk. Temple d. Cornelis Tiele d.	Sir Frederick Abel d. Edward Condon b. Alpheus Hyatt d. Baron von Krafft-Ebing d. John W. Powell d. Walter Reed d. Rudolf Virchow d. Johannes Wislicenus d.	Lord Acton d. Charles K. Adams d. Saml. R. Gardiner d. E. L. Godkin d. Philip Gove b. Alice Freeman Palmer d.	Philip Bailey d. Lucius Beebe b. Arna Bontemps b. Geo. Douglas Brown d. Katharine Brush b. Saml. Butler d. Mary H. Catherwood d. Aubrey DeVere d. Edward Eggleston d. Thos. Dunn English d. Kenneth Fearing b. Corey Ford b. Paul Leicester Ford d. Wolcott Gibbs b.	Bret Harte d. G. A. Henty d. Georgette Heyer b. Langston Hughes b. Lionel Johnson d. Ogden Nash b. Frank Norris d. Quentin Reynolds b. Horace E. Scudder d. Lady Eleanor Smith b. John Steinbeck b. Jas. B. Stephens d. Frank R. Stockton d. Tiffany Thayer b. Philip Wylie b. Emile Zola d.	B. J. J. Constant d. Jules Dalou d. Jean Flandrin d. Thos. Nast d. J. J. Tissot d. J. G. Vibert d.	Henry Josef Krips b. Eddie Peabody b.	Vittorio De Sica b. John Dillinger b. Sol Smith Russell d. Elizabeth Cady Stanton d. Ed Sullivan b.
1903	Otto Abetz b. Alexander (Serbia) d. Cassius M. Clay d. Sir Chas. G. Duffy d. Estes Kefauver b. Brien McMahon b. Peter I (Serbia) a. Marquess of Salisbury d.	Arturo Ossorio Arana b. Wm. Farrar Smith d.	Benjamin J. Davis b. Richard J. Gatling d. Abram S. Hewitt d. Leo Huberman b. Henry Demarest Lloyd d.	Alexander Bain d. Fredk. W. Farrar d. Moritz Lazarus d. Pope Leo XIII d. Pope Pius X a. Chas. Renouvier d. Herbert Spencer d. Herbert Vaughan d.	Karl Gegenbaur d. Josiah W. Gibbs d. Jas. Glaisher d. L. S. B. Leakey b. J. Peter Lesley d. John von Neumann b. Alphonse Renard d. Alexander Rollett d. Sir Geo. G. Stokes d.	Edward Cowell d. Geo. B. Hill d. W. E. H. Lecky d. Theodor Mommsen d. Gaston Paris d.	Henry de Blowitz d. Cyril Connolly b. Countee Cullen b. Benj. L. Farjeon d. Geo. Gissing d. Augustus Hare d. Wm. F. Henley d. Chas. G. Leland d.	"H. S. Merriman" d. Clare Turlay Newberry b. G. Nuñez de Arce d. Frank O'Connor b. Raymond Radiguet b. J. Henry Shorthouse d. R. H. Stoddard d. Evelyn Waugh b.	Robt. F. Blum d. Paul Gauguin d. Phil May d. Camille Pissarro d. Mark Rothko b. Jas. A. M. Whistler d.	Luigi Arditi d. Vernon Duke b. Helen Traubel b. Hugo Wolf d.	Tallulah Bankhead b. Paul Du Chaillu d. Fernandel b. Lou Gehrig b. Fulton Lewis, Jr. b. Fredk. L. Olmsted d. Stuart Robson d. Lord Rowton d.

1904–1910 A.D.

Year A.D.	Government and Law	Military, Naval, and Aviation Affairs	Industry Commerce Economics Finance Invention Labor	Philosophy and Religion	Science, Technology, and Medicine	Education Scholarship History	Literature and Journalism		Visual Arts	Music	Miscellaneous
1904	Chip Bohlen b. Ralph J. Bunche b. M. A. Hanna d. Sir Wm. V. Harcourt d. V. Plehve d. M. S. Quay d. P. Waldeck-Rousseau d.	John B. Gordon d. Paul Krüger d. Jas. Longstreet d.	Jack Frye b. Gabriel Tarde d.	Thos. Fowler d. Robert McCracken b. Sir Leslie Stephen d.	Niels R. Finsen d. George Gamow b. J. Robert Oppenheimer b. Karl Weigert d. Alexander Williamson d.	Fredk. York Powell d. Hermann Von Holst d. Henri Wallon d.	Alfred Ainger d. Margery Allingham b. Sir Edwin Arnold d. Hamilton Basso b. Anton Chekhov d. Kate Chopin d. Frances P. Cobbe d. Cecil Day-Lewis b.	Parke Godwin d. Moss Hart b. Lafcadio Hearn d. Laurence Hutton d. Maurus Jókai d. A. J. Liebling b. Nancy Mitford b. Pablo Neruda b. Clement Scott d. Saml. Smiles d. Nathanael West b.	Peter Arno b. Frederic Bartholdi d. Miguel Covarrubias b. Henri Fantin-Latour d. J. L. Gérôme d. Franz von Lenbach d. Vassili Vereshchagin d. G. F. Watts d.	Anton Dvořák d. Gladys Swarthout b.	Theodor Herzl d. Fanny Janauschek d. "Dan Leno" d. Nathan Leopold b. Peter Lorre b. Sir Henry M. Stanley d. Geo. Francis Train d.
1905	Haakon VII (Norway) a. Dag Hammarskjöld b. John Hay d.	Fitzhugh Lee d.	Jay Cooke d. Eugene Dennis b. Christian Dior b. Louise Michel d. Michael J. Quill b.	Sir Geo. Williams d.	Ernst Abbe d. Adolf Bastian d. Sir John Burdon-Sanderson d. Walther Flemming d. Albrecht von Kölliker d. Jean J. Reclus d. Baron von Richthofen d.	John Bartlett d. Sir Richard C. Jebb d. Sir Wm. Muir d. Julius Oppert d.	H. E. Bates b. Marc Blitzstein b. Jean Burton b. Mary Mapes Dodge d. "Violet Fane" d. Henry Harland d. José de Hérédia d. Manfred B. Lee ("Ellery Queen") b.	Geo. Macdonald d. John O'Hara b. Wm. Sharp d. Edgar Snow b. Albion W. Tourgée d. Jules Verne d. Lew Wallace d.	Adolphe Bouguereau d. Adolph Menzel d. Constantin Meunier d. J. Valera y Alcalá Galiano d.	Eddie Condon b. Tommy Dorsey b. Theodore Thomas d.	Gracie Allen b. Thomas J. Barnardo d. Clyde Beatty b. Clara Bow b. Comte de Brazza d. Robert Donat b. Kay Francis b. Sir Henry Irving d. Joseph Jefferson d. Mary A. Livermore d. Franchot Tone b. Alfred Waterhouse d. Margaret Webster b
1906	Susan B. Anthony d. Christian IX (Denmark) d. Michael Davitt d. Frederick VIII (Denmark) a. Hugh Gaitskell b. Fredk. W. Maitland d. Bartolomé Mitre d. Henry Pu-yi b. Duke of Rutland d. Carl Schurz d.	John M. Schofield d. Wm. R. Shafter d. Joseph Wheeler d.	Marshall Field d. Johann Most d. Russell Sage d.	Edward B. Foote d. Eduard von Hartmann d. Geo. J. Holyoake d. Chas. A. Watts d.	Marston Bates b. Ludwig Boltzmann d. Pierre Curie d. Johann Dzierzon d. W. Maurice Ewing b. Mary Putnam Jacobi d. Saml. P. Langley d. Willy Ley b. Maria G. Mayer b. Hermann Sprengel d.	Jeremiah Curtin d. Wm. R. Harper d. Albert Sorel d.	Ferdinand Brunetière d. John W. DeForest d. Paul Laurence Dunbar d. Richard Garnett d. "John Oliver Hobbes" d.	Henrik Ibsen d. Julian Klaczko d. Klaus Mann b. Clifford Odets b. José de Pereda d. W. Steward Ross d. T. H. White b. A. D. T. Whitney d.	Hercules Brabazon d. Jules Breton d. Eugène Carrière d. Paul Cézanne d. Jean Desbrosses d. Ernst Josephson d. Alfred Stevens (painter) d.	Anton Arenski d. Oscar Levant b. John K. Paine d.	Margaret Bourke-White b. Primo Carnera b. Lady Burdett-Coutts d. Agnes Moorehead b. Adelaide Ristori d Dmitri Trepov d. Stanford White d.
1907	Russell A. Alger d. J. P. Casimir-Perier d. Richard Crossman b. Marquess of Dufferin d. François Duvalier b. Viscount Goschen d. Gustav V (Sweden) a. Ramón Magsaysay b. Muzaffar-ed-Din (Persia) d. Oscar II (Sweden) d.		Ernest H. Crosby d. John K. Ingram d. Walter Reuther b. Wm. Whiteley d.	Moncure D. Conway d. John A. Dowie d. King Fischer d. Abraham Heschel b. Joshua Loth Liebman b. Hugh O. Pentecost d.	Marcellin Berthelot d. Rachel Carson b. Agnes M. Clerke d. Asaph Hall d. Angelo Heilprin d. Pierre Janssen d. Lord Kelvin d. Dmitri Mendeléyev d. Henri Moissan d. Sir Wm. H. Perkin d. Edward Routh d.	Sophus Bugge d. David Clift b. Henry F. Pelham d. Sir Spencer Walpole d.	Hugh Auden b. Thos. Bailey Aldrich d. Giousue Carducci d. "Christopher" Caudwell b. Wm. Henry Drummond d. Mary J. Holmes d. J. K. Huysmans d. "Ian Maclaren" d.	Gerald Massey d. David Masson d. Sir Lewis Morris d. R. Sully-Prudhomme d. André Theuriet d. Francis Thompson d. James R. Ullman b. Joseph Flint Willard d.	Augustus Saint-Gaudens d. Stanislaw Wyspianski d.	Edvard Grieg d. Joseph Joachim d. Jeanette MacDonald b.	Ilse Koch b. Canada Lee b. Richard Mansfield d. L. Mylius-Erichsen d. Anna May Wong b.

Year A.D.	Government and Law	Military, Naval, and Aviation Affairs	Industry Commerce Economics Finance Invention Labor	Philosophy and Religion	Science, Technology, and Medicine	Education Scholarship History	Literature and Journalism		Visual Arts	Music	Miscellaneous
1908	Salvador Allende (Chile) b. / Sir Henry Campbell-Bannerman d. / Carlos I (Portugal) d. / Grover Cleveland d. / 8th Duke of Devonshire d. / Lyndon B. Johnson b. / William Knowland b. / Manoel II (Portugal) a. / Joseph R. McCarthy b. / T. Estrada Palma d. / Adam Clayton Powell, Jr. b. / Marchese di Rudini d.	Sir Redvers Buller d. / Stephen D. Lee d.	Benj. Waugh d.	Hiram Bingham, Jr. d. / Edward Caird d. / Friedrich Paulsen d. / Otto Pfleiderer d. / Ira D. Sankey d. / Eduard Zeller d.	Wm. E. Ayrton d. / Antoine H. Becquerel d. / Jacob Bronowski b. / Friedrich von Esmarch d. / Alfred Giard d. / Oliver W. Gibbs d. / Franz Leydig d. / Chas. A. Young d.	Gaston Boissier d. / E. F. Fenellosa d. / D. C. Gilman d. / Chas. Eliot Norton d.	Edmondo de Amicis d. / John C. Collins d. / François Coppée d. / John Creasey b. / Holger Drachmann d. / Ian Fleming b. / Ludovic Halévy d. / Joel C. Harris d. / Bronson Howard d. / Jonas Lie d. / Betty MacDonald b.	Donald G. Mitchell d. / Louise Moulton d. / "Ouida" d. / Jas. R. Randall d. / Jas. J. Roche d. / Theodore Roethke b. / Victorien Sardou d. / Edmund C. Stedman d. / Amy Vanderbilt b. / Richard Wright b.	Harriet Hosmer d.	Edward A. MacDowell d. / Clara Novello d. / David Oistrakh b. / Nikolai Rimsky-Korsakov d. / Pablo de Sarasate d.	Lou Costello b. / José Limón b. / Anna Magnani b. / Ainsworth R. Spofford d.
1909	Abdul Hamid II (Turkey) dep. / Albert I (Belgium) a. / Don Carlos d. / Geronimo d. / Lalmohun Ghose d. / Jan H. Hofmeyr d. / Friedrich von Holstein d. / Marquis Ito d. / Leopold II (Belgium) d. / Cesare Lombroso d. / F. de Martens d. / Kwame Nkrumah b. / Marquess of Ripon d. / U. Thant b.	Pascual Cervera d. / O. O. Howard d. / Edmund Zalinski d.	Saul Alinsky b. / John D. Eaton b. / E. H. Harriman d. / Hinton R. Helper d. / Mike Todd b. / Carroll D. Wright d.	Wm. T. Harris d. / Eugene M. Macdonald d. / Jas. H. Stirling d. / Cyrus R. Teed d. / Geo. Tyrrell d. / Chas. B. Waite d. / Simone Weil b.	Virginia Apgar b. / Anton Dohrn d. / Theodor Engelmann d. / Emil Hansen d. / Simon Newcomb d. / Hans Thomsen d.	Francisco Ferrer d. / Henry C. Lea d.	James Agee b. / Rosa N. Carey d. / F. Marion Crawford d. / John Davidson d. / August Derleth b. / R. C. Dutt d. / Martha F. Finley d. / Clyde Fitch d. / R. W. Gilder d. / Jacob Gordin d. / Fredk. Greenwood d. / Edward Everett Hale d. / Sara Orne Jewett d. / Baron von Liliencron d.	Sir Theodore Martin d. / Catulle Mendès d. / Geo. Meredith d. / Chas. W. Stoddard d. / Algernon Swinburne d. / John M. Synge d. / John B. Tabb d. / Ernst von Wildenbruch d. / Augusta E. Wilson d.	Wm. Frith d. / Edward J. Gregory d. / Chas. F. McKim d. / Louis Prang d. / Frederic Remington d.	Isaac Albenis d. / Dudley Buck d. / Eddy Duchin b. / Gene Krupa b. / Benj. J. Lang d.	Benoît Coquelin d. / Errol Flynn b. / Helena Modjeska d. / Russell Sturgis d. / Margaret Sullavan b.
1910	Chulalongkorn (Siam) d. / Edward VII (England) d. / George V (England) a. / Joseph Kasavubu b. / Manoell II (Portugal) dep. / Pierre Nord Alexis d. / Thos. C. Platt d.		D. O. Mills d. / Wm. Graham Sumner d.	Mary Baker Eddy d. / Wm. James d.	Eric Berne b. / John W. Campbell b. / Stanislao Cannizzaro d. / Rudolf Fittig d. / Sir Wm. Huggins d. / Robt. Koch d. / Friedrich Kohlrausch d. / Giovanni Schiaparelli d. / Edouard Van Beneden d.	Elizabeth Blackwell d. / Léopold V. Delisle d. / Fredk. J. Furnivall d. / John E. B. Mayor d. / Hormuzd Rassam d. / Wm. Rolfe d. / Goldwin Smith d.	Otto Bierbaum d. / Björnsterne Björnson d. / Rebecca Harding Davis d. / "O. Henry" d. / Julia Ward Howe d. / Earl Schenck Miers b.	Wm. Vaughn Moody d. / Jean Moreas d. / Edouard Rod d. / Count Leo Tolstoy d. / "Mark Twain" d. / Comte de Vogüé d.	Andreas Achenbach d. / Sir Francis Haden d. / Winslow Homer d. / Holman Hunt d. / Ludwig Knaus d. / John La Farge d. / Sir Wm. Orchardson d. / Henri Rousseau d. / Eero Saarinen b. / Edward L. Sambourne d. / Chas. Van der Steppen d. / John Q. A. Ward d.	Mily Balakirev d. / Edouard Colonne d. / Franz Haberl d. / Karl Reinecke d. / Jennie Tourel b. / Pauline Viardot-Garcia d.	Jack Hawkins b. / Florence Nightingale d. / Jimmy Savo b.

1911–1918 A.D.

Year A.D.	Government and Law	Military, Naval, and Aviation Affairs	Industry Commerce Economics Finance Invention Labor	Philosophy and Religion	Science, Technology, and Medicine	Education Scholarship History	Literature and Journalism		Visual Arts	Music	Miscellaneous
1911	Sir Chas. W. Dilke d. Marquis Komura d. Riaz Pasha d. Georges Pompidou b. Peter Stolypin d.	Piet Cronje d. Winfield S. Schley d.	James B. Carey b.		Alfred Binet d. Sir Frances Galton d. Joseph D. Hooker d. Jacobus Van't Hoff d.	Francis A. March d.	John Bigelow d. "Anthony Boucher" b. Randolph Churchill b. Sam Walter Foss d. Sir W. S. Gilbert d. Paul Goodman b. T. W. Higginson d. Chet Huntley b. Richard Middleton d.	David Graham Phillips d. Jos. Pulitzer d. Wm. Clark Russell d. Elizabeth S. P. Ward d. Eugene F. Ware d. Joseph Widmann d. "John Strange Winter" d.	Edwin A. Abbey d. Eliot Elisofon b. Carl Hill d. Josef Israëls d. Alphonse Legros d. Howard Pyle d.	Mahalia Jackson b. Gustav Mahler d. Felix Mottl d.	Dizzy Dean b. Jack Ruby b. Denman Thompson d. Eduard Whymper d.
1912	Eugène Brisson d. Christian X (Denmark) a. Frederick VIII (Denmark) d. Milo Milovanovic d. Mutsuhito (Japan) d. Whitelaw Reid d. Winthrop Rockefeller b. Yoshihito (Japan) a.	Arthur MacArthur d. Sir Geo. S. White d.	Voltairine DeCleyre d. A. Leroy-Beaulieu d. Gustave de Molinari d. Wilbur Wright d.	Wm. Booth d. Chas. Loyson d.	Sir Geo. Darwin d. Edward Divers d. Peter Lebedev d. Lord Lister d. Jules Poincaré d. Eduard Strasburger d.	H. H. Furness d. Theodor Gomperz d. Sophia Jex-Blake d. Fredk, Seebohm d. W. W. Skeat d. Arthur Verrall d.	Herman J. Bang d. Will Carleton d. Henry Labouchère d. Andrew Lang d. Justin M'Carthy d.	Giovanni Pascoli d. Kenneth Patchen b. Margaret E. Sangster d. Wm. T. Stead d. August Strindberg d.	Sir Laurence Alma-Tadema d. Francis D. Millet d. Jackson Pollock b.	Saml. Coleridge-Taylor d. Kathleen Ferrier b. Woody Guthrie b. Jules Massenet d.	Clara Barton d. Geo. Grossmith d. Sonya Henie b. Octavia Hill d. Robert Scott d. Richard N. Shaw d.
1913	Constantine (Greece) a. George I (Greece) d. Francisco Madero d. Menelik II (Abyssinia) d. Emile Ollivier d. Marquis de Rochefort d. Prince Tokugawa d. Geo. Wyndham d. Zobeir Rahama d.	Graf von Schlieffen d. Mahmoud Shevket d. Viscount Wolseley d.	August Bebel d. Chas. H. Cramp d. Rudolf Diesel d. J.P. Morgan, Sr. d. Lester F. Ward d.	James A. Pike b. Thaddeus B. Wakeman d.	Sir Robert S. Ball d. Chas. McBurney d. L. Teisserenc deBort d. Alfred Russel Wallace d.	Robinson Ellis d. Conte de Gubernatis d.	Alfred Austin d. Albert Camus b. Jules Clarétie d. Edith E. Cooper d. Edward Dowden d. Louis Hémon d.	William Inge b. Thos. A. Janvier d. Sir John Lubbock d. Joaquin Miller d. Sir Geo. Reid d. Wm. Hale White d.	Hans von Bartels d. Walt Kelly b.	Mathilde Marchesi d.	John Garfield b. Karl Hagenbeck d. Dorothy Kilgallen b. Alan Ladd b. Vivien Leigh b. Carmen Miranda b. Harriet Tubman d. Armin Vambery d.
1914	Joseph Chamberlain d. Charles I (Rumania) d. Ferdinand I (Rumania) a. Archduke Franz Ferdinand d. Earl of Minto d. Lord Strathcona d. Marchese di Visconti-Venosta d.	General Creighton Abrams b. Jacobus De la Rey d. Alfred T. Mahan d. Earl Roberts d. Alexander Samsonov d. Danl. E. Sickles d.	Hubert Bland d. Jean Jaurès d. Jacob Riis d. Sir Joseph Swan d. Geo. Westinghouse d.	Pope Benedict XV a. Richard Heber Newton d. Pope Pius X d. Alfred Weber d.	Alphonse Bertillon d. Alexander R. Clarke d. Robt. K. Duncan d. Johann Hittorf d. Chas. Minot d. John Muir d. August Pauly d. Chas. S. Peirce d. John H. Poynting d. Eduard Suess d. Fredk. W. True d. August Weismann d.	Augustus Jessopp d. Harry Thurston Peck d. Aldis Wright d.	Stewart Alsop b. John Berryman b. Ambrose Bierce d. ? Katharine H. Bradley d. Gaston Calmette d. Madison Cawein d. Adelaide Crapsey d. Samuel R. Crockett d. Paul Dérouléde d. Alain Fournier d. Sydney Grundy d.	Paul Heyse d. Jules Lemaitre d. Ross F. Lockridge b. Frédéric Mistral d. S. Weir Mitchell d. Charles Péguy d. Baronesse von Suttner d. Dylan Thomas b. Theodore Watts-Dunton d.	Sir Hubert von Herkimer d. August Macke d. Sir John Tenniel d.	Anatol Liadov d. Lillian Nordica d. Pol Plancon d. Giovanni Sgambati d.	Theodore De Vinne d. Laurence Irving d. Gypsy Rose Lee b. Tyrone Power, Jr d. Babe Zaharias b.

Year A.D.	Government and Law	Military, Naval, and Aviation Affairs	Industry Commerce Economics Finance Invention Labor	Philosophy and Religion	Science, Technology, and Medicine	Education Scholarship History	Literature and Journalism		Visual Arts	Music	Miscellaneous
1915	Porfirio Diaz d. G.J. Gokhale d. Marquis Inouye d. Sir Chas. Tupper d. Edouard Vaillant d. Count Witte d.	Sir Andrew Noble d.	Jack Hall b. Jas. Keir Hardie d.	Thos. K. Cheyne d. Fanny Crosby d.	Theodor Bovén d. Loren D. Carlson b. Sir Arthur Church d. Paul Ehrlich d. Jean Fabre d. Jas. Geikie d. Jas. Hargreaves d. Friedrich Löffler d. Kurt Marek b. Henry G. Moseley d. Sir Henry E. Roscoe d. Sir Arthur Rücker d. Earl Sutherland, Jr. b.	Thos. R. Lounsbury d. Sir Jas. A. Murray d. Booker T. Washington d.	M.E. Braddon d. Rupert Brooke d. Chas. H. Clark d. Jas. E. Flecker d. Remy de Gourmont d. Paul Hervieu d. Elbert Hubbard d.	"Maarten Maartens" d. Thomas Merton b. Stephen Phillips d. Morgan Robertson d. "Martin Ross" d. Robert C. Ruark b. F. Hopkinson Smith d.	Walter Crane d. Henri Gaudier-Brzeska d. Wilfrid M. Zogbaum b.	Karl Goldmark d. Billie Holiday b. Rafael Josefly d. Theodor Leschetizsky d. Alexander Scriabin d.	Edith Cavell d. Anthony Comstock d. Chas. Frohman d. Wm. G. Grace d. Edith Piaf b.
1916	Roger Casement d. Jas. Connolly d. Franz Josef (Austro-Hungary) d. Sir John E. Gorst d. Karl I (Austro-Hungary) a. Seth Low d. Patrick Pearse d. Earl of St. Aldwyn d. Martinus Steyn d. Yuan Shih-K'ai d.	Jos. S. Gallieni d. Colmar von der Goltz d. Arthur Görgei d. Lord Kitchener d. Helmuth von Moltke d. John S. Mosby d.	Marshall Field 3rd. b. Hetty Green d. Benj. Kidd d. P. Leroy-Beaulieu d. Sir Hiram Maxim d.	Josiah Royce d.	Cleveland Abbe d. Prince Golitsyn d. Sir Victor Horsley d. Arnold Lang d. Percival Lowell d. Ernst Mach d. Élie Metchnikoff d. Hugo Münsterberg d. John B. Murphy d. Albert Neisser d. Sir Wm. Ramsey d. Théodule Ribot d. Julius Wiesner d.	Gaston Maspero d.	Sarah K. Bolton d. Stopford A. Brooke d. "Carmen Sylva" d. Rubén Darío d. Richard Harding Davis d. Marie von Ebner-Eschenbach d. José Echegaray d. Emilie Faguet d. Joseph Jacobs d.	Henry James, Jr. d. Jack London d. H.W. Mabie d. H.H. Munro d. J.W. Riley d. Alan Seeger d. Henryk Sienkiewicz d. J.T. Trowbridge d. Emile Verhaeren d.	Wm. M. Chase d. Thos. Eakins d.	Enrique Granados d. Clara L. Kellogg d. Hanish Maccunn d. Max Reger d. Hans Richter d. Sir Paolo Tosti d.	Betty Grable b. Sir Clements Markham d. Jean Mounet-Sully d. Grigor Rasputin d. Ada Rehan d. Tomasso Salvini d.
1917	Joseph H. Choate d. Joseph B. Foraker d. Sir Leander S. Jameson d. John F. Kennedy b. Fernand Labori d. Wayne Macveagh d. Sir Fredk. Maude d. Nicholas II (Russia) dep. Richard Olney d.	Geo. Dewey d. Fredk. Funston d. Radomir Putnik d.	Graf von Zeppelin d.	Thos. E. Hulme d. José Rodó d.	Johann von Baeyer d. Emil von Behring d. Eduard Buchner d. Gustav Jäger d. Karl Rabl d. August Rauber d. Sir Edward B. Tylor d.	Elizabeth Garrett Anderson d. Pasquale Villari d. L.L. Zamenhof d.	Jane Bowles b. Sir Francis Burnand d. Carson McCullers b. Wm. De Morgan d. Octave Mirbeau d. Harrison G. Otis d. Francis T. Palgrave d.	Franklin B. Sanborn d. Fredk. C. Selous d. Ruth McE. Stuart d. Edward Thomas d. Philip E. Thomas d. Wm. Winter d.	Carolus-Duran d. Edgar Degas d. Moses J. Ezekiel d. Auguste Rodin d. Albert P. Ryder d. Hugo Sunberg d. Wilhelm Trübner d.	Teresa Carreno d. Edouard de Reszke d. Wieland Wagner b.	Wm. F. Cody d. Belva Lockwood d. Andrew J. Still d. Sir H. Beerbohm Tree d.
1918	Victor Adler d. Boris III (Bulgaria) a. Lord Courtney d. Ferdinand I (Bulgaria) abd. Karl I (Austro-Hungary) dep. Gamal Abdel Nasser b. Walter Hines Page d. John Redmond d. Sir Cecil Spring-Rice d. Benj. R. Tillman d. Wilhelm II (Germany) abd.	Lavr Kornilov d.	Georgy Plekhanov d. Viscount Rhondda d. George Lincoln Rockwell b.	Washington Gladden d. Minor J. Savage d. Georg Simmel d. Chas. Wagner d.	Alexander Liapunov d. Henry Maudsley d. Andrew D. White d. Saml. W. Williston d.	Henry Adams d. H.H. Barcroft d.	Guillaume Apollinaire d. Arlo Bates d. Randolph Bourne d. William Wilfred Campbell d. Shirley Jackson b.	Joyce Kilmer d. Paul Margueritte d. Georges Ohnet d. Wilfred Owen d. Edmond Rostand d. Dora Sigerson d. Frank Wedekind d.	Ferdinand Hodler d.	Arrigo Boïto d. César Cui d. Claude Debussy d. Sir Chas. Parry d.	Karl Peters d.

Year A.D.	Government and Law	Military, Naval, and Aviation Affairs	Industry Commerce Economics Finance Invention Labor	Philosophy and Religion	Science, Technology, and Medicine	Education Scholarship History	Literature and Journalism		Visual Arts	Music	Miscellaneous
1919	Alfred Deakin d. Kurt Eisner d. Count Itagaki d. Aleksandr Izvolski d. Jean de Lanessan d. Sir Wilfrid Laurier d. Eva Peron b. Theodore Roosevelt d. Moise Tshombe b.	Louis Botha d. Sir Henry Wood d.	Andrew Carnegie d. Wm. Cunningham d. H.C. Frick d. Hugo Haase d. Karl Liebknecht d. Rosa Luxemburg d. John Mitchell d. Arthur Watson b. F.W. Woolworth d.	Paul Carus d. John E. Remsburg d.	Wm. Brewster d. Sir Wm. Crookes d. Baron Roland von Eötvös d. Emil Fischer d. Ernst Haeckel d. Abraham Jacobi d. Sir Wm. Osler d. Edward C. Pickering d. Lord Rayleigh d. Gustaf Retzius d. Simon Schwendener d. Richard Semon d. Alfred Werner d.	Sir John Mahaffy d.	Henry M. Alden d. Leonid Andreev d. Wm. Waldorf Astor d. Amelia E. Barr d. Bruce Cummings d. John Fox d.	Karl Gjellerup d. Ricardo Palma d. Lady Ritchie d. W.M. Rossetti d. Horace Traubel d. Ella Wheeler Wilcox d.	Kenyon Cox d. Sir Edward Poynter d. P.A. Renoir d.	Nat "King" Cole b. Noah Greenberg b. Ruggiero Leoncavallo d. Horatio W. Parker d. Adelina Patti d.	Henry B. Irving d. Jackie Robinson b. Anna Howard Shaw d. Sir Chas. Wyndham d.
1920	Venustiano Carranza d. Empress Eugénie d.	Lord John Fisher d. Alexander Kolchak d.	Carl Legien d. Jacob Schiff d. B.G. Tilak d. Theodore N. Vail d. Max Weber d.	Wm. Sanday d.	Otto Bütschli d. Moritz Cantor d. Yves Delage d. Max Fürbringer d. Wm. C. Gorgas d. Sir Norman Lockyer d. Wilhelm Pfeffer d. Augusto Righi d. E.E. Southard d. Wilhelm Wundt d.	Heinrich Friedjung d. John H. Vincent d.	Paul Adam d. Rhoda Broughton d. Arthur H. Bullen d. Adolf Frey d. J. Bruce Glazier d. Mrs. Burton Harrison d. Thos. O. Heggen b. Wm. Heinemann d. Marguerite Higgins b.	W.D. Howells d. B. Perez Galdós d. John Reed d. Marilla M. Ricker d. Olive Schreiner d. Joseph M. Stoddart d. Harvey Swados b. Mrs. Humphry Ward d.	Anders Zorn d.	Max Bruch d. Reginald DeKoven d. Chas. T. Griffes d. Maud Powell d.	Montgomery Clift b. Robert E. Peary d. Gabrielle Réjane d.
1921	Theobald von Bethmann-Hollweg d. Champ Clarke d. Matthias Erzberger d. Prinz zu Eulenberg-Hertefeld d. Philander C. Knox d. Franklin K. Lane d. Peter I (Serbia) d. Joseph Reinach d. Barone di Sonnino d.	Alexei Kuropatkin d.	Sir Ernest J. Cassel d. Henry M. Hyndman d. Prince Kropotkin d.	John B. Crozier d. Cardinal Gibbons d. Frank W. Gunsaulus d. Alexander Whyte d.	John Burroughs d. Jonathan Dwight d. Geo. T. Ladd d. Alfred Lehmann d. Max Verworn d.	Morris Jastrow d. Barrett Wendell d.	Aleksander Blok d. Austin Dobson d. John Habberton d. J.G. Huneker d. Vladimir Korolenko d. Mary L. Molesworth d.	Emilia Pardo Bazán d. Edgar Saltus d. Harriet E. Spofford d. Jacqueline Susann b. Henry Watterson d.	August Hagborg d. Adolf von Hildebrand d. Amadeo Modigliani d. Abbott Thayer d.	Enrico Caruso d. Engelbert Humperdinck d. Christine Nilsson d. Camille Saint-Saëns d.	Linda Darnell b.
1922	Michael Collins d. Constantine (Greece) d. Enver Pasha d. Faud (Egypt) a. Arthur Griffith d. Marquis Okuma d.	Christian De Wet d. Eric von Falkenhayn d. Sir Henry H. Wilson d. Prince Yamagata d.	Alexander Graham Bell d. Jules Guesde d. Ann Klein b. John Wanamaker d.	Lyman Abbott d. Pope Benedict XV d. Pope Pius XI a.	Sir W.H.M. Christie d. Giacomo Ciamician d. Haim Ginott d. Alexander Goette d. Wm. S. Halsted d. Oskar Hertwig d. Emil Holmgren d. Camille Jordan d. Jacobus C. Kapteyn d. Alphonse Laveran d. Alfred Nathorst d. Louis Ranvier d. Wm. H.R. Rivers d. Jokichi Takamine d.	Viscount Bryce d. Ernest Lavisse d. Sir George Prothero d.	John Kendrick Bangs d. Wilfrid S. Blunt d. "Nellie Bly" d. "Charles Egbert Craddock" d. "Marion Harland" d. Horace E. Hooper d. Wm. H. Hudson d.	Alice Meynell d. Thos. Nelson Page d. Josephine P. Peabody d. Marcel Proust d. Sir Walter Raleigh d. Geo. R. Sims d. Giovanni Verga d.		Artur Nikisch d. Sir Chas. Santley d.	Judy Garland b. Judy Holliday b. Marie Lloyd d. Carl Lumholtz d. Sir Ernest Shackleton d.

Year A.D.	Government and Law	Military, Naval, and Aviation Affairs	Industry Commerce Economics Finance Invention Labor	Philosophy and Religion	Science, Technology, and Medicine	Education Scholarship History	Literature and Journalism	Visual Arts	Music	Miscellaneous
1923	Théophile Delcassé d. George II (Greece) a. Warren G. Harding d. Norman Kirk b. L.Q.C. Lamar d. A. Bonar Law d. Stojan Protić d. Alexander Stambolisky d. Yakub Khan d.	Chas. D. Sigsbee d. Pancho Villa d.		Bernard Bosanquet d. John Clifford d.	Stefan Apathy d. Earl of Carnarvon d. Sir Jas. Dewar d. Wilhelm von Röntgen d. Chas. B. Steinmetz d. Sir Fredk. Treves d. J. van der Waals d. Robt. Wiedersheim d.		Maurice Barrès d. Brendan Behan b. Oscar Browning d. Geo. Cosbuc d. Louis Couperus d. Frederic Harrison d. Chas. B. Hawes d. Maurice Hewlett d. Emerson Hough d. "Pierre Loti" d. Wm. H. Mallock d. Katherine Mansfield d. Viscount Morley d. Max Nordau d. Raymond Radiguet d. Morris Rosenfeld d. Wm. R. Thayer d. Fredk. H. Trench d. Kate Douglas Wiggin d.	Palmer Cox d. Joaquin Sorolla d.		Sarah Bernhardt d. Albert Chevalier d. Tennessee Claflin d. Samuel H. Sheppard b.
1924	Teófilo Braga d. Henry Cabot Lodge d. Prince Matsukata d. Woodrow Wilson d.	Audie Murphy b. Robert Nivelle d. Sir Chas. Townsend d.	Saml. Gompers d. Clifford M. Holland d. Nikolai Lenin d. Alfred Marshall d. Maffeo Pantaleoni d.	Francis H. Bradley d.	Sir Wm. Bayliss d. Sir Archibald Geikie d. G. Stanley Hall d. Victor Hensen d. Jacques Loeb d. Georg H. Quincke d. Wilhelm Roux d. Eugen Warming d.	Alexander Bickel b. B.L. Gildersleeve d.	Wm. Archer d. S. Baring-Gould d. Valeri Bryusov d. Francis Hodgson Burnett d. Joseph Conrad d. Marie Corelli d. John R. Coryell d. Adolfo De Bosis d. Anatole France d. Iwan Gilkin d. Franz Kafka d. Grace Metalious b. Edith Nesbit d. "Margaret Sidney" d. Carl Spitteler d.	Léon Bakst d. Emile Claus d.	Julian Aguirre d. Ferruccio Busoni d. François Dubois d. Gabriel Fauré d. Victor Herbert d. Giacomo Puccini d. Sir Chas. Stanford d.	Eleonora Duse d. Rocky Marciano b.
1925	Karl Branting d. Wm. J. Bryan d. Geo. N. Curzon d. C.R. Das d. Friedrich Ebert d. Sir Geo. Goldie d. Robert F. Kennedy b. Robt. M. LaFollette d. Patrice Lumumba b. Viscount Milner d. Sun Yat-Sen d. Réne Viviani d.	F. Conrad Hötzendorf d. Viscount French d. Mikhail Frunze d. Chas. Lanrezac d. Nelson A. Miles d.	Geo. D. Herron d. Viscount Leverhulme d.	Malcolm X b. Rudolf Steiner d. Jas. Ward d.	Camille Flammarion d. Giovanni Grassi d. Oliver Heaviside d. Sir Thos. Thorpe d. August von Wassermann d.	Sir Paul Vinogradov d.	James Lane Allen d. A.C. Benson d. Geo. W. Cable d. Frank M. Colby d. Franz Fanon b. Sir Rider Haggard d. Paul Hanna d. Amy Lowell d. Frank A. Munsey d. Flannery O'Connor b. Herbert Quick d. Wladyslas Remont d. Edith M. Thomas d. Sergei Yessenin d. Stephen Zeromski d.	Geo. Bellows d. Eduard von Gebhardt d. John S. Sargent d. Jan Stursa d. Sir Wm. H. Thornycroft d.	Moritz Moszkowski d. Jean de Reszke d. Erik Satie d.	Lenny Bruce b. Georg Schweinfurth d.

1926–1933 A.D.

Year A.D.	Government and Law	Military, Naval, and Aviation Affairs	Industry Commerce Economics Finance Invention Labor	Philosophy and Religion	Science, Technology, and Medicine	Education Scholarship History	Literature and Journalism		Visual Arts	Music	Miscellaneous
1926	Giovanni Amendola d. Joseph G. Cannon d. Sanford B. Dole d. Feliks Dzerzhinski d. Sir Thomas E. Holland d. Takaakiro Kato d. Leonid Krassin d. Mahommed Riza Pahlevi(Iran) a. Alton B. Parker d. Nicholas Pašič d. Yoshihito (Japan) d.		Ernest Belfort Bax d. Eugene V. Debs d. Nikolai Tschaikovsky d.	Emile Coué d. Rudolph Eucken d. Cardinal Mercier d.	Wm. Bateson d. Emil Bose d. Luther Burbank d. John Dreyer d. Camillo Golgi d. Heike Kamerlingh Onnes d. Jas. F. Kemp d. John X. Merriam d. Sir Wm. Tilden d.	Chas. W. Eliot d.	Ronald Firbank d. W.L. George d. Marietta Holley d. Sir Sidney Lee d. Frances Newman d. Rainer Maria Rilke d.	E.W. Scripps d. Stuart P. Sherman d. Clement K. Shorter d. Geo. Sterling d. Arthur B. Walkley d. Israel Zangwill d.	Mary Cassatt d. Claude Monet d. Joseph Pennell d.	Franz Kneisel d.	Gertrude Bell d. Charles M. Doughty d. Marilyn Monroe b.
1927	Ion Bratianu d. Empress Carlotta d. John Dillon d. Ferdinand I (Rumania) d. Lyman J. Gage d. Marquess (Chas.) Lansdowne d. Luigi Luzzatti d. Countess Markievicz d. Kevin O'Higgins d. Sergei Sazonov d. Saad Zaghlul d.	Reginald Dyer d. Leonard Wood d.	Elbert H. Gary d. Henry E. Huntington d. Hudson Maxim d. Chas. Rüthenberg d. Nicola Sacco d. Bartolomeo Vanzetti d.	Francis E. Clark d. Inayat Khan d. Benj. Purnell d.	Svante Arrhenius d. Sir George Greenhill d. Victor Lenher d. Ira Remsen d. Sir Arthur E. Shipley d. Jacob Solis-Cohen d. Ernest Starling d. Adrian Stokes d. Henry D. Thompson d. Edward B. Titchener d. Jan Tschakste d. Chas. D. Walcott d.	David Hogarth d. Walter Leaf d. Lucy M. Salmon d. Benj. Ide Wheeler d.	Mikhail Artzybashev d. Solomon Bloomgarden d. Georg Brandes d. Houston Stewart Chamberlain d. Sir Sidney Colvin d. Francis Grierson d. Maximilian Harden d. J.K. Jerome d. K'ang Yu-wei d.	Wm. Le Queux d. Keith Preston d. S. Przybyszewski d. Matilda Serao d. "Feodor Sologub" d. J. St. Loe Strachey d. Lionel Strachey d. Mary Webb d.	Sir Luke Fildes d. Louis A. Fuertes d. Ambrose McEvoy d. Emily Sartain d.	Emil Mollenhauer d.	Camille Blanc d. Lizzie Borden d. John Cranko b. Arnold Daly d. John Drew d. Isadora Duncan d. Sir Harry H. Johnston d. Florence Mills d. Henry M. Taylor d. Wayne B. Wheeler d. Victoria Woodhull d.
1928	Herbert Asquith d. Delphin M. Delmas d. Chauncey M. Depew d. Giovanni Giolitti d. "Che" Guevara b. Yves Guyot d. L. Lajpat Rai d. Robt. Lansing d. Li Yuan-Hung d. Prinz von Lichnowsky d. Alvaro Obregón d. Wm. O'Brien d. Stjepan Radič d. Rushdi Pasha d. Said Pasha d. Abdel Sarwat Pasha d. Satyendro Sinha d.	Conde di Cadorna d. G.W. Goethals d. Earl Haig d. Baron de Jacques d. John McAnerney d. Alexander Protoguerov d. Baron Pyotr Wrangel d.	Sir Horace Darwin d. Wm. D. Haywood d. John H. Logan d. Louis F. Post d.	Viscount Haldane d. Augusta E. Stetson d. Reuben A. Torrey d.	T.C. Chamberlin d. John M. Coulter d. Sir David Ferrier d. Johannes Fibiger d. Hendrick Lorentz d. Finn Malmgren d. Edward W. Maunder d. Hideyo Noguchi d. Flora W. Patterson d. Theodore Richards d. Wilhelm Wien d.	Archibald Coolidge d. Henry W.C. Davis d. Wm. E. Griffis d. Wm. G. Hale d. Jane Harrison d. Théodore Reinach d. Paul Sabatier d. Sir Geo. Otto Trevelyan d. Anne H. Wharton d. Talcott Williams d.	Herbert Bashford d. Holbrook Blinn d. Donn Byrne d. Ina Coolbrith d. Frank Crane d. "Alan Dale" d. Sir Edmund Gosse d. Thos. Hardy d. Geo. B. Harvey d. Avery Hopwood d. V. Blasco Ibanez d. Basil King d. Chas. F. Lummis d. Geo. Barr McCutcheon d.	Charlotte Mew d. Chas. A. Montague d. Standish J. O'Grady d. Barry Pain d. Thos. S. Perry d. Anne Sexton b. Hermann Sudermann d. Italo Svevo d. Louis Tracy d. Stanley J. Weyman d. Richard Whiteing d. Elinor Wylie d.	Arthur B. Davies d. A.B. Frost d. Edmund Osthaus d. Richard F. Outcault d. Franz von Stuck d.	Edmond Clément d. Henry F. Gilbert d. Leos Janáček d. Leslie Stuart d.	Roald Amundsen d. Floyd Bennett d. Wm. H. Crane d. Robert Mantell d. Otto Nordenskjöld d. Emmeline Pankhurst d. Theodore Roberts d. Ellen Terry d. Sir Henry Wickham d.

Year A.D.	Government and Law	Military, Naval, and Aviation Affairs	Industry Commerce Economics Finance Invention Labor	Philosophy and Religion	Science, Technology, and Medicine	Education Scholarship History	Literature and Journalism	Visual Arts	Music	Miscellaneous
1929	Count Andrassy (Jr.) d. Myron T. Herrick d. T. P. O'Connor d. Earl of Rosebery d. Gustav Stresemann d. Baron Tanaka d. Oscar W. Underwood d.	Ferdinand Foch d. Stepan Stepanovitch d.	Victor Berger d. Millicent G. Fawcett d. Melville E. Stone d. Thorstein Veblen d. Baron von Welsbach d. Havelock Wilson d.	Branwell Booth d. Fredk. L. Hosmer d. Martin Luther King, Jr. b. John Roach Straton d. Katherine Tingley d.	Emile Berliner d. Ralph H. Curtiss d. Sir Wm. Dawkins d. Harrison G. Dyar d. Joseph Goldberger d. John W. Harshberger d. Aletta Jacobs d. Rodolfo Lanciani d. Sir E. Ray Lankester d. Chas. Sajous d. Sir Bertram Windle d. Richard Zsigmondy d.	Heinrich Delbrueck d. Emily Howland d. Alfredo Trombetti d.	Katherine Lee Bates d. Bliss Carman d. Edward Carpenter d. Leonard Cline d. Ellen Thorneycroft Fowler d. John Freeman d. Hugo von Hofmannsthal d. Arno Holz d. Henry Arthur Jones d. Mary MacLane d. Brander Matthews d. Harvey O'Higgins d. C. B. Palleri d. Flora Annie Steel d. Moorefield Storey d. Caspar Whitney d. Jesse Lynch Williams d. Harry C. Witwer d.	T. A. Dorgan d. Edward H. Garrett d. Chas. Grafly d. Robert Henri d. John Huffington d.	Anton Beer-Walbrunn d. Patrick Conway d. Istvan Kertesz b. Lili Lehmann d. Oscar Saenger d. Frank Van der Stucken d.	Serge Diaghiliev d. Wyatt Earp d. Chas. Forepaugh d. Noah Hayes d. Lillie Langtry d. Hans Meyer d.
1930	Arthur James Balfour d. Tom Mboya b. Wm. H. Taft d.	Friedrich von Bernhardi d. Tasker H. Bliss d. Alfred von Tirpitz d. Valeriano Weyler d.	Glenn Curtiss d. Melville D. Post d. Elmer A. Sperry d. Max Valier d.	Rafael Merry del Val d.	Wm. H. Bristol d. Mary W. Calkins d. J. Walter Fewkes d. Christine Ladd-Franklin d. Wm. D. Matthew d. John S. Rickard d. Wm. E. Story d.	Theodore W. Hunt d. Arthur A. Macdonnell d.	Isabella Alden d. Wm. E. Barton d. Edward W. Bok d. Wm. Bolitho d. Robt. Bridges d. Herbert Croly d. Sir A. Conan Doyle d. Mary E. Wilkins Freeman d. Lorraine Hansberry b. D.H. Lawrence d. Wm. J. Locke d. Neil Munro d. Vladimir Mayakovsky d. Kirk Munroe d. G. dePorto-Riche d. Jean Richepin d. Romer Wilson d.	J. L. G. Ferris d. F. McKinney Hubbard d. Julius Rolshoven d. Edward V. Valentine d.	Joseph Adamowski d. Leopold Auer d. Emmy Destinn d. Nathan Franko d. Cosima Wagner d. Siegfried Wagner d.	"Deadwood Dick" d. Jas. Eads How d. H. Karl Kumm d. Fridtjof Nansen d.
1931	Alfonso XIII (Spain) abd. Dwight Morrow d.	J.J.C. Joffre d.	Thos. A. Edison d. Mortimer L. Schiff d.	Brother Joseph d.	Edward G. Acheson d. Aristides Agramonte d. John H. Comstock d. Francis X. Dercum d. Hans Hoerbiger d. David Starr Jordan d. Gustave Le Bon d. Albert A. Michelson d. Per Axel Rydberg d.	E. A. Alderman d. Melvil Dewey d.	Arnold Bennett d. Sir Hall Caine d. Frank Harris d. Rossiter Johnson d. Vachel Lindsay d. "Lucas Malet" d. Ole Rölvaag d. Arthur Schnitzler d. Katharine Tynan d. Juan Zorilla d.	Ralph Barton d.	Vincent D'Indy d. Nellie Melba d. Eugène Ysaÿe d.	Maclyn Arbuckle d. Sir Thos. Lipton d. Anna Pavlova d. Tyrone Power d. Knute Rockne d. Nathan Straus d.
1932	Aristide Briand d. J.J. Jusserand d.		Eduard Bernstein d. Florence Kelley d. Ivar Kreuger d. Julia Lathrop d. Alberto Santos-Dumont d. Filippo Turati d. Graham Wallas d. William Wrigley d.		Charles Fort d. Sir Patrick Geddes d. W. W. Keen d. Graham Lusk d. Wilhelm Ostwald d. Wm. Patten d. Sir Ronald Ross d.	C. M. Gayley d. J. B. McMaster d. Salomon Reinach d. Lytton Strachey d.	René Bazin d. Gamaliel Bradford d. Eugène Brieux d. Hayden Carruth d. Chas. W. Chestnutt d. Hart Crane d. G. Lowes Dickinson d. Wells Drury d. Kenneth Grahame d. Lady Gregory d. Harold MacGrath d. John Macy d. Harold Monro d. Frederick O'Brien d. Jas. Oppenheim d. Sir Gilbert Parker d. Sylvia Plath b. Clinton Scollard d. Edgar Wallace d.		Johanna Gadski d. John Philip Sousa d.	Wm. J. Burns d. Rose Coghlan d. Geo. Eastman d. Billy Emerson d. Minnie Maddern Fiske d. Wilton Lackaye d. Chauncey Olcott d. Jesse Pomeroy d. Julius Rosenwald d. Florenz Ziegfeld d.
1933	Calvin Coolidge d.	Nikolai Yudenitch d.	Morris Hillquit d. Rose Pastor Stokes d. Claudio Treves d. Clara Zetkin d.	Felix Adler d. Irving Babbitt d. Annie Besant d. Woodbridge Riley d.	Eleanor A. M. Gamble d. Frederick Starr d.	John Grier Hibben d. A. H. Sayce d.	Earl Derr Biggers d. Stella Benson d. Augustine Birrell d. Horatio Bottomley d. Constantine Cavafy d. Robt. W. Chambers d. John Galsworthy d. Louise Closser Hale d. "Anthony Hope" d. Leonard Huxley d. Ring Lardner d. Wilson Mizner d. George Moore d. George Saintsbury d. Louis Joseph Vance d. Henry Van Dyke d.	E. W. Kemble d. Joseph Urban d.	Andreas Dippel d. Marcel Journet d. Vladimir de Pachmann d.	"Fatty" Arbuckle d. Mrs. O.H.P. Belmont d. Texas Guinan d. Knud Rasmussen d. Ernest Torrence d.

1934–1944 A.D.

Year A.D.	Government and Law	Military, Naval, and Aviation Affairs	Industry Commerce Economics Finance Invention Labor	Philosophy and Religion	Science, Technology, and Medicine	Education Scholarship History	Literature and Journalism		Visual Arts	Music	Miscellaneous
1934	Albert I (Belgium) d. Engelbert Dollfuss d. Paul von Hindenburg d. Wm. Travers Jerome d. Raymond Poincaré d.	L. H. Lyautey d. Count Togo d.	Catherine Breshkovsky d.		Marie Curie d. Yuri Gagarin b. Fritz Haber d. Santiago Ramon y Cajal d. Maynard Shipley d.		"F. Anstey" d. Mary Austin d. F. N. Doubleday d. Montague Glass d. Julian Hawthorne d. Thos. L. Masson d.	Sir Arthur Pinero d. Eugene Manlove Rhodes d. "Octave Thanet" d. Jakob Wassermann d. Brand Whitlock d.	John Collier d. Harrison Fisher d. Winsor McCay d.	Frederick Delius d. Sir Edward Elgar d. L. F. Gottschalk d. Sir Gerald DuMaurier d. Philip Hale d.	Roberto Clemente b. Maggie Cline d. John Dillinger d. Emilie Dionne b. Marie Dionne b. Marie Dressler d. Cass Gilbert d. Margaret Illington d Lou Tellegen d. Zaro Agha d.
1935	Viscount Byng d. Oliver Wendell Holmes, Jr. d. Josef Pilsudski d.	T. E. Lawrence d.	André Citroen d. E. L. Doheny d. Adolph Ochs d.	Billy Sunday d.	Henry Fairfield Osborn d. Michael Pupin d. Charles Richet d. Henshaw Ward d.		Henri Barbusse d. Thomas Boyd d. Richard Washburn Child d. Holman F. Day d. Nathan Haskell Dole d. Anna Katharine Green d.	"Vernon Lee" d. Fremont Older d. E. A. Robinson d. Arthur Somers Roche d. Will Rogers d. Geo. W. Russell d. Anne Douglas Sedgwick d. Don C. Seitz d. Sir Wm. Watson d.	Childe Hassam d. Gaston Lachaise d. Julius Meier-Graefe d. Eugene Zimmermann d.	Alban Berg d. Sophie Braslau d. Marcella Sembrich d. Herbert Witherspoon d.	Jane Addams d. Alfred Dreyfus d. DeWolfe Hopper d. Frederick Warde d. Francis Wilson d.
1936	Charles Curtis d. Edward VIII (England) a. and abd. Farouk I (Egypt) a. Fuad (Egypt) d. George V (England) d. George VI (England) a. Eleutherios Venizelos d.	Viscount Allenby d. William Mitchell d.	Alexander Berkman d. Wm. English Walling d. Sir Basil Zaharoff d.		J. S. Haldane d. Ivan Pavlov d.	Wm. F. Badé d. Anne Sullivan Macy d. Ellen Fitz Pendleton d.	Juliette Adam d. Mary Raymond Shipman Andrews d. Arthur Brisbane d. Gilbert K. Chesterton d. Grazia Deledda d. Finley P. Dunne d. F. Garcia Lorca d. Maxim Gorky d. A. E. Housman d. Rudyard Kipling d.	"Lu Hsun" d. Samuel Merwin d. Harriet Monroe d. M. W. Pickthall d. Luigi Pirandello d. Henri de Regnier d. Panteleimon Romanov d. Sir Owen Seaman d. Oswald Spengler d. Lincoln Steffens d. Miguel de Unamuno d.	Lorado Taft d. Clive Weed d.	Clara Butt d. Ossip Gabrilowitsch d. Otterino Respighi d. Ernestine Schumann-Heink d. Antonio Scotti d.	Jean Charcot d. Ben Greet d. Percy Hammond d. John Ringling d. Howard Thurston d.
1937	Frank B. Kellogg d. J. Ramsay MacDonald d. Thomas Masaryk d. Elihu Root d.	Richmond P. Hobson d.	E. A. Filene d. Andrew W. Mellon d. Émile Pathé d. John D. Rockefeller, Sr., d. Philip Snowden d.	Wm. Montgomery Brown d.	Alfred Adler d. Sir J. C. Bose d. Wm T. Hornaday d. Guglielmo Marconi d. Lord Rutherford d. Wm. Morton Wheeler d. Wm. Alanson White d.		Sir Jas. M. Barrie d. "Christopher Caudwell" d. "Ralph Connor" d. John Drinkwater d. Edward Garnett d. Norman Hapgood d. E. W. Howe d. Ilya Ilf d.	Robt. Underwood Johnson d. G. H. Lorimer d. Don Marquis d. Paul Elmer More d. Marie Van Vorst d. Francis Viele-Griffin d. Edith Wharton d.	Élie Faure d. Frederick MacMonnies d. F. B. Opper d.	George Gershwin d. Henry Hadley d. Charles Widor d.	Winthrop Ames d J. Forbes-Robertson d. Wm. Gillette d. "Little Egypt" d.
1938	Benjamin N. Cardozo d. Clarence Darrow d. E. M. House d. Kemal Atatürk d.	Erich Ludendorff d.	Harvey S. Firestone d. Andrew Furuseth d. Saml. Insull d. Karl Kautsky d. Emile Vandervelde d.	Anton Lang d.	John J. Abel d. W. W. Campbell d. J. E. Coover d. Edward M. East d. Grey Owl d. Geo. B. Grinnell d. Geo. Ellery Hale d. Wm. H. Pickering d.	Christian L. Lange d. Frank H. Vizetelly d.	Lascelles Abercrombie d. S. Alvarez Quintero d. Isaak Babel d. Gabriele D'Annunzio d. Zona Gale d. Robert Herrick d. Francis Jammes d.	Edgar Jepson d. Jas. Weldon Johnson d. Alexander Kuprin d. Aylmer Maude d. W. B. Maxwell d. Owen Wister d. Thomas Wolfe d.	Geo. Grey Barnard d. Will Dyson d. Wm. J. Glackens d.	Feodor Chaliapin d. Alma Gluck d. Leopold Godowsky d. Maurice Ravel d.	Pauline Frederick d. May Irwin d. Carl von Ossietzky d. Edward Tuck d.
1939	Feisal II (Iraq) a. Philipp Scheideman d.	Graf Johann von Bernstorff d.	Sir Henri Deterding d. Charles M. Schwab d.	Pope Pius XI d. Pope Pius XII a.	Henry Balfour d. Harvey W. Cushing d. Sir Frank Dyson d. Havelock Ellis d. Sigmund Freud d. Joseph Grinnell d. Edwin Linton d. Robt. MacDougall d. Otto Rank d. David Todd d. E. A. Westermarck d.	Benjamin G. Brawley d.	Heywood Broun d. Olav Duun d. Ford Madox Ford d. Zane Grey d. Sidney Howard d. Leonard Merrick d. Llewellyn Powys d. Opie Read d.	Rose Hartwicke Thorpe d. Ernst Toller d. Guido da Verona d. Harry Leon Wilson d. Willard Huntington Wright d. Wm. Butler Yeats d.	Arthur Rackham d.	Artur Bodanzky d. Ernest H. Schelling d.	Richard Halliburton d. Lee Harvey Oswald b. Fay Templeton d.

Year A.D.	Government and Law	Military, Naval, and Aviation Affairs	Industry Commerce Economics Finance Invention Labor	Philosophy and Religion	Science, Technology, and Medicine	Education Scholarship History	Literature and Journalism		Visual Arts	Music	Miscellaneous
1940	Manuel Azaña d. Neville Chamberlain d. Leon Trotsky d.		Emma Goldman d. Geo. Lansbury d. Lord Rothermere (Harold Harmsworth) d. Lillian Wald d.	Sir Wilfred Grenfell d. Alfred Loisy d.	Sir Oliver Lodge d. Raymond Pearl d. Wilhelm Stekel d. Sir Joseph J. Thomson d. Julius Wagner-Jauregg d. Hans Zinsser d.	Glenn Frank d. Robert R. Moton d.	Thos. Beer d. E. F. Benson d. John Buchan d. W. H. Davies d. F. Scott Fitzgerald d. Hamlin Garland d. Robert Grant d.	Werner von Heidenstam d. DuBose Heyward d. Selma Lagerlof d. Osip Mandelstam d. Edwin Markham d. Ameen Rihani d. Nathanael West d. Humbert Wolfe d.	Paul Klee d. Jonas Lie d. Janet Scudder d	Mary Anderson d. Alessandro Bonci d. Jan Kubelik d. Emma Nevada d. Luisa Tetrazzini d.	Mrs. Patrick Campbell d. Frederick Cook d. Douglas Fairbanks, Sr., d. Marcus Garvey d. Tom Mix d.
1941	Louis D. Brandeis d. Mohammed Riza Pahlevi (Iran) abd.		Simon Guggenheim d. Wm. Z. Ripley d. Werner Sombart d. Josiah Stamp d.	Henri Bergson d. Shailer Mathews d. Evelyn Underhill d.	Sir Frederick G. Banting d. Annie J. Cannon d. Hans Driesch d. Sir James G. Frazer d. Daniel W. Morehouse d. W. H. Nernst d. Elsie Clews Parsons d. John S. Plaskett d.	Everett Dean Martin d. Edward J. O'Brien d. Preserved Smith d. Henry Osborn Taylor d.	Sherwood Anderson d. "Elizabeth" d. James Joyce d. Archibald G. Macdonnell d. Dmitri S. Merezhkovski d. H. W. Nevinson d. Guy de Pourtalès d. Marcel Prévost d. Gabriele Reuter d.	Lola Ridge d. Elizabeth Madox Roberts d. Constance Rourke d. Hans Otto Storm d. Rabindranath Tagore d. Sir Hugh Walpole d. Eugene Walter d. Virginia Woolf d. Percival C. Wren d.	Gutzon Borglum d. Geo. deForest Brush d. Louis M. Eilshemius d. Sir John Lavery d.	Sir Hamilton Harty d. Mischa Levitski d. Ignace J. Paderewski d. Christian Sinding d.	Lord Robert Baden-Powell d. Daniel Carter Beard d. Lou Gehrig d.
1942		Jean Darlan d.	Robert Hunter d. Tom Mooney d.		Vernon Bailey d. Franz Boas d. Sir Wm. H. Bragg d. Raymond L. Ditmars d. Lawrence J. Henderson d. Bronislaw K. Malinowski d. C. Hart Merriam d. Sir W. M. Flinders Petrie d. Charles Schuchert d.	Guglielmo Ferrero d. Gustavus Myers d.	Rudolf Besier d. Léon Daudet d. Rachel Field d. "Cosmo Hamilton" d.	Alice Duer Miller d. Alice Hegan Rice d. Carolyn Wells d. Stefan Zweig d.	Cecilia Beaux d. Charles C. Curran d. Will James d. Gertrude Vanderbilt Whitney d. Grant Wood d.	Pasquale Amato d. Emma Calvé d. Alfred Hertz d. Arthur Pryor d. Frederick A. Stock d. Felix Weingartner d.	John Barrymore d. Geo. M. Cohan d. Ralph Adams Cram d. Michel Fokine d. Tony Sarg d. Otis Skinner d.
1943	Boris III (Bulgaria) d. Ben B. Lindsey d. Alexandre Millerand d.		Robert Blatchford d. Richard T. Ely d. J. Pierpont Morgan Jr., d. Beatrice Webb d.	Raoul deRoussy deSales d. Simone Weil d.	Geo. W. Carver d. Geo. W. Crile d. Leonard Darwin d. Ales Hrdlička d. Lillien J. Martin d. Nikola Tesla d.	Albert Bushnell Hart d. Otto Jesperson d. A. Lawrence Lowell d.	Stephen Vincent Benét d. Lawrence Binyon d. "E. M. Delafield" d. Elinor Glyn d. "Sarah Grand" d. Jackson Gregory d. Arthur Guiterman d. Zsolt de Harsányi d. W. W. Jacobs d. Eric Knight d.	Wm. Lyon Phelps d. Henrik Pontoppidan d. Laura E. Richards d. Sir Charles G. D. Roberts d. Harold E. Stearns d. Alexander Woollcott d.	Reginald B. Birch d. Marsden Hartley d. Art Young d.	Alice Nielsen d. Sergei Rachmaninoff d.	Max Reinhardt d.
1944	Joseph Cailloux d. Geo. W. Norris d. Manuel Quezon y Molina d. Alfred E. Smith d. Wendell L. Willkie d.	Sir John Dill d. Erwin Rommel d.	Ernst Thaelmann d.	Aimee Semple McPherson d.	Alexis Carrel d. Jas. McKeen Cattell d. Sir Arthur S. Eddington d. Yandell Henderson d. Joseph Jastrow d. Eugen Steinach d. Sir Arthur Smith Woodward d.	Philip Guedalla d. Ida M. Tarbell d.	George Ade d. Joaquin Alvarez Quintero d. John Peale Bishop d. James Boyd d. "Max Brand" d. Humphrey Cobb d. Irvin S. Cobb d. Katharine Fullerton Gerould d. Jean Giraudoux d. Stephen Leacock d. Wm. Ellery Leonard d. Joseph C. Lincoln d.	Filippo T. Marinetti d. A. T. Quiller-Couch d. Romain Rolland d. Antoine de St. Exupéry d. Eunice Tiétjens d. Hendrik Willem Van Loon d. Wm. Allen White d. Chas. Erskine Scott Wood d. Harold Bell Wright d. Francis Yeats-Brown d.	Cyrus E. Dallin d. Chas. Dana Gibson d.	Lina Cavalieri d. Cécile Chaminade d. Will Marion Cook d. Josef Lhévinne d. Dame Ethel M. Smyth d. Sir Henry Wood d.	Henrietta Crosman d. Yvette Guilbert d. Mikhail Mordkin d. Paul Poiret d.

1945–1953 A.D.

Year A.D.	Government and Law	Military, Naval, and Aviation Affairs	Industry Commerce Economics Finance Invention Labor	Philosophy and Religion	Science, Technology, and Medicine	Education Scholarship History	Literature and Journalism	Visual Arts	Music	Miscellaneous
1945	Plutarco E. Calles d. Heinrich Himmler d. Adolf Hitler d. Pierre Laval d. David Lloyd George d. Benito Mussolini d. Vidkun Quisling d. Franklin D. Roosevelt d.	August von Mackensen d. Geo. S. Patton d.			Walter B. Cannon d. Logan Clendening d. Hans Fischer d. Smith Ely Jelliffe d. John C. Merriam d. Thos. Hunt Morgan d.	Lord Charnwood (G. F. Benson) d. Felix E. Schelling d.	Achmed Abdullah d. Maurice Baring d. Robert Benchley d. Edouard Bourdet d. Thos. Burke d. Margaret Deland d. Lord Alfred Douglas d. Theodore Dreiser d. Caradoc Evans d. Arthur Davison Ficke d. Bruno Frank d. Gustav Frenssen d. Ellen Glasgow d. Georg Kaiser d. Ada Negri d. Charles G. Norris d. Amélie Rives d. Felix Salten d. Wm. B. Seabrook d. Lady Eleanor Smith d. Arthur Symons d. Alexei Tolstoy d. Arthur Train d. Richard Walton Tully d. Paul Valery d. Franz Werfel d.	Alexander Stirling Calder d. Sir Wm. Rothenstein d. José Maria Sert d. Ignazio Zuloaga d.	Bela Bartók d. H. C. Chatfield-Taylor d. Jerome Kern d. John McCormack d. Pietro Mascagni d. Erno Rapee d.	"Beatrice Fairfax" d. Alla Nazimova d. Ernie Pyle d.
1946	Harry L. Hopkins d. Abdullah Ibn Hussein (Jordan) a. Mikhail Kalinin d. Gustav Noske d. Gifford Pinchot d. Victor Emmanuel III (Italy) abd.	Joseph W. Stilwell d.	Francisco Largo Caballero d. Karl Haushofer d. Sidney Hillman d. John Maynard Keynes d.	Graf Hermann von Keyserling d. Charles M. Sheldon d.	Simon Flexner d. Edgar L. Hewett d. Sir James Jeans d. Gilbert N. Lewis d. Clarence E. McClung d. Hugo Obermaier d. Henry C. Plummer d. Adriaan Van Maanen d.		Octave Aubry d. Ray Stannard Baker d. Ernest Boyd d. Claude Bragdon d. Countee Cullen d. Thos. Dixon d. H. G. Granville-Barker d. Clayton Hamilton d. Gerhart Hauptmann d. Orrick Johns d. E. Phillips Oppenheim d. Channing Pollock d. "Henry Handel Richardson" d. Damon Runyon d. E. Thompson Seton d. Edward B. Sheldon d. May Sinclair d. Logan Pearsall Smith d. Gertrude Stein d. Booth Tarkington d. H. G. Wells d. Stewart Edward White d.	John Steuart Curry d. Arthur G. Dove d. Hendrik Glintenkamp d. Alfred Stieglitz d.	Carrie Jacobs Bond d. Chas. Wakefield Cadman d. Manuel DeFalla d. Paul Rosenfeld d. Moriz Rosenthal d. Leo Slezak d. Harry Von Tilzer d. Vincent Youmans d.	George Arliss d. W. C. Fields d. Wm. S. Hart d. Laurette Taylor d.
1947	Stanley Baldwin d. Christian X (Denmark) d. George II (Greece) d. Fiorello H. LaGuardia d. Lewis E. Lawes d.	Evans F. Carlson d.	Irving Fisher d. Henry Ford d. Sidney Webb (Lord Passfield) d.	Morris R. Cohen d.	Frederick Gowland Hopkins d. H. S. Jennings d. Geo. Grant MacCurdy d. Sir Halford J. Mackinder d. Max Planck d. Wm. Berryman Scott d. Alfred North Whitehead d. Clark Wissler d.	Nicholas Murray Butler d.	John D. Beresford d. Tristan Bernard d. Willa Cather d. Winston Churchill d. Lincoln Colcord d. "Hans Fallada" d. Samuel Hoffenstein d. Robert Cortes Holliday d. Ricarda Huch d. Elizabeth Jordan d. Richard Le Gallienne d. Hugh Lofting d. Marie Belloc Lowndes d. Arthur Machen d. Gregorio Martinez Sierra d. Charles B. Nordhoff d. Baroness Orczy d.	Nicholas K. Roerich d. Jo Mora d.	Louise Homer d. Grace Moore d. Ellen Beach Yaw d.	
1948	Eduard Beneš d. Count Folke Bernadotte d. Chas. Evans Hughes d. Jan Masaryk d. A. Roxas y Manuel d. Hideki Tojo d. Wilhelmina (Netherlands) d.	John J. Pershing d.	Thomas W. Lamont d. Orville Wright d.	Nikolai Berdyaev d. Msgr. Edw. J. Flanagan d. Mohandas K. Gandhi d. Rufus M. Jones d. Joshua Loth Liebman d.	Ruth F. Benedict d. Robert Briffault d. A. A. Brill d. Vladimir Karapetoff d. Abraham Myerson d. Richard C. Tolman d. Franz Weidenreich d.	Charles A. Beard d. Frederick L. Paxson d. Newman I. White d.	Antonin Artaud d. Gertrude Atherton d. Georges Bernanos d. Roark Bradford d. Alice Brown d. Susan Glaspell d. Vicente Huidobro d. Will Irwin d. Holbrook Jackson d. Ross F. Lockridge d. Emil Ludwig d. Claude McKay d. A. E. W. Mason d. Wilfred Meynell d. Meredith Nicholson d. Jessie B. Rittenhouse d. Genevieve Taggard d. Albert J. Wetjen d.		Umberto Giordano d. Franz Lehár d. John A. Lomax d. Olga Samaroff d. Oley Speaks d. Ermanno Wolf-Ferrari d.	Sergei Eisenstein d. David Wark Griffith d. Burns Mantle d. Harry Price d. Babe Ruth d.
1949	Giorgi Dimitrov d.		Amadeo P. Giannini d.	Stephen S. Wise d.	Edward L. Thorndike d.	Jas. Truslow Adams d. Burton J. Hendrick d. Douglas Hyde d. Lloyd Lewis d. Sir Bernard Pares d.	Hervey Allen d. Philip Barry d. Rex Beach d. Henry Bedford-Jones d. Lewis Browne d. Will Cuppy d. Thomas Heggen d. "Hugh Kingsmill" d. Maurice Maeterlinck d. S. S. McClure d. Klaus Mann d. Margaret Mitchell d. Axel Munthe d. Sarojini Naidu d. Edith O. Somerville d. Sigrid Undset d. Oswald Garrison Villard d. R. A. J. Walling d.	José Orozco d.	Harry T. Burleigh d. Hans Kindler d. E. Robert Schmitz d. Richard Strauss d.	Robert Ripley d. Bill Robinson (Bojangles) d.

Year A.D.	Government and Law	Military, Naval, and Aviation Affairs	Industry Commerce Economics Finance Invention Labor	Philosophy and Religion	Science, Technology, and Medicine	Education Scholarship History	Literature and Journalism		Visual Arts	Music	Miscellaneous
1950	Alice Stone Blackwell d. Leon Blum d. Gustav V (Sweden) d. MacKenzie King d. Dudley Field Malone d. Jan Smuts d. Henry L. Stimson d.	Archibald Wavell d	Sid Grauman d. Harold Laski d. Robert E. Ringling d.	Evangeline Booth d.			Irving Bacheller d. Wm. Rose Benét d. William A. Brady d. Edgar Rice Burroughs d. John Gould Fletcher d. Heinrich Mann d. Edgar Lee Masters d. Karin Michdëlis d.	Edna St. Vincent Millay d. Ernest Poole d. Max Radin d. Rafael Sabatini d. George Bernard Shaw d. James Stephens d. Michael Strange d. Michael Williams d. Clement Wood d.	Eliel Saarinen d.	Walter Damrosch d. Kurt Weill d.	Frank Buck d. Walter Huston d. Al Jolson d. Waslaw Nijinsky d.
1951	Ernest Bevin d. Charles G. Dawes d. Abdullah Ibn Hussein (Jordan) d. Liaquat Ali Khan d. Maxim Litvinov d. Henri Philippe Pétain d. Arthur H. Vandenberg d	Carl Gustav Mannerheim d.	Ella Reeve Bloor d. Wm. Randolph Hearst d.	Ludwig Wittgenstein d.	Peter H. Buck d. Serge Voronoff d .	Christian Gauss d.	Louis Adamic d. Algernon Blackwood d. Hermann Broch d. Abraham Cahan d.	John Erskine d. André Gide d. James Norman Hall d. Sinclair Lewis d. Harold Ross d.	Albert C. Barnes d. John Sloan d.	John Alden Carpenter d. Eddy Duchin d. Olive Fremstad d. Serge Koussevitzky d. Sigmund Romberg d. Artur Schnabel d. Arnold Schönberg d.	Fanny Brice d. Mady Christians d. Dorothy Dix d. Lincoln Ellsworth d. Robert Flaherty d. Cyril Maude d. Olga Nethersole d. Ivor Novello d. Vesta Victoria d.
1952	Stafford Cripps d. Farouk I (Egypt) abd. George VI (England) d. Harold Ickes d. Alexandra Kollontay d. Brien McMahon d. Vittorio Emanuele Orlando d. Eva Peron d. Chaim Weizmann d.		Stuyvesant Fish d. William Green d. Harold Harmsworth d. Philip Murray d. William E. Scripps d.	Benedetto Croce d. George Santayana d.	Edwin G. Conklin d. Karen Horney d. Sister Elizabeth Kenny d.	John Dewey d. Maria Montessori d.	Herschel Brickell d. Katharine Brush d. Jean Burton d. Norman Douglas d. Jeffery Farnol d.	Gilbert Frankau d. Knut Hamsun d. Eugene Jolas d. Ferenc Molnar d. Fulton Oursler d. Mark Sullivan d.	Jo Davidson d. Bernard Karfiol d. Rollin Kirby d. H.T. Webster d .	Emma Eames d . Alfred Einstein d.	John Garfield d. Canada Lee d. Hattie McDaniel d. Vesta Tilley d.
1953	Lavrenti Beria d. George Creel d. Ibn Saud (Saudi Arabia) d. Maud Gonne d. Robt. M. La Follette, Jr. d. Joseph Stalin d. Robert A. Taft d. Fred Vinson d . Robert Wagner, Sr. d.	Karl von Rundstedt d. Sir Francis Wingate d.	Lee Shubert d.		Robert A. Millikan d. Florence Sabin d.	Douglas Southall Freeman d.	Hilaire Belloc d. Henry Bernstein d. Ivan Bunin d. Cyril E. Joad d. Eugene O'Neill d.	T.F. Powys d. Marjorie Kinnan Rawlings d. Dylan Thomas d. Ben Ames Williams d.	Raoul Dufy d. James Earle Fraser d. Milt Gross d. John Marin d.	Kathleen Ferrier d. Serge Prokofiev d. Titta Ruffo d. Jacques Thibaud d.	Maude Adams d. James J. Jeffries d. Osa Johnson d. Jim Thorpe d.

1954–1961 A.D.

Year A.D.	Government and Law	Military, Naval, and Aviation Affairs	Industry Commerce Economics Finance Invention Labor	Philosophy and Religion	Science, Technology, and Medicine	Education Scholarship History	Literature and Journalism		Visual Arts	Music	Miscellaneous
1954	Pierre de Chambrun d. E.H. Crump d. Alcide de Gasperi d. Will H. Hays d. Robert Jackson d. Pat McCarran d. Maury Maverick d. Joseph P. Tumulty d. Hoyt Vandenberg d. Andrei Vishinski d.	Paul Ludwig von Kleist d.	Arthur Garfield Hays d. Kokichi Mikimoto d.	Irwin Edman d. Wm. R. Inge d.	Karl T. Compton d. Enrico Fermi d. Earnest Albert Hooton d.		Leonard Bacon d. Jacinto Benavente y Martínez d. Maxwell Bodenheim d. S.G. Colette d.	Joseph Hergesheimer d. James Hilton d. Alain Locke d. Frederick Lonsdale d. Grantland Rice d.	André Derain d. Reginald Marsh d. Henri Matisse d.	Wilhelm Furtwängler d. Charles Ives d. Oskar Straus d.	Lionel Barrymore d. Emilie Dionne d. Sidney Greenstreet d. Bert Lytell d. Fritzi Scheff d.
1955	John W. Davis d. Cordell Hull d. Owen J. Roberts d.	Adolfo de la Huerta d.	Julius Ochs Adler d. Dale Carnegie d. Arthur Deakin d. Samuel H. Kress d. Robert R. McCormick d. Glenn Martin d. Joseph Pulitzer, Jr. d. R.S. Reynolds, Sr. d.	Mary Katherine Drexel d. Pierre Teilhard de Chardin d.	Albert Einstein d. Alexander Fleming d. James B. Sumner d. August Vollmer d.	Mary McLeod Bethune d.	James Agee d. Paul Claudel d. Robert P.T. Coffin d. Bernard De Voto d. Elisabeth Sanxay Holding d.	Ludwig Lewisohn d. Amy Loveman d. Thomas Mann d. Robert E. Sherwood d. Wallace Stevens d.	Fernand Legér d. Carl Milles d. Willy Pogany d. Maurice Utrillo d.	Olin Downes d. Arthur Honegger d. Homer Rodeheaver d.	Theda Bara d. Constance Collier d. Ely Culbertson d. Trixie Fraganza d. Walter Hampden d. Carmen Miranda d. Harry Thurston d. Honus Wagner d.
1956	Alben W. Barkley d. Hiram Bingham d. Frank Hague d. Juan Negrin d.	Pietro Badoglio d.	Clarence Birdseye d. Henry Pratt Fairchild d. Marshall Field, Jr. d. Harry F. Sinclair d. Thomas J. Watson, Sr. d. Matthew Woll d.	Giovanni Papini d. Agnes Maude Royden d.	Irène Joliot-Curie d. Alfred C. Kinsey d. Frederick Soddy d.	George Sarton d.	Michael Arlen d. Pío Baroja y Nessi d. Max Beerbohm d. Julien Benda d. Louis Bromfield d. Owen Davis d. Walter de la Mare d. James M. Hopper d.	Rupert Hughes d. Sheila Kaye-Smith d. Christopher La Farge d. Charles MacArthur d. Percy MacKaye d. H.L. Mencken d. A.A. Milne d. Fletcher Pratt d. Leonora Speyer d. Wickham H. Steed d.	Frank Brangwyn d. Lyonel Feininger d. William Gropper d. Marie Laurencin d. Emil Nolde d. Jackson Pollock d.	Tommy Dorsey d. Walter Gieseking d.	Fred Allen d. Louis Calhern d. Hattie Carnegie d. Ruth Draper d. Elsie Janis d. Alexander Korda d. Bela Lugosi d. "Connie Mack" d. Mistinguett d. Margaret Wycherly d. Babe Zaharias d.
1957	Aga Khan III (Ismailians) d. Walter F. George d. Haakon VII (Norway) d. Eduard Herriot d. Leslie Hore-Belisha d. Nicholas Horthy de Nagybánya d. Joseph R. McCarthy d. Kenneth D. McKellar d. Ramón Magsaysay d.		Sosthenes Behn d. Howard C. Candler d. Christian Dior d. Lincoln Filene d. Frank E. Gannett d. Louis B. Mayer d. Gerard Swope d.	Msgr. Ronald Knox d.	Irving Langmuir d. John von Neumann d. Wilhelm Reich d. Albert E. Wiggam d.	Charles E. Funk d. C.K. Ogden d.	Sholem Asch d. Joyce Cary d. Lord Dunsany d. Walter Duranty d. Oliver St. John Gogarty d. Nikos Kazantzakis d. Giuseppi Tomasi di Lampedusa d.	Wyndham Lewis d. Gabriela Mistral d. Christopher Morley d. Burton Rascoe d. Kenneth Roberts d. Michael Sadleir d. John Van Druten d. Laura Ingalls Wilder d.	Constantin Brancusi d. Miguel Covarrubias d. Diego Rivera d. Maurice Stern d. Pavel Tchelitchew d. J.R. Williams. d.	Beniamino Gigli d. Ezio Pinza d. Jean Sibelius d. Arturo Toscanini d.	Humphrey Bogart d. Richard E. Byrd d. Joe Gould d. Oliver Hardy d. Peggy Hopkins Joyce d. Elizabeth Kingsley d. Norma Talmadge d. Erich Von Stroheim d.

Year A.D.	Government and Law	Military, Naval, and Aviation Affairs	Industry Commerce Economics Finance Invention Labor	Philosophy and Religion	Science, Technology, and Medicine	Education Scholarship History	Literature and Journalism		Visual Arts	Music	Miscellaneous
1958	Otto Abetz d. Feisal II (Iraq) d.	Claire L. Chennault d. Maurice Gamelin d.	Lucien Lelong d. Malcolm Lockheed d. Christabel Pankhurst d. Mike Todd d. H.B. Warner d.	Pope John XXIII a. G. E. Moore d. Pope Pius XII d.	Frédéric Joliot-Curie d. Charles F. Kettering d. Ernest O. Lawrence d. Wolfgang Pauli d. Marie C. Stopes d. John B. Watson d.	Mary G. Beard d. Claude G. Bowers d. Louise Pound d.	Zoë Akins d. Elmer Davis d. Lion Feuchtwanger d. Dorothy Canfield Fisher d. Wolcott Gibbs d. Louis Golding d. Juan Ramón Jiménez d. Rose Macaulay d. Betty MacDonald d.	George Jean Nathan d. Alfred Noyes d. Elliott Paul d. Mary Roberts Rinehart d. Robert W. Service d. Elsie Singmaster d. John C. Squire d. Herbert Bayard Swope d.	Guy Pène Du Bois d. Georges Rouault d. Maurice de Vlaminck d.	W.C. Handy d. Artur Rodzinski d. Ralph Vaughan Williams d.	Margaret Anglin d. Ronald Colman d. Robert Donat d. Norman Bel Geddes d. Burton Holmes d. Doris Humphrey d. Douglas Mawson d. Tyrone Power, Jr. d. Sir Hubert Wilkins d.
1959	Hitoshi Ashida d. William J. Donovan d. John Foster Dulles d. Maurice Duplessis d. Earl of Halifax (Edward Wood) d. Daniel François Malan d.	Wm. F. Halsey d. Wm. D. Leahy d. George C. Marshall d.	Cecil B. DeMille d. Jack Frye d. Harold Vance d.	Paul Radin d.	Sir Henry Tizard d. Gregory Zilboorg d.	Abraham Flexner d. Albert L. Guérard d.	Maxwell Anderson d. Raymond Chandler d. Sarah N. Cleghorn d. Octavus Roy Cohen d. Ashley Dukes d.	Edgar A. Guest d. Laurence Housman d. Wallace Irwin d. Edwin Muir d. Sax Rohmer d. Tiffany Thayer d.	Bruce Bairnsfather d. Bernard Berenson d. Jacob Epstein d. Georg Grosz d. Frank Lloyd Wright d.	George Antheil d. Eduard van Beinum d. Ernest Bloch d. Billie Holiday d. Wanda Landowska d. Heitor Villa-Lobos d.	Ethel Barrymore d. Lou Costello d. Errol Flynn d. Duncan Hines d. Willie (Wm. F.) Hoppe d. Edna Wallace Hopper d. Napoleon Lajoie d. Victor McLaglen d.
1960	Oswaldo Aranha d. Aneurin Bevan d. Joseph N. Welch d.	Albert Kesselring d.	E. Sylvia Pankhurst d. John D. Rockefeller, Jr. d. Beardsley Ruml d. Walter Dorwin Teague d.	"Daddy Grace" d.	Roy Chapman Andrews d. Eric T. Bell d. A.L. Kroeber d. Leonard Woolley d.	Lewis B. Namier d.	Franklin P. Adams d. Vicki Baum d. Albert Camus d. Gene Fowler d. M.A. De Wolfe Howe d. Zora N. Hurston d. Harry Kemp d.	John P. Marquand d. Boris L. Pasternak d. Eden Phillpotts d. Emily Post d. "Nevil Shute" d. Richard Wright d.	James Montgomery Flagg d.	Lucrezia Bori d. Oscar Hammerstein, II d. John Charles Thomas d. Laurence Tibbett d.	Luis Angel Firpo d. Clark Gable d. Gregory Ratoff d. Jimmy Savo d. Mack Sennett d. Margaret Sullavan d. Clara Kimball Young d.
1961	Luigi Einaudi d. Dag Hammarskjöld d. Learned Hand d. Patrice Lumm Patrice Lumumba d. Sam Rayburn d. Rafael Leonidas Trujillo Molina d. Sumner Welles d.		Eugene Dennis d. William Z. Foster d.	Carl G. Jung d.	Lee De Forest d. Arnold Gesell d.		Emily G. Balch d. Konrad Bercovici d. Henry Seidel Canby d. Louis-Ferdinand Céline d. Whittaker Chambers d. Mazo De la Roche d. Hilda Doolittle d. Franz Fanon d. Kenneth Fearing d. Dashiell Hammett d.	Moss Hart d. Ernest Hemingway d. Robert Hillyer d. George S. Kaufman d. Isaac F. Marcosson d. Oliver Onions d. Julia Peterkin d. Angela Thirkell d. Dorothy Thompson d. James Thurber d.	Augustus John d. "Grandma Moses" d. Eero Saarinen d.	Sir Thomas Beecham d.	Leo Carrillo d. Ruth Chatterton d. Ty Cobb d. Gary Cooper d. Marion Davies d. Elsie Ferguson d. Barry Fitzgerald d. Blanche Ring d. Anna May Wong d.

1962–1968 A.D.

Year A.D.	Government and Law	Military, Naval, and Aviation Affairs	Industry Commerce Economics Finance Invention Labor	Philosophy and Religion	Science, Technology, and Medicine	Education Scholarship History	Literature and Journalism		Visual Arts	Music	Miscellaneous
1962	Eleanor Roosevelt d.		René Coty d. Owen D. Young d.		William Beebe d. Niels Bohr d. Arthur H. Compton d.		Ludwig Bemelmans d. William S.B. Braithwaite d. E.E. Cummings d. William Faulkner d. Sir Philip Gibbs d.	Francis Hackett d. Hermann Hesse d. Robinson Jeffers d. Nina Wilcox Putnam d. Victoria Sackville-West d. Hannen Swaffer d.	"Ding" Darling d. Ivan Mestrovic d.	Alfred Cortot d. Kirsten Flagstad d. Eugene Goosens d. Fritz Kreisler d. Bruno Walter d.	Juan Belmonte d. Frank Borzage d. Louise Fazenda d. Charles Laughton d. Charles ("Lucky") Luciano d. Marilyn Monroe d. Vilhjalmur Stefannson d. Grover A. Whalen d.
1963	Sir William Beveridge d. Tom Connally d. Ngo Dinh Diem d. Hugh Gaitskell d. Theodor Heuss d. Estes Kefauver d. John F. Kennedy d. Herbert H. Lehman d.		Irénée DuPont d. Jacob J. Shubert d. Evelyn John Strachey d.	Sherwood Eddy d. Pope John XXIII d. G. Bromley Oxnam d. Abba Hillel Silver d.	Jean F. Piccard d.	Edith Hamilton d.	Herbert Asbury d. Van Wyck Brooks d. Jean Cocteau d. W.E.B. Dubois d. Robert Frost d. Aldous Huxley d. Oliver La Farge d. C.S. Lewis d.	A.J. Liebling d. Frances Lockridge d. Clifford Odets d. Sylvia Plath d. Theodore Roethke d. William Carlos Williams d. Stark Young d.	Georges Braque d. Jimmy Hatlo d. John La Farge d. David Low d.	Amelita Galli-Curci d. Paul Hindemith d. Rosa Raisa d.	Richard Barthelmess d Monte Blue d. Elsa Maxwell d. Adolphe Menjou d. Lee Harvey Oswald d. Edith Piaf d. ZaSu Pitts d.
1964	Emilio Aguinaldo d. Josephus Daniels, Jr. d. Herbert Hoover d. Jawarlahal Nehru d. Wm. O'Dwyer d.	Douglas MacArthur d. Henry Maitland Wilson d. Sgt. Alvin C. York d.	Giuseppe Amato d. Lord Beaverbrook d. Pascal Covici d. Benjamin J. Davis d. Elizabeth Gurley Flynn d. Roy W. Howard d. Maurice Thorez d. Palmiro Togliatti d. John Haynes Holmes d. Alexander Meiklejohn d.		Rachel Carson d. J.B.S. Haldane d. Leo Szilard d. Norbert Weiner d.		Hamilton Basso d. Brendan Behan d. Marc Blitzstein d. J. Frank Dobie d. Ian Fleming d. A.Hamilton Gibbs d. Herman Hagedorn d. Ben Hecht d. Archibald Henderson d. Stewart H. Holbrook d.	Clarence Budington Kelland d. Grace Metalious d. Sean O'Casey d. Flannery O'Connor d. Hesketh Pearson d. Donald Culross Peattie d. Roscoe Pound d. Frank Scully d. Franz Sillanpaa d. Carl Van Vechten d. T. H. White d.	Alexander Archipenko d. Percy L. Crosby d. Stuart Davis d.	Pierre Monteux d. Cole Porter d.	Gracie Allen d. Eddie Cantor d. Sir Cedric Hardwicke d. Alan Ladd d. Peter Lorre d. Harpo Marx d. Joseph Schildkraut d.
1965	Sir Winston Churchill d. Herbert V. Evatt d. Felix Frankfurter d. Joseph C. Grew d. Ruth Sears (Baker) Pratt d. Syngman Rhee d. Moshe Sharett d. Adlai Stevenson d. Henry A. Wallace d.	Maxime Weygand d.	Bernard M. Baruch d. Marshall Field 3rd d. John M. Lewis d. Frances Perkins d. Helena Rubenstein d. David O. Selznik d.	"Father Divine" d. Malcolm X d. Clarence E. Pickett d. Paul J. Tillich d.	John Hays Hammond, Jr. d. Albert Schweitzer d.	Virginia Gildersleeve d. Angelo Patri d.	Thomas B. Costain d. T.S. Eliot d. Lorraine Hansberry d. Shirley Jackson d. Sophie Kerr d. Alexander King d.	W. Somerset Maugham d. Dawn Powell d. Quentin Reynolds d. Robert C. Ruark d. Howard Spring d.	"Le Corbusier" d. Charles Sheeler d. Wilfrid M. Zogbaum d.	Nat "King" Cole d. Jeanette MacDonald d. Tito Schipa d. Sigmund Spaeth d. Edgar Varese d.	Clyde Beatty d. Mary Boland d. Clara Bow d. Sidney Chaplin d. Linda Darnell d. Louise Dresser d. Judy Holliday d. Dorothy Kilgallen d. Stan Laurel d. Mae Murray d. Nance O'Neil d. Branch Rickey d.

Year A.D.	Government and Law	Military, Naval, and Aviation Affairs	Industry Commerce Economics Finance Invention Labor	Philosophy and Religion	Science, Technology, and Medicine	Education Scholarship History	Literature and Journalism		Visual Arts	Music	Miscellaneous
1966	Theodore Francis Green d. Paul Reynaud d. Henrik Verwoerd d.	Chester W. Nimitz d.	Elizabeth Arden d. Bernard F. Gimbel d. Blanche Wolf Knopf d. Sebastian Kresge d. Michael J. Quill d. Alfred P. Sloan d. Alexander Trachtenberg d.	Daisetz T. Suzuki d. Harry F. Ward d.	Wm. Menninger d. Margaret Sanger d.	Moses Hadas d.	Anna Akhmatova d. Margery Allingham d. Lucius Beebe d. Georges Duhamel d. C.S. Forester d. Lewis Gannett d. Marguerite Higgins d.	Wm. McFee d. Lee Meriwether d. Anne Nichols d. Kathleen Norris d. Frank O'Connor d. Mari Sandoz d. Lillian Smith d. Arthur Waley d. Evelyn Waugh d.	Walt Disney d. Alberto Giacometti d. Don Herold d. Hans Hoffman d. Paul Manship d. Maxfield Parrish d. Russ Westover d. William Zorach d.	Noah Greenberg d. Deems Taylor d. Wieland Wagner d.	Lenny Bruce d. Francis X. Bushman d. Montgomery Clift d. Raymond Duncan d. Hedda Hopper d. Buster Keaton d. Fulton Lewis, Jr. d. Helen Menken d. Erwin Piscator d. Billy Rose d. Sophie Tucker d. Ed Wynn d.
1967	Konrad Adenauer d. Clement Attlee d. William C. Bullitt d. John Nance Garner d. "Che" Guevara d. Henry Pu-yi d.		Sir Norman Angell d. Roger Babson d. Bruce Barton d. J. Frank Duryea d. Victor Gollancz d. Henry J. Kaiser d. Willard M. Kiplinger d. Henry R. Luce d. Albert John Luthuli d. A.J. Muste d. George Lincoln Rockwell d.	Francis Cardinal Spellman d.	Hugo Gernsback d. Hermann J. Muller d. J. Robert Oppenheimer d. Béla Schick d.		Ilya Ehrenberg d. Martin Flavin d. Waldo Frank d. Michael Gold d. Alice Tisdale Hobart d. Vyvyan Holland d. Langston Hughes d. Carson McCullers d.	John Masefield d. André Maurois d. Max Miller d. Dorothy Parker d. Elmer L. Rice d. Carl Sandberg d. Siegfried Sassoon d. Alice B. Toklas d.	Edward Hopper d.	Nelson Eddy d. Geraldine Farrar d. Mary Garden d. Woody Guthrie d. Zoltán Kodály d. Louis Persinger d. Paul Whiteman d.	Primo Carnera d. Mischa Elman d. Ilse Koch d. Vivien Leigh d. Tommy Manville d. Edison Marshall d. Paul Muni d. Evelyn Nesbit d. Francis Ouimet d. Clementine Paddleford d. Claude Rains d. Basil Rathbone d. Jack Ruby d. Spencer Tracy d. Felix Youssoupoff d.
1968	Francis Biddle d. Gerhart Eisler d. Robert F. Kennedy d. Trygve Lie d. Stewart G. Menzies d. Michael A. Musmanno d. Harold Nicolson d. George Papandreou d.	Arturo Ossorio Arana d. Hanford MacNider d.	Leo Huberman d. Homer Martin d. Arthur Hays Sulzberger d. Norman Thomas d.	Karl Barth d. Augustin Cardinal Bea d. Bob Jones, Sr. d. Martin Luther King, Jr. d. Daniel Poling d.	Yuri Gagarin d. George Gamow d. Charles W. Mayo d. Lise Meitner d. Thomas Parran d.	Crane Brinton d.	"Anthony Boucher" d. Paul Vincent Carroll d. Randolph Churchill d. Edna Ferber d. Vardis Fisher d. Dudley Fitts d. Fannie Hurst d. Howard Lindsay d. Thomas Merton d.	Sarah Gertrude Millin d. Pierre van Paassen d. Salvatore Quasimodo d. Herbert Read d. Conrad Richter d. Laurence Stallings d. John Steinbeck d.	Peter Arno d. Adolf Dehn d. Marcel Duchamp d.	Charles Münch d.	Tallulah Bankhead d. Kay Francis d. Dorothy Gish d. Duke Kahanamoku d. Helen Keller d. Mae Marsh d. Ruth St. Denis d. Earl Sande d. Eleanora Sears d. Raymond Swing d. Franchot Tone d. Walter Wanger d.

1969–1974 A.D.

Year A.D.	Government and Law	Military, Naval, and Aviation Affairs	Industry Commerce Economics Finance Invention Labor	Philosophy and Religion	Science, Technology, and Medicine	Education Scholarship History	Literature and Journalism		Visual Arts	Music	Miscellaneous
1969	Thurman W. Arnold d. Dwight David Eisenhower d. Ramon Grau San Martin d. Ho Chi Minh d. Joseph Kasavubu d. Tom Mboya d. Franz von Papen d. Moise Tshombe d. Klementii E. Voroshilov d.	Harold R.L. Alexander d.	Louis Dublin d. Raoul Fleischmann d. John L. Lewis d.	Harry Emerson Fosdick d. Karl Jaspers d. James A. Pike d.	Willy Ley d. Hans Rademacher d. Theodor Reik d. Vesto M. Slipher d.	Leonard Woolf d.	John Mason Brown d. Ivy Compton-Burnett d. Floyd Dell d. Max Eastman d. Corey Ford d. Josephine Herbst d. Maurice Hindus d.	Jack Kerouac d. Drew Pearson d. Westbrook Pegler d. Stephen Potter d. Osbert Sitwell d. B. Traven d.	Arthur ("Bugs") Baer d. Walter Gropius d. Ludwig Mies van der Rohe d. Ben Shahn d.	Ernest Ansermet d. Wilhelm Backhaus d. Vernon Duke d. Giovanni Martinelli d. Gladys Swarthout d.	Judy Garland d. Walter C. Hagen d. Sonya Henie d. Rex Ingram d. Boris Korloff d. Rocky Marciano d. Nicholas M. Schenck d. Joseph von Sternberg d. Charles Winninger d.
1970	Lázaro Cárdenas d. Edouard Daladier d. Charles De Gaulle d. Alexander Kerenski d. Gamal Abdel Nasser d. Antonio Salazar d. Hjalmar Schacht d. Sukarno d.	Wladyslaw Anders d. Marie Pierre Koenig d. B.H. Liddell Hart d.	Agnes E. Meyer d. Walter Reuther d. Anna Louise Strong d.	Richard Cushing d. David de Sola Pool d. Bertrand Russell d.	Eric Berne d. Max Born d. Leslie Groves d. John T. Scopes d. Otto H. Warburg d.		S.Y. Agnon d. John Dos Passos d. Guy Endore d. E.M. Forster d. Erle Stanley Gardner d. John Gunther d. Francis Parkinson Keyes d. D.B. Wyndham Lewis d. François Mauriac d.	Clare Turlay Newberry d. John O'Hara d. Harry A. Overstreet d. Eric Maria Remarque d. Nelly Sachs d. Franz Schoenberner d. Gilbert Seldes d. Wilbur D. Steele d.	Beniamino Bufano d. Rube Goldberg d. Henry Varnum Poor d. Mark Rothko d.	John Barbirolli d. Eddie Peabody d. Clare Sheridan d.	Billie Burke d. Marie Dionne d. Edward Everett Horton d. Gypsy Rose Lee d. Chester Morris d. Marjorie Rambeau d. Samuel H. Sheppard d. Lenore Ulric d.
1971	Dean Acheson d. Adolf A. Berle d. Hugo L. Black d. Thomas E. Dewey d. François Duvalier d. Nikita S. Khrushchev d. Elmo Roper d. T.V. Soong d.	Audie Murphy d.	"Coco" Chanel d. Jack Hall d. György Lukács d. Robt. S. Lynd d. James Cash Penney d. Spyros Skouras d. J. David Stern d. Thomas M. Storke d.	Reinhold Niebuhr d.	John W. Campbell d. Paul De Kruif d. Cesar Searchinger d.	Alvin Johnson d. Hans Kohn d. Allan Nevins d.	Bennett A. Cerf d. August Derleth d. St. John Ervine d. Helen Hull d. Manfred B. Lee ("Ellery Queen") d.	Ogden Nash d. Giorgos Seferis d. Samuel Spewack d. James F. Stevens d. James R. Ullman d. Philip Wylie d.	Rockwell Kent d.	Louis ("Satchmo") Armstrong d. Marcel Dupré d. Igor Stravinsky d.	Margaret Bourke-White d. Spring Byington d. Chester Conklin d. Bebe Daniels d. Fernandel d. Nathan Leopold d. Ted Lewis d. Paul Lukas d. John S. Sumner d.
1972	Ralph J. Bunche d. James F. Byrnes d. Martin Dies d. Edward VIII (England) d. J. Edgar Hoover d. Kwame Nkrumah d. Lester B. Pearson d. Adam Clayton Powell, Jr. d. Paul-Henri Spaak d. Harry S. Truman d.	Matvei Zakharov d.	Saul Alinsky d. Warren K. Billings d. Louis Budenz d. Lord Arthur Rank d. Igor Sikorsky d.	Geoffrey Francis Fisher d. Abraham Heschel d. Eugène Cardinal Tisserant d.	Loren D. Carlson d. Eleanor Glueck d. Edward Kendall d. L.S.B. Leakey d. Kurt Marek d. Maria G. Mayer d. Harlow Shapley d.	Sanford Bates d. Philip Gove d.	Daisy Ashford d. John Berryman d. Cecil Day-Lewis d. Paul Goodman d. L.P. Hartley d. Yasunari Kawabata d. Compton Mackenzie d.	Earl Schenck Miers d. Marianne Moore d. Kenneth Patchen d. Ezra Pound d. Jules Romains d. Edgar Snow d. Harvey Swados d. Mark Van Doren d. Edmund Wilson d.	Eugene Berman d.	Robert Casadesus d. Rudolf Friml d. Ferde (von) Grofé d. Mahalia Jackson d. Oscar Levant d. Alexander Smallens d. Helen Traubel d.	Charles Atlas d. Maurice Chevalier d. Sir Francis Chichester d. Roberto Clemente d. Gladys Cooper d. Jennie Grossinger d. José Limón d. Basil O'Connor d. Louella Parsons d. Jackie Robinson d. Dame Margaret Rutherford d. Ted Shawn d. Margaret Webster d. Walter Winchell d.

Year A.D.	Government and Law	Military, Naval, and Aviation Affairs	Industry Commerce Economics Finance Invention Labor	Philosophy and Religion	Science, Technology, and Medicine	Education Scholarship History	Literature and Journalism		Visual Arts	Music	Miscellaneous
1973	Salvador Allende (Chile) d. Fulgencio Batista y Zaldivar d. David Ben-Gurion d. Georges Bonnet d. Earl Browder d. Gustav VI Adolf d. Ismet Inönü d. Lyndon B. Johnson d. Liu Shao-Chi d. ? Jeannette Rankin d. Samuel I. Rosenman d. Louis S. St. Laurent d. Walter Ulbricht d. Charles Whittaker d.	Erich von Manstein d. Arthur (Wm.) Radford d. Eddie Rickenbacker d.	James B. Carey d. Norman Chandler d. John D. Eaton d. Ragnar Frisch d. Alfred C. Fuller d. Laurens Hammond d. Charles S. Mott d. Winthrop Rockefeller d. Elsa Schiaparelli d.	Cardinal Amleto Cicognani d. Charles H. Dodd d. Maurice Eisendrath d. Eli Stanley Jones d. Cardinal Achille Lienart d. Robert McCracken d. Jacques Maritain d. Gabriel Marcel d.	Bernt Balchen d. Haim Ginott d. Walter R. Hess d. Louis S. Katz d. Artturi I. Virtanen d. Selman A. Waksman d. Paul Dudley White d. Karl Ziegler d.	Howard Aiken d. Samuel Flagg Bemis d. William B. Benton d. David Clift d. Alexander S. Neill d.	Conrad P. Aiken d. Hugh Auden d. S.N. Behrman d. Arna Bontemps d. Elizabeth Bowen d. Jane Bowles d. Pearl S. Buck d. Whit Burnett d.	Mary Ellen Chase d. Sir Noel Coward d. John Creasey d. William Inge d. David Lawrence d. Cornelia L. Meigs d. Nancy Mitford d. Pablo Neruda d. J.R.R. Tolkien d.	Eliot Elisofan d. Philip Evergood d. Anna Hyatt Huntington d. Walt Kelly d. Jacques Lipchitz d. Pablo Picasso d. Edward Steichen d.	Pablo Casals d. Eddie Condon d. Istvan Kertesz d. Otto Klemperer d. Gene Krupa d. Lauritz Melchior d. Joseph Szigeti d. Jennie Tourel d.	John Cranko d. John Ford d. Betty Grable d. Jack Hawkins d. Sessue Hayakawa d. Anna Magnani d. Paavo J. Nurmi d. E. G. Robinson d. Mary Wigman d.
1974	Marshal Mohammad Ayub Khan d. Chip Bohlen d. Richard Crossman d. Ernest Gruening d. Haj Amin el-Husseini d. Norman Kirk d. William Knowland d. V.K. Krishna Menon d. Wayne Morse d. Sir Leslie Munro d. Karl Mundt d. Juan Perón d. Georges Pompidou d. Kotaro Tanaka d. U. Thant d. Earl Warren d.	General Creighton Abrams d. Admiral Nikolai Kuznetsov d. Charles Lindbergh d. General Carl Spaatz d. Lewis Strauss d. Marshall Georgi Zhukov d.	John C. Garand d. Daniel Gerber d. Seymour Harris d. Paul G. Hoffman d. H.L. Hunt d. Anne Klein d. Edward H. Molyneux d. Arthur Watson d.	Samuel Hepburn d.	Virginia Apgar d. Marston Bates d. Jacob Bronowski d. Vannevar Bush d. Sir James Chadwick d. Edward Condon d. W. Maurice Ewing d. Karl F. Meyer d. Earl Sutherland, Jr. d.	Alexander Bickel d. Sir Denis Brogan d. Sidonie Gruenberg d. James Muilenburg d.	Stewart Alsop d. Miguel Asturias d. H.E. Bates d. Cyril Connolly d. Georgette Heyer d. Chet Huntley d. Erich Kästner d. George E. Kelly d. Arthur Krock d. Pär Fabian Lagerkvist d. Lois Lenski d.	Walter Lippmann d. Marcel Pagnol d. Olive Prouty d. Margaret Pulitzer d. John Crowe Ransom d. Anne Sexton d. Vincent Starrett d. Jacqueline Susann d. Amy Vanderbilt d. Samuel Goldwyn d.	Louis I. Kahn David Siqueiros d.	Duke Ellington d. Henry Josef Krips d. Darius Milhaud d. David Oistrakh d. Harry Partch d. Harry Ruby d.	Jack Benny d. Katharine Cornell d. Dizzy Dean d. Alexander De Seversky d. Vittorio De Sica d. Alan Guttmacher d. Sol Hurok d. Harold Loeb d. Agnes Moorehead d. Ed Sullivan d.

INDEX

(Where it has been impossible to find the date of birth, the date of death only is given, or possibly just a date when the person flourished. The first date given for popes and ruling monarchs is the date of accession rather than date of birth; and if the monarch abdicated or was deposed that date is given rather than date of death.)

Baring, Sir Francis 1740-1810
Baring, Maurice 1874-1945
Baring-Gould, Sabine 1834-1924
Barkley, Alben W. 1877-1956
Barlow, Joel 1754-1812
Barnard, Lady Anne 1750-1825
Barnard, Frederick A. P. 1809-1889
Barnard, George Grey 1863-1938
Barnard, Henry 1811-1900
Barnardo, Thomas J. 1845-1905
Barnato, Barnett (Isaacs) 1852-1897
Barnave, Antoine 1761-1793
Barnes, Albert C. 1872-1951
Barnes, Thomas 1786-1841
Barnes, William 1800-1886
Barneveldt, Jan van O. *See* Oldenbarneveldt, Jan van
Barnum, Phineas T. 1810-1891
Baroja y Nessi, Pío 1872-1956
Baronius, Caesar 1538-1607
Barr, Amelia E. 1831-1919
Barras, Comte de (Paul) 1755-1829
Barrès, Maurice 1862-1923
Barrett, Elizabeth. *See* Browning, Elizabeth Barrett
Barrett, Lawrence 1838-1891
Barrie, Sir James M. 1860-1937
Barros, João de 1496-1570
Barrow, Isaac 1630-1677
Barry, James 1741-1806
Barry, John 1745-1803
Barry Philip 1896-1949
Barrymore, Ethel 1879-1959
Barrymore, John 1882-1942
Barrymore, Lionel 1878-1954
Bartels, Hans von 1856-1913
Barth, Heinrich 1821-1865
Barth, Jean 1651-1702
Barth, Karl 1886-1968
Barthelmess, Richard 1897-1963
Barthez, Paul 1734-1806
Bartholdi, Frédéric 1834-1904
Bartholin, Thomas 1616-1680
Bartlett, John 1820-1905
Bartók, Béla 1881-1945
Bartolommeo, Fra (Baccio della Porta) 1475-1517
Bartolommeo, Veneto 1480-1555
Barton, Bernard 1784-1849
Barton, Bruce 1886-1967
Barton, Clara 1821-1912
Barton, Elizabeth (Maid of Kent) 1506-1534
Barton, Ralph 1891-1931
Barton, William E. 1861-1930
Bartram, John 1699-1777
Bartram, William 1739-1823
Baruch, Bernard 1870-1965
Bary, Heinrich de 1831-1888
Barye, Antoine 1795-1875
Basedow, Johann 1723-1790
Bashford, Herbert 1871-1928
Bashkirtsev, Marie 1860-1884
Basil, Saint 329-379
Basil I (Emperor of East) 866-886
Basil II (Emperor of East) 960-1025
Basilicus (Emperor of East) 475-477
Baskerville, John 1706-1775
Bassano, Jacopo (Giacomo da Ponte) 1510-1592
Basso, Hamilton 1904-1964
Bassompierre, François de 1579-1646
Bastian, Adolf 1826-1905
Bastiat, Frédéric 1801-1850
Bastien-Lepage, Jules 1848-1884
Bates, Arlo 1850-1918
Bates, H. E. (Herbert Ernest) 1905-1974
Bates, Henry W. 1825-1892
Bates, Katharine Lee 1859-1929
Bates, Marston 1906-1974
Bates, Sanford 1884-1972
Bateson, William 1861-1926
Bathe, Lady de. *See* Langtry, Lillie
Batista y Zaldivar, Fulgencio 1901-1973
Batthyànyi, Count (Lajos) 1806-1849
Baudelaire, Charles 1821-1867
Baudry, Paul 1828-1886
Bauer, Bruno 1809-1882
Bauhin, Gaspard 1556-1624
Baum, Vicki 1888-1960
Baumé, Antoine 1728-1804
Baumgarten, Alexander ..1714-1762
Baur, Ferdinand 1792-1860
Bax, Ernest Belfort 1854-1926
Baxter, Richard 1615-1691
Bayard, Pierre de (Chevalier) 1473-1524
Bayard, Thomas F. 1828-1898
Bayazid (Bajazet) I (Turkey) 1389-1403
Bayazid (Bajazet) II (Turkey) 1481-1512
Bayle, Pierre 1647-1706
Bayliss, Sir William M. ..1860-1924
Bayly, Thomas H. 1797-1839
Bazaine, Achille François 1811-1888
Bazán, Álvaro de. *See* Santa Cruz, Marquis of
Bazin, René 1853-1932
Bazzi, Giovanni de'. *See* Sodoma, Il
Bea, Augustin Cardinal ..1881-1968
Beach, Michael Hicks. *See* St. Aldwyn, Earl of
Beach, Rex 1877-1949
Beaconsfield, Earl of. *See* Disraeli, Benjamin
Beard, Charles A. 1874-1948
Beard, Daniel Carter 1850-1941
Beard, Mary G. 1876-1958
Beardsley, Aubrey 1872-1898
Beaton, David (Bethune) 1494-1546
Beatrice (Portinari) 1266-1290
Beattie, James 1735-1803
Beatty, Clyde 1905-1965
Beatus Rhenanus 1485-1547
"Beau Brummell." *See* Brummell, George
"Beau Nash." *See* Nash, Richard
Beauchamp, Kathleen. *See* Mansfield, Katherine
Beauchamp, Richard. *See* Warwick, 13th Earl of
Beaufort, Edmund. *See* Somerset, 2nd Duke of
Beaufort, Henry 1377-1447
Beauharnais, Eugène de ..1781-1824
Beaumarchais, Pierre de ..1732-1799
Beaumont, Charles d'Éon de. *See* Éon de Beaumont
Beaumont, Francis 1584-1616
Beaumont, Jean de 1798-1874
Beaumont, Sir John 1583-1627
Beauregard, Pierre G. T. ..1818-1893
Beaux, Cecilia 1863-1942
Beaverbrook, Lord (William Maxwell Aitken) 1879-1964
Bebel, August 1840-1913
Beccaria, Marchese di (Cesare) 1738-1794
Becher, Johann 1635-1682
Becker, Nicolaus 1810-1845
Beckett, Gilbert á. *See* á Beckett
Beckford, William 1759-1844
Becquerel, Antoine C. ...1788-1878
Becquerel, Antoine H. ...1852-1908
Beddoes, Thomas Lovell ..1803-1849
Bede of Jarrow (Venerable) 673-735
Bedford, Duke of (John Plantagenet) 1389-1435
Bedford-Jones, Henry 1887-1949
Beebe, Lucius 1902-1966
Beebe, William 1877-1962
Beecham, Sir Thomas 1879-1961
Beecher, Catherine 1800-1878
Beecher, Henry Ward 1813-1887
Beecher, Lyman 1775-1863
Beechey, Sir William 1753-1839
Beer, Jakob Meyer. *See* Meyerbeer, Giacomo
Beer, Thomas 1889-1940
Beer-Walbrunn, Anton ...1865-1929
Beerbohm, Max 1872-1956
Beers, Ethel Lynn 1827-1879
Beethoven, Ludwig van ..1770-1827
Behan, Brendan 1923-1964
Behn, Aphra 1640-1689
Behn, Sosthenes 1882-1957
Behring, Emil von 1854-1917
Behring, Vitus 1680-1741
Behrman, S. N. 1893-1973
Beinum, Eduard van 1900-1959
Béla IV (Hungary) 1235-1270
Bel Geddes, Norman 1893-1958
Belisarius 505-565
Bell, Alexander Graham ..1847-1922
Bell, Andrew 1753-1832
Bell, Sir Charles 1774-1842
Bell, Eric T. 1883-1960
Bell, Gertrude 1868-1926
Bell, Robert 1800-1867
Bell, Thomas 1792-1880
Bellamy, Edward 1850-1898
Bellarmino, Roberto 1542-1621
Bellini, Gentile 1429-1507
Bellini, Giovanni 1430-1516
Bellini, Jacopo 1400-1470
Bellini, Vincenzo 1801-1835
Bellmann, Karl 1740-1795
Belloc, Hilaire 1870-1953
Bellows, George 1882-1925
Belmont, August 1816-1890
Belmont, Mrs. Oliver H. P. (Alva) 1853-1933
Belmonte, Juan 1892-1962
Belon, Pierre 1518-1564
Beltrami, Eugenio 1835-1900
Belzoni, Giovanni 1778-1823
Bembo, Pietro 1470-1547
Bemelmans, Ludwig 1898-1962
Bemis, Samuel Flagg 1891-1973
Benavente y Martinez, Jacinte 1866-1954
Benbow, John 1653-1702
Benchley, Robert 1889-1945
Benda, Julien 1867-1956
Benedict of Nursia, Saint..480-543
Benedict XIV (Pope) 1740-1758
Benedict XV (Pope) 1914-1922
Benedict, Sir Julius 1806-1885
Bénedict, Ruth F. 1887-1948
Beneke, Friedrich 1798-1854
Beneš, Eduard 1884-1948
Benét, Stephen Vincent ...1898-1943
Benét, William Rose 1886-1950
Benfey, Theodor 1809-1881
Ben-Gerson, Levi. *See* Gersonides
Ben-Gurion, David 1886-1973
Benjamin, Judah P. 1811-1884
Benjamin, Park 1809-1864
Bennet, Henry. *See* Arlington, Earl of
Bennett, Arnold 1867-1931
Bennett, Floyd 1890-1928
Bennett, James Gordon ..1795-1872
Benny, Jack 1894-1974
Benson, Arthur C. 1862-1925
Benson, E. F. 1867-1940
Benson, Edward W. 1829-1896
Benson, Stella (Mrs. J. C. O'G. Anderson) 1892-1933
Bentham, Jeremy 1748-1832
Bentinck, Lord (George) 1802-1848
Bentinck, William. *See* Portland, Earl of
Bentley, Richard 1662-1742
Benton, Thomas H. 1782-1858
Benton, William B. 1900-1973
Beranger, Pierre de 1780-1857
Bercovici, Konrad 1882-1961
Berdyaev, Nikolai 1874-1948
Berengarius 924
Berenson, Bernard 1865-1959
Beresford, John 1738-1805
Beresford, John D. 1873-1947
Beresford, Viscount (William Carr) 1768-1854
Berg, Alban 1885-1935
Berger, Victor 1860-1929
Bergerac, Cyrano de 1619-1655
Bergh, Henry 1811-1888
Bergman, Torbern 1735-1784
Bergson, Henri 1859-1941
Beria, Lavrenti 1899-1953
Berkeley, George (Bishop) 1685-1753
Berkeley, Sir William ...1608-1677
Berkman, Alexander 1870-1936
Berle, Adolf A. 1895-1971
Berlichingen, Goetz von ..1480-1562
Berliner, Emile 1851-1929
Berlioz, Hector 1803-1869
Berman, Eugene 1899-1972
Bernadotte, Count Folke ..1895-1948
Bernadotte, Jean. *See* Charles XIV (Sweden)
Bernanos, Georges 1888-1948
Bernard de Clairvaux, Saint 1090-1153
Bernard de Menthon, Saint 923-1008
Bernard, Claude 1813-1878
Bernard, Simon 1779-1839
Bernardin de St. Pierre, Jacques 1737-1814
Bernardine, Saint 1380-1444
Berne, Eric 1910-1970
Berners, Lord (John) ...1469-1533
Berners, Juliana 1388
Bernhardi, Friedrich von 1849-1930
Bernhardt, Sarah 1844-1923
Bernini, Giovanni 1598-1680
Bernoulli, Daniel 1700-1781
Bernoulli, Jacques 1654-1705
Bernoulli, Jean 1667-1748
Bernstein, Eduard 1850-1932
Bernstein, Henry 1876-1953
Bernstorff, Graf von (Andreas) 1735-1797
Bernstorff, Graf von (Christian) 1769-1835
Bernstorff, Graf von (Johann) 1712-1772
Bernstorff, Graf von (Johann) 1862-1939
Berossus ................B.C. 250
Berry, Mary 1763-1832
Berryman, John 1914-1972
Berthelot, Marcellin 1827-1907
Berthier, Louis F. 1753-1815
Berthollet, Claude de 1748-1822
Bertillon, Alphonse 1853-1914
Bertin, Pierre 1751-1819
Berton, Henri 1761-1844
Bertrand, Jacques 1807-1841
Berwick, Duke of (James Fitzjames) 1670-1734
Berzelius, Jöns J. 1779-1848
Besant, Annie 1847-1933
Besant, Sir Walter 1836-1901
Besier, Rudolf 1878-1942
Bessarion, John 1395-1472
Bessel, Friedrich 1784-1846
Bessemer, Sir Henry 1813-1898
Bessières, Jean Baptiste ..1766-1813
Bestuzhev, Count (Aleksei) 1693-1768
Bethell, Richard. *See* Westbury, Lord
Bethlen, Gábor 1580-1629
Bethmann-Hollweg, Theobald von 1856-1921
Bethune, David. *See* Beaton, David
Bethune, Mary McLeod ..1875-1955
Betterton, Thomas 1635-1710
Betty, Henry (Infant Roscius) 1791-1874
Bevan, Aneurin 1897-1960
Beveridge, Sir William ...1879-1963
Bevin, Ernest 1881-1951
Beyle, Henri-Marie. *See* "Stendhal"
Beza, Theodore 1519-1605
Biagio, Bernardino di. *See* Pinturicchio
Bichat, François 1771-1802
Bickel, Alexander 1924-1974
Biddle, Francis 1886-1968
Biddle, John 1615-1662
Bierbaum, Otto 1865-1910
Bierce, Ambrose 1842-1914
Bigelow, John 1817-1911
Biggers, Earl Derr 1884-1933
Bilderdijk, Willem 1756-1831
Bilfinger, Georg 1693-1750
Billaud-Varenne, Jean ...1756-1819
Billaut, Adam 1662
"Billings, Josh." *See* Shaw, Henry Wheeler
Billings, Warren K. 1893-1972
"Billy the Kid." 1859-1881
Bilney, Thomas 1495-1531
Binet, Alfred 1857-1911
Bingham, Hiram, Sr. 1789-1869
Bingham, Hiram, Jr. 1831-1908
Bingham, Hiram (Senator) 1875-1956
Binyon, Laurence 1869-1943
Bion ....................B.C. 100
Biot, Jean 1774-1862
Birch, Reginald B. 1856-1943
Bird, Robert M. 1806-1854
Birdseye, Clarence 1886-1956
Birgitta, Saint. *See* Bridget of Sweden, Saint
Birkbeck, George 1776-1841
Birney, James G. 1792-1857
Biron, Armand de 1747-1793
Birrell, Augustine 1850-1933
Bischoff, Theodor 1807-1882
Bishop, Sir Henry Rowley 1786-1855
Bishop, John Peale 1892-1944
Bismarck, Prinz von (Otto) 1815-1898
Bizet, Georges 1838-1875
Björnson, Björnsterne 1832-1910
Black, Adam 1784-1874
Black, Hugo L. 1886-1971
Black, Joseph 1728-1799
Black, William 1841-1898
Black Hawk 1767-1838
Blackie, John S. 1809-1895
Blackmore, Richard D. ..1825-1900
Blackstone, Sir William ..1723-1780
Blackwell, Alice Stone ...1857-1950
Blackwell, Elizabeth 1821-1910
Blackwell, Lucy Stone. *See* Stone, Lucy
Blackwood, Algernon 1869-1951
Blackwood, Frederick. *See* Dufferin and Ava, Marquess of
Blackwood, William 1776-1834
Blaine, James G. 1830-1893
Blainville, Henri 1777-1850
Blair, James 1655-1743
Blair, Robert 1699-1746
Blake, Robert 1599-1657
Blake, William 1757-1827
Blanc, Camille 1846-1927
Blanc, Louis 1811-1882
Blanchard, François 1753-1809
Blanchard, Jacques 1600-1638
Bland, Hubert 1914
Blanqui, Louis 1805-1881
Blasco Ibáñez 1867-1928
Blatchford, Robert 1851-1943
Blavatsky, Helena 1831-1891
Bleek, Wilhelm 1827-1875
Blennerhasset, Harman ..1765-1831
Blessington, Countess of (Marguerite) 1789-1849
Bligh, William 1753-1817
Blind, Mathilde 1841-1896
Blind Harry. *See* Harry the Minstrel
Blinn, Holbrook 1872-1928

Meredith, George 1828-1909
"Meredith, Owen" (Earl Lytton) (Edward R. Bulwer) ..1831-1891
Merezhkovski, Dmitri S. 1865-1941
Mergenthaler, Ottmar ...1854-1899
Mérimée, Prosper 1803-1870
Merivale, Charles 1808-1893
Merivale, Herman 1806-1874
Meriwether, Lee 1862-1966
Merriam, C. Hart 1855-1942
Merriam, John C. 1869-1945
Merrick, Leonard 1864-1939
"Merriman, Henry Seton" (Hugh S. Scott) 1862-1903
Merriman, John X. 1841-1926
Merry del Val, Rafael ...1865-1930
Merton, Thomas 1915-1968
Merwin, Samuel 1874-1936
Meryon, Charles 1821-1868
Mesmer, Franz 1733-1815
Messalina, Valeria 22-48
Messier, Charles 1730-1817
Mestrovic, Ivan 1883-1962
Metalious, Grace 1924-1964
"Metastasio" (Pietro Trapassi) ... 1698-1782
Metchnikoff, Élie 1845-1916
Metternich-(Winneburg), Prinz Klemens von 1773-1859
Meulen, Adam van der ..1632-1690
Meunier, Constantin 1831-1905
Mew, Charlotte 1870-1928
Meyer, Agnes E. 1887-1970
Meyer, Conrad 1825-1898
Meyer, Hans 1858-1929
Meyer, Julius L. 1830-1895
Meyer, Karl F. 1884-1974
Meyer, Victor 1848-1897
Meyerbeer Giacomo (Jakob Meyer Beer) 1791-1864
Meynell, Alice 1849-1922
Meynell, Wilfred 1852-1948
Mézières, Philippe de ...1327-1405
Mezzofanti, Giuseppe 1774-1849
Michael VIII (Emperor of East) .. 1260-1282
Michaëlis, Johann 1717-1791
Michaelis, Karin 1872-1950
Michel, Louise 1830-1905
Michelangelo (Buonarroti) 1475-1564
Michelet, Jules 1798-1874
Michell, John 1724-1793
Michelson, Albert A. 1852-1931
Mickiewicz, Adam 1798-1855
Middleton, Conyers 1683-1750
Middleton, Richard 1882-1911
Middleton, Thomas 1570-1627
Midhat Pasha 1822-1884
Mierevelt, Michiel van ..1567-1641
Mieris, Franz van 1635-1681
Miers, Earl Schenck 1910-1972
Mies van der Rohe, Ludwig 1886-1969
Mifflin, Thomas 1744-1800
Mignard, Pierre 1610-1695
Migne, Jacques 1800-1875
Mignet, François 1796-1884
Miguel, Don 1802-1866
Mikhail (Russia) 1613-1645
Mikimoto, Kokichi 1858-1954
Miklošić, Franz von **1813-1891**
Milan IV (Obrenovic) (Serbia) .. 1882-1889
Miles, Nelson A. 1839-1925
Milhaud, Darius 1892-1974
Mill, James 1773-1836
Mill, John Stuart 1806-1873
Millais, Sir John E. 1829-1896
Millay, Edna St. Vincent 1892-1950
Miller, Alice Duer 1874-1942
Miller, Cincinnatus Hiner. *See* Miller, Joaquin
Miller, Hugh 1802-1856
Miller, Joaquin (Cincinnatus Hiner) 1839-1913
Miller, Joe 1684-1738
Miller, Max 1901-1967
Miller, William 1782-1849
Millerand, Alexandre 1859-1943
Milles, Carl 1875-1955
Millet, Francis D. 1846-1912
Millet, Jean François 1814-1875
Millikan, Robert A. 1868-1953
Millin, Sarah Gertrude ..1889-1968
Mills, Darius Ogden 1825-1910
Mills, Florence 1895-1927
Milman, Henry H. 1791-1868
Milne, A. A. 1882-1956
Milne-Edwards, Henri ...1800-1885
Milner, Viscount (Alfred) 1854-1925
Milnes, Richard Monckton. *See* Houghton, Lord
Milos I (Obrenovich) (Serbia) ... 1817-1860
Milovanović, Milovan ...1863-1912
Miltiades .... B.C. 488
Milton, John 1608-1674
Minghetti, Marco 1818-1886
Minin, Nikita. *See* Nikon
Mino di Giovanni 1431-1484
Minot, Charles S. 1852-1914
Minot, Laurence ....-1350
Minto, Earl of (Gilbert) 1845-1914
Minto, William 1845-1893
Minuit, Peter 1580-1638
Miquel, Johann von 1829-1901
Mirabeau, Comte de (Gabriel Riqueti) 1749-1791
Miranda, Carmen 1913-1955
Miranda, Francisco 1750-1816
Miranda, Francisco de Sá de. *See* Sá de Miranda, Francisco de
Mirandola, Pico della. *See* Pico della Mirandola
Mirbeau, Octave 1850-1917
Mirbel, Charles 1776-1854
Mistinguett 1875-1956
Mistral, Frédéric 1830-1914
Mistral, Gabriela 1889-1957
Mitchel, John 1815-1875
Mitchell, Donald Grant ("Ik Marvel") 1822-1908
Mitchell, John 1870-1919
Mitchell, John T. W. ...1828-1895
Mitchell, Margaret 1900-1949
Mitchell, Maria 1818-1889
Mitchell, S. Weir 1829-1914
Mitchell, William 1879-1936
Mitford, Mary Russell ...1787-1855
Mitford, Nancy 1904-1973
Mithradates VI (The Great) (Pontus) .... B.C. 121-63
Mitre, Bartolomé 1821-1906
Mitscherlich, Eilhardt ...1794-1863
Mivart, St. George J. 1827-1900
Mizner, Wilson 1876-1933
Möbius, August 1790-1868
Modigliani, Amadeo 1884-1921
Modjeska, Helena 1840-1909
Mohammed 570-632
Mohammed Ali (Egypt) 1833-1849
Mohammed II (Turkey) 1451-1481
Mohammed Ahmed (The Mahdi) .. 1843-1885
Mohammed al-Batani 850
Mohl, Hugo von 1805-1872
Möhler, Johann 1796-1838
Mohun, Lord (Charles) ..1675-1712
Moir, David 1798-1851
Moissan, Henri 1852-1907
Mokanna, al- (Hashim ibn-Hakim) .. 780
Molay, Jacques de 1243-1314
Moleschott, Jacob 1822-1893
Molesworth, Mary L. 1839-1921
Molière (Jean Baptiste Poquelin) 1622-1673
"Molina, Tirso de." *See* "Tirso de Molina"
Molinari, Gustave de ...1819-1912
Molinos, Miguel de 1640-1697
Mollenhauer, Emil 1855-1927
Molnar, Ferenc 1878-1952
Moltke, Graf von (Helmuth) (uncle) 1800-1891
Moltke, Helmuth von (nephew) ... 1848-1916
Molyneux, Edward H. 1894-1974
Mommsen, Theodor 1817-1903
Monboddo, Lord (James Burnett).. 1714-1799
Moncrieff, Lord (James) 1776-1851
Mond, Ludwig 1839-1900
Monet, Claude 1840-1926
Monge, Gaspard 1746-1818
Monk, George 1608-1669
Monmouth, Duke of (James Scott) 1649-1685
Monro, Alexander 1697-1767
Monro, Harold 1879-1932
Monroe, Harriet 1861-1936
Monroe, James 1758-1831
Monroe, Marilyn 1926-1962
Montacute, Thomas de. *See* Salisbury, Earl of
Montagna, Bartolomeo ...1450-1523
Montagu, Basil 1770-1851
Montagu, Charles. *See* Halifax, Earl of
Montagu, Edward. *See* **Sandwich**, Earl of
Montagu, Lady Mary Wortley 1689-1762
Montague, Charles E. 1867-1928
Montaigne, Michel de ...1533-1592
Montalembert, Comte de (Charles) 1810-1870
Montcalm, Marquis de (Louis Joseph) 1712-1759
Montcorbier, François de. *See* Villon, François
Montecorvino, Giovanni di 1247-1348
Montefiore, Sir Moses ...1784-1885
Montemayor, Jorge 1520-1561
Montespan, Marquise de (Françoise) 1641-1707
Montesquieu, Baron de (Charles) .. 1689-1755
Montessori, Marie 1870-1952
Monteux, Pierre 1875-1964
Monteverdi, Claudio 1567-1643
Montez, Lola 1818-1861
Montezuma II (Mexico) 1503-1520
Montfaucon, Bernard de 1655-1741
Montfort, Simon de (Earl of Leicester) 1208-1265
Montgolfier, Joseph 1740-1810
Montgomerie, Alexander 1550-1610
Montgomery, James 1771-1854
Montgomery, Richard ...1736-1775
Montgomery, Robert 1807-1855
Montmorency, Duc de (Anne) 1493-1567
Montmorency-Bouteville, François de. *See* Luxembourg, Duc de
Montpensier, Duchesse de (Anne) 1627-1693
Montrose, Marquess of (James Graham) 1612-1650
Montserrat, Viscountess. *See* Claflin, Tennessee
Moody, Dwight L. 1837-1899
Moody, William Vaughn 1869-1910
Mooney, Tom 1885-1942
Moorcraft, William 1770-1825
Moore, Albert J. 1831-1896
Moore, Clement C. 1779-1863
Moore, G. E. 1873-1958
Moore, George 1852-1933
Moore, Grace 1901-1947
Moore, Sir John 1761-1809
Moore, Marianne 1887-1972
Moore, Thomas 1779-1852
Moorehead, Agnes 1906-1974
Mora, Jo 1876-1947
Morales, Luis de 1509-1586
Moray, Earl of. *See* Murray, Earl of
Mordaunt, Charles. *See* Peterborough, Earl of
Mordkin, Mikhail 1881-1944
More, Hannah 1745-1833
More, Paul Elmer 1864-1937
More, Sir Thomas, Saint 1478-1535
Moréas, Jean 1856-1910
Moreau, Jean 1763-1813
Morehouse, Daniel W. ...1876-1941
Morel. *See* Deschamps, Eustache
Morelli, Giovanni 1816-1891
Moretto, Il (Alessandro Bonvicino) 1498-1554
Morgagni, Giovanni 1682-1771
Morgan, Sir Henry 1635-1688
Morgan, John Hunt 1825-1864
Morgan, John Pierpont, Sr. 1837-1913
Morgan, John Pierpont, Jr. 1867-1943
Morgan, Lewis H. 1818-1881
Morgan, Lady Sydney ...1783-1859
Morgan, Thomas Hunt ...1866-1945
Morghen, Raphael 1758-1833
Morisot, Berthe 1841-1895
Morland, George 1763-1804
Morley, Christopher 1890-1957
Morley, Henry 1822-1894
Morley, Viscount (John) 1838-1923
Morley, Thomas 1557-1603
Mornay, Philippe de (du Plessis-Marly Mornay) 1549-1623
Morny, Duc de (Charles) 1811-1865
Morris, Chester 1901-1970
Morris, Gouverneur 1752-1816
Morris, Sir Lewis 1833-1907
Morris, Robert 1734-1806
Morris, William 1834-1896
Morrison, Robert 1782-1834
Morrow, Dwight 1873-1931
Morse, Jedidiah 1761-1826
Morse, Samuel F. B. 1791-1872
Morse, Wayne L. 1900-1974
Morton, Earl of (James Douglas) .. 1525-1581
Morton, John 1419-1500
Morton, Thomas (of Merrymount) 1590-1646
Morton, William T. G. ...1819-1868
Mosby, John S. 1833-1916
Moschus .... B.C. 150
Mosely, Henry G. 1887-1915
Moses, Anna Mary ("Grandma") 1860-1961
Most, Johann 1846-1906
Moszkowski, Moritz 1854-1925
Motherwell, William 1797-1835
Motley, John Lothrop 1814-1877
Moton, Robert R. 1867-1940
Mott, Charles S. 1875-1973
Mott, Lucretia 1793-1880
Motte-Fouqué, Baron de la. *See* Fouqué, Baron de la Motte
Motteux, Pierre 1663-1718
Mottl, Felix 1856-1911
Mouchez, Amédée 1821-1892
Moulton, Louise Chandler 1835-1908
Moultrie, William 1731-1805
Mounet-Sully, Jean 1841-1916
Mowatt, Anna Cora 1819-1870
Mowbray, Thomas. *See* Norfolk, 1st Duke of
Mozart, Wolfgang Amadeus 1756-1791
Mudie, Charles Edward ..1818-1890
Muggleton, Lodowick ...1609-1698
"Muhlbach, Luise" (Klara Mundt) 1814-1873
Muhlenberg, Henry Melchior 1711-1787
Muhlenberg, John P. G. ..1746-1807
Muhlenberg, William A. 1796-1877
Muilenburg, James 1896-1974
Muir, Edwin 1887-1959
Muir, John 1838-1914
Muir, Sir William 1819-1905
Müller, Ferdinand von ..1825-1896
Muller, Fritz 1821-1897
Muller, Hermann J. 1890-1967
Müller, Johann. *See* Regiomontanus
Müller, Johannes von ...1752-1809
Müller, Johannes Peter ..1801-1858
Muller, Julius 1801-1878
Müller, Max 1823-1900
Müller, Otto 1720-1784
Mulready, William 1786-1863
"Multatuli." *See* Dekker, Edward
Münch, Charles 1891-1968
Munchhausen, Baron von (Hieronymus) 1720-1797
Mundt, Karl E. 1900-1974
Mundt, Klara. *See* "Muhlbach, Luise"
Muni, Paul 1895-1967
Munkácsy, Mihály von (Michael Lieb) 1844-1900
Munro, Hector Hugh ("Saki") 1870-1916
Munro, Hugh A. J. 1819-1885
Munro, Sir Leslie 1901-1974
Munro, Neil 1864-1930
Munroe, Kirk 1850-1930
Munsey, Frank A. 1854-1925
Münster, Sebastian 1489-1552
Münsterberg, Hugo 1863-1916
Munthe, Axel 1857-1949
Münzer, Thomas 1489-1525
Murad I (Turkey) 1359-1389
Murad III (Turkey) 1574-1595
Murad IV (Turkey) 1623-1640
Murat, Joachim (Naples) 1808-1815
Muratori, Ludovico 1672-1750
Muraviëv, Count Mikhail 1845-1900
Murchison, Sir Roderick I 1792-1871
Murdock, William 1754-1830
Murfree, Mary. *See* "Craddock, Charles Egbert"
Murger, Henri 1822-1861
Murillo, Bartolomé 1617-1682
Murphy, Audie 1924-1971
Murphy, John B. 1857-1916
Murray, Lord (George) ..1694-1760
Murray, Sir James A. ...1837-1915
Murray (Moray), Earl of (James Stuart) 1531-1570
Murray, John 1778-1843
Murray, Lindley 1745-1826
Murray, Mae 1889-1965
Murray, Philip 1886-1952
Murray, Wm. *See* Mansfield, Earl of
Murry, Mrs. John Middleton. *See* Mansfield, Katherine
Musäus, Johann August ..1735-1787
Musmanno, Michael A. ..1897-1968
Musset, Alfred de 1810-1857
Mussolini, Benito 1883-1945
Mussorgsky, Modest 1835-1881
Mustafa Kemal. *See* Kemal Atatürk
Muste, A. J. 1885-1967
Mutis, José 1732-1808
Mutsuhito (Meiji Tennu) (Japan) 1867-1912
Muzaffar-ed-Din (Persia) 1896-1907
Myers, Frederic W. H. ..1843-1901
Myers, Gustavus 1872-1942
Myerson, Abraham 1881-1948
Mylius-Erichsen, Ludwig 1872-1907

N

Nabis .... B.C. 207-194
Nabu-rimanni .... B.C. 500
Nachtigal, Gustav 1834-1885
Nadir Shah 1688-1747
Nadson, Semion 1862-1889
Naevius, Gnaeus ..... B.C. 264-194
Nageli, Karl von 1817-1891
Naidu, Sarojini 1878-1949
Nairne, Lady (Caroline) 1766-1845
Namier, Lewis B. 1888-1960

Razin, Stenka 1671
Read, Herbert 1893-1968
Read, Opie 1852-1939
Read, Thomas Buchanan 1822-1872
Reade, Charles 1814-1884
Reade, Winwood 1838-1875
Realf, Richard 1834-1878
Réaumur, René de ...1683-1757
Réaux, Gédéon Tallemant des. *See* Tallemant des Réaux, Gédéon
Récamier, Jeanne 1777-1849
Rechberg und Rothenlöwen, Graf von (Johann) ...1806-1899
Reclus, Jean J. 1830-1905
Recorde, Robert **1510-1558**
Red Jacket (Sagoyewatha) ......
.................**1758-1830**
Redcliffe, Stratford de. *See* Stratford de Redcliffe, Viscount
Redgrave, Richard 1804-1888
Redi, Francesco 1626-1697
Reding, Aloys von ...1755-1818
Redmond, John 1856-1918
Redpath, James 1833-1891
Reed, John 1887-1920
Reed, Thomas B. 1839-1902
Reed, Walter 1851-1902
Reeve, Clara 1729-1807
Reger, Max 1873-1916
Regiomontanus (Johann Müller) ....
.................1436-1476
Regnard, Jean Francois ..1656-1710
Regnault, Henri Victor ..1810-1878
Régnier, Henri de ...1864-1936
Régnier, Mathurin ...1573-1613
Regulus, Marcus Atilius .. B.C. 250
Rehan, Ada 1860-1916
Reich, Wilhelm 1897-1957
Reichenbach, Baron von (Karl) ..
.................1788-1869
Reichert, Karl 1811-1883
Reichstadt, Duc de (Napoleon II) ("l'Aiglon") 1811-1832
Reid, Sir George ...1841-1913
Reid, Samuel Chester ..1783-1861
Reid, Thomas 1710-1796
Reid, (Thomas) Mayne ..1818-1883
Reid, Whitelaw 1837-1912
Reik, Theodor 1888-1969
Reil, Johann 1759-1813
Reimarus, Hermann ...1694-1768
Reinach, Joseph 1856-1921
Reinach, Salomon ...1858-1932
Reinach, Théodore ...1860-1928
Reinecke, Karl 1824-1910
Reinhardt, Max 1873-1943
Reiske, Johann 1716-1774
Réjane, Gabrielle (Charlotte Réju) 1857-1920
Réju, Charlotte. *See* Réjane, Gabrielle
Remak, Robert 1815-1865
Remarque, Erich Maria 1898-1970
Rembrandt (van Rijn) ..1606-1669
Remenyi, Ede 1830-1898
Remigius, Saint 440-533
Remington, Frederic ...1861-1909
Remington, Philo 1816-1889
Remsburg, John E. ...1848-1919
Remsen, Ira 1846-1927
Remusat, Jean P. 1788-1832

Renan, (Joseph) Ernest ..1823-1892
Renard, Alphonse 1842-1903
Renaudot, Théophraste ..1586-1653
René I (Anjou) 1409-1480
Reni, Guido. *See* Guido Reni
Renoir, Pierre Auguste ..1841-1919
Renouvier, Charles ...1815-1903
Renwick, James 1662-1688
Repnin, Prince (Nikolai) 1734-1801
Respighi, Otterino ...1879-1936
Reszke, Edouard de ...1856-1917
Reszke, Jean de **1850-1925**
Retz, Baron de. *See* Rais, Gilles de Laval, Baron de
Retz, Jean de (Cardinal) 1614-1679
Retzius, Anders 1796-1860
Retzius, Gustaf 1842-1919
Reuchlin, Johann 1455-1522
Reuter, Fritz 1810-1874
Reuter, Gabriele 1859-1941
Reuter, Baron de (Paul) 1821-1899
Reuther, Walter 1907-1970
Reventlow, Count (Christian) .....
.................1784-1827
Revere, Paul 1735-1818
Reybaud, Marie Roch ...**1799-1879**
Reymond, Emil Dubois. *See* Dubois-Reymond, Emil
Reymont, Wladyslas **1867-1925**
Reynaud, Paul **1876-1966**
Reynolds, John F. 1820-1863
Reynolds, Sir Joshua ...1723-1792
Reynolds, Quentin ...1902-1965
Reynolds, R. S., Sr. **1881-1955**
Rezanov, Nikolai de ...1764-1807
Rhazes. *See* Bubacher
Rhee, Syngman 1875-1965
Rhigas, Constantine ...1760-1798
Rhodes, Cecil 1853-1902
Rhodes, Eugene Manlove 1869-1934
Rhondda, Viscount (David Thomas) 1856-1918
Riaz Pasha 1835-1911
Ribaut, Jean **1520-1565**
Ribeiro, Bernardim **1482-1552**
Ribera, José ("Lo Spagnoletto") ..
.................1588-1652
Ribot, Théodule 1839-1916
Ricardo, David 1772-1823
Ricci, Lorenzo 1775
Ricci, Matteo 1552-1610
Ricciarelli, Daniele. *See* Volterra
Rice, Alice Hegan 1870-1942
Rice, Edmund 1762-1844
Rice, Elmer L. 1892-1967
Rice, Grantland 1880-1954
Rice, James 1843-1882
Rich, Barnabe 1540-1617
Rich, Edmund, Saint. *See* Edmund Rich, Saint
Rich, Henry. *See* Holland, Earl of
Rich, John 1692-1761
Rich, Robert. *See* Warwick, Earl of
Richard, Saint 1197-1253
Richard I ("Coeur de Lion") (England) 1189-1199
Richard II (England) ...1377-1399
Richard III (England) ..1483-1485
Richard de Bury (Richard Aungervyle) 1282-1345
Richard, John S. 1850-1930

Richards, Laura E. 1850-1943
Richards, Theodore 1868-1928
Richardson, Sir Benjamin Ward ...
.................1828-1896
Richardson, Henry H. ...1838-1886
"Richardson, Henry Handel" (Ethel L. Robertson) 1880-1946
Richardson, Sir John ...1787-1865
Richardson, Samuel ...1689-1761
Riche, Georges de Porto. *See* Porto-Riche, Georges de
Richelieu, Cardinal de (Armand Jean du Plessis) ...1585-1642
Richelieu, Duc de (Armand Emmanuel du Plessis) 1766-1822
Richepin, Jean 1849-1930
Richet, Charles 1850-1935
Richter, Conrad 1890-1968
Richter, Hans 1843-1916
Richter, Jean Paul ...1763-1825
Richthofen, Baron von (Ferdinand) 1833-1905
Rickenbacker, Edward Vernon ....
.................1890-1973
Ricker, Marilla M. 1840-1920
Rickey, Branch 1881-1965
Ridge, Lola 1883-1941
Ridley, Nicholas 1500-1555
Ridpath, John Clark ...1840-1900
Riel, Louis 1844-1885
Riemann, Georg 1826-1866
Riemenschneider, Tilman 1515
Rienzi, Cola di 1313-1354
Riesener, Jean 1734-1806
Righi, Augusto 1850-1920
Rihani, Ameen 1877-1940
Riis, Jacob 1849-1914
Riley, James Whitcomb ..1849-1916
Riley, Woodbridge ...1869-1933
Rilke, Rainer Maria ...1875-1926
Rimbaud, Arthur 1854-1891
Rimsky-Korsakov, Nikolai 1844-1908
Rinehart, Mary Roberts ..1876-1958
Rinehart, William Henry 1825-1874
Ring, Blanche 1871-1961
Ringling, John 1866-1936
Ringling, Robert E. 1897-1950
Ripley, George 1802-1880
Ripley, Robert L. 1893-1949
Ripley, William Z. 1867-1941
Ripon, Marquess of (George Robinson) 1827-1909
Riqueti, Gabriel. *See* Mirabeau, Comte de
Rishanger, William 1250-1312
Ristori, Adelaide 1822-1906
Ritchie, Lady (Anne Thackeray) ..
.................1837-1919
Ritschl, Albrecht 1822-1889
Ritschl, Friedrich ...1806-1876
Rittenhouse, David ...1732-1796
Rittenhouse, Jessie B. ..1869-1948
Ritter, Karl 1779-1859
Rivas, Duque de (Angel de Saavedra) 1791-1865
Rivera, Diego 1886-1957
Rivera, José Fructuoso ..1790-1854
Rivers, Earl (Anthony Woodville) 1442-1483
Rivers, William H. R. ...1864-1922

Rives, Amélie (Princess Troubetzkoy) 1863-1945
Rivinus, Augustus ...1652-1723
Rizal, José 1861-1896
Rizzio, David 1533-1566
Rob Roy (Robert MacGregor) ....
.................1671-1734
Robert I (Franks) 922-923
Robert II (Franks) 996-1031
Robert I (Scotland). *See* Bruce. Robert
Robert II (Scotland) ...1371-1390
Robert the Devil (Robert of Normandy) 1035
Robert of Gloucester ...1260-1300
Roberts, Sir Charles G. D. 1860-1943
Roberts, Elizabeth Madox 1886-1941
Roberts, Earl (Frederick) ("Bobs") 1832-1914
Roberts, Kenneth ...1885-1957
Roberts, Owen J. 1875-1955
Roberts, Theodore 1861-1928
Robertson, George Croom 1842-1892
Robertson, Morgan ...1861-1915
Robertson, Thomas William 1829-1871
Robertson, William ...1721-1793
Roberval, Gilles de ...1602-1675
Robespierre, Maximilien de 1758-1794
Robins, Benjamin ...1707-1751
Robinson, Bill ("Bojangles") ....
.................1878-1949
Robinson, Edward G. 1893-1973
Robinson, Edwin Arlington 1869-1935
Robinson, George. *See* Ripon, Marquess of
Robinson, Henry Crabb ..1775-1867
Robinson, Hercules. *See* Rosmead, Lord
Robinson, Jackie 1919-1972
Robsart, Amy (Lady Dudley) ....
.................1532-1560
Robson, Stuart 1836-1903
Robusti, Jacopo. *See* Tintoretto
Roch, Saint 1327
Rochambeau, Comte de (Jean) ...
.................1725-1807
Roche, Arthur Somers ...1883-1935
Roche, James Jeffrey ...1847-1908
Roche, Regina Maria ...1764-1845
Rochefort, Marquis de (Henri) ...
.................1830-1913
Rochester, Earl of (John Wilmot) 1648-1680
Rochester, Earl of (Lawrence Hyde) 1641-1711
Rockefeller, John D. (Sr.) 1839-1937
Rockefeller, John D. (Jr.) 1874-1960
Rockefeller, Winthrop ...1912-1973
Rockne, Knute 1888-1931
Rockwell, George Lincoln 1918-1967
Rod, Edouard 1857-1910
Rodbertus, Johann Karl 1805-1875
Rodeheaver, Homer ...1880-1955
Roderic (Visigoths) 711
Roderick (Ireland) 1198
Rodgers, John 1773-1838
Rodin, Auguste 1840-1917
Rodney, Caesar 1728-1784
Rodney, Lord (George) ..1718-1792

Rodó, José 1872-1917
Rodzinski, Artur 1894-1958
Roe, Edward P. 1838-1888
Roe, Sir Thomas 1580-1644
Roebling, John A. 1806-1869
Roederer, Comte de (Pierre) .....
.................1745-1835
Roemer, Ole 1644-1710
Roerich, Nicholas ...1874-1947
Roethke, Theodore ...1908-1963
Roger I (Sicily) 1072-1101
Roger II (Sicily) 1130-1154
Roger of Salisbury 1139
Roger of Wendover 1236
Rogers, James E. T. ...1823-1890
Rogers, John (Earlier) ..1500-1555
Rogers, John (Later) ...1627-1665
Rogers, Robert 1731-1795
Rogers, Samuel 1763-1855
Rogers, Will 1879-1935
Roget, Peter M. 1779-1869
Rogier, Charles 1800-1885
Rohan, Cardinal (Louis) **1734-1803**
Rohan, Benjamin de. *See* Soubise, Duc de
Rohlfs, Mrs. Charles. *See* Green, Anna Katharine
Rohmer, Sax 1886-1959
Rokitansky, Carl von ...1804-1878
Roland de La Platière, Jean ......
.................1734-1793
Roland de la Platière, Manon (Madame Roland) 1754-1793
Rolfe, William J. 1827-1910
Rolland, John 1560
Rolland, Romain 1866-1944
Rolle de Hampole, Richard ......
.................1290-1349
Rollett, Alexander ...1834-1903
Rollin, Charles 1661-1741
Rolshoven, Julius ...1858-1930
Rölvaag, Ole 1876-1931
Romains, Jules (Louis Farigoule) 1885-1972
Romanes, George John ..1848-1894
Romano, Giulio. *See* Giulio Romano
Romanov, Panteleimon ..1884-1936
Romberg, Moritz 1795-1873
Romberg, Sigmund ...1887-1951
Romilly, Sir Samuel ...1757-1818
Rommel, Erwin 1891-1944
Romney, George 1734-1802
Romney, Earl of (Henry Sidney) ..
.................1641-1704
Romulus, Augustulus (Emperor of West) 475-476
Roncalli, Angelo. *See* John XXIII (Pope)
Rondelet, Guillaume ...1507-1556
Ronsard, Pierre de ...1524-1585
Röntgen, David 1743-1807
Röntgen, Wilhelm von ..1845-1923
Rooke, Sir George ...1650-1709
Roon, Graf von (Albrecht) ....
.................1803-1879
Roosevelt, Eleanor ...1884-1962
Roosevelt, Franklin Delano 1882-1945
Roosevelt, Theodore ...1858-1919
Root, Elihu 1845-1937
Root, George F. 1820-1895

Roper, Elmo 1900-1971
Rops, Félicien 1833-1898
Rosa, Carl 1842-1889
Rosa, Salvator 1615-1673
Rosas, Juan de 1793-1877
Roscellinus 1050-1122
Roscher, Wilhelm 1817-1894
Roscius, Infant. *See* Betty, Henry
Roscius, Quintus ....B.C. 126-62
Roscoe, Sir Henry E. ...1833-1915
Roscoe, William 1753-1831
Rose, Billy 1899-1966
Rose, Ernestine 1810-1892
Rose, Hugh. *See* Strathnairn, Lord
Rosebery, Earl of (Archibald Primrose) 1847-1929
Rosecrans, William S. ..1819-1898
Rosenfeld, Morris ...1862-1923
Rosenfeld, Paul 1890-1946
Rosenhof, August von ..1705-1759
Rosenkranz, Karl ...1805-1879
Rosenman, Samuel I. ..1896-1973
Rosenthal, Moriz 1862-1946
Rosenwald, Julius ...1862-1932
Rosmead, Lord (Hercules Robinson) 1824-1897
Rosmini-Serbati, Antonio 1797-1855
Ross, Betsy 1752-1836
Ross, Harold 1892-1951
Ross, Sir John 1777-1856
Ross, John (Kooweskoowe) ......
.................1790-1866
"Ross, Martin" (Violet Martin) 1862-1915
Ross, Sir Ronald ...1857-1932
Ross, W. Stewart ("Saladin") ...
.................1844-1906
Rosse, Earl of (William Parsons) 1800-1867
Rossetti, Christina ...1830-1894
Rossetti, Dante Gabriel ..1828-1882
Rossetti, William Michael 1829-1919
Rossi, Conde di (Pelligrino) 1787-1848
Rossini, Gioachino ...1792-1868
Rosslyn, Earl of (Alexander Wedderburn) 1733-1805
Rostand, Edmond 1868-1918
Roswitha. *See* Hrotsvitha
Rothe, Richard 1799-1867
Rothenlöwen, Graf von Rechberg. *See* Rechberg-Rothenlöwen
Rothenstein, Sir William 1872-1945
Rothermere, Lord (Harold Harmsworth) 1868-1940
Rothko, Mark 1903-1970
Rothschild, Meyer Amselm ......
.................1743-1812
Rotrou, Jean de 1609-1650
Rouault, Georges ...1871-1958
Roubillac, Louis 1695-1762
Rouget de Lisle, Claude ..1760-1836
Rourke, Constance ...1885-1941
Rous, Francis 1579-1659
Rousseau, Henri ("Douanier") ...
.................1844-1910
Rousseau, Jean Baptiste ..1670-1741
Rousseau, Jean Jacques ..1712-1778
Rousseau, Pierre Waldeck. *See* Waldeck-Rousseau, Pierre
Rousseau, Théodore 1812-1867

Wallace, Lew 1827-1905
Wallace, Sir William ...1272-1305
Wallack, Lester 1820-1888
Wallas, Graham 1858-1932
Wallenstein, Albrecht von 1583-1634
Waller, Edmund 1606-1687
Walling, R. A. J. 1869-1949
Walling, William English 1877-1936
Wallis, John 1616-1703
Wallon, Henri 1812-1904
Wallqvist, Olaf 1755-1800
Walpole, Horace (4th Earl of Orford) 1717-1797
Walpole, Sir Hugh 1884-1941
Walpole, Sir Robert (1st Earl of Orford) 1676-1745
Walpole, Sir Spencer ...1839-1907
Walpurgis, Saint 780
Walsingham, Sir Francis 1530-1590
Walter of Coventry 1290
Walter of St. Victor 1180
Walter, Bruno 1876-1962
Walter, Eugene 1887-1941
Walter, Hubert 1205
Walter, John 1739-1812
Walther von der Vogelweide 1198-1228
Walton, Izaak 1593-1683
Wanamaker, John 1828-1922
Wanger, Walter 1894-1968
Waquidi 745-823
Warbeck, Perkin 1474-1499
Warburg, Otto 1883-1970
Warburton, William 1698-1779
"Ward, Artemus." *See* Browne, Charles Farrar
Ward, Elizabeth Stuart Phelps 1844-1911
Ward, Harry F. 1873-1966
Ward, Henshaw 1872-1935
Ward, Mrs. Humphry (Mary Arnold Ward) 1851-1920
Ward, James 1843-1925
Ward, John Q. A. 1830-1910
Ward, Lester F. 1841-1913
Ward, William George ..1812-1882
Warde, Frederick B. 1851-1935
Ware, Eugene Fitch ("Ironquill") 1841-1911
Warham, William 1450-1532
Warming, Eugen 1841-1924
Warner, Charles Dudley 1829-1900
Warner, H. B. 1876-1958
Warner, Seth 1743-1784
Warner, Susan B. ("Elizabeth Wetherell") 1819-1885
Warren, Earl 1891-1974
Warren, Gouverneur K. ..1830-1882
Warren, John. *See* De Tabley, Lord
Warren, John Collins 1778-1856
Warren, Joseph 1741-1775
Warren, Mercy 1728-1814
Warren, Samuel 1807-1877
Warriston, Lord (Archibald Johnston) 1611-1663
Warton, Thomas 1728-1790
Warwick, 13th Earl of (Richard Beauchamp) 1382-1439
Warwick, Earl of (Richard Neville) ("The Kingmaker") ..1428-1471
Warwick, Earl of (Robert Rich) 1587-1658
Washburne, Elihu B. 1816-1887
Washington, Booker T. ..1856-1915
Washington, George 1732-1799
Wassermann, August von 1866-1925
Wassermann, Jakob 1873-1934
Waterhouse, Alfred 1830-1905
Waterhouse, George 1810-1888
Watson, Arthur K. 1919-1974
Watson, John. *See* "Maclaren, Ian"
Watson, John B. 1878-1958
Watson, Thomas 1557-1592
Watson, Thomas J., Sr. ...1874-1956
Watson, Sir William 1858-1935
Watt, James 1736-1819
Watteau, Antoine 1684-1721
Watterson, Henry 1840-1921
Watts, Alaric Alexander 1797-1864
Watts, Charles A. 1836-1906
Watts, George Frederic ..1817-1904
Watts, Isaac 1674-1748
Watts-Dunton, Theodore 1832-1914
Waugh, Benjamin 1839-1908
Waugh, Edwin 1817-1890
Waugh, Evelyn 1903-1966
Wavell, Archibald 1883-1950
Wayne, Anthony 1745-1796
Waynflete, William of 1395-1486
Webb, Beatrice 1858-1943
Webb, Mary 1881-1927
Webb, Sidney (Lord Passfield) 1859-1947
Weber, Alfred 1835-1914
Weber, Carl Maria von ..1786-1826
Weber, Ernst H. 1795-1878
Weber, Max 1864-1920
Weber, Wilhelm 1804-1891
Webster, Daniel 1782-1852
Webster, H. T. 1885-1952
Webster, John 1580-1625
Webster, Margaret 1905-1972
Webster, Noah 1758-1843
Wedderburn, Alexander. *See* Rosslyn, Earl of
Wedekind, Frank 1864-1918
Wedgwood, Josiah 1730-1795
Weed, Clive 1884-1936
Weed, Thurlow 1797-1882
Weelkes, Thomas 1575-1623
Weems, Mason Locke (Parson Weems) 1760-1825
Weenix, Jan Baptist 1621-1660
Weidenreich, Franz 1873-1948
Weierstrass, Karl 1815-1897
Weigert, Karl 1845-1904
Weil, Simone 1909-1943
Weill, Kurt 1900-1950
Weingartner, Felix von ...1863-1942
Weir, Robert 1803-1889
Weishaupt, Adam 1748-1830
Weismann, August 1834-1914
Weizmann, Chaim 1874-1952
Welch, Joseph N. 1890-1960
Weld, Thomas 1595-1660
Welles, Sumner 1892-1961
Wellesley, Arthur. *See* Wellington, Duke of
Wellesley, Marquis of (Richard Cowley) 1760-1842
Wellington, Duke of (Arthur Wellesley) 1769-1852
Wells, Carolyn ....1872?-1942
Wells, Charles J. 1799-1879
Wells, David A. 1828-1898
Wells, H. G. 1866-1946
Wells, Horace 1815-1848
Welsbach, Baron von (Karl) 1858-1929
Welsh, John 1570-1625
Wenceslaus (Holy Roman Empire) 1378-1400
Wendell, Barrett 1855-1921
Wentworth, Thomas. *See* Strafford, Earl of
Wentworth, William C. ..1793-1872
Werfel, Franz 1890-1945
Werlhof, Paul 1700-1767
Werner, Abraham 1750-1817
Werner, Alfred 1866-1919
Werner, Friedrich 1768-1823
Werve, Claus de 1425
Wesley, Charles 1707-1788
Wesley, John 1703-1791
Wesley, Samuel 1766-1837
Wesley, Samuel Sebastian 1810-1876
Wessel, Johann (Gansfort) 1420-1489
Wessex, Earl of. *See* Godwine
West, Benjamin (astronomer) 1730-1813
West, Benjamin (painter) 1738-1820
West, Nathanael 1904-1940
West, Thomas. *See* Delaware, Lord
Westbury, Lord (Richard Bethell) 1800-1873
Westcott, Brooke Foss ...1825-1901
Westcott, Edward Noyes 1847-1898
Westermarck, Edward A. 1862-1939
Westinghouse, George ...1846-1914
Westmacott, Sir Richard 1775-1856
Westover, Russ 1886-1966
"Wetherell, Elizabeth." *See* Warner, Susan B.
Wetjen, Albert R. 1900-1948
Weyden, Rogier van der (Roger de la Pasture) 1400-1464
Weygand, Maxime 1867-1965
Weyler y Nicolau, Valeriano 1838-1930
Weyman, Stanley J. 1855-1928
Weyprecht, Karl 1838-1881
Whalen, Grover A. 1886-1962
Wharton, Countess of (Anna) 1632-1685
Wharton, Anne H. 1845-1928
Wharton, Edith 1862-1937
Wharton, Francis 1820-1889
Wharton, Thomas (anatomist) 1614-1673
Wharton, Marquess of (Thomas) (political writer) 1648-1715
Whately, Richard 1787-1863
Wheatley, Phillis 1753-1784
Wheaton, Henry 1785-1848
Wheatstone, Sir Charles ..1802-1875
Wheeler, Benjamin Ide ..1854-1927
Wheeler, Joseph 1836-1906
Wheeler, Wayne B. 1869-1927
Wheeler, William Morton 1865-1937
Wheelock, Eleazer 1711-1779
Whetstone, George 1544-1587
Whewell, William 1794-1866
Whichcote, Benjamin ...1609-1683
Whistler, James A. M. ..1834-1903
Whiston, William 1667-1752
Whitby, Daniel 1638-1726
White, Andrew D. 1832-1918
White, Sir George Stuart 1835-1912
White, Gilbert (of Selborne) 1720-1793
White, Henry Kirke 1785-1806
White, Hugh Lawson ...1773-1840
White, Joseph Blanco ...1775-1841
White, Newman I. 1892-1948
White, Paul Dudley 1886-1973
White, Richard Grant ...1821-1885
White, Stanford 1853-1906
White, Stewart Edward ..1873-1946
White, T. H. 1906-1964
White, William A. P. *See* "Boucher, Anthony"
White, William Alanson..1870-1937
White, William Allen ..1868-1944
White, William Hale ("Mark Rutherford") 1831-1913
Whitefield, George 1714-1770
Whitehead, Alfred North 1861-1947
Whitehead, Charles 1804-1862
Whitehead, William 1715-1785
Whiteing, Richard 1840-1928
Whiteley, William 1831-1907
Whitelocke, Bulstrode ...1605-1675
Whiteman, Paul 1891-1967
Whitgift, John 1530-1604
Whitlock, Brand 1869-1934
Whitman, Walt 1819-1892
Whitney, Adeline D. T. ..1824-1906
Whitney, Casper 1862-1929
Whitney, Eli 1765-1825
Whitney, Gertrude Vanderbilt 1878-1942
Whitney, William Dwight 1827-1894
Whittaker, Charles Evans 1901-1973
Whittier, John Greenleaf 1807-1892
Whittington, Richard (Dick) 1423
Whymper, Edward 1840-1911
Whyte, Alexander 1837-1921
Whyte-Melville, George J. 1821-1878
Wickham, Sir Henry 1846-1928
Widmann, Joseph 1842-1911
Widor, Charles 1844-1937
Wiedersheim, Robert ...1848-1923
Wieland, Christopher Martin 1733-1813
Wien, Wilhelm 1864-1928
Wiener, Norbert 1894-1964
Wieniawski, Henri 1835-1880
Wier, Johann 1516-1588
Wiertz, Antoine 1806-1865
Wiesner, Julius 1838-1916
Wigand, Albert 1812-1886
Wiggam, Albert E. 1871-1957
Wiggin, Kate Douglas ...1856-1923
Wigglesworth, Michael ..1631-1705
Wigman, Mary 1886-1973
Wilberforce, Samuel 1805-1873
Wilberforce, William ...1759-1833
Wilbye, John 1574-1638
Wilcox, Ella Wheeler 1850-1919
Wild, Jonathan 1682-1725
Wilde, Oscar 1854-1900
Wilde, Richard Henry ...1789-1847
Wildenbruch, Ernst von ..1845-1909
Wilder, Laura Ingalls 1867-1957
Wilfrid, Saint 635-709
Wilhelm I (Germany) ...1871-1888
Wilhelm II (Germany) ..1888-1918
Wilhelm, Karl 1815-1873
Wilhelmina (Netherlands) 1898-1948
Wilkes, Charles 1798-1877
Wilkes, John 1727-1797
Wilkie, Sir David 1785-1841
Wilkins, Sir (George) Hubert 1888-1958
Wilkins, John 1614-1672
Wilkins, Mary E. *See* Freeman, M. E. W.
Wilkinson, James 1757-1825
Wilkinson, John (ironmaster) 1728-1808
Wilkinson, Sir John (Egyptologist) 1797-1875
Wilkinson, Robert 1490
Willard, Emma 1787-1870
Willard, Frances E. 1839-1898
Willard, Josiah Flint 1869-1907
Willem I (Holland) 1815-1840
Willem II (Holland) ...1840-1849
Willem III (Holland) ...1849-1890
Willems, Jan Frans 1793-1846
William I (The Conqueror) England) 1066-1087
William II (Rufus) (England) 1087-1100
William III (England) ..1689-1702
William IV (England) ..1830-1837
William I (The Silent) (Orange) 1533-1584
William II (Orange) 1626-1650
William (The Lion) (Scotland) 1165-1214
William (Guglielmo) I (Sicily) 1154-1166
William (Guglielmo) II (Sicily) 1166-1189
William of Auvergne 1249
William of Champeaux 1121
William of Malmesbury ..1080-1143
William of Occam 1300-1349
William of Rubruquis 1215-1293
William of Wykeham 1323-1404
Williams, Ben Ames 1889-1953
Williams, Eleazar ("Lost Dauphin"?) 1789-1858
Williams, Ephraim 1715-1755
Williams, Sir George 1821-1905
Williams, Isaac 1802-1865
Williams, J. R. 1888-1957
Williams, Jesse Lynch ...1871-1929
Williams, John (archbishop) 1582-1650
Williams, John (missionary) 1796-1839
Williams, Michael 1877-1950
Williams, Ralph Vaughan. *See* Vaughan Williams, Ralph
Williams, Roger 1604-1683
Williams, Talcott 1849-1928
Williams, William Carlos 1883-1963
Williamson, Alexander ..1824-1904
Willibrord, Saint 657-738
Willis, Nathaniel Parker 1806-1867
Willis, Thomas 1621-1675
Williston, Samuel W. ...1852-1918
Willkie, Wendell L. 1892-1944
Willobie, Henry 1575-1596
Willoughby, Sir Hugh 1554
Wills, William Gorman ..1828-1891
Wills, William John 1834-1861
Willughby, Francis 1635-1672
Wilmot, David 1814-1858
Wilmot, John. *See* Rochester, Earl of
Wilson, Alexander 1766-1813
Wilson, Augusta Evans ..1835-1909
Wilson, Sir Daniel 1816-1892
Wilson, Edmund 1895-1972
Wilson, Sir Erasmus 1809-1884
Wilson, Francis 1854-1935
Wilson, George 1819-1859
Wilson, Harry Leon 1867-1939
Wilson, Havelock 1858-1929
Wilson, Sir Henry Hughes 1864-1922
Wilson, Henry Maitland ..1881-1964
Wilson, James 1742-1798
Wilson, John (composer) 1595-1674
Wilson, John ("Christopher North") (critic) 1785-1854
Wilson, Richard 1714-1782
Wilson, Romer 1891-1930
Wilson, Woodrow 1856-1921
Winchell, Alexander 1824-1891
Winchell, Walter 1897-1972
Winchilsea, Countess of (Anne Finch) 1666-1720
Winckelmann, Johann ...1717-1768
Windham, William 1750-1810
Windle, Sir Bertram 1858-1929
Windsor, Duke of. *See* Edward VIII (England)
Wingate, Sir Francis 1861-1953
Winifred, Saint 650
Winneburg, Prinz von Metternich. *See* Metternich-(Winneburg)
Winninger, Charles 1884-1969
Winslow, Edward 1595-1655
Winslow, Jacob 1669-1760
Winsor, Justin 1831-1897
Wint, Peter de 1784-1849
"Winter, John Strange" (Mrs. Arthur Stannard) 1856-1911
Winter, William 1836-1917
Winthrop, John (Elder) 1588-1649
Winthrop, John (Younger) 1606-1676
Winthrop, Robert C. 1809-1894
Winwood, Sir Ralph 1563-1616
Winzet, Ninian 1518-1592
Wirt, William 1772-1834
Wise, Henry A. 1806-1876
Wise, Isaac M. 1819-1900
Wise, Stephen S. 1874-1949
Wiseman, Nicholas (Cardinal) 1802-1865
Wishart, George 1513-1546
Wislicenus, Johannes 1835-1902
Wissler, Clark 1870-1947
Wistar, Caspar 1761-1818
Wister, Owen 1860-1938
Wither, George 1588-1667
Witherspoon, Herbert ...1873-1935